THE OAKWOOD LIBRARY OF RAILWAY HISTOR

The Atock ...ock Family

A Worldwide Railway Engineering Dynasty

by

Ernie Shepherd

THE OAKWOOD PRESS

British Library Cataloguing in Publication Data
A Record for this book is available from the British Library
ISBN 978 0 85361 681 8

Typeset by Oakwood Graphics.
Repro by PKmediaworks, Cranborne, Dorset.
Printed by Cambrian Printers, Aberystwyth, Ceredigion.

Dedication

This book is dedicated to the memory of Robin (Bob) Clements, without whose inspiration it would most likely never have seen the light of day.

Rear cover: The Atock family crest. The name Atock is derived from the old Anglo-Saxon word 'ac', suggesting that the holder lived beneath or close to an oak tree.

Courtesy Alex Atock

Published by The Oakwood Press (Usk), P.O. Box 13, Usk, Mon., NP15 1YS.
E-mail: sales@oakwoodpress.co.uk
Website: www.oakwoodpress.co.uk

Contents

Portrait photograph of Martin Atock. The date and the occasion are unknown. The original hangs in Alex Atock's living room. *Alex Atock Collection*

Foreword

by Alex Atock

I am deeply honoured to have been asked to write a foreword to this superb biography, which has been dedicated to my ancestors whom I tend to refer to as the 'Railway Atocks'.

Like so many before me it was not until I had become a grandfather that I commenced showing any interest in the lives of my predecessors or in what they had achieved and by this time most of those who could have answered my queries had long since departed. However, I started to research the family tree and, with the aid of information supplied by my cousins and a detailed scrapbook created and maintained by my grandfather, Tom Atock, I managed to trace the family back to Martin Atock, described as a coachman, who married on Christmas Day 1811. His grandsons included Martin Atock (1834-1901), whose photograph hangs in our drawing room, and his siblings George and William Henry Attock. The different spelling of the names of the latter had me mystified until one morning, totally out of the blue, a letter arrived from Ernie Shepherd wanting to know my connection to the family. He commented that he planned to write a book covering the lives of this unique family of railway engineers dating back over almost 200 years.

Over a period of time we exchanged letters, emails, photographs and copies of my grandfather's scrapbook before finally meeting in person on several occasions. Running parallel with this, Ernie, assisted by his colleague and friend, Gerald Beesley, undertook extensive and detailed research, which finally put meat on all the bones to create this wonderful record of the Atock family's contribution to the railway systems of the United Kingdom, Ireland, Latin America and the Far East. The emphasis is very much on the personal lives of the personalities concerned although it is ably balanced by information on their technical expertise, administrative abilities and details of the engines and carriages they built, many of which have remained in service until comparatively recently.

This book has answered many of my questions. I now know why there are two spellings of the Atock/Attock name; Martin Atock's photograph on the wall now has added significance as has Arthur George Atock's signet ring which I wear on my finger and also his Military Cross, which I have in my possession and which he won posthumously following the campaign in which he lost his life in France in 1918. I am proud to learn that my grandfather travelled on the footplate of the engine which took the Prince of Wales, later King George V, from Dublin to, and back from, the West of Ireland during the latter's visit in 1903. As a child I recall on many occasions meeting Tom Atock's great friend and colleague, W.H. Morton, and still miss the passing of my father at such a young age before I fully appreciated what he did in life.

Finally, and I believe I speak on behalf of my cousins, Denis Bryce, Pam Holmes, Katherine Atock and their families, I am immensely grateful to Ernie Shepherd for writing this wonderful and fitting tribute to our predecessors. There are now no excuses why our children's generation should plead ignorance of their forefathers as I once did. Thank you Ernie!

Ross-on-Wye, 2007

Foreword

by Bill Attock

When I received the first email out of the blue from a complete stranger expressing an interest in researching my family, I think I can be excused for having been more than a little suspicious. Why I thought would anyone want to research *my* family? However, as more emails were exchanged I realised that I was corresponding with a real Railway enthusiast, if not fanatic! As you will read in the book, I come from a long line of railway engineers, and I have always felt a twinge of regret that I was the first generation to break the connection not only with the railways, but also with engineering. However, I consoled myself with the fact that as I chose the Motor Trade as my career, at least it had transport in common.

Although not a trained engineer, I spent many hours 'helping' my father (Martin Oldacres) in his workshop, usually working on one of his vintage cars. My father was a stickler for doing things the right way - not for nothing was his nickname at work 'half a thou. Attock'. Many a time I have been chastised for using the wrong tool for a job, or even worse not cleaning and putting away tools after using them.

I have been amazed at the detail that Ernie Shepherd has collected; I can safely say that he knows more about my family than I do. His research into our family has been an eye opener for me, as although I knew of the existence of the Atock family as opposed to our spelling Attock, I had no idea that we come from the same ancestors. The other thing that has become apparent is the similar way our two families have developed down the generations - there are many similarities, such as the Christian names like Martin and George being common to both families, as you will read in the book, even to the fact that Alex Atock is also the first one of his family to break the family's link to the railways.

Obviously this book is not destined to be a best seller but any railway enthusiast will be privileged to receive the detailed information that Ernie has put together; he could never be rewarded for the amount of work he has invested in this book. I am sure, however, that the fact that everything is now on record will be reward enough.

Bingley, 2007

Introduction

The origins of this biography can be traced back more than 20 years. The late Bob Clements, one of the founding fathers of the Irish Railway Record Society (IRRS), spent a lifetime researching the history of the Midland Great Western Railway of Ireland (MGWR), and more particularly its locomotive stock. Generally regarded as the most Irish of the railway companies, the MGWR was commonly referred to in Ireland simply as the Midland, although in this work it will be referred to as the MGWR to avoid confusion with the English Midland Railway. When the present author approached Bob in the late 1980s proposing the writing and publication of a general history of the MGWR, he received unstinting support and assistance from him; it is much to be regretted that Bob did not live long enough to see the work in print (*see Bibliography*).

Shortly before his death, Bob invited myself and the late Norman McAdams, at the time Treasurer of the IRRS, to his home at Killadoon, near Celbridge. During the course of a lengthy discussion on various railway matters, including his beloved MGWR, Bob produced a hand-written manuscript consisting of 10 spiral-bound notebooks and comprising some 220 pages. This manuscript outlined in great detail the complete locomotive history of the MGWR. He expressed a wish that at some stage in the future this manuscript might be published. For various reasons nothing was done with the manuscript, no doubt in part due to various typists' inability to decipher Bob's distinctive style of handwriting!

Nearly three years ago the present author, having had the general history of the MGWR published, in addition to the more recent completion of a similar history of the Waterford Limerick & Western Railway (WL&WR), decided to borrow the manuscript from the IRRS, in whose care it had been entrusted, and undertook to put it into an electronic format. The significance of the above two histories is that Martin Atock served as locomotive, carriage and wagon superintendent of the latter company from 1861 until 1872 and of the former for the next 28 years up until 1900.

It was quickly realised, however, with the passage of time, that the manuscript, in its original form, might appeal to few people; it is now more than 40 years since steam traction disappeared from the Midland section of Córas Iompair Éireann (CIE), and with each year's passing there were fewer enthusiasts who would have seen an ex-MGWR steam locomotive, much less be interested in knowing, e.g. when a particular locomotive received a new boiler. Nevertheless, the manuscript was typed up exactly as it was written, with some minor alterations for the sake of clarity. For example, Bob used the word 'lubers', which I have substituted with lubricators; similarly Bob always referred to 'Multy', arguing that anyone reading a locomotive history of the MGWR would recognise this as Multyfarnham, a small station on the Sligo line. Otherwise, an exact transcription of the original was made, with the inclusion of Bob's subsequent additions and corrections inserted as footnotes. A CD of this has been presented to the IRRS for the use of future researchers.

Having established that Martin Atock had served part of his apprenticeship at the Stratford works of the Eastern Counties Railway (ECR), where his father George was in charge of carriages and wagons for 29 years on both that company and its successor, the Great Eastern Railway (GER), and where his brothers Frederick and George had also worked, the author decided to follow up the trail, incorporating as much as possible of the material in Bob Clements' manuscript in order to follow Martin's progress at the Broadstone works of the MGWR. Little did he know that some two years later he would have traced four generations and 13 members of the family involved in railways and spanning a period of nearly 130 years, not only in Britain and Ireland, but also in Australia, Burma, Ceylon, Cuba, Egypt, Malaya, New Zealand, Sudan and Venezuela – truly a great, worldwide, railway dynasty! In addition, some further members of the family led (or lead) exciting lives apart from the railway scene and are worthy of some mention.

This is the present author's first attempt at writing a biography and initially he experienced some difficulties in tracing the family background. The Internet has proved most useful in relation to family history research, at least as far as England and Wales are concerned; the situation in Ireland, however, falls far short of what is available in Britain. Inevitably, there are some gaps in our information. Whereas locomotive engineers like Sir Nigel Gresley and Richard Maunsell had long-established family backgrounds, which have been reasonably well documented, the Atock family came from a humble background and left little evidence of their passing.

In addition, carriage and wagon matters are frequently regarded as less glamorous than those relating to locomotives and have received scant attention in the past. Indeed, few references were found in the ECR and GER minutes to the four members of the family who served on those railways for more than 30 years. Likewise, the Waterford & Limerick Railway (W&LR, and predecessor to the WL&WR) and MGWR records have few references to Martin Atock, and even fewer to Thomas and Martin Leslie in the case of the latter railway. This has made it difficult to judge the full extent of their involvement in company matters. On the other hand, the Lancashire & Yorkshire Railway (L&YR) minutes have a profusion of entries about Frederick, although his son Frederick William receives little mention (and even fewer in London Midland & Scottish Railway (LMS) records).

That said, the author made contact in October 2004 with two surviving members of the family, Alex Atock and Bill Attock (reference will be made in Chapter One to the two spellings used). Both Alex and Bill have proved to be most enthusiastic about the project and have freely provided the author with whatever relevant material they had in their possession, including collections of family photographs. I believe it has been a two-way experience as they also discovered additional information about their respective families. To both of them I am extremely grateful, also to Katherine Atock of Cambridge. As regards the Australian branch of the family, Pamela Holmes, her son Warwick and Gaynor Gastmeier all produced material and family photographs, which proved useful.

Assistance has been received from many other sources. I am reluctant to single out individuals as every one has given so freely of their time and knowledge. However, the author's friend and research colleague of many years, Gerald Beesley, must receive special mention. Such was his assistance and support that Gerald's name should by rights be the one to appear on the cover

Alex Atock

Bill Attock

of this book. Gerald carried out research on the author's behalf through his contacts at the Institution of Civil Engineers, the Institution of Mechanical Engineers and the British Library in London, for which I am most grateful; he also accompanied the author on fact-finding trips to Doncaster to meet up with Bill Attock, and to the National Archives at Kew, later meeting up with Alex Atock. Gerald's Australian friend, Dick Bullock, generously made his extensive library available and also made many constructive comments regarding some of the early draft chapters.

The late Bob Clements also deserves special mention, as without his manuscript the seeds of the idea for the present work might never have germinated. It is hoped in time to continue the MGWR story with a biography of William Herbert Morton, who was in charge at Broadstone from 1915 until the end of 1924, later becoming general manager of the Great Southern Railways.

Fellow IRRS member Padraig O'Cuimin presented a series of papers to that august body dealing with the history of the carriage and wagon stock of the MGWR, these being published in the Society's Journal in the early 1970s. Padraig very generously allowed me to utilise whatever I wished from these articles, also making available additional material in his possession. Regarding WL&WR rolling stock, Barry Carse, another member of the IRRS, kindly loaned the author a carriage and wagon register, which had recently come into his possession; this proved of enormous value in correcting some previously erroneous and inadequate information regarding that company's stock. Tim Moriarty and Brendan Pender, respectively Librarian and Archivist of the IRRS, kindly allowed access to material in the Society's care. Other IRRS members who have assisted include Desmond Coakham and Sean Kennedy, for the use of photographs from their extensive collections, and the late Norman McAdams.

Another enthusiast group deserving of mention is the Great Eastern Railway Society (GERS), founded in 1973 to cater for those interested in the history of that company and its predecessors. One of its members, the late Harry Jones, spent long hours in what was then known as the Public Record Office (now the National Archives) at Kew transcribing the various minute books of the GER and its constituent companies. Subsequently this material was typed up by volunteers and made available both in hard copy and on CD; these transcripts have proved most useful in the author's researches. Individual members of the GERS who have assisted include the Publications Officer, Barry Jackson, and John Watling, current President and the acknowledged carriage and wagon expert. Noel Coates of the Lancashire & Yorkshire Railway Society, likewise, very kindly provided the author with drawings of L&YR wagons; these are duly acknowledged.

Thanks are due to Córas Iompair Éireann, the holding company for the present-day Irish railway Company, Iarnród Éireann (IE); CIE is the body charged with the holding and preservation of the statutory records of all the railway companies in the Republic, which were predecessors to IE. Various Secretarial Services Managers, including Dympna Kelledy, Mary Oliver, Marcella Doyle, and the present incumbent, Ann Neary, have over the years kindly allowed access to the various minute books etc. in the company's care; thanks are also due to Frances Sugrue. The National Archives in Kew hold similar records for the British railway companies, and thanks are due to them for enabling research into the minute books of the L&YR and the LMS.

John Callanan, the Archivist of the Institution of Engineers of Ireland also provided valuable assistance. Other organizations that have provided valuable assistance include the Australian War Memorial in Canberra, Doncaster Record Office, Kendal Record Office, Lancashire Record Office in Preston, Lutterworth Museum, Mountjoy School (now Mount Temple Comprehensive), The High School, Dublin and Trinity College, Dublin. My wife also deserves special mention for her patience and understanding during many evenings 'widowed' whilst research continued. Finally, the author wishes to thank his good friend, Loraine Rösler, for her final proofreading of the manuscript. A primary school principal by profession, Loraine gave the author a clearer understanding of the correct use of the comma!

Throughout the manuscript the author has almost exclusively used given names for the various members of the family. Although this may appear rather informal on the author's part, it has been done to avoid possible confusion when dealing with so many individuals, particularly as first names were perpetuated in succeeding generations.

In relation to photographs, reference has already been made to IRRS members. Many of those used have come from Atock/Attock family collections. Particularly in the case of those provided by Bill Attock from his collection, it is believed that a number of these may have been taken by the English Electric Company's official photographer. Due acknowledgement is made to that company. The author apologises for any illustrations which have been incorrectly acknowledged and would appreciate being so advised so that it can be corrected in any future editions.

Any errors or omissions are the sole responsibility of the author.

Chapter One

Origins of the Family

There are two schools of thought regarding the origins of the Atock/Attock family name. The Historical Research Center in the United States and Cottle's *A Dictionary of English and Welsh Surnames* both refer to the family name as being of local origin. It is said to derive from the old Anglo-Saxon word 'ac', meaning oak. The original bearer of the name may have lived at or near an oak tree. Various derivations are documented, including Atack, Atock, Attack, Attick and Attock. The surname is first recorded in England as early as 1273 when a reference is made in the *Hundred Rolls* to 'Adam At the Ocke' in Shropshire. Twenty-three years later, Geoffrey atte Ock appears in the *Subsidiary Rolls* for Sussex.

The second theory put forward is that the name Atock and its various permutations are connected to the Lancashire names of Eatock and Eatough. It has been suggested by Colin Eatock of Toronto that the Lancashire dialect led to the corruption of the name Atock. Alison Murray, whose great-grandmother Jane Atock was born in 1856 in the village of Trawden in Lancashire, cites various spellings of the name; this branch of the family settled in the Burnley area and became cotton weavers. *A Dictionary of English and Welsh Surnames* also includes the name Eatock, but, interestingly, makes no mention of Atock derivations. Whether the Lancashire Atocks have any distant connection with the railway dynasty is unknown, but seems unlikely, as very few first names are common between the Lancashire and Yorkshire Atocks. It must be remembered that many people were illiterate at that time and clergy who might be comparative newcomers to an area wrote down what they heard, thus leading to derivations of names. As we shall shortly see, the different spellings of Atock and Attock are encountered in the case of the family with which we are dealing.*

The 1881 Census lists almost 500 instances of the name with various spellings (excluding the Eatock variations). Of this number some 80 per cent show their county of birth as Yorkshire, with a comparatively small number in Lancashire. The author has also found approximately 150 instances of the family resident in Yorkshire in the period encompassing the 17th and 18th centuries; the majority of these used the spelling Atack. In all there were 14 different spellings of the Atock name, 82 out of the 150 being Atack, whilst 14 were Atock (the spelling Atocks was also found). It is interesting to note that by far the majority of these people were to be found in a compact rectangular area some 25 miles long and 16 miles wide. This area runs east from Bradford to meet the present M1 motorway at Micklefield, then turns south as far as Ackworth and then west again to a point just south of Huddersfield before returning north to Bradford. Within this area, by far the largest concentration (115) was in the village of Crofton just to the south-east of Wakefield.

* An Attock family of Sandal Magna, just south of Wakefield, included a Martin Attock who was christened there on 1st May, 1714, his father also being called Martin. Although there is no evidence that the Atock family from Crofton had any connection with those from Sandal Magna, it should be noted that one of Martin's siblings was recorded as Thomas Atock. The similarity of family first names is also noteworthy.

Research of the parish registers for Crofton for the above two centuries has, however, failed to uncover a definite connection to the subject of the present biography. Crofton was for many years a coal-mining centre and a number of entries show the occupation of residents as collier or labourer. We do not know how Martin Atock, who was born in the 1750s, came to reside in the City of York, or even if he came from Crofton, as it has not been possible to trace his parents. He was married to Dinah and lived in the parish of St Helen's, Stonegate, an ecclesiastical parish in the City of York adjacent to the Minster. They had several children, including Diana, born on 10th February, 1781, Thomas, born in 1782, Mary, christened on 17th March, 1783 and Esther, christened at Saint-Michael-le-Belfry, York, on 23rd April, 1785. The family could also possibly have included Martin (b.1778). Thomas Atock married Ann in 1804 and they had at least two children, including Anne (b.1805) and Elizabeth (b.1816).

Although it has not been possible to verify that Martin and Dinah were the parents of Martin Atock born in 1778, the fact that all of the Christian names, with the exception of Diana, were regularly used by the Atock/Attock family in later generations, there seems a strong likelihood that he was a member of that family. Our story moves onto solid ground with the marriage on Christmas Day 1811 of Martin Atock to Phoebe Foss in St George's church, Doncaster.* Today it seems strange that the marriage ceremony took place on Christmas Day, but we should remember that holidays were virtually unknown at the beginning of the 19th century in Britain and this was one of the few free days available to the working classes. Martin's occupation was shown in the parish register as a coachman, but as all later references show him as a coachmaker it has been assumed that the earlier entry is in error.

So what were the circumstances that brought Martin Atock to Doncaster? The answer probably lies in the situation of the town at the time of his marriage. In 1811 it was a thriving market town situated on the river Don in the West Riding of Yorkshire with a population of just under 7,000. Located in the centre of a large agricultural district, it had one of the largest corn-markets in the kingdom but, strangely, there was no corn exchange. Attempts to make Doncaster a manufacturing town at the beginning of the 19th century were unsuccessful so, whilst the nearby towns of Leeds and Sheffield underwent great industrial and social change, Doncaster remained largely unaltered. The famous Great North Road, which was the main route north from London to York, passed through the whole length of Doncaster. It was also, to use railway parlance, a 'junction' town where routes to Sheffield, Leeds and Hull diverged. The coaching trade provided business in the coaching inns and related trades, and the town derived a considerable amount of its income from that source.

Although a coach had called at the 'Red Lion' inn since 1785, it was not until about 1790 that the first mail coach ran from the 'Old Angel' inn. The popularity of the 'Old Angel' as a posting house was short-lived as the 'New Angel' on the opposite side of the road secured the majority of the business when it opened in 1810. Coach services which connected London and Leeds, and which stabled and changed horses at the time, were the 'Diligence' and 'Rockingham'. Within the town there were two coach-making firms, James & John Anderton of Frenchgate, and Thomas Clement at West Laith Gate. Ralph Foss, who was christened at

* Work started on the original church in the late 12th century and took more than 250 years to complete. The building was destroyed by fire on the night of 28th February, 1853. Many of the parish records were badly damaged as a result.

Kirkby Fleetham, Yorkshire, on 8th December, 1782, was a coachmaker at Frenchgate and was most probably working for the Andertons. He married Phoebe Lambert at Doncaster on 23rd November, 1801, and their first child Ann was born on 9th May, 1802 and christened at Doncaster. Phoebe Foss who married Martin Atock may have been a younger sister of Ralph's and, in view of Martin's known trade, it is more than likely that he also worked with the same coach-making firm at Frenchgate. Martin was 33 years of age when he married Phoebe, and it is just possible that he was previously married and widowed.

Phoebe Atock, who was born about 1801 in Doncaster, may have been a close relative of Martin's, or even his daughter by an earlier marriage. On 12th August, 1822 she married a William Adams at Doncaster and, jumping ahead some years, we find William Adams living in Factory Lane where he was shown as a shopkeeper in the Doncaster Directory for 1837. Phoebe Adams was widowed by 1851 and was working as a laundress. She was residing at Halifax's Yard close to Frenchgate and her granddaughter Ann Trugman was living with her. Ann later married Charles Street in June 1862; he was born in Wanstead about 1841 and was an engine fitter in the Great Northern Railway (GNR) Works at Doncaster, generally known at that time as 'The Plant'.

Phoebe Adams died on the night of 1st February, 1868 when she either fell from or was blown off the Plant Bridge, which crossed the railway line near Factory Lane. A local newspaper gives a lengthy description of an accident to Phoebe, recording that she had gone to the Plant to collect Charles' pay and was found lying at the bottom of the steps leading to the bridge by a labourer. She was removed to St James's Hospital where she died of her injuries during the night. Her granddaughter gave evidence to the subsequent inquest of identifying Phoebe. The Coroner for Doncaster, John Lister, in announcing a verdict of accidental death, criticised the GNR for failing to provide adequate lighting at the bridge. Charles and Ann had quite a large family and one of their sons, Harry, was a milling machine mechanic, most likely at the Plant works.

Now we must return to Martin Atock and his family, for in June or July 1812 their first son, George, was born. We do not have the precise date for this momentous event in our story, but we do know that he was baptised in St George's church, Doncaster on 19th July. Martin and Phoebe had at least two other children, a daughter Harriet, who was christened in St George's church on 9th October, 1814, and another son William born in January 1817; he was christened in St George's church on 23rd February. Tragically, Martin died in Doncaster on 24th December, 1818 at the young age of 40, leaving a widow to bring up three young children. It appears that Phoebe and her children remained in Doncaster; the fact that William (who was barely a year old when his father died) lived there for the rest of his life lending some credence to this assumption.

The public charities of Doncaster were numerous and Phoebe may have turned to them for assistance. In 1804 Quintin Kay, of Ludgate-hill, London, who may have been a member of the Religious Society of Friends (Quakers), had bequeathed bank annuities, producing £300 per annum, which was chiefly devoted to the relief of poor and reduced persons, and to the apprenticing of six poor children to mechanical or handicraft trades in Doncaster. Although we have no details of George Atock's education and early career, it is not beyond

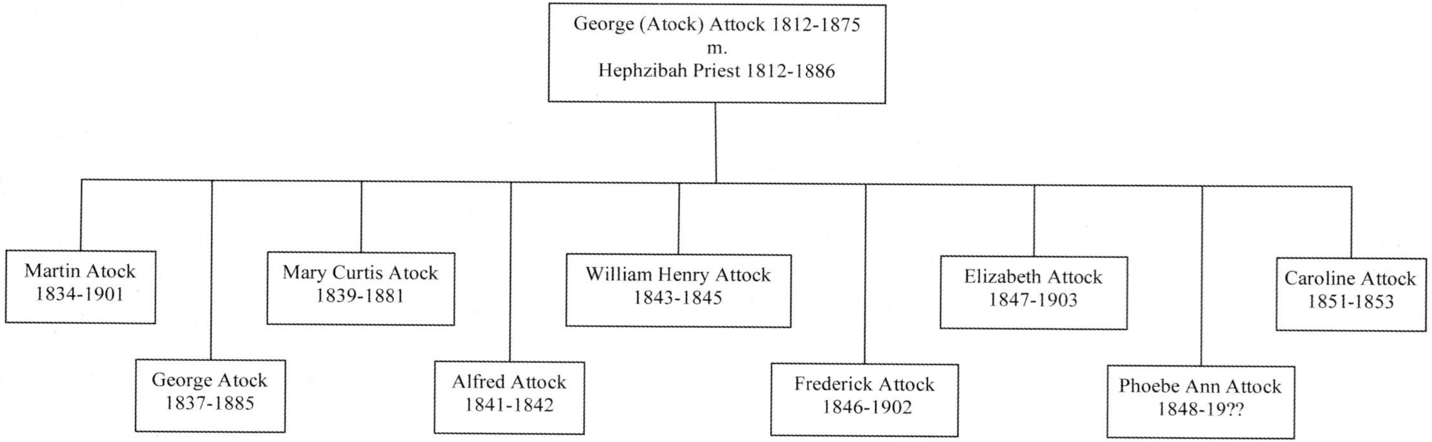
George (Atock) Attock 1812-1875
m.
Hephzibah Priest 1812-1886
Martin Atock
1834-1901
George Atock
1837-1885
Mary Curtis Atock
1839-1881
Alfred Attock
1841-1842
William Henry Attock
1843-1845
Frederick Attock
1846-1902
Elizabeth Attock
1847-1903
Phoebe Ann Attock
1848-19??
Caroline Attock
1851-1853

the bounds of possibility that it was through the application of such resources and the assistance of Ralph Foss that George Atock was apprenticed to the coach-making trade, probably with the firm of James & John Anderton in Doncaster. There was a strong Quaker influence in the coach-making trade and they had a significant presence in Doncaster.* Although the Atock family were Anglicans, Martin's work as a coach-maker would have brought his family to their notice. Whatever the case, there is no doubt that Quaker contacts were to play a part in George's future career, as we shall shortly see.

We have no further information regarding George's sister, Harriet, but we do know that his brother William married Tabitha, daughter of Henry Ellis, a shoemaker. The wedding took place in Doncaster parish church on 20th November 1837, William's occupation at that time being shown as a printer. The couple had two children, Eliza, who was born in 1838 but died when she was less than a year old, and Mary Ellis, born in 1839. For some years prior to her marriage in 1862 Mary Ellis helped in her father's shop, William employing two boys in the printing business about that time. William's occupation had changed to that of parcel agent by March 1871, and the family was residing at West Villa in Doncaster. His niece, Mary Hutton, described as a scholar aged 12, was living with them. Mary's parents were John and Mary Hutton from Derbyshire, his occupation being shown as a sicklemaker. Following Tabitha's death in 1889 Mary stayed on with William to look after him. He contracted cancer and passed away on 26th June, 1891 at his home, No. 18 Balby Road. Shortly afterwards, Mary Hutton married Thomas William Turnell, a railway shunter.

The next time we hear about George is on the occasion of his marriage to Hephzibah Priest at Manchester parish church on 5th November, 1832, where the chaplain, Revd R. Remington, conducted the service. Hephzibah, who was born in Lincoln on 24th January, 1813, was the daughter of George and Mary Priest. The name Hephzibah is biblical in origin, meaning 'in her is my delight', diminutives being Hespie and Eppie. They may possibly have met in Doncaster as a George Priest died in that town in 1851, although we do not know whether or not he was Hephzibah's father. The marriage ceremony was celebrated following publication of Banns, the record of which shows both bride and groom as belonging to the parish. George's occupation is shown in the parish register as a coach-maker and, for the first time, his surname is spelt as Attock. We do not have any explanation for the change in spelling other than to assume that the clergyman wrote the name in the register as he heard it, the differences in Yorkshire and Lancashire accents possibly contributing.

The author has found no information to throw light on where George was employed at the time of his marriage. It is quite possible that members of the Quaker community in Doncaster encouraged him to move to the north-west where his coach-making skills could be applied to the benefit of the budding railway industry. One scenario is that he was working for Richard Melling at No. 5 Coupland Street, Greenheys in the Walkden district of Manchester. Melling built coaches for the Liverpool & Manchester Railway (L&MR) where his brother, Thomas, was locomotive superintendent from 1837 to 1839. Richard Melling together with his brother John and William H. Beeston were partners in the firm of Beeston & Melling who supplied twenty open second-class carriages for the

* The Balby district, the suburb of Doncaster where William Atock later lived, was where George Fox the founder of the Society of Friends and his followers held their first meetings, and where they suffered persecutions very little short of those of the inquisition.

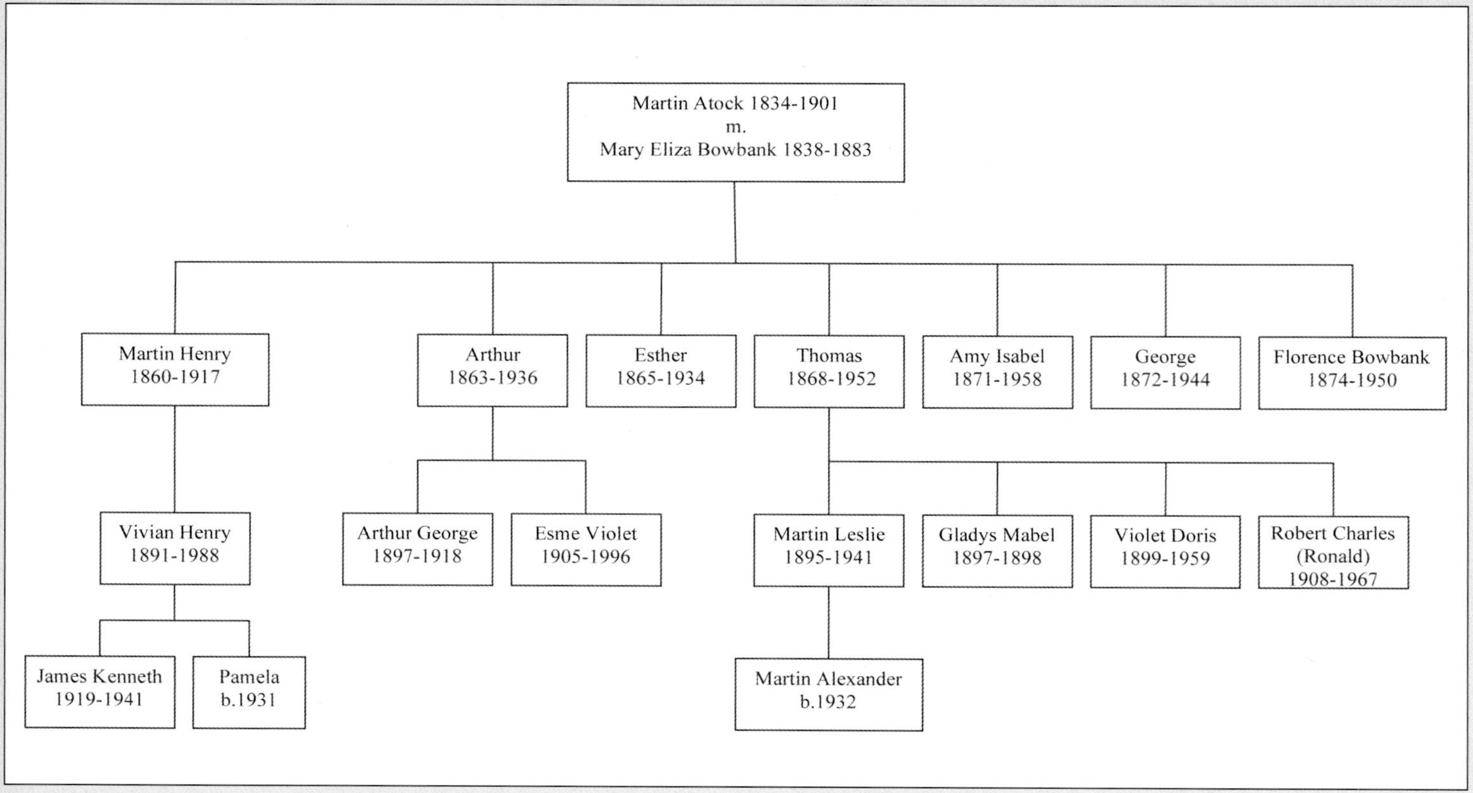
Martin Atock 1834-1901
m.
Mary Eliza Bowbank 1838-1883
Martin Henry 1860-1917
Arthur 1863-1936
Esther 1865-1934
Thomas 1868-1952
Amy Isabel 1871-1958
George 1872-1944
Florence Bowbank 1874-1950
Vivian Henry 1891-1988
Arthur George 1897-1918
Esme Violet 1905-1996
Martin Leslie 1895-1941
Gladys Mabel 1897-1898
Violet Doris 1899-1959
Robert Charles (Ronald) 1908-1967
James Kenneth 1919-1941
Pamela b.1931
Martin Alexander b.1932

opening of the Dublin & Kingstown Railway that were virtually identical to those built for the L&MR. Alternatively, George may have been employed directly by the L&MR to look after their carriages at the Manchester end of the line. At that time T.C. Worsdell was in charge of the L&MR coach shops at Liverpool.

Thomas Clarke Worsdell was born at Hayes, near London, in 1788 and apprenticed to a London firm of coachbuilders. Some time about 1812 he moved to Lancashire and took up employment with Jonathan Dunn, where he refined his coach-making skills at Dunn's coach works in Lancaster. By 1816 he was running his own coach building business in Bolton, and whilst in that town he became associated with the Quakers. Five years later he had moved to Preston, and in 1827 he set up another branch of his business at Crown Street in Liverpool, which later became the L&MR coach shops. It is not clear whether this venture was at his own instigation (as a result of being left a bequest of £1,000), or because he was persuaded by James Cropper, a Quaker Director of the L&MR, to build some of the first passenger carriages for that railway. It was through his work for the L&MR that Worsdell came to the attention of none other than George Stephenson, who later described him as 'the best coach-maker I ever knew'. In addition to carriages and wagons for the L&MR, he had built the tender for Stephenson's *Rocket* and was involved in the Rainhill Trials.

In 1832 the Directors of the L&MR decided to dispense with some staff due to a decrease in passenger traffic; further staff being discharged in 1833 as part of on-going economy measures. It may have been those particular circumstances that resulted in George Attock moving to Preston where he was probably accommodated in one of the coach works there through the good offices of Worsdell. We know for certain that George and Hephzibah were living at Church Street in Preston by June 1834 when their first child, Martin, was born. He was baptised on 26th June in the parish church of St John the Evangelist, the ceremony being performed by the vicar, Revd Wilson. Roger Carus Wilson had been appointed vicar of St John's in 1817 at the early age of 25 and was one of the most remarkable incumbents in Preston. The great increase of churches in Preston was due to his energy and initiative, no fewer than five additional churches being built during his incumbency, namely St Peter, 1825, St Paul, 1826, Christ Church, 1836, St Mary, 1838, and St Thomas, 1839. These churches are shown in a monument erected to his memory on the south wall of the chancel in the church of St John the Evangelist following his death in 1839.

Despite the fact that George's surname had been shown as Attock at the time of his marriage, his son's baptism was recorded in the parish register as Martin Atock. It is unlikely that a clergyman with the standing of Revd Wilson would have changed his mind and used anything other than the traditional Atock spelling of the surname when he made the entries for the baptism of the next two children, George and Mary Curtis, and the significance of this will become apparent in the next chapter. George was born on 17th November, 1837, when the family was living in Oxford Street, but by the time that Mary Curtis arrived their address was shown as Ribblesdale Place. Preston was not served by a railway line until the North Union Railway (NUR) was opened northwards from Wigan on 21st October, 1838, however, there were three coach-making businesses operating in the town in 1834. They were Robert Kerr, Woodcock's Court, Messrs Leece & Son, Library Street and John Penny of the Bull Inn Yard. These facts seem to

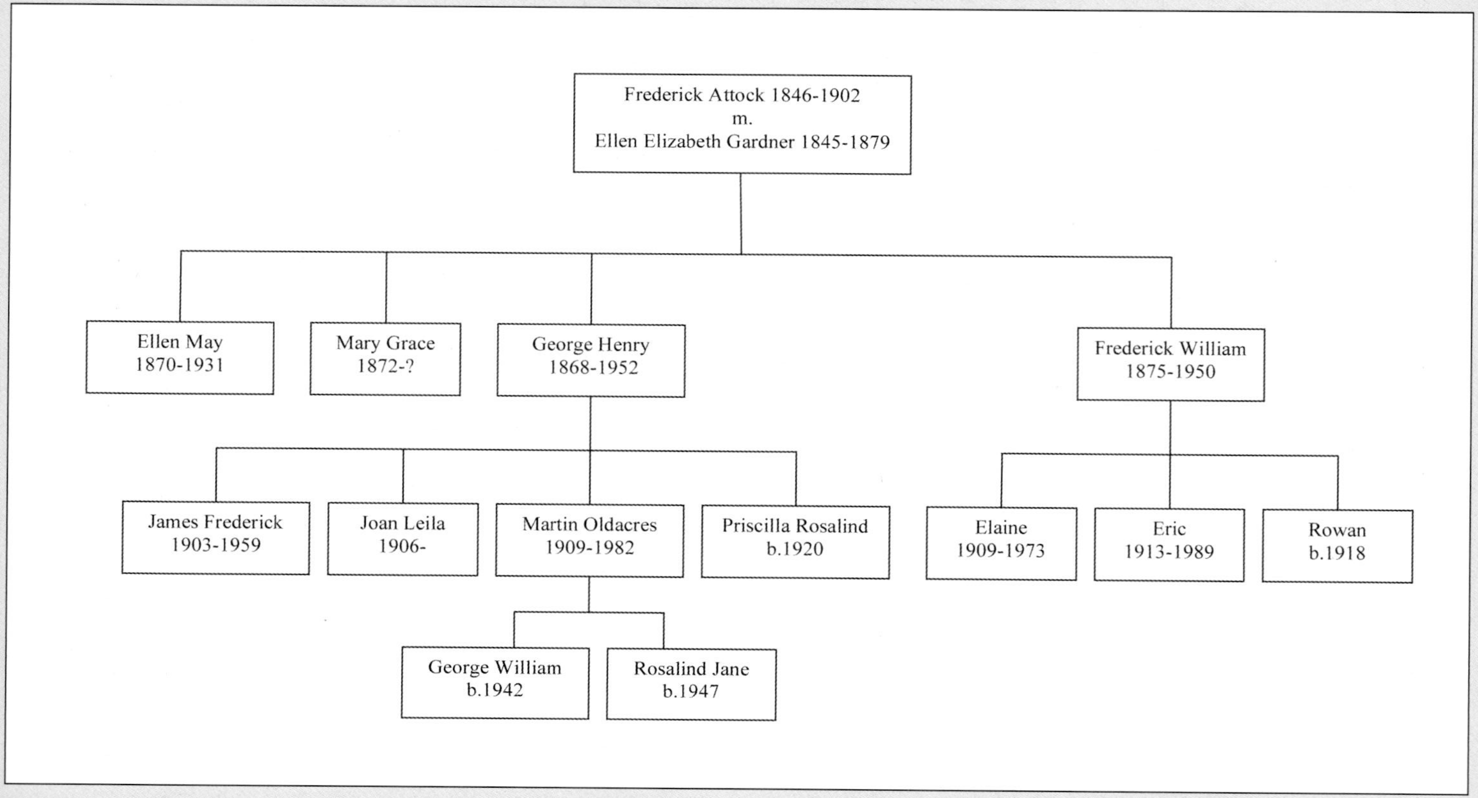
Frederick Attock 1846-1902
m.
Ellen Elizabeth Gardner 1845-1879
Ellen May
1870-1931
Mary Grace
1872-?
George Henry
1868-1952
Frederick William
1875-1950
James Frederick
1903-1959
Joan Leila
1906-
Martin Oldacres
1909-1982
Priscilla Rosalind
b.1920
Elaine
1909-1973
Eric
1913-1989
Rowan
b.1918
George William
b.1942
Rosalind Jane
b.1947

indicate that, for most of the period that George and his family were in Preston, he was probably engaged in the construction of road coaches. Of course he could have returned to the railway industry in Preston with the arrival of the NUR.

The opening of the NUR brought a corresponding increase in traffic to the L&MR and additional carriages had to be built in the company's workshop. This resulted in the L&MR recruiting extra coach-makers in 1839 and may well have been the reason behind George's move from Preston to Liverpool. Once again it is quite possible that Quaker contacts had a hand in the process, the L&MR in particular having Directors of that persuasion. We know for certain that George Attock and his family were living at Fairclough Street, Liverpool, when their son Alfred Attock was born on 11th April, 1841. The family's stay in Liverpool was not to be a happy one as both Alfred and another son, William, died there at very young ages. Alfred succumbed to a chest infection when he was only nine months old, his death occurring at No. 54 Warren Street in the Mount Pleasant district of the city on 15th January, 1842. William Henry Attock was born on 16th December, 1842 at No. 15 Edward Street, also in the Mount Pleasant district. William Henry died of pneumonia after contracting whooping cough and, at the time of his death on 28th November, 1845, the family had moved to No. 8 Anson Terrace in the Islington district. Both Mount Pleasant and Islington are close enough to Crown Street where the L&MR and the Grand Junction Railway had their respective workshops, the former district lying just to the east of Central station and to the south of Lime Street; in fact Fairclough Street meets up with Crown Street at its south end. Islington lies to the north of the railway, but still close enough for George to have travelled to work at the railway workshops.

George and Hephzibah must have been devastated by the death of a second son within a space of less than four years. Hephzibah was in fact pregnant at the time of William Henry's death, Frederick Attock being born at Anson Terrace on 10th February, 1846. It will have been noted that all three children born in Liverpool were registered with the Attock surname, which was also to be the case for all subsequent births. At the same time as these family happenings, things in Liverpool were becoming less predictable for George. The amalgamation that was to bring about the formation of the London & North Western Railway (LNWR) was imminent, which undoubtedly would have brought redundancies at Crown Street with the rationalisation of the two workshops.

Whether it was George's own decision, or whether he was once again pointed in the right direction by Quaker friends, the move that he was about to make was dramatic. We shall see in the next chapter that there had already been a Quaker participation in the affairs of the Carriage & Wagon Department of the Eastern Counties Railway at Stratford, with Thomas Clarke Worsdell's son being employed there until January 1845. Such connections may have had an influence, but there is no doubt that George Attock's capabilities were sufficient in their own right to secure him a good position on a railway at the opposite end of the country. It is not clear if he was appointed chief foreman of the Wagon Department immediately, or promoted to that position soon after his arrival at Stratford. In either case, his early attainment of a responsible role is further evidence that he must have had considerable experience of railway work earlier in his career. In Chapter Two we shall deal with George's days on the Eastern Counties Railway and the early events in the lives of two of his sons who had notable railway careers.

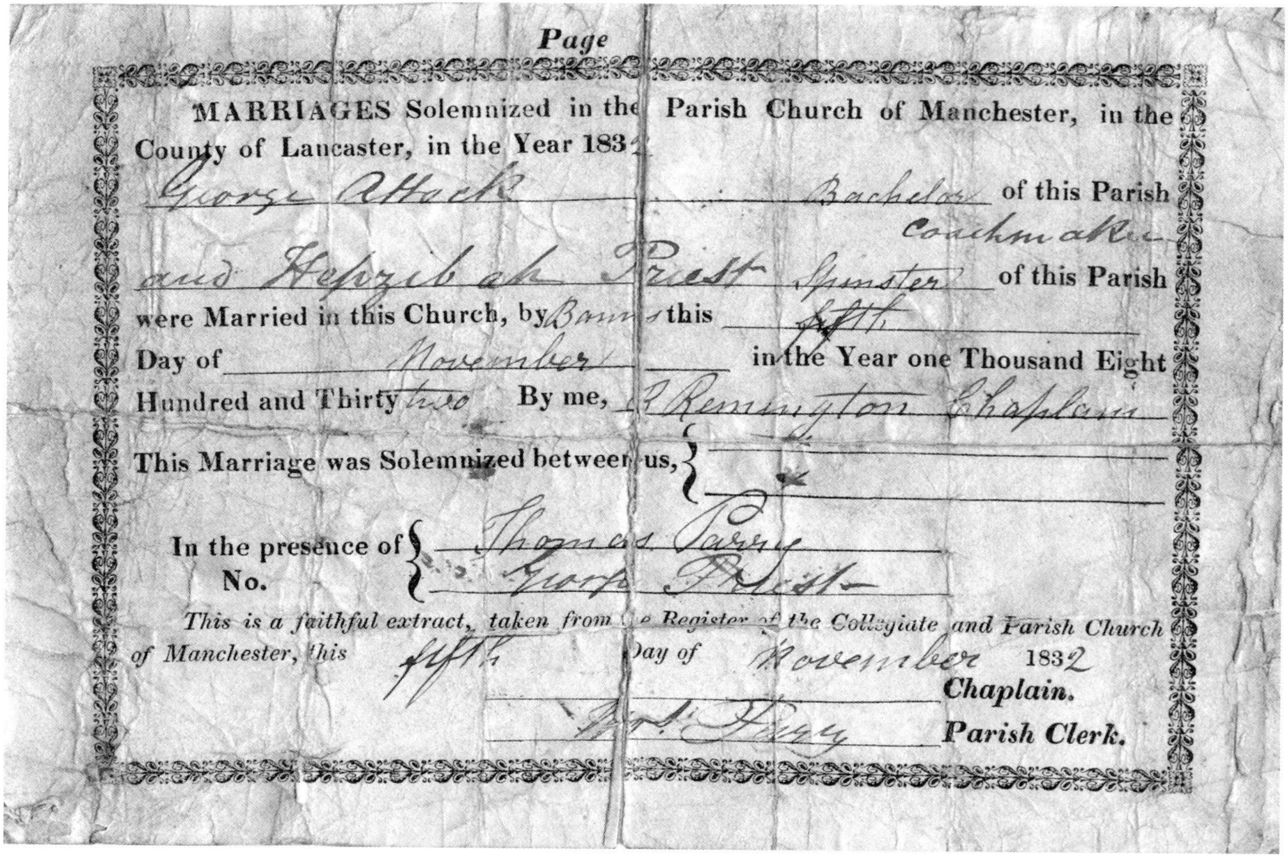
Page

MARRIAGES Solemnized in the Parish Church of Manchester, in the County of Lancaster, in the Year 1832

George Attock Bachelor of this Parish
Coachmaker
and Hepzibah Priest Spinster of this Parish
were Married in this Church, by Banns this fifth
Day of November in the Year one Thousand Eight Hundred and Thirty two By me, R Remington Chaplain

This Marriage was Solemnized between us, {

In the presence of { Thomas Parry
No. { George Priest

This is a faithful extract, taken from the Register of the Collegiate and Parish Church of Manchester, this fifth Day of November 1832

Chaplain.

Jno. Parry Parish Clerk.

The start of the 'Railway Dynasty'. Entry in the Manchester Parish Register recording the marriage on 5th November, 1832 of George Attock to Hephzibah Priest. Note spelling of surname with two 'Ts'.

Bill Attock Collection

Chapter Two

The Family moves to East Anglia

Before we look at events following George Attock's arrival at Stratford works, it is as well to acquaint ourselves briefly with the origins and circumstances of the company that he was joining. Early in 1834 plans were drawn up for the formation of a line of railway from London to York and Edinburgh, passing through Cambridge. The proposed scheme was not well received by the former cities, being considered too long a route to complete as a single undertaking. Suggestions were then put forward for a line from London to Norwich and Yarmouth. Further consideration of the matter produced a scheme for a route via Chelmsford, Colchester and Ipswich, which it was felt would best serve the counties of Essex, Suffolk and Norfolk; a Prospectus for such a line was published in July 1834, the Consulting Engineer being Charles Blacker Vignoles, with John Braithwaite as the Resident Engineer. The Prospectus referred to the fact that Vignoles was Engineer to the Dublin & Kingstown Railway, 'one of the most difficult and splendid works of this description which has been executed'. The unexpected indisposition of John Braithwaite at a critical time meant that a Bill for the scheme was not presented to Parliament until the 1835/36 Session.

The Eastern Counties Railway was incorporated by Act of Parliament, which received Royal Assent on 4th July, 1836. The ECR got no further than Colchester; the remainder of the line originally authorized by the Act had to be built by three different companies and was not completed until 1849. The first 10¼ mile section was opened on 18th June, 1839 between a temporary terminus at Devonshire Street, in the Mile End district of London, and Romford. It was extended to Brentford on 1st July, 1840, an extension to Shoreditch at the London end being opened on the same day. Opening of the final extension of the line to the London terminus at Liverpool Street did not take place until 1st November, 1875, after George Attock had retired. The Northern & Eastern Railway (N&ER), also incorporated on 4th July, 1836, was opened from Angel Lane, Stratford, to Broxbourne on 15th September, 1840, extended to Harlow on 9th August, 1841, to Spelbrook on 22nd September of that year, and to Bishop's Stortford on 16th May, 1842. Running powers were exercised over the ECR into London. The N&ER was subsequently leased by the ECR as from 1st January, 1844.

Both the ECR and the N&ER were constructed to a gauge of 5 ft 0 in., and as early as October 1836 consideration had been given to the most suitable gauge for the ECR. Pending a resolution of this matter it was agreed that no contracts could be awarded for bridges and viaducts, or even the purchase of land. Isambard Kingdom Brunel of the Great Western Railway (GWR) was approached seeking his views on the advantages of the 7 ft 0¼ in. gauge as proposed by him for that line. By April 1837 the GWR gauge had been rejected by the two companies as being too expensive, but it was not until February of the following year that the decision was finally taken to adopt the 5 ft 0 in. gauge. The ECR system was re-gauged to the standard 4 ft 8½ in. gauge between 5th September and 7th October, 1844.

The ECR established a locomotive works on spare land on the Hare Hall estate to the east of Romford. An article in *The Locomotive Magazine* for May 1901 attributes its location as being convenient to Braithwaite's residence - it had been agreed on 16th October, 1838 that he should reside at Hare Hall rent-free for seven years. It seems more likely, however, that the works were established there simply because the company had surplus land available at that location; in any event, Braithwaite's contract was terminated in February 1843. The N&ER had, meanwhile, established its works at Angel Lane, Stratford, the nearest point on its system to London. The lease of the latter company in January 1844 resulted in the ECR having two locomotive works at its disposal. The re-gauging of all locomotives and rolling stock was undertaken at the Romford works; however, on 30th October, 1845 the Directors finally decided to concentrate their workshop facilities at Stratford, the necessary plans being ready by July 1846. The Romford facility was retained for the manufacture and repair of wagon tarpaulins, the buildings there remaining in use into British Railways days.

George Hudson, originally a successful draper from York, had, at the age of 27 years, been bequeathed the not inconsiderable sum (for 1827) of £30,000 which he decided to invest in North Midland Railway (NMR) shares. In 1837 he was appointed Chairman of the York & North Midland Railway (Y&NMR), a position that brought him into contact with the Stephensons. Later, Hudson was instrumental in the amalgamation of the NMR with its rival, the Birmingham & Derby Junction Railway, the result being the formation of the Midland Railway, of which he quickly became Chairman. He was at the height of his fame in the mid-1840s, being frequently referred to as the 'Railway King'.

Hudson's interests soon brought him into conflict with the proposed Great Northern Railway. When the ECR Directors invited Hudson to join the Board of the Company in an attempt to solve its financial problems, he saw an opportunity to gain alternative access to London. The incorporation of the GNR in 1846, however, put an end to any prospect of a line from London to connect with his empire in the North East. Hudson was elected Chairman of the ECR on 30th October, 1845, his deputy being David Waddington, originally from Liverpool. It was not long, however, before serious criticisms were being voiced as to Hudson's style of management; it transpired that whilst the shareholders were benefiting from increased dividends, these were not being paid out of revenue, as was normal, but from capital. An investigating committee of shareholders was set up early in 1849, leading to Hudson being ousted as Chairman on 28th February of that year and his replacement by Waddington. Hudson's period as Chairman of the ECR has been described as one in which 'the Eastern Counties Railway pursued a ruthless policy of blackmail, obstructionism, rate wars and sheer dishonesty'. Even after the formation of the Great Eastern Railway in 1862 the situation was not to change for some years to come.

It is now necessary to take a brief look at the various locomotive superintendents and the provision of rolling stock prior to George Attock's arrival. As referred to above, John Braithwaite was Resident Engineer from 1834 until February 1843; during this period he had also been responsible for locomotive and rolling stock matters. The resolution of the gauge question in 1837 enabled advertisements to be placed in March 1838 for carriages, tenders being sought for four first class, six second class and six third class vehicles, with orders being placed in the following July. In February 1839 further orders were placed, with six first class carriages coming from Messrs Dunn & Son of Lancaster, a firm that we have already come across in Chapter One.

Also included in the 1839 order were two first class carriages from Mr Dawson of Dublin at £420 each. This was the firm of J.S. Dawson (later trading as Rogerson, Dawson & Russell) of Phibsborough Road in Dublin; their workshops were later taken over by the Midland Great Western Railway and incorporated in the latter's works at Broadstone. As far as is known, this was the only export order ever given to Dawsons. The Manchester firm of Richard Melling, with whom George Attock may have had early connections, also supplied carriages during 1839, as did two local firms, Messrs McVey and Mr Gower of Stratford. It was ordered that the four third class carriages from the former builder were to have buffer springs.

An article in the *Railway Times* for 22nd June, 1839, in connection with the opening of the ECR line, gives us some information on the early carriage stock. Three classes were provided: first class carriages were similar to those in use on the London & Croydon and the Grand Junction Railways. It was stated that they could accommodate six persons each (presumably per compartment), and were divided into compartments with comfortable lining, cushions and the like. Second class compartments were without cushions and were open at the sides, while the third class had been provided without any covering at the top or sides. The article commented that there was no doubt they would, 'during fine weather, obtain a fair share of passengers'. All three classes of carriage were painted a bright blue, with the company coat of arms emblazoned on the sides, and were said to be extremely comfortable and substantial.

It was not very long, however, before complaints were being made in regard to the third class carriages. A letter in the *Railway Times* in September 1839 referred to a lady who had 'her tippet (scarf) set on fire'; in extinguishing this she severely burnt her hand. The *Railway Times* was led to believe that the open carriages were attached next to the engine in order to drive passengers into the higher classes of carriage. Worse was to come: the *Essex Mercury* reported in June 1840 that third class passengers were being further discomforted by the removal of seats and their replacement by railed divisions down the centre of the carriages similar to those in sheep wagons. This is confirmed by a Board minute of 16th June, 1840 which gives details of a new fare structure. As an example, fares from London to Brentwood were 4*s*. 6*d*. first class, 3*s*. 0*d*. second class and 1*s*. 6*d*. third class (no seats); a week later, another minute refers to a third class fare of 2*s*. 3*d*. with seats. Whether or not a decision had been taken to revert to seating is not known, or perhaps there were in effect four classes, as was the case on some of the Irish railways about that time.

Following Braithwaite's departure in February 1843, William Fernihough, who came from Messrs Bury, was appointed locomotive superintendent. Fernihough was responsible for altering the gauge of the locomotives and rolling stock in 1844. It is alleged that following a serious accident near

Littlebury on 4th August, 1845, William Fernihough resigned. Whatever the reason, Thomas Scott was appointed on 28th October, 1845 to replace him, Scott's tenure of office being less than 12 months.* A Board Minute for 10th December, 1844 refers to a Mr Worsdell of the Carriage Department quitting as from 4th January, 1845. This was Thomas Worsdell, who had spent some time with his father, Thomas Clark Worsdell, on the Leipzig & Dresden Railway, being offered the position of locomotive and rolling stock superintendent on that railway in 1838. He returned to England in May 1842, married in Lancaster in January of the following year and then moved to the ECR at Stratford. The above minute is the only reference in the Board Minutes to Thomas Worsdell and it appears that he may have been in charge of carriage & wagon affairs during Fernihough's period in office.

Thomas Scott had been apprenticed to Thomas Cabry,† locomotive superintendent of the Y&NMR since 21st November, 1836, and had latterly been in charge of the Midland Railway's locomotive depot at Leeds. Following Hudson's arrival on the ECR, Thomas Cabry was called in to report on the company's locomotives and rolling stock, being paid a fee of 100 guineas in May 1846. Scott was a Hudson appointee, as was his successor, John Hunter, who came from Newcastle in May 1846. At that time it was ordered that Scott was to have 'an assistant to act as relief'. Hunter was put in charge of the works at Stratford and Romford with Scott appointed to supervise the operation of locomotives, i.e. the running superintendent. Hunter was responsible for the erection of the new running sheds and repair shops at Stratford. These buildings formed the nucleus of Stratford works as they were in later days.

There are few references in the Board Minutes to the provision of new carriage stock during the period between 1839 and 1850. It was decided in October 1844 to provide lighting in first class, while three years later second-class carriages from Joseph Wright of Birmingham were to have armrests 'to standard pattern'. In regard to upholstery, it was agreed in October 1850 that linings and trimmings in first class were to be blue instead of drab as previously. One further group of carriages worthy of mention are the 10 'improved' carriages introduced in 1847 for the North Woolwich branch. Built by Messrs Adams at their Fairfield works in Bow, these carriages were noteworthy in that they were eight-wheeled (not bogie); they were 40 ft in length and 9 ft wide, with a 30 ft wheelbase. They were semi-rigid with a flexible joint between the two halves. Divided into four compartments, they were first/second composites providing accommodation for some 110 passengers. As eight-wheelers they only lasted for three years, each of the bodies being separated in 1850 to provide 20 four-wheeled composites.

On the wagon front, the usual stock was provided in the early years. Hudson's arrival late in 1845 saw wagons being procured in large numbers

* John Marshall in his *Biographical Dictionary of Railway Engineers* states (p.51) that John Chester Craven came to the ECR in May 1845 as locomotive engineer (but not as superintendent), before moving to the London Brighton & South Coast Railway (LB&SCR) in December 1847. Craven was born near Leeds on 11th September, 1813 and worked on the Manchester & Leeds Railway and later on the ECR before going to the LB&SCR as their locomotive superintendent in December 1847.

† Thomas Cabry's nephew, Joseph, born in Cheshire about 1831, was one of Martin Atock's predecessors as locomotive superintendent on the MGWR in Ireland.

from the North of England. For example, 20 were purchased from the Newcastle & Darlington Railway and 50 from the Y&NMR in October 1845. Also in October 1845 it was agreed to order 200 wagons with zinc tops. Further batches of coal wagons, totalling 550, came from Messrs Payne & Burn and Messrs G. & M. Palmer, Messrs Barnap & Co., all of Newcastle, Messrs Hawks, Crawshay of Gateshead, Mr Hudson of Shields, Mr Burlinson of Sunderland and Messrs A. Fletcher of Darlington.

The exact date of George Attock's move to Stratford is unknown. We do know from a presentation made to him on the occasion of his retirement in November 1874 that he had 29 years' service and that the Act of Parliament that created the London and North Western Railway received Royal Assent on 16th July, 1846. His third son, Frederick, was born at No. 8 Anson Terrace in the Islington district of Liverpool on 10th February of that year, so it is likely that he began his career at Stratford works as chief foreman of the Wagon Department sometime between March and July 1846. The family, now consisting of George and Hephzibah and their four children, Martin, George, Mary Curtis and Frederick, took up residence at No. 1 Angel Place, Leyton Road, close to the works. As recorded above, Thomas Scott was in charge of rolling stock matters, although John Hunter was to take over, as locomotive, carriage & wagon superintendent, within a few months of George's arrival.

The *Railway Times* for 2nd January, 1847 makes reference to a dinner and ball, provided by the Directors two nights previously for the workmen at Stratford, an event no doubt attended by George and Hephzibah. Some 1,500 invitations were sent out for the dinner, which was provided by Messrs Bathe & Breach of the London Tavern in Bishopsgate Street, close to the line's terminus. The repast was held in the new repairing shop, described as 'a building of great extent, ...tastefully decorated and containing a dining-room quite capable of accommodating the pretty large party who were invited'. After dinner, tea and coffee were served, the ladies retiring to a gallery provided for their use. After some speeches, approximately 3,000 people attended the ball. It was recorded that dancing was kept up until a late hour with an unflagging spirit, which was highly pleasing to behold; one can imagine George and Hephzibah dancing into the early hours.

On a more serious note, the shareholders' half-yearly meeting, held at the beginning of February 1847, gave some details of the company's progress to that date. Mr Hunter, in his report, referred to the carriage and wagon stock being in a 'much improved state' and generally in good condition. Apart from a stock of 58 passenger and 13 goods engines, additions to the carriage stock during the half-year included 27 firsts, 51 seconds, 74 thirds, 82 other coaching vehicles and 406 goods, cattle, coal and timber trucks. The Chairman reported that suitable sheds had been provided at all stations where carriages were stored, for their better protection. In April 1850 John Hunter gave six months' notice that he was to resign and advertisements were placed for his replacement. No less than 30 applications were opened at the Board meeting on 16th May. These included William Fernihough, who was by then with the South Eastern & Chatham Railway, and Henry L. Corlett, who was carriage superintendent of the Great Southern & Western Railway (GS&WR) at Inchicore in Dublin since the

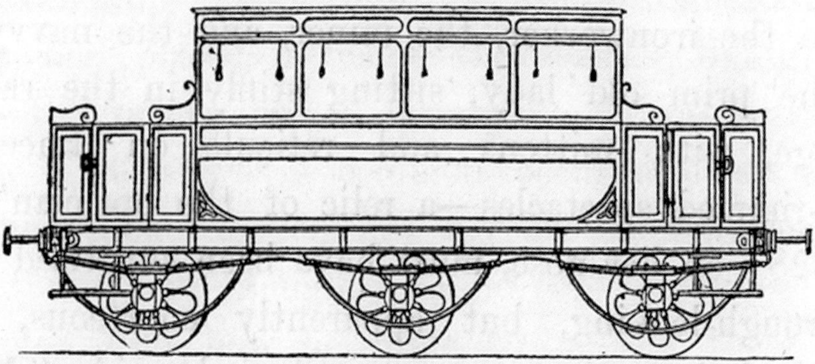

EXTERIOR OF AN EASTERN COUNTIES SMOKING CARRIAGE OF 1846.

Wood cuts of the interior and exterior of an Eastern Counties Railway smoking carriage of the mid- to late-1840s. Some artist's licence has doubtless been incorporated.

Gerald Beesley Collection

A SMOKING CARRIAGE ON THE EASTERN COUNTIES LINE IN 1846.

dismissal of Edward Lean on 1st March, 1849. Edward Lean had been appointed in place of Charles Fay following his move from the GS&WR to the Lancashire & Yorkshire Railway in October 1846. Henry Corlett was to remain with the GS&WR as carriage superintendent until his resignation on 20th April, 1877 when the post was combined with that of locomotive superintendent under Alexander McDonnell. Two other persons who applied for the position at Stratford are worth mentioning, viz. Thomas Lunt of Liverpool and Robert Andrews of the GWR, both of whom were later to hold the post of locomotive superintendent on the Waterford & Limerick Railway.

The successful candidate, John Viret Gooch, was duly appointed as from 22nd July, 1850. Gooch was born in 1813 in Bedlington, 12 miles north of Newcastle; he was the second of three children of John Gooch. His younger brother, Daniel born in 1816, rose to prominence with the GWR. John Viret served his apprenticeship with Joseph Locke, in due course becoming locomotive superintendent of the Manchester & Leeds Railway. Locke had been responsible for the construction of the London & Southampton Railway, renamed the London & South Western Railway (LSWR) in 1839, and it was his influence which saw the young Gooch appointed as their locomotive superintendent in 1841; there he was responsible for the setting-up of the company's works at Nine Elms, opened in 1843. Pending Gooch's arrival at Stratford, Messrs Hunter and Kitson* were instructed to prepare a complete listing of all locomotives, carriages and wagons, showing mileages run and state of repair.

A survey of wagons carried out three months earlier, in April 1850, listed a total of 2,836 goods and cattle wagons in stock, of which 1,103 had spring buffers at both ends, 650 had spring buffers at one end, while the remaining 1,083 had 'dead' buffers only. In addition, there were 64 ballast wagons and 49 goods brake vans with spring buffers at one end; finally there were 612 coal wagons with 'dead' buffers. Also about this time it was reported that John Ashbury of Manchester had been overpaid £2,000 on the Wagon Account, £1,400 of which was to be repaid, the balance of £600 being offset against future orders. This overpayment is a hint as to the mismanagement of the company's financial affairs, details of which were to surface before too long.

On his arrival, Gooch immediately set about improving operating methods that had been allowed to deteriorate over a period of time; an attempt was also made to standardise pay amongst drivers and firemen as well as removing perks, which had been in operation for many years. These developments were, quite understandably, resented by the men, who in a body petitioned the Board seeking Gooch's removal from office. This demand was quite unacceptable to the Directors and as a result the men were dismissed on 18th August, 1850. Replacements were obtained both from the North British Railway and from Gooch's old employer, the LSWR. It was also reported that some damage was caused to engines due to the use of inexperienced enginemen.

January 1851 saw orders placed for additional carriage stock. These were initially for 18 first class and 22 second class carriages from Joseph Wright at £358 and £248 each respectively; a Board Minute, dated 21st January, stated that

* William Kitson was born in Leeds about 1814 and was the brother of James Kitson, founder of the Airdale Foundry in the Hunslet district of Leeds where the locomotive building firm of Kitson & Co. was located.

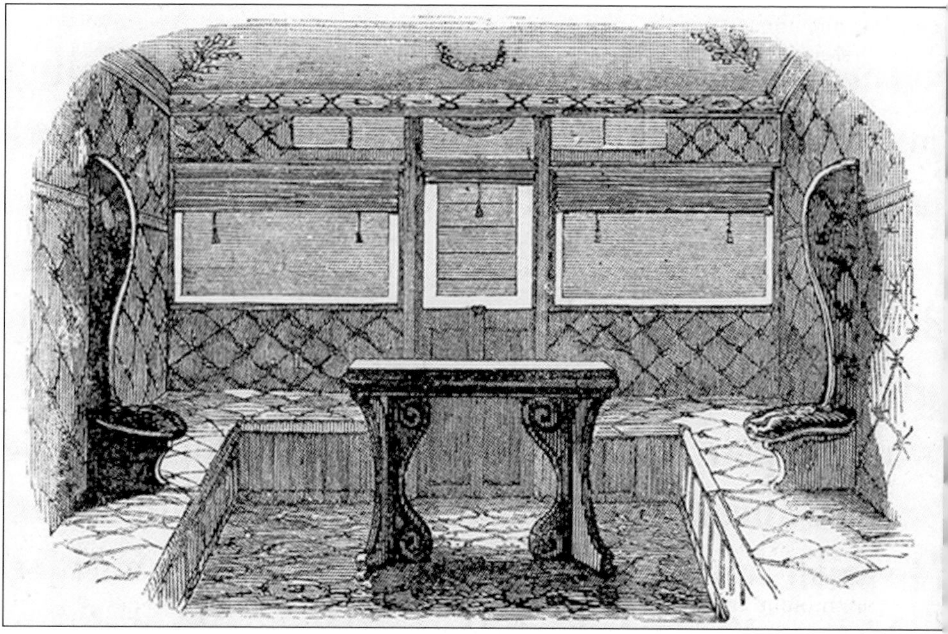

A wood cut of an Eastern Counties Railway first class carriage of 1847, typical of what George Attock would have seen when he arrived at Stratford. *Gerald Beesley Collection*

Wood cut of an Eastern Counties Railway second class carriage of 1847. *Gerald Beesley Collection*

an amendment was made for 20 composite carriages, although there is no reference to revised numbers of firsts and seconds. In October of the same year George Attock was requested to proceed at once with a new first class and new second-class bodies, to be placed on new iron frames. We know that Gooch experimented with iron underframes in the early 1850s before reverting to wood. The latter were used exclusively by Gooch's successor, Robert Sinclair, and it was not until 1879 that the first steel underframes were used by the GER. Apart from the two carriages mentioned above, 20 iron underframes 21 ft 8 in. in length were made and were placed under 20 old Newmarket Railway carriage bodies; the old wooden frames from these carriages were shortened and in turn placed under old Northern & Eastern Railway vehicles.

In June 1852 Gooch submitted a statement to the Board listing payments due to his various assistants in the Locomotive Department for savings effected in the 18 month period ending 4th January, 1852, totalling £2,098 15*s.* 4*d.* This total included £143 10*s.* 0*d.* to Frederick Trevethick,* £27 3*s.* 0*d.* to George Attock and no less than £1,552 7*s.* 4*d.* to Gooch himself. Such payments were to be the subject of considerable concern to shareholders some three years later and were to lead in part to Gooch's resignation.

In the following December the Board decided that all new locomotives, carriages and wagons were to be built by the company at Stratford works, an aspiration which proved to be somewhat optimistic. About this time a programme commenced of rebuilding low-sided wagons and coal wagons to increase capacity to 6 tons; the total cost of raising wagon sides was estimated at £15,000, whereas new wagons equal to the gain in carrying capacity would cost £80,000.

Complaints regarding shortages of wagons, excessive rates for the carriage of coal and other concerns regarding the company's financial affairs led to the setting up of a shareholders' committee of investigation in September 1855; this investigation, like the earlier one into Hudson, was instigated by Horatio Love, a solicitor. A number of matters were reviewed, some interest focusing on the Stores Department, when it transpired that the Chairman's personal clerk, Alfred Williams, described by one witness as 'an unsuccessful farmer and Army Officer', had been appointed as storekeeper. It was quickly ascertained that the Chairman, David Waddington, and Williams controlled all stores, while blank spaces and pencilled entries were to be found in the Stores Accounts; furthermore, items such as grease and horsehair had been sold at a loss. A discrepancy of £12,000 was found in these accounts.

When the investigation into Williams was instigated, Waddington angrily referred to it as being 'an affront on a gentleman'. It also transpired that Williams and one of the Directors, a Mr Hawkins, MP for Colchester, had married sisters; subsequent to this the former had ordered timber from Hawkins without any tendering process. There was also evidence to show that Williams appeared to be living well beyond his salary, although, in response to this allegation, he spoke of an annual allowance from his parents and a sum left by his aunt in her will. In regard to the company's shipping operations, it was

* Frederick Trevethick, son of Richard Trevethick the inventor of the high-pressure steam engine, was born about 1817 in Penzance, Cornwall. Frederick had at least two sons, Frederick and James G., as well as a daughter Maria.

found that the two vessels employed on the Harwich to Antwerp service were totally unsuited to the operation due to their shallow draft. There was also some question as to whether the company was legally authorized to operate such steamer services, which had to that date incurred large losses.

The bulk of the criticism in the report, however, was levelled against John Viret Gooch, this falling under various headings. At the time of his appointment in July 1850 to the post of locomotive, carriage & wagon superintendent, he had negotiated an agreement with the Chairman allowing him 5 per cent on all savings effected over £10,000 per annum. As we have already noted above, this amounted to more than £1,500 for the first 18 months of Gooch's tenure, although his annual salary was only £600. Peter Ashcroft, the way & works superintendent until November 1854, was very critical of Gooch, referring to the savings being 'a fallacy used to his (Gooch's) own advantage'.

It came to light that Gooch was a senior partner in the North & East Coal Company, of which Alfred and Edward Prior were the owners. The Prior brothers had negotiated a contract with the ECR in 1853 to transport coal over the company's lines at a preferential rate, a fact known to the Chairman; the ECR were also obliged under the agreement to provide 200 wagons, storage depots and sidings. Gooch, without any reference to the Board, soon interfered with the rates charged to other companies. Other coal companies made regular complaints in this regard and also about shortage of wagons; at one stage it transpired that some 500 wagons were tied up in Priors' enterprise. Mr Young, the Mayor of Wisbeach (modern spelling - Wisbech) and a coal merchant, found it necessary to purchase his own wagons; although these were exactly the same as the company's wagons, Young was refused permission to use them on the grounds of safety. It was found that station staff, many of whom were working under Gooch's direction unloading Prior's coal, were encouraged to sell that firm's products and were receiving commission from Gooch. He was also the owner of four steamships operating out of Lowestoft and engaged in Prior's traffic; all the ECR men at that port worked for Gooch.

There was also evidence that locomotives were being ordered from outside firms, while others were being built at Stratford works for the Royal Danish Railway. Two of the outside orders were with Kitsons of Leeds and the Canada Company in Birkenhead, the latter described as 'not a good Company'. The Canada Company was an enterprise established by George Harrison following consultations with Messrs Peto, Brassey & Betts concerning construction of locomotives for the Grand Trunk Railway of Canada, hence the title. Mention was made of the fact that William Kitson, Gooch's principal assistant at Stratford, was a brother of James Kitson. The Royal Danish Railway had been established in 1852/53 with a Royal concession, granted to Messrs Peto & Betts in perpetuity, for a system of railways. The first section, 69 miles in length, was opened from Tonning to Hussum, Flensburg and Rendsburgh on 17th May, 1855. Much of this line ended up in what later became German territory. It was built and equipped with rolling stock by the contractors, and the North of Europe Steam Navigation Company set up a comprehensive system of steamer communication. It was known that Gooch had visited Denmark and had there met with the King.

This was a damning report, not only for the various individuals investigated, but it also showed how the company's financial state had deteriorated and how little the Directors knew of day-to-day happenings within the company. Frederick Trevethick, who had been one of Gooch's assistants, resigned in January 1856, William Kitson taking over his responsibilities. As regards Gooch himself, it was decided to terminate his contract as from the end of June 1856. It was reported that he was unavailable in connection with the half-yearly report to shareholders and it transpired that he was staying with the Earl of Caithness at Barrogill Castle in Thurso, quaintly shown as being in North Britain. Although only 44 years of age, John Viret Gooch appears to have retired from railway work at that time and spent his remaining years with his family at his country residence, Cooper's Hill House, Easthampstead in Berkshire, where he died on 8th June, 1900. Records indicate that he did have some financial involvement with the Lintz Colliery Company in Co. Durham up to at least December 1867, a company also part-owned by his old friend and business partner, Alfred Prior.

Gooch's position as locomotive superintendent was taken by Robert Sinclair, who came from the Caledonian Railway, where he had held a similar position since 1847. He also later took on the additional responsibilities of Chief Engineer, following the resignation of Peter Bruff, a role that he was to retain until 1866. Robert Sinclair was born in London on 1st July, 1817, the son of Alexander Sinclair, a merchant and founder of the firm of Sinclair, Hamilton & Co. He was educated at Charterhouse School in London before serving an apprenticeship with the firm of Scott, Sinclair & Co., engineers and shipbuilders in Greenock. He obtained employment on the Liverpool & Manchester Railway at Edge Hill and later on the Grand Junction Railway, serving under Joseph Locke. Sinclair subsequently spent some time in France before returning to Scotland as locomotive superintendent of the Glasgow, Paisley & Greenock Railway, moving into a similar position on the Caledonian Railway when the former was absorbed into that company; in 1851 he also took charge of civil engineering matters.

In September 1856 David Waddington resigned his positions as Chairman and a Director of the ECR. It appears that Mr Davies of the superintendent's office was instrumental in issuing a circular to staff regarding 'a gift of esteem for David Waddington'; he was severely reprimanded for this and ordered at once to withdraw the circular, and he resigned in November. Waddington was replaced on the Board by Horatio Love, who was elected Chairman in February 1857. It must be stressed that there was never any suggestion that George Attock was in any way involved in any of these underhand dealings; neither his name nor any reference to improprieties in relation to rolling stock is mentioned anywhere in the shareholders' report.

On the family front, George and Hephzibah had three more children following their move to Stratford, all girls. Elizabeth was born on 1st November, 1847, Phoebe Ann on 8th May, 1849 and Caroline on 17th October, 1851. We know that Elizabeth and Phoebe Ann subsequently married, but Caroline initially proved to be a mystery, all searches failing to find any trace of her subsequent to her birth. Only recently has the author discovered that Caroline died in October 1853, she was buried at Brickfields Congregational Chapel in

West Ham. George's second son, also George, started as a boy at Stratford works on the occasion of his 14th birthday, 17th November, 1851. His older brother, Martin, had already started his railway career there, presumably also on his 14th birthday in 1848. It is known that Martin spent two years as a draughtsman with Messrs Mather & Platt at their works in Manchester; we have no dates for his move to Manchester, but he was back at Stratford works as a draughtsman in May 1854 when he was earning 2*s*. 4*d*. a day.

A couple of other people working with the ECR at Stratford during the 1850s are worthy of mention, Thomas Conran and James Thomas Rowe. Thomas Conran, born in Co. Longford about 1831, was a draughtsman there in July 1853. He moved shortly afterwards to take up a position on the Cork & Bandon Railway. When that company's locomotive superintendent resigned his position in April 1857, he recommended Conran, by then the senior fitter, as fully competent to take his place, a position he held for some 30 years. James Thomas Rowe began his career as a boy at Stratford in May 1854 and we shall hear more of him in later chapters.

The chief draughtsman at Stratford, a Mr Tigors, resigned on 8th July, 1857 and Martin was appointed to succeed him. By that time he had met Mary Eliza, the daughter of Henry and Eliza Bowbank of Cambridge, where her father was a baker. The couple married at the Church of St Andrew's the Great in Cambridge on 16th August, 1859, the ceremony being conducted by the Vicar, Revd John Martin. By then Martin had been promoted foreman of the running shed at Stratford and was earning 50*s*. a week, sufficient to support a young wife. A son, Martin Henry, was born to the happy couple on 30th June, 1860 at Stratford. Martin remained at Stratford from that time until he moved to Limerick in 1861.

It is not clear what prompted Martin to leave the ECR and move to Ireland, but the family tradition of a rift is given credence by Martin's decision to adopt the ancestral spelling of his surname. We know that Martin, George and Mary Curtis, who were all born in Preston, had been recorded in the parish register with the Atock surname. What gives added significance to the theory that the rift had occurred around 1861 is the fact that by March of that year George had also left Stratford, where, as a fitter, he had been earning 3*s*. 11*d*. a day. He too reverted to the Atock surname and was living at No. 33 Kensington Place, Brighton, at the home of John H. Davis, a wagon maker; so presumably by then he had secured employment with the London Brighton & South Coast Railway at its Brighton works.

Ten years later, young George Atock was boarding at the home of John Fitton, a glasscutter, at 6 Chapman Street in Manchester. He now described himself as an engineer; whilst we do not know where he was employed, it seems likely that he was with either Messrs Beyer, Peacock & Co. or the Manchester Sheffield & Lincolnshire Railway, both of whose works were located in Gorton. George had retired by the time of the 1881 census, as he was living with his sister Elizabeth, who might also have taken Martin and George's side in whatever rift may have occurred in the family. She and George were the witnesses at the wedding of their sister Mary Curtis to Edward Stevens at the Parish Church at West Ham on 31st August, 1863, the siblings spelling their name Atock!

George Atock's gravestone in Aldeburgh, Suffolk. Note spelling of surname with the single 'T'. *Photographer unknown*

Elizabeth had married a John Strutt, in 1865 and was residing at High Street, Saxmundham. George Atock never married and he died on 14th January, 1885 at the home of John and Elizabeth. By that time they had become the proprietors of the West Suffolk Hotel in High Street, Aldeburgh,* on the coast some seven miles south-east of Saxmundham.

Edward Stevens, who married Mary Curtis, was also on the staff of the Locomotive Department at Stratford where he held the position of cashier. Edward, born about 1835, was one of seven children of Joseph and Hannah Stevens of High Street, Hadleigh in Suffolk, where his father was for many years an innkeeper. When Edward entered employment at Stratford works he took lodgings nearby, at No. 5 Phillip Terrace, with Stephen and Mary Franklin. Stephen was a coach body maker by trade and it was most likely through his employment in her father's department that Mary Curtis had become acquainted with Edward. At the young couple's marriage on 31st August, 1863, in addition to George and Elizabeth, a Robert Wardle was a witness. As we shall see later in our narrative, Wardle was to cause some upset at Stratford works.

Following their marriage, Edward and Mary Curtis moved to Lay Cottage, which was very close to where Martin had lived prior to his move to Limerick. They had three children, Mary, born in 1865, George Edward in 1866 and Nellie in 1869. Tragically Mary Curtis died early in 1881 at the young age of 42, leaving Edward to bring up three young children, although he had a 19-year-old servant, Alice Bradman, to assist him. By that time George Edward had entered on an engineering apprenticeship at Stratford works. Ten years later, George Edward, by then calling himself Edward, was an engine fitter and was boarding with Henry Furze (a retired engine driver) and his family at 74 Windmill Lane, situated close to the GER works at Stratford. On the night of the 1891 census,

* Orford Ness just to the south of Aldeburgh became the site of the world's first radar research station in 1935.

Mary Stevens was staying with her uncle, Frederick Attock, at 185 High Street, Chorlton-on-Medlock, Manchester.

Here it might be mentioned that John Strutt's first cousin, William Strutt, married Elizabeth's sister, Phoebe Ann at Leyton Parish Church on 15th September, 1879, the ceremony being performed by the Vicar, Revd W.J. Bettison; one of the witnesses was Phoebe Ann's mother, Hephzibah. William, who was himself a farmer, was the eldest of six children born to William and Sophia (née Ennals) Strutt of Layham in Suffolk. William and Phoebe had five children, viz. Alice, William, Nellie, Frederick and Stanley. By March 1901 William was a stonemason's labourer living in Main Street, Hadleigh, with his wife Phoebe Ann and their son Stanley who was then 15 years of age and serving his time as a groom's apprentice. In yet another coincidence in the Attock story, Hadleigh was the birthplace of Edward Stevens who had married Mary Curtis.

Reverting to matters on the ECR, working of the smaller concerns, under agreement or by acquisition, had put the company in command of the entire railway traffic of East Anglia by the early 1860s. The chief weakness lay in management; the direction of the smaller companies was imperfectly co-ordinated, and little effective control was applied to the whole group. Although arrangements for through working had been made between them, the companies were never on easy terms, and they squabbled continuously. A necessary step to rectifying the situation was made when Parliament agreed to the ECR, the Eastern Union Railway, the East Anglian Railway, and the East Suffolk & Norfolk Railway companies, along with their subsidiary undertakings, being incorporated into the GER on the 7th August, 1862.

Robert Sinclair approached the GER Board in October 1865 stating that he wished to relinquish the post of locomotive, carriage & wagon superintendent, although he was prepared to remain on as the company's Chief Engineer. The Directors were sympathetic to Sinclair's request suggesting, however, that he should remain on in his full capacity until the following January. He was also requested to act in an advisory capacity on rolling stock matters, being granted a retainer of £100 per annum; in addition, he was to receive two-thirds of his salary as Chief Engineer. William Kitson assumed the responsibility for locomotives and rolling stock pending the selection of a successor.

On 7th December, 1865 it was announced that 28 applications had been received for the post of locomotive superintendent, these in due course being whittled down to two candidates, viz. William Kitson and Samuel Waite Johnson. Johnson, who had been with the Edinburgh & Glasgow Railway, was duly appointed on 3rd May, 1866 at a salary of £750 per annum. Some other staff changes occurred about that time. Early in January 1866 it was announced that Mr Kitson was leaving the company; this was William's son, William Henry, who was the foreman at Stratford running shed. Mark Wardle was appointed to take his place and George Macallan was instructed to go to Cambridge as running superintendent to replace Wardle there. However, Wardle declined to move to Stratford and resigned his position, the vacancy at Stratford being filled by a Mr A. Kier. Johnson remained with the GER until 15th July, 1873 when he left to take up an appointment as locomotive superintendent of the Midland Railway, where he was to distinguish himself.

Brief reference has been made earlier to Robert Wardle, and an interesting entry relating to a Mr Wardle appears in the GER minutes for 23rd November 1870, which is quoted here in full, viz.

> Conviction. Also from the Law Clerk re case at the Central Criminal Court on 22nd inst. Mr Wardle charged with sending threatening letter to Mr Johnson (Locomotive Superintendent). Found guilty, sentenced to three months and security of £200 for 18 months.

On discovering this, the author was initially of the opinion that this might have been Mark Wardle who had left the company in 1866 following his refusal to move to Stratford, as related in the preceding paragraph. However, it transpired that it was Robert Wardle, a locomotive fitter, aged 51, who had sent written threats of death to S.W. Johnson. He had been employed by the GER as a foreman of smiths for many years prior to 1867. In Court, evidence was given that Wardle had written 'under a morbid state of feeling, to which the defendant had become subject'. He had apparently sustained losses as a shareholder in the GER, and this resulted in him 'taking stimulants, to which he at times addicted'. It was also commented that ordinarily he was a most humane man, but that if not then legally insane, he was very nearly so when he wrote the letters. In possible mitigation, it was stated that he had accidentally received two blows to the head with a heavy hammer in the course of his work and that he had been dismissed in 1867 for drunkenness. Robert Wardle served out his three months' sentence at Springfield Prison in Essex. It is not known if he was in any way related to Mark Wardle.

Meanwhile, George Attock had continued with his duties as carriage & wagon superintendent. He was one of four members of the wider family to have inventions patented, and in 1863 he had come up with an idea for improvements in assistant bearing springs for use on locomotives and rolling stock (Patent No. 2145, 1863). Basically the improvement he suggested consisted of a mode of applying India rubber or steel springs between the underframe and body of the vehicles so as to diminish vibrations and shocks normally imparted to them due to uneven permanent way. George expressed himself in favour of using George Spencer's patented India-rubber cones, considering them to give the best action and to be safe in use. Spencer's Patent was dated 22nd July, 1853, No. 1733.

On 20th October, 1874 George Attock announced his resignation from the GER on the grounds of ill health. A ceremony was held at Stratford on 23rd December when he was presented with a silver cup, silver salver and a sum of £200 for his dedicated services to the company over the previous 29 years. Regrettably George did not live long to enjoy his retirement as he passed away at his residence on Leytonstone Road on 23rd August of the following year. He died of heart disease at the comparatively young age of 63. George's son Frederick, who had joined the ECR as an apprentice on his 14th birthday in February 1860, and who, prior to his father's retirement, had been acting as his assistant, was duly promoted at a salary of £250, while Massey Bromley was appointed works manager.

In taking over the role of carriage & wagon superintendent of the GER from his late father, Frederick became responsible for some 2,000 carriages, between 11,000 and 12,000 wagons, nearly 600 road vans, as well as 1,150 men. His new position also carried responsibility for the design of all carriages and wagons and during his short tenure of two years he received a compliment on the GER saloon from the Prince of Wales, who commented that it was the best he had ever travelled in. Quite a deal of additional machinery was installed in the carriage & wagon shops at Stratford during 1876/77 and there is little doubt that Frederick would have been instrumental in the decision-making leading to its procurement.

Away to the north-west, Charles Fay, the carriage & wagon superintendent of the Lancashire & Yorkshire Railway, wrote to the Board of that company in November 1876 tendering his resignation. Advertisements were duly placed seeking applicants for the position and Frederick Attock was one of ten outsiders and five company people who responded. The 'insiders' included James Howarth, foreman of the coach body makers at Miles Platting, and Jonathan B. Mellor, the wagon shop superintendent at Bury, both of whom we shall come across again in Chapter Eleven. Frederick was eventually selected for the position, his resignation from the service of the GER being submitted to the Board on 9th January, 1877. He set about arranging his affairs at once in readiness for his move northwards and in Chapters Ten, Eleven and Twelve we shall follow Frederick's career on the L&YR.

Silver Cup and Salver presented to George Attock on the occasion of his retirement from the position of carriage & wagon superintendent of the Great Eastern Railway in 1874. Apart from the foregoing, George also received a sum of £200, a not inconsiderable sum at that time, showing the esteem in which he was held. *Steve Myers*

Chapter Three

A Decade at Limerick

Martin Atock's appointment to the Waterford & Limerick Railway officially dated from 1st November, 1861, but he had obviously been persuaded to take up his position as early as possible; evidence of this comes from his report to the Board on 22nd October on the state of the locomotive stock. Limerick must have seemed a very different place to the young Martin as he settled down to a new beginning in a strange country with his wife and young son. In addition, it is almost certain that Martin had no idea of the short tenure enjoyed by all of his predecessors at Limerick. It says a lot for Martin's character that he stayed there for 11 years and left of his own accord rather than being persuaded to do so by the Board. Indeed, his first five successors also had short tenures, only J.G. Robinson equalling Martin's stay there. In fairness, Henry Appleby, who took up the post in 1883, might have remained longer had he not suffered ill health as a result of a fall during a Directors' inspection of the line and taken early retirement in 1889.

Incorporated by Act of Parliament dated 21st July, 1845 the W&LR had been opened in stages between the cities named in its title, reaching the outskirts of Waterford in August 1854.* Suffice here to state that it was a company constantly strapped for cash and due to this the locomotives and rolling stock were deficient in number and starved of proper maintenance, giving rise to poor timekeeping and failures. This resulted in complaints being constantly made against successive locomotive superintendents and it is not surprising, therefore, to learn that few stayed long in the company's service; in fact there were no less than six holders of the position between 1848 and 1861. Of these one might mention Thomas Lunt, who was locomotive superintendent from 1853 to 1857. Lunt had come to Limerick from the Liverpool & Manchester Railway and was an unsuccessful candidate for the position of locomotive superintendent on the ECR when a vacancy had occurred there in 1850. Dissatisfied with the manner in which Lunt was conducting the department, the Board gave him three months' notice in December 1856. Although he had been almost four years in the situation, he had outlasted his predecessors by a good margin. Despite the complaints against him, Lunt was presented with a silver breakfast plate set in a testimony of high appreciation of his skill, ability and unassuming upright character; he was also granted a sum of £30 to enable him to remove his family back to Liverpool.

Lunt's replacement at Limerick was Jonathan Pim, the son of James Pim, Secretary of the Dublin & Kingstown Railway. He does not appear to have distinguished himself in locomotive matters, frequent complaints being made as to the poor condition of the engines in his care. Early in November 1860 Pim was ordered to furnish the Board with a schedule of all rolling stock. This schedule showed 21 passenger and five goods engines, 55 carriages, 29 other

* Full details of the history of this fascinating railway can be found in the author's work published in 2006 (*see Bibliography*).

coaching vehicles and 425 goods vehicles of various categories. These figures were soon increased as the company took over the working of the Limerick & Ennis (L&ER) and Waterford & Kilkenny (W&KR) companies. The W&LR locomotive stock included six 2-2-2 outside cylinder tender engines supplied by Messrs Stothert, Slaughter & Co. of Bristol in 1846 for the opening of the line. By 1861 these locomotives were in poor mechanical condition and were in the course of being withdrawn.

William Dargan, who had constructed the line, had also worked it under a haulage contract in the early 1850s and had added four second-hand locomotives to stock in 1853. Three of these were old Bury singles dating from 1848 which, remarkably, remained in service until the 1880s. Messrs Fairbairn of Manchester supplied a total of six 2-4-0 passenger locomotives between 1853 and 1855, and Sharp, Stewart built four 0-4-2 goods locomotives for the company in 1853. In addition to their own stock, the W&LR took over six locomotives from the W&KR, which system they worked between 1st July, 1860 and 1st June, 1867. Pim was requested to prepare a report on the W&KR stock, this being submitted in March 1861. It showed all six locomotives as requiring repairs, estimated to cost in excess of £2,500. Only one of the six was in working order, while another was in pieces at Kilkenny and Limerick; much of the W&KR rolling stock was also in poor condition. The W&LR took over the working of the L&ER in April 1861, inheriting a further three locomotives in the process.

By September 1861 a decision had been taken not to renew Jonathan Pim's contract which was due to expire at the end of the year. A Board Minute of 23rd September refers to correspondence between Robert Shaw, a W&LR Director from Portlaw in Waterford, and Mr Armstrong (of the GWR) who had been approached for his advice in regard to a suitable replacement. It is not clear whether this reference was to Joseph Armstrong or his brother George.* It seems likely that it was in fact Joseph Armstrong who was approached for his advice in view of his close association with Daniel Gooch. It will be recalled that the latter's elder brother, John Viret Gooch, had been appointed locomotive carriage and wagon superintendent of the ECR in August 1850, a post which he retained until 1856, so he would have known both George Attock and Martin Atock at Stratford.

Although the GWR had not, at that time, entered into any formal agreements with the W&LR its associate, the South Wales Railway, had reached New Milford by means of a branch from Haverfordwest on 15th April, 1856. The GWR, W&LR and W&KR agreed to establish a steam packet service between New Milford and Waterford. This service was initially operated by Messrs Ford & Jackson of London on behalf of the GWR, and was taken over by the latter in 1872. It must also be mentioned that the W&LR company's first Secretary, William Septimus Saunders, was a brother of Charles Saunders, Secretary of the GWR. So it was that the GWR through Armstrong came to recommend a Mr Attock [*sic*] for the post of locomotive superintendent at Limerick. With such a recommendation, Martin's appointment was assured, and it was confirmed by

* Joseph Armstrong was born in Cumberland in September 1816, and by 1853 was in charge of GWR locomotives in the Northern Division based at Wolverhampton. He was directly responsible to Daniel Gooch, that company's locomotive superintendent. George Armstrong, some six years younger than Joseph, also worked for the GWR and took over as Northern Division locomotive superintendent at Wolverhampton when Joseph succeeded Gooch at Swindon in 1864.

the W&LR Board at their meeting on 10th October, 1861. Martin's salary was fixed at £300 per annum, to include ordinary travelling expenses while out on the line in the performance of his duties. He was to occupy, when at liberty, the company's cottage at Limerick at a rent of £1 per month. This may have been the property known as Hamilton House later occupied by J.G. Robinson, which was just a few minutes walk from the works.

As already recorded, Martin reported to the Board on 22nd October on the condition of the W&LR locomotive stock. He indicated that nine engines were in good working order, four others required slight repairs, 11 were not in good working order and required expenditure estimated at £3,443, while six engines were not worth repairing at all (the Stothert, Slaughter engines referred to above). It is clear that Martin had inherited a very run-down collection of locomotives. To be fair to Jonathan Pim and his predecessors, as already alluded to, the Locomotive Department had been starved of capital investment almost from the day the line opened, while they were being constantly exhorted by the Directors to reduce the number of breakdowns and improve the timekeeping of trains. While the Board considered the longer-term implications of the report, Martin employed nine fitters, two boilermakers, a smith and a machinist as additional staff to effect repairs.

The Board's response to Martin's report was to direct him to prepare specifications and plans for two new locomotives and to send the same to Slaughter, Grunning & Company, also suggesting that, as part payment, they take back three of their old locomotives.* Interestingly, Pim had in fact suggested to the Board in December 1860 the requirement for a more powerful class of locomotive to work goods and mineral traffic more effectively. He had been ordered to prepare drawings and specifications for two locomotives, Slaughter, Grunning offering to supply them at £2,650 each, 'free on board' Bristol. This offer was not accepted and further tenders were obtained in March 1861, but again not acted upon. It is unlikely that Martin would have ignored the earlier drawings, but it was in fact to Sharp, Stewart that the order went for the two 0-4-2 tender locomotives, their Order No. 419. W&LR Nos. 4 & 5 were delivered in June 1862; far from being of a more powerful type, they turned out to be almost identical to the four locomotives supplied to the company in 1853-54. Sharp, Stewart submitted their invoice in June 1862 at £2,134 each; however, it was ordered that 'trials be first conducted and a report submitted by Atock before payment was made'.

At the same Board meeting as the locomotive report was submitted, Martin submitted an up-to-date scale of wages for footplate men, viz.

	Drivers	*Firemen*
For first year	4*s.* per day	2*s.* 6*d.* per day
For second year	5*s.*	2*s.* 9*d.*
For third year	5*s.* 6*d.*	3*s.*
For fourth year	6*s.*	3*s.* 6*d.*†

* The origins of Stothert, Slaughter & Co. lay in the establishment of a locomotive manufacturing business at Bristol by Henry Stothert in 1837. Edward Slaughter joined him in 1841, and in 1851 Stothert took charge of a newly acquired shipbuilding yard. Slaughter was joined by Henry Grunning in 1856 when the firm was re-styled Slaughter, Grunning & Co; finally becoming the Avonside Engine Company Ltd. in 1864.

† For a fireman having a certificate for occasional driving.

One of the earliest known railway photographs in Ireland, this depicts one of the Stothert, Slaughter locomotives of the W&LR at Clonmel on a Limerick-bound train. All six members of the class were withdrawn in 1861/62, shortly after Martin Atock's arrival at Limerick.

Hemphill Collection Image courtesy South Tipperary County Museum

This scale was approved, but the matter was left for Martin to gradually carry it out 'as he knows better his staff'. In February 1862 the locomotive superintendent reported that alterations in the train service had enabled him to dispense with the services of three men at Waterford and two at Limerick. Two months later the Board were once again asking Martin to consider and decide on the best mode of reducing the heavy working expenses, agreeing to defer pressing for a reduction of staff in the Locomotive Department until after 1st May, when it was hoped the new locomotives would have arrived. By the time of Martin's next report on the locomotives in mid-March, 16 were in good working order, four were running but requiring repairs, five were laid up for repairs and two locomotives were condemned.

In August 1863 Martin proposed a rearrangement of machinery in the works as he was unable to do much wheel-turning with the one-wheel lathe; it was also suggested that a lathe and planing machine be moved from the Limerick & Ennis railway shops at Ennis and that a small screwing machine be requisitioned. The question of further new locomotives was raised in December 1863, tenders from various makers being submitted for two goods locomotives. One was from Sharp, Stewart for two similar to those supplied in June 1862 and one from Kitson of Leeds for locomotives similar to one supplied to the W&KR in 1853. The Board, in their wisdom, decided that only 'the one most pressing for the present' be obtained, this being ordered on 10th December, 1863 from Sharp, Stewart. No. 6 was virtually identical to Nos. 4 & 5 and was delivered on 10th August, 1864. January 1864 saw more complaints from the Board regarding recent failures. For example, a special failed on Clonmel bank with a broken frame, coupling rod and crank pin on 29th December, 1863. Martin attributed these failures to the rough state of the permanent way, the Engineer's personal attention to the matter being requested. Yet again in February 1864 reductions in working expenses were sought, directions being issued for a revision of the timetable to effect improvements.

We must now take a brief look at developments in W&LR carriage and wagon stock during Martin's time at Limerick. On his arrival he inherited 62 passenger carriages, 33 other coaching vehicles, 468 goods wagons and 10 goods brake vans; the total included stock recently taken in from the W&KR and L&ER. The situation was similar to that pertaining with the locomotive stock, viz. constant shortages of equipment and lack of repairs due to the excessive parsimony imposed by the Board. The only new carriages built during Martin's tenure were two third class vehicles constructed at the Limerick workshops in 1865. Although some minor alterations were carried out, the Board seemed reluctant to do anything else. For example, they decided to do nothing in respect of a Board of Trade directive of September 1868 obliging companies to provide separate smoking compartments on each train where there was more than one carriage of each class. Again, when in March 1870 it was reported that only 10 of 23 third class carriages had backrails fitted, and that to provide them would cost £9 per carriage and reduce the seating capacity by 10 per carriage, it was decided to defer the work until carriages came in for repairs.

The traffic manager was constantly requesting the provision of additional wagons to cater for increased traffic requirements. Even when 25 open goods wagons and a similar number of covered goods wagons were ordered in September 1864 they were deemed to be insufficient. Martin was ordered to attend to all old stock requiring repairs and to employ extra hands, if required. Twelve months later, he advised the Board that he could build a wagon £10 cheaper than outside builders. Wagons were in fact built in the W&LR workshops and in April 1866 it was ordered that production be increased from two to three wagons per month, 27 open goods wagons being completed during 1866-67.

Martin organised a census of stock, which was carried out in July 1867, instructing one of his staff to brand all of the stock. As a result of that exercise it was discovered that seven coal wagons and one covered goods wagon had apparently gone missing. Following investigation Martin came to the conclusion that six of the coal wagons had probably never existed, and the other had been broken at Clonmel nearly seven years previously. The other vehicle was probably on some other company's system and might well turn up. The problems of carrying out even basic repairs to wagons were highlighted in May 1868 when Martin advised that he required a minimum of 12 additional men; the Board surprisingly agreed to this request.

Two locomotives were added to stock in 1865. No. 28 *South of Ireland*, a 2-2-2, came from Kitson; it will be recalled that this firm had tendered to supply a locomotive in December 1863 based on similar ones supplied to the W&KR in 1853. In December 1864 the W&LR offered a bond for £2,000 and £400 in cash by way of payment, this being declined by Kitsons who insisted on 'net cash on delivery'; the matter was finally resolved when Kitsons agreed to accept a Bill at three months. The second locomotive purchased in 1865 was 0-4-0ST No. 29, which was procured from Sharp, Stewart at a cost of £1,335 delivered at Liverpool, for shunting at Waterford. It arrived on the W&LR on 4th December, 1865, but in actual fact it spent precious little time at Waterford, being soon transferred to work the Markets' Siding at Limerick.

Martin also found himself involved in various staff matters during 1865. It had been the practice to grant a premium to drivers, who kept the best time, and firemen, with the lowest coal consumption. The Board agreed in February to grant £3 each to five drivers and £1 each to five firemen. During the course of discussion on this matter, thoughts were directed to the necessity for the mail trains to keep good time. In July it was announced that foreman Teal at Limerick was leaving the service after 4½ years, Martin being ordered to write to Mr Armstrong of the GWR - who had recommended Teal who hailed from Birkenhead - regarding a possible successor. It may have been these circumstances that prompted Martin to invite James Thomas (Jimmy) Rowe to leave Stratford and join him at Limerick. He was the son of Joseph Rowe, himself an engineer originally from Truro in Cornwall, and had commenced his career on the ECR at Stratford as a boy in 1854. Although he was some six years younger than Martin, Jimmy Rowe was to remain his closest aide, first at Limerick and later on the Midland Great Western Railway at Broadstone, Dublin. By the time he retired from the MGWR at the end of 1899 he had risen to the position of principal assistant locomotive engineer.

Also in July 1865, Martin sought leave to take on one or two apprentices, from whom he would obtain fees, as was customary on most railways and in private firms at the time; the Board seemed reluctant to agree but gave permission for not more than two to be taken on. In November a tender was submitted by Messrs Tobin of Limerick for the supply of 46 overcoats for enginemen at 35*s*. each, Martin requesting that the men be given these free, as it was more than three years since they got the previous supply. Once again the Directors sought to extract payment, reluctantly agreeing on that occasion, but stipulating that in future the men should pay a proportion of the cost. When the overcoats were replaced again, at the end of 1870, the enginemen were obliged to pay half of the cost.

On 14th April, 1866 James Tighe, the company's Engineer, submitted a sketch for raising a portion of Martin's house by 12 ft and adding three bedrooms at an estimated cost of £130. Martin and Mary Eliza had already increased the size of their family with the arrival of a second son, Arthur, who was born on 31st July, 1863 and a daughter, Esther, born on 15th April, 1865. It was agreed that the work should be carried out so long as the estimate was not exceeded, Martin having agreed to pay 5 per cent on the outlay. The extension to the house was put to good use with the birth of two more children at Limerick, Thomas, who arrived on 8th June, 1868, and Amy Isabel born on 23rd January, 1871.

One of the benefits accruing to the staff of the Locomotive Department suggested by Martin was the provision of a Reading Room at Limerick, the site for which was given free in November 1867, not by the company, but by the Lunatic Asylum which adjoined the railway workshops at Limerick. The Board's only apparent contribution was to allocate a sum of £30 out of their subscription to the Friendly Society.

An Outlay Investigation Committee was set up by the W&LR in February 1868, the company's officers being ordered to submit a return of their staff with comparisons of wages and material expenditure over each of the preceding three years. Martin's return was, in addition, to show the working of each engine over the previous fortnight and how or on what line each driver was engaged. A rather more thorough investigation was carried out into running costs early in 1869, Martin being ordered to furnish a comparison of such expenses on the W&LR with those on other companies. Having provided this information in March, he was informed that the Board could not see how the GS&WR could return a lower cost and sought his early attention to such reforms in staff and running expenses so as to place them in a more satisfactory state. In due course he submitted a fresh report containing proposals which, if implemented, would result in a 10 per cent reduction in wages, partly through dismissal of staff and partly by a reduction in rates of pay. By November 1869 a total of 13 of the workshop staff had been given notice to quit by Martin, in pursuance of an order from the Stores Committee. In view of these reductions it was decided to send wheels and ironwork to England for renewals of wagons. One must question the ultimate financial benefit to the company of such a move.

As part of the same economy drive the decision was taken to withdraw separate trains on the Foynes branch and to combine the services to and from Newcastle West and Foynes. Thus the passengers from the early morning train from Foynes were obliged to wait for 80 minutes at Ballingrane Junction while

Waterford & Limerick Railway 2-2-2 No. 28 outside the works and shed at Limerick. Built by Kitson in 1864, she was later named *South of Ireland* and was withdrawn by the GS&WR as their No. 280 in 1902. *H. Fayle, courtesy Irish Railway Record Society Collection*

Ex-W&LR four-compartment four-wheeled third at Kingsbridge station, Dublin (now Heuston) following the absorption of the W&L system by the GS&WR in January 1901. As second No. 2, this 21 ft 6 in.-long vehicle was built by Ashbury in 1872 and was withdrawn in 1908. Note windows with rounded top corners. They are, however, rather more curved than the Atock designs. *The late L.E. Bastable, courtesy Irish Railway Record Society Collection*

the engine was sent to Newcastle West to bring up the train from there. Having arrived at Ballingrane Junction, the two trains were combined and then headed for Limerick; the total time for the 26¼ mile journey from Foynes to Limerick was 2 hours 50 minutes. The evening service was even worse in that intending Foynes passengers from Limerick were put off the train at Ballingrane Junction and forced to wait there for 85 minutes, often in inclement weather, while the train made the round trip to Newcastle West. Needless to say this caused a storm of protest from the residents of Foynes, who soon had their own train reinstated. It has to be said that the idea for this rather illogical move came not from the locomotive superintendent but from the Board.

On the locomotive front, Martin submitted recommendations in December 1870 that two goods locomotives should be purchased to meet increased traffic requirements, it being ordered that he prepare specifications and seek tenders. These would most likely have been the first locomotives in which Martin and his able assistant Jimmy Rowe had a major influence on design. They were also the last locomotives to be obtained during Martin's time at Limerick. Four tenders were duly submitted in March of the following year; whilst that of the Yorkshire Engine Company was the lowest at £3,010, it was to Kitsons that the order went for two engines and one tender at a combined figure of £4,000 with delivery in six months. The prospective delivery date was not met and in October 1871 Kitsons advised that they could not deliver the engines before the beginning of December at the earliest due to 'disaffection of employees'.

Martin Atock as the sportsman. He was apparently a 'good shot' judging by the cups and trophies. *Alex Atock Collection*

Martin Atock, locomotive superintendent of the W&LR from 1861 to 1872 and of the MGWR from 1872 to 1900. Martin was responsible for introducing standardisation to locomotive, carriage and wagon building on the MGWR. *Alex Atock Collection*

It is not entirely clear when these 0-4-2 goods locomotives actually arrived although Kitsons referred to trials taking place in February 1872. It is worth noting that after their withdrawal both were extensively rebuilt at Limerick. In fact, No. 7 emerged from the works in Limerick in 1888 as an 0-6-0 goods locomotive bearing the name *Progress* in recognition of the fact that it was the first locomotive built there. No. 3 remained in service until 1892; parts of this locomotive were used in the construction of *Zetland*, a similarly numbered 0-4-2 tank locomotive at Limerick in the same year.

Whether Martin realised that his future prospects at Limerick were rather limited, or he had become disillusioned with the parsimonious attitude of the Board we shall never know. Whatever the circumstances, he wrote to the Board on 14th March, 1872 tendering his resignation on his appointment to the position of locomotive, carriage & wagon superintendent of the MGWR in Dublin. Whilst appreciating that he was required to give a month's notice, he sought to leave the W&LR before that period expired, but the Board declined to agree to this. On the other hand, they immediately set about advertising for his replacement at a proposed salary of £400 per annum. The selection of a successor to Martin was deferred pending review of a letter received from Sir Daniel Gooch relating to Robert Andrews. Whatever transpired, it was Mark Wardle who was appointed on 3rd May on a six months' trial at £16 13*s*. 4*d*. per month, subject to one month's notice on either side.

Both Andrews and Wardle were previously involved with the ECR, albeit a tenuous connection in the case of Robert Andrews; he had been one of 28 applicants for the post of locomotive superintendent submitted to the ECR Board in May 1850. Mark Wardle's connection with the ECR/GER was, however, somewhat longer. Born in Newcastle-upon-Tyne in 1821, he was working at the Romford works in 1848 and later that year he moved to the new works at Stratford. In January 1866 Wardle was ordered to move from Cambridge (where he had been locomotive inspector since 1859) to become shed foreman at Stratford running shed in place of William Kitson who had resigned his position. For some unknown reason, Wardle refused to move to Stratford and announced his resignation in February.

There is a possibility that Mark Wardle might have gone to the W&LR as a foreman at that time, as there is no further record of him in England. This might explain his initial appointment at a much lower salary than Martin, his position as locomotive superintendent being formally ratified from 1st November, 1872 at a salary of £300 per annum, still £100 less than that referred to in the advertisement published earlier in the year. Only three months later the Board advised Wardle that they were ready to accept his resignation or to give the necessary three months' notice with full pay. In the event he resigned, and his replacement was none other than Robert Andrews, who was elected unanimously by the Board and given a salary of £400 per annum! From this it seems evident that the W&LR Board had favoured Andrews from the start.

Chapter Four

Martin Atock moves to Dublin

Martin Atock was one of five candidates for the position of locomotive, carriage & wagon superintendent of the Midland Great Western Railway who was called to attend the Board Meeting at Broadstone on 6th March, 1872. The others who attended were J.M. Budge, GNR (of England); J. Holden, GWR; A.L. Mumford, LNWR; and J.C. Park, GS&WR.* The successful candidate was Martin Atock, whose appointment at a salary of £500 per annum with house and gas, and a coal allowance was confirmed by the Board on 13th March, 1872. The appointment was to be terminable by three months' notice on either side. He arrived at his new residence, Royal Canal House, adjacent to Broadstone station, in mid-April 1872 with his wife Mary Eliza, who was pregnant at the time, and his four young children: Martin Henry, Arthur, Esther and Thomas. Martin and Mary Eliza's fifth child, George, was born in Dublin on 22nd May, 1872.

The MGWR was a much larger concern than the W&LR and, although the workshops at Limerick had been a busy place, Broadstone works must have seemed quite large by comparison. In order to give the reader an idea of what Martin Atock faced when he arrived at Broadstone, a brief summary of the history and extent of the MGWR, and a review of locomotive developments prior to his arrival, would not go amiss. The Midland Great Western Railway of Ireland Company, incorporated by Act of Parliament dated July 1845, was authorized to construct a line of railway from Dublin to Mullingar with a branch to Longford. The Act contained provisions for the new company to purchase the Royal Canal, beside which the line ran virtually all the way to Mullingar. The first section of line was opened from Broadstone to Enfield on Monday 28th June, 1847, a distance of 26½ miles. The main line was gradually extended westwards, the final section from Mullingar through Athlone to Galway being opened on 1st August, 1851.

The powers for the branch to Longford were allowed to lapse, fresh powers for it and a branch to Cavan being obtained by Act of May 1852. The line to

* J.M. Budge was district locomotive superintendent of the GNR at Peterborough.
James Holden was born in Whitstable, Kent, in July 1837. He served an apprenticeship under his uncle, Edward Fletcher, on the York, Newcastle & Berwick Railway, moving to the C&W Department of the GWR in 1865. Eventually, after some other placements, he was appointed chief assistant to William Dean at Swindon. He became locomotive superintendent of the GER in July 1885.
A.L. Mumford later became locomotive running superintendent of the LNWR.
John Carter Park was born in Aberdeen on 2nd January, 1822 and educated in Italy. He was appointed locomotive superintendent of the Lucca, Pisa & Pistoja Railway in 1853, resigning in the following year to take part in the Crimean War. He spent some time at Longsight (LNWR) under Ramsbottom, before his appointment as locomotive superintendent of the Buffalo & Lake Huron Railroad in Canada. He was with the GS&WR as works manager at Inchicore from 1865 to 1873, when he left on becoming locomotive superintendent of the North London Railway.

Longford was opened on 8th November, 1855, the opening of the Cavan branch, which diverged from the latter at Inny Junction, following on 8th July, 1856. Other extensions to the system saw Longford connected with Sligo, this line being opened on 3rd December, 1862, and a long branch from Athlone opened in stages to Westport, the latter point being reached on 29th January, 1866. In later years referred to as the Mayo Road, this line was financed and constructed by a separate company, the Great Northern & Western Railway; the line was always worked by the MGWR, who purchased it under the provisions of an Act of August 1890. The final piece of the jigsaw of relevance to Martin Atock's time at Broadstone was the construction of the three western branches during the 1890s, bringing the system to a total length of 538½ miles.

When Martin Atock took over at Broadstone, there were 80 locomotives in stock, with a further six on order. The oldest locomotives dated from the 1847-52 period, the earliest survivors being two Grendon 2-2-2s, Nos. 30 & 33, delivered in 1847, which Martin had withdrawn from service in 1875. The next oldest were six Fairbairn 2-2-2s dating from 1848, which were also withdrawn in 1875. These early locomotives had been delivered during the tenure of the MGWR's first locomotive superintendent, John Dewrance. He had come to Ireland in 1845 from the Liverpool & Manchester Railway to take an appointment as locomotive superintendent of the GS&WR at Inchicore, but his stay there was short-lived, as it appears he resented interference by the Directors in the running of his department. He moved to a similar position on the MGWR in 1847, but his only contribution to locomotive matters before his departure in 1849 was the six Fairbairns mentioned above.*

The MGWR was worked under haulage contracts until the end of 1852, which was a frequent enough arrangement at the time, but seldom successful. Initially J.S. Dawson of Dublin worked the line, but from March 1851 the haulage contract was undertaken by Messrs William Johnson & Thomas William Kinder of the Bromsgrove Carriage & Wagon Company. A number of locomotives were introduced during the haulage contract phase, including three 2-2-2 well tanks that came from Fairbairn in 1851 for the opening of the Galway extension. It would be reasonable to assume that Martin would have also dispensed with them fairly quickly, but in fact he had Nos. 27-29 rebuilt as saddle tanks with new boilers in 1874-76.

It is not clear whether the haulage contractors or the MGWR ordered the locomotives that were delivered during the contract phase. As far as can be ascertained, drawings were prepared by a draughtsman on instructions from G.W. Hemans, the company's Engineer. Two groups of engines came from Messrs Longridge in 1852, Nos. 18-23 being 2-2-2 passenger engines, while Nos. 25 & 26 were 2-4-0s. At least three, and possibly four of the singles had been rebuilt about 1854-55 as 2-4-0s. One Longridge locomotive was scrapped before Martin's time, possibly No. 19, which had suffered a boiler failure at Float on the Cavan branch in January 1872. Martin had disposed of four others by July 1875 and the last survivor, No.18, was withdrawn in May 1880. Nos. 25 & 26 were the

* Other candidates who applied for the post at that time included Robert Andrews of the Edinburgh & Glasgow Railway (not the Robert Andrews on the W&LR), who was later to have connections with the Eastern Counties Railway (ECR), and William Fernihough of the ECR. Martin's father, George Attock, would have known both of these men at Stratford.

A period shot taken at Broadstone station in the 1890s showing one of the three Fairbairn locomotives introduced in 1851. One of Martin Atock's earliest tasks was their rebuilding in the summer of 1874 with new boilers and saddle tanks to replace the original well tanks. They remained in service until 1897, being then used on boiler wash-out duties until being finally scrapped in 1906. *H. Fayle, courtesy Irish Railway Record Society Collection*

Another view of one of the Fairbairn tanks, this time No. 29 *Elf* in use as a boiler wash-out at Broadstone in the early years of the 20th century. Although officially withdrawn in 1897, she still carries her nameplate and lined livery. *H. Fayle, courtesy Irish Railway Record Society Collection*

first coupled goods engines on the MGWR and by 1876, with a plentiful supply of 0-4-2 goods engines in stock, Martin was able to transfer them to passenger duties on the Mayo road; both were also withdrawn in May 1880.

An unusual locomotive arrived on the MGWR in May 1852 in the shape of an 0-4-0 tender engine, the only one of this type known to have run in Ireland. It was supplied by R. & W. Hawthorn (No. 24 was also the first Hawthorn engine to be delivered to Ireland) and was one of eight locomotives ordered from that company by the Glasgow & South Western Railway (G&SWR) in July 1851. The explanation for its appearance on the MGWR is that Longridge had contracted to supply three goods engines, but in 1852 they announced that they were ceasing to build engines. Thus the MGWR found themselves in urgent need of an additional engine and found that Hawthorn could oblige. No. 24 was loaned in 1861 to the W&LR and worked for a time between Limerick Junction and Waterford, so Martin would have already been familiar with the locomotive. Whether that influenced his decision in 1873 to make it one of his first locomotive withdrawals is worth considering, but it is also of interest to note that the G&SWR locomotives of that type were also withdrawn in 1872-73.

Two 2-4-0 goods locomotives, Nos. 31 & 32, almost certainly ordered by Johnson & Kinder, came from Fairbairn in December 1852. They were identical with a series of locomotives supplied by the same builder to the W&LR between 1852 and 1855, apart from having cylinders 1 in. larger in diameter. In April 1854 Fairbairn delivered two identical locomotives, Nos. 34 & 35, to the MGWR. It was reported that No. 35, named *Wren*, was used on the occasion of the opening of the Ballaghaderreen branch on 2nd November, 1874 and remained there until withdrawn in 1886, co-incidentally driven by a man named Ben Partridge! From his W&LR days Martin would also have been familiar with the capabilities of that type of locomotive and, although he had No. 32 withdrawn in July 1875, Nos. 31 & 34 lasted until May 1880.

With the cancellation of the haulage contract, the MGWR sought to recruit a resident Engineer, Edward Wilson of the York & North Midland Railway being appointed in September 1853. He was put in charge of both the Permanent Way and Locomotive Departments, but he seems to have had no distinct policy other than to purchase such locomotive designs as the makers offered. Four 0-6-0 goods engines, introduced between October 1855 and April 1856, were built at the Drogheda Iron Works by Thomas Grendon & Company. Two identical engines were built for the Dundalk & Enniskillen Railway. They were by far the largest engines built by Grendon, and among the largest in Ireland when built. A lengthy contemporary press description attributes the design to Wilson, but this was probably no more than the usual courtesy to the Engineer of the railway concerned. The locomotives were more than likely designed by Messrs R. Stephenson & Company, as that firm had sub-contracted the construction to Grendon's. They were initially used on main line goods trains, but by Martin's time were employed as pilot engines at North Wall and on banking duties from there up to Liffey Junction. Three of the four were withdrawn in 1881, but the remaining engine may have lasted until about 1883.

Edward Wilson left the MGWR in August 1856 to go to the Oxford, Worcester & Wolverhampton Railway. The one point on which he does appear to have had some views was that locomotives should have four coupled wheels for passenger and six coupled wheels for goods work. The eight Grendon 2-4-0s supplied in August 1856 (Nos. 40 & 41) and February 1860 (Nos. 1-6) were obviously influenced by this policy. We know virtually nothing about them except that by Martin's time they had been relegated from the main line (all being on the Sligo road by 1875) and that they were withdrawn during the 1880s. The only other locomotive delivered during Wilson's time was another 2-4-0, No. 42. This locomotive is something of a mystery, being supplied at short notice in August 1856 by R. Stephenson. It appears to have been one of four engines ordered by the South Australian Government Railways (SAGR). Stephenson's Order Book notes 'date of order, August 1856, finished 19th August, 1856. Taken from another order'. Interestingly, the chief engineer of the SAGR referred to the 'C' class as 'these small handy engines', but to the 'B' class (one of which came to the MGWR) as 'a perfect beast of an engine'. In Martin's time No. 42 worked the Cavan branch from at least 1876 until 1879, but by May of the following year it had been relegated to shunting duties at Liffey Junction prior to withdrawal in November 1880.

Wilson's successor was Joseph Cabry, who arrived on the MGWR in October 1856, and was a member of an important North of England family of railway engineers. He was born at Ness, Cheshire in about 1831, the eldest of four brothers. He was at first employed by his uncle, Thomas Cabry, locomotive superintendent of the Y&NMR, before coming to the MGWR. On leaving the MGWR he spent some time in London, before he became Manager of the Blyth & Tyne Railway in October 1865, which line was amalgamated with the North Eastern Railway on 7th August, 1874. He was appointed Engineer of the NER's Central Division on 5th April, 1883 and retired in 1891. He died in Newcastle on 22nd October, 1897.

Three locomotive classes were introduced in Cabry's time on the MGWR, and there was enough similarity between the classes to indicate that he supplied a fairly detailed specification and a drawing of sorts when ordering his engines, although probably all of the detailed drawings were still prepared by the respective makers. The priority on Cabry's arrival was for more goods engines, and so six were ordered from Fairbairn. All but one were delivered in 1860 and they were the first 0-4-2 locomotives on the MGWR. After about 15 years on goods work they were reported to be in bad order and they finished their days on ballast and pilot workings. In May 1877 Martin reported that they were 'very defective as to boilers, cylinders and frames', proposing to rebuild them as standard six-coupled goods engines. As so few components of the original locomotives were used, other than the coupled wheels and crank axles, they were always treated as new engines and so will be dealt with later in our narrative.

Six passenger 2-2-2s were supplied in 1862 by Hawthorn. They had 6 ft 6 in. wheels, a big jump from the then standard MGWR 5 ft 6 in. passenger wheels; they were in fact the largest diameter driving wheels ever used by the MGWR. These were probably the first MGWR locomotives built specifically to burn coal instead of coke. (It is not clear when coal was first used on the MGWR, but it was probably not before 1858; the use of coke in older engines came to an end sometime between 1868 and 1872.) They were also the first MGWR engines to have an attempt at cabs, but they sheltered only the faceplate and the back of the firebox; even the top of the regulator handle stuck out beyond the roof and sides. Having ended their days on the Mayo road, Martin had them withdrawn between 1881 and 1887. Six further 0-4-2s to Cabry's specification were ordered from Neilson & Company, but they were not delivered until 1863 after Cabry's departure. The Neilson locomotives do not appear to have differed very much from the Fairbairn ones except that the boiler was rather larger and almost the same as the Hawthorn's singles. However, the boiler differed in construction, being telescopic instead of having the largest ring in the middle. These locomotives also had cabs of the same type as the Hawthorn singles. Rather surprisingly they seem to have worked almost the same duties as Ramage's larger 0-4-2 engines (livestock specials, a very occasional passenger or excursion working, and all but the heaviest goods trains) until 1885 when Martin replaced the whole class with his new 'L' class locomotives. The tenders, with one exception, were all scrapped with the engines; the odd one was not officially written-off until 1947, and no one knows if it actually existed at any time during those 62 years!

Joseph Cabry left under a cloud in 1862, having been accused of corruption due to the letting of contracts for rolling stock and permanent way materials without sufficient competition. The Board then decided to separate the civil engineering and locomotive functions and appoint a locomotive superintendent with full time responsibility for the department. Robert Ramage, who had been chief draughtsman on the Caledonian Railway (CR), first under Robert Sinclair at the old Greenock works, and then under Ben Conner at St Rollox, was chosen for the job. With that background it was natural that Ramage's designs would owe much to Caledonian practice. He started preparing drawings for a new batch of 0-4-2 engines very soon after his appointment, although it is clear that what was given to Neilson's was little more than a general drawing.

Shortly before Ramage left St Rollox, an outside-cylinder 0-4-2 locomotive had been introduced on the CR. The design of his MGWR locomotives is believed to have been a combination of that locomotive and an earlier batch of outside-cylinder 0-6-0s built by the CR. The MGWR locomotives had the long boiler of the 0-6-0 applied to 0-4-2 frames. This resulted in a longer wheelbase version goods locomotive than their CR counterparts that were required to work over tightly curved colliery branches. Typical CR features were the heavy 1¼ in. frames, stovepipe chimneys, and dome positioned on the firebox. The tenders were so evidently CR in every respect that it seems as if Ramage had asked the makers to supply the same tender as produced for the CR. Nos. 61-66 arrived in late 1864, several months after they were due to be delivered. A second batch, Nos. 67-72, was ordered from Dübs in November 1866 at £2,536 each, these being delivered in October of the following year. There were minor differences between the two classes, probably in part due to improvements found necessary from experience with the Neilsons, but also arising from differences in the detail drawings produced by the respective makers. The 12 locomotives worked goods trains all over the MGWR system as well as occasional passenger specials, and for their size they were capable of hauling big loads. Martin must have considered them to be fairly good locomotives as he did not consider having the first of them replaced until 1887.

Broadstone had only one draughtsman at the time, William Wakefield, who Ramage had recruited from Inchicore in June 1863.* Early in 1867 Ramage was ordered to prepare specifications and drawings for six or eight new, coupled, passenger locomotives, without delay. However, it was not until January 1869 that tenders were invited for four locomotives, the order going to the Avonside Engine Co. at £2,200 each, two more being ordered in December 1869. No drawings or photographs of the class are known to exist, neither are the principal dimensions known. The tenders were of the CR type with a water capacity of 1,600 gallons. These particular locomotives spent their entire lives on the main line, but do not seem to have been used on the Limited Mails. Despite that slight limitation, Martin did not consider it necessary to have them withdrawn and replaced until 1889-90.

The last locomotives to be ordered during Ramage's time, and indeed the last 0-4-2s to be introduced on the MGWR, were 12 engines that were supplied in two batches by Neilson. The first order was placed in November 1870, described in the maker's order book as 'Six goods engines and tenders to specification and tracing of last order delivered by us'. In fact, Ramage must have reconsidered the matter for the engines as delivered were quite different from the 1864 lot. The cylinders, wheels and motion were the same, but the boilers were completely different, frames considerably modified, and the whole external styling altered. The new arrangement of splashers, platforms, cab and safety valve casing was so typical of Neilson's designs that it suggests the changes were recommended by them and not by the MGWR drawing office. For the first time on the MGWR a screw reverser replaced the lever.

The second order, placed with the same maker in December 1871, was not delivered until September - November 1872. They incorporated some alterations from the first batch, no doubt on instructions from Martin, who had taken over by the time design details were being finalised. The modifications included re-positioning of the springs and the fitting of a pair of Friedmann No. 9 injectors, which were attached outside the frames beside the ashpan. The class worked goods trains and fair specials all over the MGWR system, although they were not much used on the Sligo and Mayo roads after Martin's standard six-coupled locomotives became available. From about 1887 they were mostly to be found on pilot and ballast train duties.

One further early locomotive remains to be mentioned as it survived on the MGWR well into Martin's time. In June 1869 the MGWR had leased the Dublin & Meath Railway (D&MR). Although they purchased all the carriages and wagons they refused to take more than one of the D&MR locomotives; their No. 7, a 2-4-0 which became No. 11 on the MGWR and named *Meath*. Whilst the D&MR men had thought it to be a powerful engine, unofficially named *Drag-All*, and it most likely was, compared with the remainder of that company's stock, this was not the case when compared with the MGWR locomotives. The late Bob Clements

* William Wakefield had come from the GS&WR drawing office at Inchicore and left Broadstone to take an appointment as senior foreman at the Grand Canal Street works of the Dublin, Wicklow & Wexford Railway (DW&WR) under his father, John. He was appointed locomotive superintendent of the Waterford, Dungarvan & Lismore Railway in March 1878 but returned to Grand Canal Street in May 1880 as assistant to his father. Following John Wakefield's death William was appointed locomotive superintendent from 1st June, 1882, but resigned from the DW&WR on 12th August, 1894.

mentioned that she was the only engine never to be recorded in the Locomotive Department Report Book. He found it hard to believe that it was so reliable that it never failed, and thought it more likely that it was hardly ever in steam! Nevertheless, it remained on the books until 1886 when it was scrapped.

Robert Ramage appears to have been on good terms with the Board until the end of 1871 when serious complaints of delays, breakdowns and 'irregularity of drivers' were raised. The Board wrote to Ramage on 8th November, 1871 informing him that if more experienced drivers were required, he should obtain their services. In the future, however, the Directors 'required that no one shall be given charge of an engine until his name, age and length of service have been submitted to the Board and approved of'. A week later Ramage confirmed that six additional drivers were about to be employed. It appears that two months later Ramage was still under pressure, and on 14th February, 1872 he submitted his resignation, the Board immediately ordering that advertisements be placed in the newspapers for a replacement. Ramage obviously regretted his precipitate action and a week later sought permission to withdraw his resignation. He was politely informed that, as advertisements had been placed, the Directors could see no justification for making any change.

We have now come full-circle to Martin's appointment as locomotive superintendent on the MGWR. Having dealt with the locomotives that he inherited, it is now time to consider his contribution to MGWR locomotive design and the development of the workshops at Broadstone. One of the first moves that Martin made was to recruit a replacement for William Wakefield, and for that purpose he persuaded Jimmy Rowe, his trusted assistant at Limerick, to come up to Broadstone and fill the important post of locomotive draughtsman. The new team started work at once on the design of a 2-4-0 passenger locomotive ('D' class) to replace old locomotives dating from 1848-52, which were still in use on the company's secondary lines. Although only a few of the original drawings have survived, they are sufficient to show that the design was fully worked out, with all detail drawings made at Broadstone.

Martin introduced the right-hand driving position to the MGWR, the same as he had done on the W&LR. The typical reversing wheel with pointer working on a brass strip above it made its first appearance whilst the regulator handle was of the two-armed butterfly type. The only notable feature of the Stephenson valve motion, and one that persisted as long as Martin used it, was the placing of the swing links below instead of above the pulling links which supported the swing links. The 1 in. thick iron frames were somewhat shallow, and wheels and axles were also of iron. The boiler, which was in three rings and butt jointed, was attached to the smokebox tubeplate by an angle iron, while the firebox casing was joined by a stepped lap-joint, the same as Ramage's arrangement. The safety valves, which were of a type invariably used by Martin, possibly owed their origins to William Cowan of the Great North of Scotland Railway. A completely new design of tender was prepared with frames on the same vertical line as the axleboxes and springs, openings being cut in the frameplates for the latter. The tank, with a water capacity of 1,600 gallons, was of horseshoe shape, enclosing the bunker which had vertically-sliding doors; coal capacity was 2½ tons.

The design of the 'D' class clearly showed most of the features of Martin's locomotive design that were to remain standard for many years. In November 1872 tenders were sought for the supply of 12 of these locomotives. The order went to Neilson's for eight with copper fireboxes and brass tubes at £2,620 each and four with fireboxes and tubes of 'Howell's Metal' at £2,450 each. In April 1876 a further five locomotives of the same class were delivered by Messrs Dübs. Externally these locomotives had the typical Atock outline save for the absence of a cab. This was surprising for, as we have already noted, all new MGWR engines since 1862 had been built with at least an attempt at a cab. Their absence supports an old MGWR tradition that there was once a locomotive superintendent who disapproved of cabs for fear his enginemen might fall asleep! Indeed, there was some reason for this fear, considering the very excessive hours often worked by MGWR men in those days. The decision to fit cabs was made not later than the summer of 1875, so the Neilson locomotives probably got them at their first or second shopping. The 'D' class were used mainly on the Mayo, Cavan and Meath roads and on Enfield or Mullingar locals, together with the short branches, occasionally venturing as far as Sligo.

It had been proposed in 1873 that drawings be prepared for new goods locomotives ('L' class), but in the event details were not ready until September 1875, when seven 0-6-0 goods locomotives were ordered from R. Stephenson & Co. for delivery in the following March - April at £2,777 each. Three more were ordered in February 1876 at £2,800 each, to be delivered at one per month after completion of the first order. The first seven actually arrived between May and July, the three additional locomotives being delivered in August 1876. They were the MGWR's first six-coupled engines since the Grendons of 1855. Ramage's attachment to the 0-4-2 type may have been due to his Scottish origins, as four-coupled goods locomotives were almost universal there; it may also be remarked that Atock had not found six-coupled locomotives necessary on the W&LR. The 'L' class is not well documented, but there is enough evidence to show that the class differed in many ways from the 'D' class. When new Nos. 86-88 and No. 93 went to the Sligo road, Nos. 89-92 to the Mayo road, and Nos. 94-5 were put to work on the Cavan and Galway goods.

Martin submitted a report to the Board on 22nd November, 1876, referring to a number of tube failures with the new locomotives and, in an effort to ascertain what might be causing the problem, he entered into correspondence with Messrs Allen Everitt & Sons of Smethwick, the manufacturers of the tubes. The fireboxes also gave more trouble than they should have done. These problems were never actually cured as a result of which the renewal commenced in 1893; none of the locomotives lasted a full 20 years in their original condition. However, the 'D' and 'L' classes set a standard for MGWR locomotive design during the Atock period. Later types were, of course, larger and incorporated various alterations and developments. Although his designs differed very greatly from those of his predecessors, it is also evident that Martin adopted such features of Ramage's practice as he considered worth retaining.

Coincidental with Martin's arrival at Broadstone, George Wilkinson, the company's architect, submitted plans for proper new engine sheds and workshops. The Board ordered, on 15th May, 1872, that Wilkinson and Atock should visit the most modern workshops in England and the most likely to suit the company. Arising from their visit, Wilkinson was instructed, on 19th June, 1872, to prepare specifications and to advise the Board when these were ready so that advertisements could be placed for tenders. In December tenders were read for the building of a new engine shed and circular shed, those of Samuel H. Bolton at £8,250 for the former and £6,750 for the latter being accepted. With the new running sheds approaching completion, it was ordered, on Martin's recommendation of 14th January, 1874, that granite flags be used for flooring instead of brick as suggested by Wilkinson. The original estimate did not include the construction of inspection pits, Bolton being requested in March 1874 to provide an estimate for them. At about this time he had also submitted proposals to erect a clock tower, offices and stores for £257 14*s*. 4*d*., which was accepted. Bolton, in due course, submitted his tender for providing five pits, complete with the necessary sewers, in an amount of £350, this also being accepted. In July 1874 the tender of Messrs T. Ritchie & Sons of Edinburgh to supply an electric clock for the locomotive yard in an amount of £47, exclusive of erection, was considered too costly, a turret clock being in due course supplied by Francis Moore, in December, for £30.

On a more personal note, Martin was elected a member of the Institution of Civil Engineers of Ireland (ICEI), on 22nd April, 1874, having been proposed by John Bailey (of the firm of Courtney, Stephens & Bailey, of Dublin), and seconded by John Challoner Smith (Engineer of the DW&WR), supported by James Dillon. In July 1874 Bolton agreed to enlarge Martin's residence at Royal Canal House, Broadstone, for the sum of £213. By that time Mary Eliza was expecting again, and the final addition to the family, Florence Bowbank Atock, was born on 14th September, 1874. Florence never married and passed away in Tunbridge Wells, Kent, on 13th December, 1950. Shortly before her birth, in August 1874, Martin had registered his Patent for *A Combined Machine or Tool for Boring, Turning and Key Bed Grooving*, (Patent No. 2716, 1874), the first of three Patents in his name. The machine was intended for boring out and facing the bosses of two wheels or boring two-wheel tyres, or boring, facing or turning any other two pieces of work at the same time. It could also be used for turning the two journals of a straight axle or shaft at one time, or for cutting and grooving two key beds at one time. In addition to his duties as locomotive superintendent, Martin was appointed Head of the Stores Department in November 1874, his salary being increased by £100 per annum to take account of the added responsibility.

Brief reference has already been made above to the rebuilding of three Fairbairn tank locomotives dating from 1851. In June 1874 Martin had been ordered to obtain estimates for new boilers for them from various manufacturers. In November an order was placed with the Vulcan Foundry not only for the boilers, but also for three saddle tanks and three pairs of frame plates at a combined price of £1,845 delivered on Quay at Dublin. In addition, new cylinders were obtained from Grendon of Drogheda at £45 each. No. 27 returned to service in June 1875, No. 28 six months later and No. 29 early in 1876. The old boiler from No. 27 was sold in September 1874, for £85, to Messrs Browne & Nolan, stationers of Dublin. As the only passenger tank locomotives

Institution of Civil Engineers
OF IRELAND.

Certificate of Candidate.

(Name) Martin Atock

(Title or Designation) Locomotive Superintendent

(Usual Place of Residence) Broadstone Station Dublin

being desirous of admission into the INSTITUTION OF CIVIL ENGINEERS OF IRELAND, *I recommend him from personal knowledge as a person in every respect worthy of that distinction.* Because he served a Pupilage on the Eastern Counties Railway under Messrs Gooch & [illegible]. Was two years as Draughtsman under Messrs Mather & Platt of Manchester. Was appointed in 1861 Loco Superintendent of the Waterford & Limerick Railway & now holds a similar appointment on the Midland Gt Western of Ireland.

(Here state distinctly the Qualifications of the Candidate, according to the spirit of Articles 2, 3, 4, 5, Section 11.)

On the above grounds, I beg leave to propose him to the Council as a proper person to be admitted into the Institution.

John Bailey *Member.*

Dated this 10 *day of* Feby 1874

We, the undersigned, concur in the above recommendation, being convinced that Mr Atock *is in every respect a proper person to be admitted into the Institution.*

John C Smith

James Dillon

Mr Atock *The Council having considered the above recommendation, present to be ballotted for as* Member *of the Institution of Civil Engineers of Ireland.*

J. B. Stoney *Chairman.*

Dated this 5 *day of* March 1874

Read to the Institution, *day of* 185

Martin Atock's application for membership of the Institution of Civil Engineers of Ireland dated 5th March, 1874. The proposer was John Bailey of the well-known Dublin engineering firm of Courtney, Stephens & Bailey. Martin was recommended by John Challoner Smith, Engineer to the Dublin Wicklow & Wexford Railway, and James Dillon.

Courtesy John Callanan, Archivist, Institution of Engineers of Ireland

to run on the MGWR prior to 1890, they were used on the Edenderry and Athboy branches. After their withdrawal from service in 1897 they were employed on boiler washout duties at Broadstone until 1906.

Martin reported in September 1874 that the fitting shop roof was 'much out of repair' and instructions were given for necessary remedial work to be carried out. However, even more important moves were afoot for the construction of new workshops at Broadstone. On 10th February, 1875 Wilkinson submitted plans for new locomotive shops, and was requested to prepare a specification and estimate for the same. It is clear from the minutes that Martin had not been consulted as to his requirements and, in January 1877, the architect was requested to report on revised plans as suggested by the locomotive superintendent. In the interim, Messrs T. & C. Martin of Dublin had tendered, in April 1875, for the removal of the old engine shed at Broadstone and its erection at the North Wall for £436 17*s.* 0*d.*, this tender being accepted. A little over a year later, on 31st May, 1876, James Price, the MGWR Engineer, informed the Board that the facilities available for the repair of engines were inadequate, and he was requested to submit a report as to the building of new fitting shops.

The total cost for the construction of the new locomotive erecting shop buildings, as agreed with Samuel Bolton, amounted to £17,262 17*s.* 0*d.* Although the main workshop buildings had been completed by early 1878, plans for some of the ancillary facilities, including an enlarged boiler house, coal yard, urinals and WCs, were only submitted to the Board in April of that year, estimates not being ready until 26th June; Bolton's tender for this work at £365 5*s.* 7*d.* was accepted at the Board meeting held on that day. The fitting-up of the workshops and installation of the necessary machinery was not completed. In fact tenders had been sought for the supply and erection of four hydraulic gantries, but Sir W.G. Armstrong & Co. and Messrs Eastons & Anderson declined to tender for these. Eventually, the tender of Messrs Tannett, Walker & Co. in an amount of £3,240 was accepted on 15th May. Tenders for various other machine tools, deemed by Martin to be essential, were approved in July 1878 as follows:

Item	*Proposed supplier*	*Amount* £
Wheel Lathe	Craven Bros	344
Crank Axle Lathe	Craven Bros	420
Cylinder Boring Machine	Craven Bros	115
Wheel Drilling Machine	Shaw Hossack & Co.	108
Slotting Machine	J. Buckton & Co.	155
Shaping Machine	Shaw Hossack & Co.	322
Boring Machine	Fairbairn, Kennedy & Naylor	375
Slide Lathe	Smith & Coventry	97
Slot Drilling Machine	Sharp, Stewart & Co.	106
Total		*£2,042*

Messrs Sharp, Stewart & Co. agreed to supply a locomotive-type boiler for the new workshops in July 1878 at a cost of £547, and Messrs Wren & Hopkins's tender for a 3 ton travelling crane at £395 was accepted in the following month.

Reverting to 1872, one of the other engineering tasks to which Martin had to turn his attention was to have the engine of one of the company's disabled canal

Broadstone running shed photographed not long before its final closure, hence the rather untidy appearance. Martin Atock would have been quite familiar with this view, but would hardly have countenanced such a scene of desolation. Note clock tower, referred to in the text.

Seán Kennedy

MGWR class 'H' 0-6-0 No. 99 *Cambria* at Broadstone, one of four locomotives purchased from Messrs Avonside in 1878. Originally intended for the Waterford Dungarvan & Lismore Railway, that company refused delivery due to their not being ready on time. Later rebuilt with larger boilers, three of the class remained in service until 1949.

H. Fayle, courtesy Irish Railway Record Society Collection

steamers put into proper working order. Whether or not this was one of two cargo steamers ordered from Grendon in August 1870 is not certain, but we do know that one of them had been the subject of correspondence between Ramage and the makers in August 1871. At that time Grendons had stated that they saw no reason for supposing that any defects existed in the design, or with either imperfect materials or workmanship. In any event, specifications were prepared in June 1872 for new engines and boilers for the canal steamers, Harland & Wolff of Belfast and Courtney & Stephens of Dublin tendering in October. The latter firm were successful, two engines and boilers being ordered from them in December 1872 for £1,850, with £300 allowed for old machinery. No. 1 canal steamer was reported as disabled in March 1874, due to the main shaft having been broken, the matter being referred to Martin for a report.

Shortly after his arrival at Broadstone, Martin had found himself immersed in staff matters; an application by the men in his department, requesting to be paid weekly instead of monthly, being submitted on 3rd July, 1872. The Board sought a list of the men who wished for the change, probably anticipating that not many would want it, and that they would be able to persuade them to remain with the existing system. However, when it became clear that no less than 316 out of a total of 466 men had signed the memorial, it was the Directors who agreed to consider how best to implement the change. Another staff matter that surfaced about this time was the dismissal of driver Williams in November 1872 because he was keeping a public house, a matter that was in contravention of the company's rules.

It was the practice on the MGWR, as it had been on the W&LR, to offer a premium to drivers and firemen who returned better than average coal consumptions. A sum of £55 was so distributed in August 1873, although Martin had the unpleasant duty of informing drivers Keenan and Martin that they would be discharged if they were unable to improve their figures. Later, in December 1879, the Board decided that such premiums should only be paid to drivers, firemen in future to be rewarded by promotion as vacancies arose. In December 1873 Martin lost his wagon examiner at Mullingar, a man by the name of Cullen, who was run over by an engine and subsequently died from his injuries. A request for assistance for Cullen's children was met by a donation of £5, which Martin was ordered, 'to see applied in a proper way'.

Martin's second Patent, *An Improved Hydraulic Gantry*, dated 16th May, 1878 (Patent AD 1878 No. 1961), was for a design of equipment intended to be used in the lifting of locomotives, rolling stock and other heavy weights, by means of a hydraulic cylinder, chains, pump and cistern worked by hand. The framework to take the hoisting gear was to be mounted on four flanged wheels, to enable it to travel upon lines of rail. There is no doubt that Martin would have put such equipment to use on the MGWR, but it is not known how many other railways might have adopted lifting gantries based on his Patent.

The MGWR's standard goods was the 'L' class. A slightly modified version was the 'LM' represented here by No. 84 *Dunkellen*, a Broadstone-built locomotive of 1891. She was withdrawn in 1925 as GSR 'J18' No. 572, although she never actually carried her new number. They were rather larger than the famous '101' or 'J15' class of the GS&WR.

H. Fayle, courtesy Irish Railway Record Society Collection

Another member of the 'LM' class, this time No. 136 *Cavan*, built by Kitson in 1895. She lasted right to the end of the steam era, being withdrawn in 1961 as CIE No. 590. She was photographed at Broadstone. *H. Fayle, courtesy Irish Railway Record Society Collection*

Chapter Five

Twenty Years of MGWR Locomotive Development

The year 1879 saw the introduction of a policy that was to remain in force during the ensuing 20 years of Martin Atock's time with the MGWR, namely the complete renewal of every locomotive, carriage and wagon after 20 years' service. This looks more like an accountant's rule than an engineer's. It was hardly likely that the same period would suit all types of rolling stock, and for engines 20 years was definitely awkward – on the long side for one copper firebox but definitely too short for two. Though Atock followed the rule for the items mentioned, he ignored it in regard to tenders. With the opening of the new workshops it became possible for the MGWR to undertake its own locomotive construction. The first examples actually built at Broadstone were the 'LN' class 0-6-0s, Nos. 49-54. They were designed as a new standard class of goods locomotive and were built as renewals of the Fairbairn 0-4-2s introduced by Cabry in 1860. As such, they incorporated the crank axles and non-standard 5 ft 1½ in. coupled wheels of the original locomotives. An important development in this class was the provision of steam brakes on both engine and tender; at first this was worked by a small handle at the three-way cock, centrally positioned on the faceplate, but the inconvenience of this arrangement when shunting saw its replacement by a hand wheel on the fireman's side. (It should be noted that it had always been the fireman's duty on the MGWR to take charge of the hand brake.) When new, they all went to the Sligo road and they spent most of their time there; the smaller wheels were probably found more suitable for the steep banks on that line although one worked the Mayo road from time to time. They appear to have been rather more reliable engines than the 'L' class, averaging 53 months against only 29 months between reported failures.

Early in 1878 work commenced on drawings for a class of 0-6-0 tank locomotives to replace the old Grendon long-boiler locomotives on North Wall pilot duties. The 'P' class were essentially a tank version of the 'LN' class with smaller wheels. In January 1880 four sets of boilers, frame plates, wheels and axles were ordered from Beyer, Peacock & Co. at £1,037 per set. Four locomotives, Nos. 100-103, were completed at Broadstone during 1881. The 'L' class motion was used and appears to have remained largely unaltered, although Martin did substitute steel for iron in the slidebars, piston rods and crossheads; in addition, a solid-eye little end replaced the old strap and cotter type. The 'LN' boiler was retained, apart from an alteration in the feed arrangement. One might have expected Martin to follow Inchicore practice for tank locomotives and make the front, roof, and back of the cab from one plate, but an ordinary square cab was provided. It was certainly a mistake to use the standard screw reverser, for a big lever would have been far handier for shunting.

In the meantime, four locomotives had arrived in January 1880 from Avonside of Bristol, the only ones to be supplied by that firm to the MGWR

MGWR class 'P' 0-6-0T No. 105 *Hercules* at Broadstone. Four locomotives to this design entered service in 1881 for banking goods trains up the steep incline from North Wall goods yard in Dublin. No. 105 followed in 1891. Withdrawn in 1949 as CIE class 'J10' No. 618.

H. Fayle, courtesy Irish Railway Record Society Collection

'D' class 2-4-0 No. 5 *Mars* on the turntable at Broadstone. No. 5 is in full lined livery and sports a tall chimney and large polished brass dome. Clearly visible is the 'elephant's trunk' brake piping around the front of the smokebox, as designed by Jimmy Rowe. It is easy to understand how a fireman could inadvertently grab the trunk rather than the handrail.

H. Fayle, courtesy Irish Railway Record Society Collection

during Martin's time. They were not built to a Broadstone design, and we must go back some 2½ years to trace their origins. In August 1877 the Waterford Dungarvan & Lismore Railway ordered four 0-6-0s from Avonside for delivery in April 1878. Daniel McDowell, locomotive superintendent of the Waterford & Central Ireland Railway, had prepared the specification and drawings, and he may have based the design on a couple of excellent Avonside 0-4-2s that he had working on his line, but with smaller driving wheels to suit the steep gradients on the Dungarvan line. The WD&LR was almost ready for opening by May 1878, but none of the locomotives had arrived. The WD&LR locomotive superintendent, William Wakefield, had meanwhile arranged to hire two locomotives from the DW&WR, through the good offices of his father, John, who was their locomotive superintendent. As a result, the WD&LR refused to take delivery of the Avonside locomotives, which were offered to the W&LR in July 1879 and to the DW&WR in the following November. Both companies refused the offer, allegedly on the grounds that the locomotives were too heavy. They were then offered to the MGWR at £1,800 each, delivered at Bristol, Martin successfully negotiating a price of £1,600 each, delivered at North Wall, Dublin.

The few drawings that have survived of the Avonside locomotives show the use of steel for frames, straight axles and axleboxes; all examples of its early use in such components, which was unusual at that date. The fireboxes had sloping grates, the only known examples on the MGWR until the arrival of the Woolwich 2-6-0s in 1924. Martin reported favourably on the new locomotives apart from tyre fastenings, and the underhung trailing springs which were too low. Nameplates were probably affixed at Broadstone, although they were placed, unusually, a considerable distance above the boiler centre-line. Nos. 96-99 had hand brakes only as delivered, a situation that lasted until 1888 when drawings were made for the fitting of steam brakes to engines and tenders. When delivered they were put to use mainly on the Galway, Cavan and Meath goods trains, although No. 98 had a couple of failures reported when working on the Ballaghaderreen branch in 1885. About 1900 they were transferred to North Wall, working out their time there until rebuilt. Rebuilding was carried out after Martin's retirement, and the details are not relevant to this volume, except to note that little of the original locomotives survived the rebuilding.

Six more 'D' class passenger engines were ordered from Beyer, Peacock in January 1880 at £2,260 each (Order No. 3924). They were generally very similar to the 1876 batch except that, due to the use of a longer boiler, the leading wheels were moved forward increasing the wheelbase by 1 ft. Their duties included practically every passenger job except for the heaviest main line trains. Fourteen more examples of this type of locomotive were added between 1883 and 1887, four of which came from Kitson of Leeds in 1886, the remainder being built at Broadstone. The only known alterations in the first four locomotives built at Broadstone in 1884, as compared to the Beyer, Peacock ones, was the use of steel for various parts and the fitting of simple vacuum brakes operated from the fireman's side.

The four Kitson locomotives were ordered in May 1885 at £2,160 each and, although due for delivery in October of that year, they did not arrive until

'D' class 2-4-0 No.48 *Connaught*, built at Broadstone in 1887 and withdrawn in 1922. One of a class of 39 locomotives, they came from various builders.

H. Fayle, courtesy Irish Railway Record Society Collection

'D' Class No. 2 *Jupiter*, built by Beyer, Peacock in 1880 as a 2-4-0. Four came from Kitson, six from Beyer, Peacock while a further 12 came from Broadstone. The six Beyers were rebuilt in 1900-01 as 4-4-0s, the first bogie locomotives on the MGWR. Although Martin was reported to be averse to bogies, possibly because he did not wish to pay royalties for using them, the drawings are dated August 1899 and must therefore be attributed to him. As CIE 'D16' class No. 534, No. 2 lasted until 1949. *H. Fayle, courtesy Irish Railway Record Society Collection*

March-April 1886. They probably had steel frameplates and new cast-iron chimneys. The company was criticised for importing locomotives rather than having them built at Broadstone, a spokesman making the rather inane comment that facilities did not exist there for building mail engines. In fact, Kitson also supplied the steel frameplates and wheels for the last six 'D' class locomotives, which were built at Broadstone in 1886-87. In addition to the duties covered by the Beyer, Peacock locomotives, the later deliveries also worked the Limited Mail from 1885 to 1893. The Beyer, Peacock examples and those built at Broadstone in 1884 shared a common weakness, namely the frequent breakage of their side rods, which were later replaced by a heavier type. This was a fault that was not known in the Kitson locomotives or the 1886-87 Broadstone batch, which suggests that Kitson may also have supplied the side rods for the latter.

During the 1870s and the early 1880s the MGWR, in common with other railways, suffered greatly from burst and leaking tubes. Reference has already been made in the previous chapter to the tube failures suffered with locomotives delivered by Robert Stephenson in 1876. Over the years various ideas had been put forward to explain the phenomenon and, on 5th April, 1882, Martin presented a paper on the subject in Dublin to the Institution of Civil Engineers of Ireland in which he outlined his thoughts on the matter. Strangely, failures were occurring with tubes in perfectly new engines; the tube makers were of high repute and there was little doubt that the tubes were of first-class quality. The defects virtually all occurred after the engines had only been in service a matter of weeks and showed up (as far as the MGWR was concerned) on the inside of the tubes about 1 in. in from the front end, corresponding with the inside face of the front tubeplate, and, coincidentally, at about the point reached by the ends of the rollers of the tube expander. Examination of failed tubes, following their removal, revealed cracks around the circumference and working in from the outside.*

Martin had initially thought that the swelled ends of the tubes had been drawn at too low a temperature or without sufficient previous annealing, rendering them brittle. Various experiments had been carried out, and he had come to the conclusion that the fault lay in the fact that the tube ends had not been sufficiently softened prior to expansion and that there had also been an over-zealous use of the tube expanders. J.A.F. Aspinall contributed at length to the discussion that followed. He was of the view that, whilst an abuse of the expander could indeed cause damage, the tubes that were being made by even the best manufacturers were by no means as good as they used to be; therein, in his opinion, lay the problem. He was particularly interested to hear that the MGWR tube failures occurred at the smokebox end of the boiler, as the GS&WR experience was that such failures occurred at the firebox end.

Between 1885 and 1889 twenty new 'L' class locomotives were built at Broadstone to replace 19 older Cabry and Ramage 0-4-2 goods locomotives and provide one additional locomotive for stock. The locomotives only differed

* At the same meeting, Henry Alfred Ivatt was elected a Member of the Institution. He was district locomotive superintendent on the GS&WR at Cork at the time, and later became that company's locomotive superintendent in 1886. He succeeded Patrick Stirling on the GNR at Doncaster in 1896.

from the 1876 batch in minor details introduced since that date. Drawings were prepared in January 1885 for a new style of cast-iron chimney instead of the built-up chimneys with copper cap used up to that time, but these were not fitted to the six locomotives introduced in that year. It is quite probable that all of the 'L' class locomotives built from 1887 onwards would have had steel frames and wheels, and we know for certain that those of 1888-89 had cast-steel motion-plates. Eight locomotives received new 1,600 gallon tenders, the remainder being paired with old Ramage tenders. They did not work the main line goods trains for very long, being replaced in 1891-2 by the 'LM' class (*see below*) and, not being equipped with ejectors, they could not work passenger trains after 1889.

In August 1889 Martin was severely censured for deficiencies that had come to light in locomotive coal stocks. This matter had first been mentioned in December 1885 when he confirmed a shortfall of upwards of 500 tons at Athlone; he was unable to give a satisfactory explanation for this discrepancy. As a consequence, inspector Bateson and foreman Deane had their pay permanently reduced by 5s. a week, and coalman Maguire was severely reprimanded. Stocktaking figures taken in July 1889 showed that by then the overall shortfall amounted to 2,968 tons, but all store books and vouchers, which had been gone over from 1880 up to the end of June 1889, proved to be strictly accurate and well kept. However, certificates furnished by the Locomotive Department were described as 'altogether erroneous'. In response, Martin attributed the discrepancies to the negligence of Archibald Reid, his late chief clerk, who had omitted to charge off coal used in working the cranes at North Wall when discharging coal from steamers into railway wagons.

As head of the department involved, the Directors held Martin personally responsible, particularly as, for several years, he had failed to exercise proper supervision over his officials, and his salary was reduced by £100 per annum as a consequence. The 1889 investigation led to the removal from their positions of Kirwan, the chief clerk, and James Bateson, the outdoor inspector, with the former being transferred to the Traffic Department. In the case of Bateson, it was decided to appoint a person 'of superior education and experience, qualified to take monthly stocks of coal'. The storekeeper, a Mr Storen, and Jimmy Rowe were ordered to take overall charge of coal stocks. This appears to be the only time that Martin Atock incurred the displeasure of the Board during his 28 years in charge of the Locomotive Department and shows an uncharacteristic lapse in his usual high standards.

Following on the terrible accident at Armagh on the Great Northern Railway (Ireland) (GNR(I)) on 12th June, 1889, emergency legislation was rushed through Parliament making it mandatory for railway companies to fit passenger trains with continuous automatic brakes. Smith's non-automatic continuous vacuum brake had been applied to some MGWR stock since 1879. A conference of locomotive superintendents had been arranged by the Board of Trade (BoT) in 1882 to discuss braking systems. Both the GS&WR and the GNR(I) declined to send their representatives as they were already using the Smith brake, the MGWR also notifying the BoT that they were using the same brake. Martin Atock recommended the adoption of the automatic vacuum brake, this being approved at a Board Meeting on 10th July, 1889 (Traffic Committee Minute No. 1040). Drawings were made immediately providing for a 20 in. vacuum cylinder and a vacuum bag at the front of the locomotives, as a front bag had not been provided for the simple vacuum brake.

The equipping of the locomotives for operating the automatic vacuum brake started in 1891 and had two design points requiring mention. Externally, a new front vacuum bag arrangement was designed by Jimmy Rowe, which became famously known on the MGWR as the 'elephant's trunk'. None of the engines were long enough at the front to allow a fixed vacuum pipe and bag in the normal position without fouling the smokebox door. Rowe's solution was to bring the vacuum pipe (which was polished copper) up round the front of the smokebox above the door. At the top he provided a swivelling joint, the corresponding portion of which carried a long vacuum bag. When out of use the vacuum bag was placed on a dummy at the base of the smokebox. The arrangement had the obvious fault that anyone on the front of the locomotive might easily catch the swivelling part of the vacuum bag instead of the handrail, which was immediately above it. Internally, the new blastpipes were of an annular type, probably based on Adams' 'Vortex' design, the internal circular opening, 2½ in. diameter for all locomotives, was for the ejector exhaust only. The cylinder exhaust was brought through a surrounding annular orifice that varied in size according to the diameter of the cylinders. In all cases its area was less than that of the plain blastpipe it replaced, by amounts varying from 18 to 24 per cent.

It is a practical certainty that all of the '7-12' class 2-4-0 locomotives were equipped with the automatic vacuum brake from new, with the possible exception of No. 7.* The renewal of the '7-12' class locomotives during 1889-90 was also the point of other important changes in design. For 16 years Martin had designed and built all his locomotives to the same basic design, subject only to the continuous introduction in the different batches of the various changes and improvements described above. Now there was a complete change, and it is clear from its extent that every part of locomotive design was considered afresh; retained where it was found satisfactory, or altered where it was felt that improvements could be made. Boilers were made larger and, by using steel instead of iron, the working pressure was increased from 130 to 150 psi. The motion was redesigned, with slidebars moved back clear of the cylinder covers and centrally supported by a cast steel motion-plate incorporating valve spindle guides, thus permitting the swing links to be eliminated. The slidebars were also moved further apart to allow the use of larger crossheads, and Adams balanced slide valves were introduced. At the same time Martin introduced marine big ends instead of the cottered arrangement formerly used. Cabs were improved and the whole external outline of the engines made simpler and less ornamental.

The fruit of all this thought and effort first appeared in the renewal of the Avonside Mail engines of 1869-70. The use of steel instead of iron for the '7-12' class boiler should have enabled a good increase in working pressure to be

* No MGWR engine ever had a really good vacuum brake; it was always liable suddenly not to work, which did not matter so much when there was a train brake as well, but was very awkward when a passenger engine was working a goods train.

MGWR '7-12' class 2-4-0 No. 9 *Emerald Isle* of 1890. The six members of the class were intended as replacements for the Avonside Mail engines of 1869-70. No. 9 was withdrawn in 1912. Of note is the very distinctive Atock flyaway cab.

H. Fayle, courtesy Irish Railway Record Society Collection

'K' Class 2-4-0 No. 33 *Arrow* standing at Clifden, Co. Galway at the head of the up Tourist Express. The train is in the short-lived blue and cream livery introduced by Martin's successor, Edward Cusack. The third coach is a typical Cusack design with distinctive roof profile, whilst the fourth carriage is the famous MGWR 12-wheeled dining car No. 3. The 'K' class were, arguably, Martin's best locomotive design.

H. Fayle, courtesy Irish Railway Record Society Collection

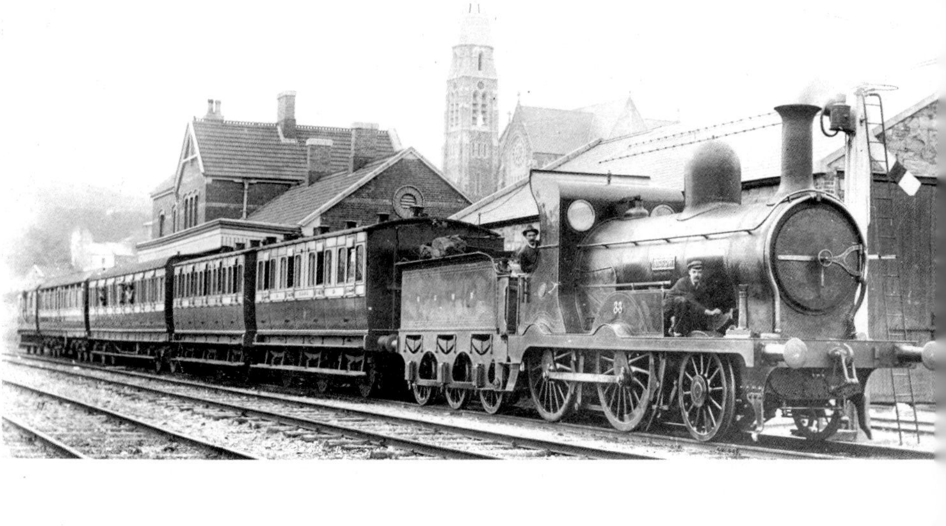

made without the use of thicker plates, but Martin was cautious and increased the boiler and casing plates from ½ to 9/16 inches thick. These new boilers were otherwise virtually identical to the 'L' class with the outside diameter increased by 1 in. Likewise, the cylinders differed hardly at all from the 'L' class, apart from the use of balanced slide valves. The two slidebars were made to a heavier section and supported centrally by the new design of cast-steel motion plate. With the elimination of the swing links, the pulling links were altered to work in guides in the motion plate, on top of which was a row of six oilcups for lubricating the motion. After the previous use of 1¼ in. steel for frame plates it was surprising that the '7-12' class had iron frame plates only 1 in. thick, as used in the small passenger engines. Wheels were, however, cast steel and, taking account of the experience with the 'D' class side rods, a heavier section design was provided.

The many improvements in various fittings included injectors of a new type and the application of the 'top feed' arrangement used on the 'P' class. The sliding firedoor was replaced by a modified version of the Ramage type, while sight-feed lubricators were provided on the driver's side in the cab instead of on the smokebox. Apart from the 'technical' changes, the appearance of the engines was also altered, whether due to simple economy measures or a change in Martin's taste we do not know. Several years previously the copper-capped chimneys had given way to cast-iron ones; now the polished brass dome and safety valve covers used on all passenger engines were replaced with painted iron ones. Brass beading disappeared from around the driving splashers, which were combined with the sandboxes. A new outline of cab appeared, the rectangular lower panel being suppressed. Any illusion that the new cab provided better protection for the men was just that, an illusion; the distance from the faceplate to the back of the roof was exactly the same as before. Finally, the old Ramage tenders were retained, the old wheels being fitted on to new axles.

We have few records of the work done by the renewed '7-12' class in MGWR days, as they appear to have suffered few failures in their early days. It must be supposed that they took turns on the Limited Mail trains once the 'D' class were replaced on those workings, but there are few reports of them on the Mayo and Meath roads. They shared the working of the Limited Mail between Athlone and Galway with the 'K' and 'LM' classes even after the 'A' class 4-4-0s appeared, as the latter were not allowed over the bridges west of Athlone when new. The decision to use 1 in. iron frame plates caused problems in later years, and as a result these locomotives had relatively short lives, the last one being withdrawn in 1922.

Martin had fitted an expansion ring into one of the Broadstone stationary boilers in July 1882. This experiment undoubtedly led to him taking out a Patent in June 1889 for *Improvements in the Shells or Barrels of Locomotive and similar Boilers* (Patent No. 10,826, also American Patent 423,406 dated 18th March, 1890). This invention was intended to provide elasticity to locomotive boiler barrels so as to obviate undue strains arising from expansion and contraction. For this purpose the smokebox tubeplate (which could be manufactured of steel, iron or copper) was to be made with a corrugated flange that was

(No Model.) 6 Sheets—Sheet 6.

M. ATOCK.

LOCOMOTIVE BOILER.

No. 423,406. Patented Mar. 18, 1890.

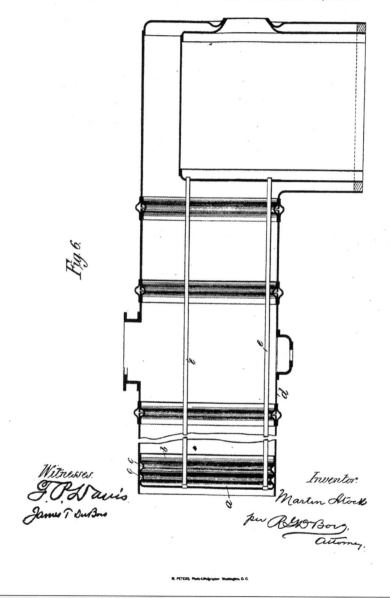

Fig. 6.

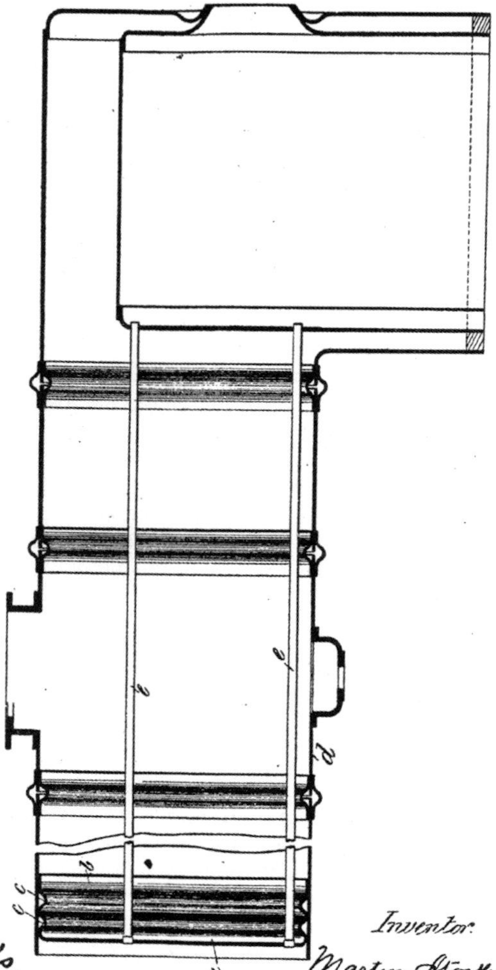

Witnesses.
G. P. Davis
James T. DuBois

Inventor:
Martin Atock
per [illegible]
Attorney.

R. PETERS, Photo-Lithographer, Washington, D.C.

Martin Atock's American Patent for his 'Corrugated Boiler', dated 18th March, 1890. Apart from Martin's own signature, that of Jimmy Rowe, his long-time friend and assistant, both at Limerick and Broadstone, will be noted. The drawing also clearly shows the nature of the corrugated front tubeplate. *R.N. Clements, Irish Railway Record Society Collection*

arranged to turn inwards within the boiler barrel or, indeed, might be reversed and turned outward. The flange was to have one or more corrugations and the corrugated part could be either entirely within the barrel or could project beyond the front tubeplate. At one or more of the circumferential joints the barrel was provided with two corrugated rings; in Martin's design there was, at each joint so provided, both inner and outer rings, the former being made of copper or other non-corrosive material. The object of these was to add strength to the joint and also to protect the outer ring from pitting.

A fifth 'P' class locomotive, No. 105, was built at Broadstone in 1890. By that time one might also have expected it to have a boiler based on the '7-12' design principles, but this was not so, and the boiler that was fitted seems to have been the last of the old type made. The period 1891-95 was an exceptionally busy one for Martin, with the introduction of three new locomotive designs, an increase in the locomotive stock from 105 to 127, and the introduction of the automatic vacuum brake for passenger trains. Two new classes were introduced in 1891: the 'E' class 0-6-0T locomotives for branch lines, and the 'LM' class goods locomotives, which were a modernised version of the 'L' class. In both classes a wheel and handle was adopted for the smokebox door in place of twin handles, a feature that remained standard on the MGWR until 1916.

Apart from the Edenderry and Athboy branches, which were worked by the three rebuilt Fairbairn tank locomotives referred to in the previous chapter, the MGWR possessed no passenger tank locomotives. By 1890 four other branch lines were worked by tender locomotives (not exactly an ideal situation) and the Ballinrobe and Loughrea branches were under construction. A passenger service had also been introduced between Broadstone and North Wall. Work on the design of new tank locomotives commenced in early 1890 and drawings for the boilers clearly show the details of Martin's 'Elastic Boiler'.

Normally, the steel boiler would have been made up from three equal butt-jointed rings. With the patent tubeplate, however, the front ring was cut short by 1 ft 3¾ in. from the front, where there was a double lap joint. Inside was the corrugated ring 1 ft 7¾ in. long, the rear end of which was riveted to the boiler barrel and the front to the flange of the tubeplate, which was therefore free to move according to expansion of the corrugations. The idea was ingenious but the extra cost of the boilers must have been considerable and their real advantage (if any) very slight. Still, inventors always believe in their own devices and Martin Atock was no exception! It is difficult to say what the life of the corrugated rings was; in spite of trouble from cracks and pitting at the root of the corrugations, some may have lasted nearly 30 years.*

Orders were placed at the end of April 1890 for six 'E' class locomotives, three each from Kitson's and Sharp, Stewart. The boilers used were of 4 ft outside diameter, butt-jointed to a firebox similar to the '7-12' class. Gresham & Craven No. 6 injectors were specified, mounted, for the first time, on the faceplate. Frames were of 1 in. steel with standard suspension and axleboxes; the motion was based on the '7-12' class, but with single slidebars. The cab was more spacious and

* Martin Atock's US Patent 423,406-423,700 *Locomotive Boiler*. What the late Bob Clements referred to as 'some quite mad boilers', 56 ft long with a flexible joint in the middle, made for Mallet engines on the Santa Fe Railroad in 1911, might have used corrugated rings based on Atock's idea. Otherwise, no reference has been found to the idea being tried other than on the MGWR.

An unidentified 'E' class 0-6-0T on a Killeshandra branch train at Crossdoney Junction. Twelve of these small locomotives were built between 1891 and 1894, nine by Kitson and three by Sharp, Stewart (1891). They were specifically designed by Martin Atock as 'light tanks' for the three new Western branches. Their distinguishing feature was the tall chimney. *H. Fayle, courtesy Irish Railway Record Society Collection*

provided better shelter than the 'P' class, although it could be unpleasantly hot in summer. They were equipped with vacuum brakes only, and they were the first engines to have the new standard buffers (2 ft instead of 18 in. long).

Three more 'E' class tank locomotives were ordered from Kitson, in January 1891, followed by a final batch of three from the same builder, in July 1893. With these orders improvements were made to the boilers and motion, and, in the 1893 batch, the balanced slide valves were abandoned; in addition, annular blast pipes were fitted, while all axleboxes were made of solid brass. In addition to their normal branch line duties the 'E' class worked the Achill road for a time, for which the last three were obviously specifically ordered. No. 114 was derailed on points at Newport when working the 5.32 pm ex-Achill on 5th September, 1896. Following a number of such incidents, T.J. Myles, the District Engineer, stated his belief that the engines were unsuitable for use on the Western extensions, being backed up in this view by the Chief Engineer, W. Purcell O'Neill. This resulted in their replacement on the Western branches by four-coupled tender engines.

We now turn to Martin's final development of the standard goods locomotive design. The 'LM' class 0-6-0 did not differ greatly from the 'L' class apart from various alterations introduced with the '7-12' and 'E' classes. Between 1891 and 1893 twelve 'LM' class locomotives were built at Broadstone, at a cost of £2,500 each, to replace the last of the Ramage 0-4-2s, three of the new locomotives having boilers supplied by Kitson. Ten further 'LM' class were ordered in 1894 for delivery the following year, five each from Sharp, Stewart and Kitson, which were additions to capital stock. The 'LM' class had steel frames and boilerplates. The motion, except for shorter pulling links, was the same as the '7-12' class, including the use of four centrally supported slidebars. Steam brakes were provided on the Broadstone locomotives, whereas those from the outside builders were equipped with vacuum brakes.

The Broadstone-built locomotives were given reconditioned tenders assembled from old bodies, built during the Ramage period to Cabry's design, mounted on new frames to the same general design that Martin had been using for his new tenders. On the other hand, the Sharp, Stewart and Kitson locomotives received tenders of a new design with a nominal capacity of 2,000 gallons of water and four tons of coal, actual figures being closer to 2,100 gallons of water and seven tons of coal. For the new tenders Martin modified his standard design of frame, increasing the wheelbase by 1 ft, which resulted in frames that were 9 in. longer. The 'LM' class were the principal main line goods locomotives during Martin's last years on the MGWR. The locomotives with vacuum brakes did a good deal of passenger work in their early days, including the Limited Mails, until the bridges west of Athlone were strengthened to permit the 'A' class to run to Galway. With the arrival of the 'B' class in 1904, and the rebuilding of the Avonsides in 1906-8, they were no longer required for the heaviest goods trains and were downgraded to working branch line goods trains and livestock specials.

By 1892 the last of the Ramage goods engines had been withdrawn and this left the entire MGWR locomotive stock to Atock's design with the exception of the four WD&LR locomotives bought in 1880 and the three saddle tank rebuilds of the old Fairbairn 2-2-2 well tanks. Except for the latter no locomotive was more than 19 years old. During 1894-95 Martin rebuilt the 10 old Stephenson 'L' class locomotives of 1876 to 'LM' class specification. The drawings show the use of thicker tyres on the original wheels to obtain the standard 5 ft 3 in. driving wheel diameter of the 'LM' class. It appears that the use of these wheels was intended only to be a temporary measure, but the small wheel centres were never subsequently changed.

The renewal of the 'L' class involved new 18 in. cylinders, motion, boiler and cab to bring them into line with the 'LM' class built in 1891-3. The rebuilt locomotives had an ordinary lap joint between the boiler barrel and the firebox casing, presumably stepped, as was Atock's normal practice. The last four boilers differed in having the length of the corrugated ring increased from 1 ft 7¾ in. to 3 ft 2 in., the remainder of the barrel being presumably made in one ring. The smokebox doors were of an improved type as fitted to the 'K' class. The motion was of the centrally supported four-slidebar type introduced on the '7-12' class in 1889. New connecting rods were of the 1891 pattern, but the old side rods were retained. They were the first MGWR goods engines to have vacuum ejectors, just preceding the 'LM' class locomotives supplied by Sharp, Stewart and Kitson. Early drawings indicate that it was intended to fit only steam brakes, but probably all were rebuilt from the start with vacuum brakes. After renewal they were used mostly on the Sligo and Mayo roads, their normal goods duties being varied by occasional passenger jobs. Re-boilering of the later 'L' class did not constitute so heavy a rebuild and, as that work took place after Martin Atock's retirement, it is omitted from this chapter.

In 1893, as the first batch of the 'LM' class were being finished at Broadstone, renewal of the 17 older 'D' class locomotives of 1873-76 was commenced. The 20 'K' class 2-4-0 locomotives, also referred to in official records as the '13-24' class, included nominal replacements for the three saddle tank rebuilds of 1874-76. The 17 'D' class replacements inherited the numbers and names of their predecessors as well as the coupled wheels, tenders and some smaller parts of the original locomotives. From the dimensions one might be forgiven for thinking they were the same as the '7-12' class. However, the new frames were thicker and the balanced slide valves were not adopted. The boilers were the same size as the '7-12' class but differed in construction. The first three had one elastic and two ordinary rings and were butt-jointed to the firebox casing. The same design of barrel was used for the next four, but they were joined to the firebox casing by a stepped lap-joint, while the remainder had one elastic and one ordinary ring. The lead locomotive of the class, No. 13, went to Mullingar to work the Sligo Limited Mail, and as others became available they were soon working all three Limited Mail trains. In the summer of 1903 they worked the Tourist Express to and from Clifden, the fastest train ever run by the MGWR.

Following the completion of the design work on the 'K' class the Broadstone drawing office had a quiet spell, at least as far as locomotive design was concerned, until the time came for the rebuilding of the 'LN' class of 0-6-0s and renewal of the Beyer, Peacock 2-4-0s of 1880-1. The 'LN' class were rebuilt to 'LM' standard during 1898-99, at which time any remaining Fairbairn wheels were replaced, the new ones at 5 ft 1½ in. diameter still being 1½ in. smaller than the standard 'LM' class wheels. A boiler barrel identical with that used in rebuilding the Stephenson 'L' class locomotives was used; the smokebox was divided horizontally by a spark arrestor level with the top of the blast pipe, which was 3 in. above the top row of tubes. The old Fairbairn tenders were finally scrapped and replaced by Martin's 2,000-gallon type. After renewal the 'LN' class returned to much the same duties as before.

Drawings for the renewal of the Beyer, Peacock 2-4-0s were started in the summer of 1898 and there were two major changes from the practice of the previous 10 years, of which the most conspicuous point was the introduction of leading bogies to MGWR locomotives. Why Martin should have adopted bogies at that particular time is not clear. The 2-4-0 locomotives were quite satisfactory and there was no question of bigger designs that might be too heavy for a single axle at the leading end. It has been said that Martin was attracted for some years to the idea of using Adams bogies, but was discouraged by the necessity of paying royalties in addition to the increased cost of construction. In designing his bogie Martin appears to have followed the Adams type just as far as he could without infringing the patent; this presumably referred to the side-control system and the question was solved by the use of swing-links for side control instead of springs. His bogie design was to remain the standard for all subsequent MGWR 4-4-0 engines.

The other noticeable design change was the replacement of Martin's famous cab with upswept roof. The original intention was for the class to have the standard Atock cab, but only No. 36, the third locomotive completed, was so fitted. The five other rebuilds had the square cab as used in rebuilding the later 'L' class, the drawings for which date from August 1899, proving their design belongs to the Atock period. The new design had full-length lower panels and a separate outside grab-rail; the roofs were of tongued and grooved pitch-pine covered with canvas, serving the double purpose of reducing both noise and condensation. The cab appears to have been influenced by Stroudley-

Drummond ideas, but Martin used a more artistic eye in eliminating a very ugly junction between side sheets and the roof of the Drummond design. The use of side doors, first introduced in Scotland, may indicate that the idea came from St Rollox. Apart from the GS&WR pay-carriage *Sprite*, the 'D BOGIE' 4-4-0 rebuilds were the first locomotives in Ireland to have side doors fitted between cab and tender, although these may not have lasted very long. The cab had a half-round piece cut out of the back of the roof at the centre, which was done to give clearance for a chain when the engine was being lifted; however, it was a dangerous trap for a fireman coming down off the tender bunker who would naturally look to swing off the cab roof at that point.

Although officially considered to be new locomotives, the 'D BOGIE' class of 1900-01 were very much on the border of being rebuilds, incorporating much more material from their predecessors than either the '7-12' or 'K' classes. The frames would deceive anyone examining them for they were in two separate plates, of which the rear one was very similar in profile to the old Beyer, Peacock frames, but deeper from driving horns to motion plate. The splice was at the motion plate, where the front and rear parts were both riveted to a 1 in. thick intermediate plate. The cylinders, which had been horizontal in all previous passenger engines, were inclined at 1 in 10, the casting being narrower to suit the frames; otherwise, apart from being cast in one piece, they were identical to the Beyer, Peacock cylinders.

The motion was of the long slide-bar type, altered to have the pulling links suspended by swing links placed above instead of below the motion and balanced by a spring instead of a weight. Steel connecting rods, of a much heavier design than those on the original Beyer, Peacock locomotives, were provided. It is believed that the side rods came from the old engines, although they were not the original rods of 1880-81. The boiler barrel was 5 in. shorter but otherwise identical to that used for the 'K' class. As rebuilt, the 'D BOGIE' class were essentially Mayo road locomotives, rarely appearing in Dublin. The first of the class, No. 2, was turned out in March 1900, just as Martin was retiring from the MGWR, suitably marking the end of 20 remarkable years of locomotive development at Broadstone.

From the foregoing account, the reader will have observed the remarkable degree of standardisation that Martin achieved in his locomotive designs. In fact, by 1900 the average number of engines per class was greater on the MGWR than the GS&WR, and (due partly to the renewal policy of the MGWR) there was a smaller variation in age between different engines of the same class. Although both companies strived for standardisation, there was a great contrast between their locomotive policies. The MGWR was not so conscious of standardisation and Broadstone would produce a separate drawing of the same basic design of part as sized for different classes. On the other hand, Inchicore would make one drawing of the basic design of part indicating the different sizes for the applicable classes. Martin was, on the whole, more willing to incorporate continuous improvements into his designs than any of the GS&WR locomotive engineers, but the advantages of Broadstone standardisation were largely confined to the manufacturing side. Martin Atock would not have approved of the interchange of parts from one locomotive to another, frequent at Inchicore.

Chapter Six

Carriage, Wagons and Retirement

When Martin Atock took over as locomotive, carriage & wagon superintendent of the MGWR in April 1872 the mileage operated by the company stood at 375, and he inherited a rolling stock fleet comprised of 166 carriages of all classes and 78 other coaching vehicles, as well as 1,579 goods wagons and a collection of departmental vehicles. By the time of his retirement the respective figures were 538 miles, 186 carriages, 200 other coaching vehicles and 2,713 goods wagons; there were also 48 goods brake vans. As a result of the MGWR policy of renewing its rolling stock at 20 year intervals, the actual number of new vehicles introduced during Martin's 28 year period in charge was, however, in excess of the difference between the two sets of figures. The rolling stock inherited by Martin was of mixed origins and included vehicles acquired from the Dublin & Meath Railway, when the working of that line was taken over by the MGWR, in 1869.

New workshops for carriages and wagons had been completed at Broadstone during 1870, which included conversion of the former goods shed into a wagon shop. The new facilities were additional to the workshops on Phibsborough Road that had been purchased from J.S. Dawson in 1851. However, no carriages had been built in the enlarged premises prior to Martin's arrival. Indeed, the first coaching stock introduced during his time came from the Bristol Wagon & Carriage Works in 1873-74, the order comprising 10 four-wheeled vehicles - three first class and three second class carriages, each having four compartments, and four combined post office, luggage and brake vans. They were, in fact, the only carriages ever purchased from the Bristol company by the MGWR. No other details have survived of these particular vehicles and, although their basic design may have originated prior to his time, it is quite possible that Martin had a hand in their final specification.

Within four months of taking up his appointment Martin had thoroughly assessed the situation and was in a position to report to the Board, stating that in his opinion the MGWR was not renewing its rolling stock at a fast enough rate. In regard to the goods stock he recommended an increase in the renewal rate to 100 wagons per year, and an order was placed that same month with the Metropolitan Carriage & Wagon Company (Metropolitan) for 100 covered wagons, which were additions to stock. The general policy that was followed from that time onwards was to renew goods stock at 20 years life by vehicles built at Broadstone and, with a few minor exceptions, to increase the capital stock through procurement of wagons from outside builders. Insofar as stock increase was concerned, Metropolitan supplied 12 timber trucks in 1873, 20 coal hoppers in 1874, 186 covered wagons in 1876-77, and 50 open coal wagons in 1877, the latter for the Locomotive Department. Later in 1877 the Ashbury Railway Carriage & Iron Company built two 'Boiler and Furniture Trucks' and in 1878 the Birmingham Railway Carriage & Wagon Company (BCW) delivered 26 ballast wagons.

Meanwhile, Martin had recommenced the construction of carriages at Broadstone, in 1875, which were turned out at the rate of eight per year. Although built to the same 22 ft 6 in. length as those constructed during the Cabry-Ramage period, certain details in the design of these third class four-wheeled carriages may well have been altered to Martin's specification. By the end of 1878 Broadstone had completed 32 of these two-compartment vehicles, and 12 additional carriages to the same design, Nos. 77-88, were purchased in 1878 from Metropolitan as additions to stock. With the latter delivery continuous footboards were introduced for the first time, and these became a standard feature on all MGWR carriages introduced thereafter. Despite being built to a dated design, these 44 third class carriages clearly demonstrated Martin's intention to produce vehicles to standard designs whenever possible.

In 1879 the MGWR obtained two family saloons from Metropolitan. They were 30 ft long and carried on 22 ft 11 in. Cleminson flexible wheelbases, the only MGWR vehicles to be so equipped. These carriages had a rather distinctive appearance for, in addition to the two central first class saloons with their large windows, each vehicle had a small second class compartment for family servants at one end and a luggage space at the opposite end. The saloon compartments were furnished with armchairs, upholstered in maroon velvet and with woodwork of Moulmein teak. Indian carpets were provided, the tints and design reportedly matching the upholstery. Wall panels were of sycamore, bordered with tulipwood and edged with black and gold mountings. Nos. 52 & 53 appear to have remained pretty well unaltered during their working lives, albeit reclassified several times. In 1880 they were renumbered as saloons 1 & 2 and were included in the first class carriage totals until reverting to composite designation as Nos. 29 & 30 around 1886-87. They finally became first class vehicles once again in 1914 when second class was abolished by the MGWR.

Also in 1879 Martin introduced the first of his standard six-wheeled carriage designs. The four-compartment first class and five-compartment second class carriages were mounted on 29 ft 11 in. underframes, their bodies being 1 in. longer. Headstocks were 8 ft 10 in. by 11 in. by 4 in. and were capped with D-shaped cast-iron blocks. The buffing gear was of the long-spindle variety, taken to rubber shock absorbers attached to the inner transoms; the buffer stock was 1 ft 5 in. long, of consistent tapering shape, and with a head diameter of 1 ft 0¾ in. This was the standard during Martin's period in office, combined buffing and drawgear later being applied to new six-wheeled firsts. Side chains were fitted to all stock until 1905, these being 2 ft 8 in. apart and centred on the drawhook. When it was fitted, the vacuum brake train pipe was offset 6 in. from the centre to clear the coupling, bending above the headstock to locate the bag centrally. The six-compartment third class carriages, introduced from 1881 onwards, had bodies one foot longer on 30 ft 11 in. underframes.

With the increase in size of the six-wheeled vehicles the rate of construction dropped, six carriages per year being built until the end of 1883. The 30 vehicles built up to that year included six first class (1879), one first class and five second class (1880), six third class (1881), one first class and five third class (1882), and two first class and four third class (1883). In 1881 Martin had advised the Board that it was not possible to increase the annual output at Broadstone unless the carriage and wagon shops were enlarged. The Board decided to follow his advice and a new carriage shop was built by Samuel H. Bolton in 1883 at a cost of £5,600. In the same year Martin suffered a personal loss on 14th May when his wife, Mary Eliza, died, her burial taking place in Brompton Cemetery, London.

Martin carried out a trial with electric lighting in the new carriage shop early in 1884, but, as the results showed no distinct advantages, it was decided to persevere with gas lighting. The introduction of the new facility enabled the rate of carriage construction to be increased, the old workshop thereafter being devoted entirely to the construction and rebuilding of wagons. In stepping up the production of carriages there was little visible effect in 1884, only five first class and two second class carriages being turned out from the Broadstone shops in that year. There was a slight change in the design of the two second class carriages in that the width of the four passenger compartments was increased, the resultant smaller centre compartment being used for luggage. From 1885 onwards, with increased facilities at his disposal, Martin was able to turn out an average of over 13 carriages per year. He maintained that rate until the end of 1891, and with five third class carriages under construction at Broadstone and six others on order from Ashbury, Martin was able, in early 1892, to report that the entire stock built before his arrival on the MGWR had been renewed.

During the seven years from 1885 to 1891 two first class, 10 second class, 18 third class, and 26 composite carriages were turned out from the Broadstone shops. The six third class carriages of 1890 marked a new departure in comfort for the lower-fare passengers with the compartment width increased to 6 ft. This allowed a reduction of one foot in the overall length of the new design compared with the earlier third class carriages. In addition to the carriages built at Broadstone during 1885-91, eight 1st & 2nd class composite carriages were purchased from the Midland Carriage & Wagon Company (MCW), in 1886. These vehicles, which were 29 ft long, were built on 28 ft 11 in. underframes, a standard length for composite carriages that Martin had introduced in the previous year. Although not strictly a part of our story, it might be mentioned that two of the Midland composites were rebuilt as slip carriages to cater for the Edenderry branch traffic, the slip being made from the down Limited Mails at Enfield. Nos. 35 & 36 were respectively converted in 1903 and 1908 and, as rebuilt, had a guard's brake compartment in place of one of their first class compartments.

Martin also used the 28 ft 11 in. underframe for four additional post office, luggage and brake vans built at Broadstone in 1885. They were equipped with outside mail collecting nets, and the 12 ft-long post office compartment contained the usual letter-sorting racks. The luggage compartment was 10 ft 8 in. long with double doors on each side, whilst the guard occupied the remaining 5 ft 7 in. The latter section had a raised roof with a 'birdcage' lookout, later replaced by the more conventional side lookouts. The combined post office, luggage and brake vans were used on the MGWR mail services until 1887. However, complaints were received from the postal authorities in that year to the effect that the existing vans were proving inadequate, accommodation provided for postal activities being considered too small. The matter was referred to Martin who pointed out that the original design of van had been approved by the Post Office Surveyor and the vehicles had been built to GPO requirements! The outcome of further discussions between Martin and the Post Office was the appearance of four 30 ft Travelling Post Office (TPO) vans in 1887-88.

Brown Marshall's of Birmingham supplied three branch line third brakes and three main line passenger brake vans in 1890. These two designs of brake van were both 30ft long, and had first appeared from Broadstone in 1887-88 when eight branch line third brakes and 12 main line passenger brake vans were completed. The design of the guard's compartment of both types differed from the standard Atock contour in that the height of the roof was raised above that of the rest of the carriage to provide a 'birdcage' lookout, and there was no tumblehome in the lower portion of the sides. Ten further branch line third brakes were built in 1889. Third class travel could not be described as comfortable in Martin's time; seating simply consisted of flush-finished wooden benches. It was not until long after his retirement that a strip of carpeting material was provided on the benches with the abolition of second class in 1914, this material surviving in use in some third class carriages until the 1940s.

The bodywork of all Martin's six-wheeled carriages was of a uniform standard. They were 9 ft wide overall, the sides being parallel from the cantrail to a point 2 ft 4½ in. above the solebar, a 3 in. tumblehome then reducing the width to 8 ft 6 in. at the solebar. The ends were made up of five panels, and the roof radius was 12 ft giving a height from rail to roof apex of 11 ft 4 in. Atock windows were distinctive, with rounded top corners and square bottom ones. While similar windows were also to be found on GER carriages during George Attock's period there, they do not appear to have been an Atock/Attock design. R.W. Rush, in his work on Lancashire & Yorkshire Railway passenger stock, suggests that Charles Fay introduced this type of window on that railway in the late 1850s. However, the Ashbury Railway Carriage & Iron Company had supplied third class carriages to the Manchester & Leeds Railway in 1840, and first and third class carriages to the East Lancashire Railway in 1854 with this feature, and it could be found on vehicles supplied by Ashbury to other companies.*

Window size varied depending on compartment size, doors being a standard 2 ft wide. Louvred timber ventilators were originally provided over the door droplights, these being replaced from 1880 onwards by pressed-steel bonnets. Messrs Defries & Sons' oil lamps were used in later years; an interesting point was that no fixed steps were provided for lamp servicing, access having to be gained by means of an ordinary ladder. Syphon type ventilators were used on the roof until about 1890 when a change was made to Laycock torpedo ventilators.

Martin had very definite ideas on the matter of carriage wheelbase. In a paper read to the Institution of Civil Engineers of Ireland in 1891 he referred to experiments carried out on the GER which showed that '0.57 of the length of the

* The Ashbury Railway Carriage & Iron Company was established by John Ashbury in 1837 with workshops at Knott Mill in Manchester, near original terminus of the Sheffield, Ashton-under-Lyme and Manchester Railway (incorporated 1837, opened 1841, and which became a constituent of the Manchester Sheffield & Lincolnshire Railway in 1846). Ashbury moved to Openshaw in 1841 and became a limited company in 1862.

No. 182M, a 31 ft four-compartment composite saloon, originally built at Broadstone in 1893 as coupé No. 8 first and converted in 1939. She remained in service until 1960.

Desmond Coakham

Five-compartment six-wheeled Third No. 2M built at Broadstone in 1893 and finally withdrawn in 1956. Probably the best known of Martin Atock's carriage designs. Note distinctive Atock style windows.

Desmond Coakham

Above: Another, unidentified, five-compartment third, in CIE livery and sporting the 'flying snail' crest. Livery was dark green with eau-de-nil waist strip and numbers. Note smoking labels on three of the compartments.
Desmond Coakham

Left: Uncovered wooden seating in a compartment of an ex-MGWR third class six-wheeler in 1947. Most of these carriages had by then been fitted with a rudimentary covering over the seats. Also note plain wooden flooring and distinctive Atock window.
R.N. Clements, courtesy Irish Railway Record Society Collection

Ex-MGWR six-wheeled, five-compartment second No. 45M at an unknown location. Note Atock-style windows with curved top corners and square bottom corners. *Desmond Coakham*

Branch line third brake No. 11M built at Broadstone in 1883 at a cost of £446. Seating was provided for 24 passengers. Note distinctive straight sides to the guard's van section, whereas the balance of the sides sport the usual tumblehome. *Desmond Coakham*

carriages was the correct thing'. Martin had, however, adopted a 20 ft wheelbase for his 30 ft carriages, i.e. 0.67 of the body length. He contended that this produced carriages that travelled with the greatest possible smoothness, as it approximated to the distance apart of the centres of percussion and spontaneous rotation. The GER Board Minutes make no references to such experiments having taken place, but it is interesting to record that carriages introduced during George Attock's time there conformed more or less to the old formula. Mansell wooden-centred wheels, 3 ft 7½ in. in diameter, were adopted by the MGWR as standard in 1879, and up until about that time, grease boxes were generally used for axle journal bearings, a change to oil boxes being made in 1880.

During the period from 1872 to 1892 Martin had also renewed all of the 1,579 goods vehicles that he had inherited when he joined the MGWR. At the same time the capital stock was increased by 844 vehicles, as illustrated below:

Wagon type	*12/1871*	*Renewals*	*Capital*	*12/1892*
Open Box	117	151	50	201
Covered Goods	1,045	1,045	406	1,451
Cattle Trucks	305	255	250	505
Timber Trucks	30	30	18	48
Boiler Trucks			4	4
Powder Vans	2			2
Ballast Trucks	80	76	26	102
Loco Coal Trucks		20	90	110
Totals	*1,579*	*1,579*	*844*	*2,423*

The wagon stock produced at Broadstone or procured from outside builders during Martin's 28 year tenure exhibited standard features. Prior to 1893 all of the covered goods, open cattle and ballast wagons were built to a length of 13 ft 6 in. over headstocks. Open box wagons of all types were 16 ft in length, whilst timber trucks were 13 ft long. Plank size for covered and cattle wagons was 6½ in., open box wagons had sides 3 in. thick, the number of planks depending on the class of wagon. Throughout the Atock period the MGWR used 3ft 3½ in. diameter eight-spoke wagon wheels, with either cast-iron or steel centres, wrought-iron spokes and steel tyres. Grease boxes were generally used for axle journal bearings, oil boxes on wagons not appearing until well after Martin's time. Prior to 1885 a single wooden brake block was used, applied by a single lever and operating on one wheel. In that year hand braking on a pair of wheels using cast-iron blocks was introduced. During the 1870s the MGWR used the Spencer self-contained buffer with a continuous drawhook and two rubber shock absorbers. About 1885 that arrangement was replaced by long-spindled buffers taken to rubber shock absorbers, anchored to a massive cast-iron box bolted to the centre of the solebars.

The 7-ton covered goods wagons were the most numerous type in the fleet and were used not only for ordinary goods but also for livestock traffic. In 1891 a new design was introduced, which although of the same dimensions as earlier covered goods wagons, incorporated simplified side framing, 120 being built at Broadstone to this design. The next most numerous class were the open cattle wagons, the 305 vehicles that Martin inherited being progressively replaced by

A typical scene at Liffey Junction, Dublin, at the turn of the 20th century, showing large numbers of cattle wagons - this was the nearest point to the Dublin cattle markets. The locomotive is an unidentified 'P' class 0-6-0T which has brought a train of assorted cattle wagons up from the North Wall yard. *Photographer unknown, courtesy Seán Kennedy*

covered goods wagons such that none remained by 1885. In that year work started on the construction of a new series of open cattle wagons at Broadstone, a total of 505 having been completed by the end of 1892, of which 250 were additions to wagon stock, 100 of which were obtained from Ashbury in 1890. The same builder had earlier supplied two 'Boiler and Furniture Trucks' in 1877 for the transport of extraordinary loads. They were 20 ft long over headstocks with a 12 ft wheelbase and a carrying capacity of 7 tons. Two more were built to the same design at Broadstone in 1892.

Livestock traffic was fundamental to the existence of the MGWR and fairs at the principal market towns were considered very important. The principal fair was that held at Ballinasloe in the first week of October each year at which the Directors of the company entertained friends and customers. Tatlow describes the 1891 Ballinasloe fair in detail and, in particular, mentions the attendance of the senior officers. On that occasion he shared rooms with Martin, noting that he had slept in the same room in part of the original station premises for many years on the occasion of the fairs. Martin had recorded his attendance in 'Robinson Crusoe' fashion by cutting notches in the beams of the ceiling! Martin told Tatlow that an old jackdaw that perched outside their skylight every morning had perched there all the years that he had been attending the fair.

The transport of locomotive coal was also important and for that traffic 20 wooden coal hopper wagons were supplied by Metropolitan in 1873 for movements between Spencer Dock and Broadstone. These wagons measured 16 ft over headstocks with a 9 ft 6 in. wheelbase and a tare weight of 6 t 7 cwt. The double hopper doors were operated simultaneously by means of a rotating shaft. Four years later Metropolitan also delivered 50 open box wagons for carriage of locomotive coal between Broadstone and the outlying depots. They were three-plank vehicles with 'cupboard' doors, and a capacity for 8 tons of coal. A further 20 wagons to the same design were built as renewals at Broadstone in 1881 and a similar batch was turned out in 1892. Metropolitan also supplied 12 timber trucks in 1873, but we have no technical details of these vehicles. They were most likely similar to another batch of 20 timber trucks built at Broadstone as renewals in 1875. Six timber trucks were built as additions to stock in 1892.The timber loads were secured using screw-adjusted chains, the wagons normally operating in pairs or as three together depending on the length of the loads.

In 1873 Martin was instructed to 'make up Mr Rowan's train to 20 wagons and have *Western District* painted on each'. (Devonshire J. Rowan resigned his position as District Engineer on 31st May, 1876.) The result was that 10 ballast wagons were turned out from Broadstone as renewals in the same year. A drawing of 1874 shows a ballast wagon equipped with a brake and a 'sentry box' superimposed on the outline of the wagon for a guard's compartment. It is believed that one of the 10 wagons, possibly No. 1259, was so fitted. A further 26 ballast wagons were obtained from BCW in 1877 as additions to stock, and four others were renewed at Broadstone in the same year. These 30 vehicles had a single brake and self-contained buffers, and both the sides and the ends could be dropped for the discharge of loads. Twenty more renewals came from Broadstone in 1881, the last new ballast wagons to appear during the period under review. The ballast wagon with the brake compartment must have outlived its usefulness as four purpose-built ballast brake vans were completed at Broadstone in 1882-83.

Before returning to the passenger stock we must consider the goods brake vans that were introduced by Martin prior to 1891, such vehicles being numbered in a separate series to the goods wagons. Two incline brake vans were supplied by Metropolitan in 1873 for use on the steeply-graded Liffey branch, these being augmented by two more from the same builder in 1877; they had also built a similar brake van for the Westport Quay line in 1875. The MGWR had renewed six goods brake vans during 1874 and a further eight came from the Bristol Wagon & Carriage Works in 1876. These 8-ton goods brake vans were 17 ft 6 in. long over headstocks, with a veranda at the rear, off which was the guard's compartment with a 'birdcage' lookout and an adjoining compartment for cattle drovers with a 13 in. deep bench fitted to the end wall. The braking was by wooden brake blocks acting on all wheels, operated by a large vertical wheel in the guard's compartment. A further six goods brake vans were built by Metropolitan in 1878, three as renewals and three as additions to stock. BCW supplied eight more in 1881, whilst Broadstone turned out another 10 goods brake vans in the following year.

The braking of passenger trains always required attention and, following the Newark brake trials of 1875, the MGWR gave consideration to providing continuous brakes.* In September 1878 Martin had a train of five carriages and a van equipped with Smith's non-automatic vacuum brake. Trials were carried out between Dublin and Kingscourt and, the outcome having been considered satisfactory, four locomotives and 25 carriages were also equipped with the

* As part of a Royal Commission set up in 1874 to inquire into the whole question of railway safety, brake trials were arranged near Newark on the Midland Railway line from Nottingham in June 1875. Eight railway companies participated in the trials, including the L&YR with Fay's brake. The results of the trials were inconclusive.

Smith's brake in the following year. By 1884 vacuum brake equipment had been applied to 25 locomotives and 180 carriages and vans. The Armagh accident of 12th June, 1889, which resulted in the passing of the Regulation of Railways Act of 1889, made it mandatory for railway companies to fit passenger trains with continuous automatic brakes. Martin tackled the matter with his usual energy and within four years most of the MGWR passenger stock had been converted to the automatic vacuum brake.

Although Martin was on the point of achieving the complete renewal of the passenger carrying stock in 1892, the imminent opening of the various western branches brought about a need for additional rolling stock. We have already noted the introduction of eighteen 30 ft five-compartment third class carriages in 1890-91. They were the first of what was perhaps the best known of Martin's designs, a further 60 being added over the ensuing nine years. Apart from 11 supplied by Ashbury in 1892 they were built at Broadstone, five of the former vehicles being part of an order for 24 vehicles for the western branch traffic. The entire order placed with the Ashbury Carriage & Iron Company consisted of five first class, five second class and five third class carriages and nine main line passenger brake vans. Two further main line passenger brake vans were built in 1900, differing from the previous deliveries only in having a droplight added to one leaf of each set of the double doors.

The first and second class carriages were to the new designs introduced by Martin for the replacement of the 1873 Bristol carriages. The three second class carriages with lavatories that were built at Broadstone in 1892 as replacements were the first of this type to appear on the MGWR. Water tanks were situated internally at cantrail level under the roof, one to each pair of lavatories. One of the compartments with access to a lavatory was reserved for ladies, whilst the compartment next to it was for smokers. The five second class carriages supplied by Ashbury as additions to stock in 1894 were similar; it would appear that the original intention was for them to also have internal water tanks, but as delivered the tanks were placed on the roof. These eight second class carriages had 1 ft 6 in. seats with cushions and sprung backrests, and each compartment was equipped with siphon ventilators and oil lamps.

The new design of first class carriage was a more radical departure from previous designs. For these, Martin increased the length to 31 ft and provided two lavatories in the centre of the vehicle, the inclusion of which resulted in the compartment at one end being re-designed as a coupé with large end windows. Instructions contained in the Appendix to the MGWR Working Timetable stated that the coupé end of these carriages 'must not be marshalled next the engine'. Eight first class carriages were built to this design, three at Broadstone in 1893 as replacements for the old Bristol carriages, and five by Ashbury in 1894 as additions to stock for the western branch traffic. The latter differed from the Broadstone batch in that the water tanks for the lavatories were placed on top of the roof, whereas the earlier ones had them placed internally in the same way as the 1892 second class carriages.

A solitary 29 ft composite carriage was built to the standard design at Broadstone in 1893. No. 10 was the last six-wheeled composite built for the MGWR as the final lot of composite carriages to be turned out in Martin's time were a complete departure from previous practice. Drawings were prepared in 1897 for tri-composite carriages to a new contour with a high elliptical roof. The principal change, however, was that they were to be 53 ft long and mounted on two four-wheeled bogies. The bogies were positioned at 36 ft between centres and had an 8 ft wheelbase. An order was placed with MCW for the construction of four carriages to the new design and Nos. 39-42, the first bogie carriages on the MGWR, were delivered in 1900. Two compartments were provided for each of the three classes of passengers, arranged symmetrically about a central luggage compartment and four lavatories were included, two each for first and second class.

Martin first carried out experiments with electric lighting in July 1895. Instructions were given in the following March for 12 carriages and the four TPO vans to be equipped. By the time of Martin's retirement, 63 carriages, four TPOs and four passenger brake vans were equipped with electric lighting. Foot-warmers were the sole means of heating for passengers in six-wheeled stock until 1912, when steam heating was introduced.

Under Martin Atock's direction, the usual array of non-passenger coaching stock was provided. A total of 17 carriage trucks were built between 1872 and the end of 1889, but we know nothing more about them. Four new vehicles appeared in 1890 to replace early stock, and four additions followed in 1891. A further four carriage trucks were built in 1893, two on revenue and two on the capital account. All 12 of those built from 1890 were 15 ft 8 in. long over headstocks, and had fixed three-plank sides. The first vehicles to be used by the MGWR specifically for perishable traffic were six vehicles supplied by Metropolitan in 1874, which were described as 'Meat & Fish Vans'. They were 14 ft 8 in. long over headstocks, on an 8 ft 6 in. wheelbase with outside-framed, horizontally-sheeted bodies and horizontal louvres on the sides and at the ends. They were equipped with double doors, and a double roof was provided to assist with ventilation. The same builder supplied a further 14 similar vans in 1877-78. In 1882 Martin introduced a new design of meat & fish van, and had a prototype built at Broadstone in that year. Thirty-five additional vans were built to his improved design, 10 by the Midland Carriage & Wagon Company in 1883, followed by 25 from Metropolitan in 1889.

The MGWR horsebox design was easily recognisable by its dog box at one end, which gave it the appearance of an old-fashioned lorry, the dog box forming the 'bonnet'. The standard horsebox with protruding extension probably appeared as early as 1873 on a 9 ft wheelbase. It measured 15 ft in length, the body being divided into three compartments: a small groom's compartment at one end, a three-stall horse compartment and the dog box at the other end, the latter with its roof sloping at about 30°. Seating for the groom consisted of a plain bench devoid of back support. In 1899 a slightly longer version (16 ft 6 in.) was introduced. The only other coaching vehicles requiring mention are the mortuary vans, Nos. 42 & 58, rebuilt from withdrawn four-wheeled third class carriages. No. 42 appeared in 1893 and No. 58 in 1896. New body panels were provided and there was a large sliding door to the single compartment.

In regard to the liveries applied to rolling stock, orders were given as early as October 1868 that the third class carriages should be painted in a more

The typical MGWR horsebox with its dogbox at one end and groom's compartment at the other. They have been described as being like an old fashioned front-engined lorry. The groom's compartment had little in the way of creature comforts. *Desmond Coakham*

MGWR covered goods open centre (CGOC) No. 937 in an unidentified rural setting. Although built in 1906, she was typical of a MGWR wagon of Martin's period in office. No. 937 was broken up in 1935. The chalk marks on the right-hand door indicate that she was either going to or had recently been in Mallow, Co. Cork. *Desmond Coakham*

economical livery, possibly brown. E.L. Ahrons stated that the MGWR brown was 'not unlike that of the old Great Eastern stock'. GER stock was varnished teak when new, becoming a pale brown-umber shade when repainted. If this is so, and if Martin suggested the colour, it must date from no earlier than 1872. This would have been the livery used until Edward Cusack took over from Martin in 1900, following which he introduced blue and white on some stock. However, Cusack's livery did not wear well, and a reversion was made to brown, passenger carriages being lined out in straw. The livery of wagons is not as clearcut as that for coaching stock, as there are no contemporary descriptions to help us. It is believed, however, that the standard colour was dark slate, coal wagons (both traffic and locomotive) were black, permanent way vehicles sand-beige (yellow clay), brake vans and passenger train wagons were probably painted in the carriage brown.

In 1893 the length of covered goods and cattle wagons was increased to 14 ft 2 in., to comply with the Irish Railway Clearing House order of 1st October, 1892 that the minimum inside dimensions for goods wagons should be fixed at 14 ft by 7 ft 3 in. In Martin's time 130 covered goods wagons constructed to the new dimensions were added to stock. Of these 30 were built at Broadstone in 1893 and 100 were supplied by Metropolitan in 1895-96. The last 100 open cattle wagons were also built to the revised dimensions, being supplied by Metropolitan in 1895. Drawings for covered cattle wagons were prepared in 1898, the first of this type, entering service in the following year, being part of a batch of 100 built by Metropolitan.

As early as 1854 two vans had been built for the carriage of gunpowder. It seems as if these were replaced by two new vans built in 1898 and 1899. They were of timber-frame construction with the underframes similar to those used for the covered cattle wagons. They were sheeted outside with 12 swg steel plate, joints being covered by 2 in. mild steel strips. The interiors were lined with 1 in. timber sheeting while the floor and walls, up to a height of 1 ft 10½ in., were covered with lead sheeting. The last goods wagons to be added to stock in Martin's time were 30 open coal wagons for the Locomotive Department supplied by Ashbury in 1899, which brought the stock of goods wagons to 2,713.

Martin was a member of the Council of the Institution of Civil Engineers of Ireland for eight years between 1889 and 1896, and was elected its Vice-President from 1891 to 1894. In 1895 the MGWR celebrated the 50th anniversary of its incorporation, and a dinner was held on Saturday 3rd August for the workmen, in the Workmen's Institute at No. 21 Phibsborough Road, Dublin, nearly 200 members being present. A press report stated that the hall was 'prettily decorated, and a small scroll bearing the inscription "Prosperity to the Midland Great Western Railway" occupied the place of honour'. Martin Atock, President of the Workmen's Institute, occupied the chair. Letters of apology were read from *inter alia* Thomas and Arthur Atock and Henry Ivatt of the GS&WR.

After a sumptuous dinner, Martin rose to loud applause and, ever modest, said that he did not think he was the fittest person to hold the post, not being as eloquent as others. He went on to talk of the company's development over the past 50 years, having grown from a line 26½ miles in length when opened to

ADDRESS

Presented to

Martin Atock Esq.

Locomotive Engineer
Midland Great Western
Railway of Ireland.
Upon his retirement from
that Office on March 31st 1900.

Dear Mr Atock, We your Colleagues and friends avail ourselves of the opportunity afforded by your retirement from the responsible position of Locomotive Engineer to this Company, which you have filled with great ability for the last 28 years, to testify to the respect and esteem in which you are deservedly held and to wish you many years of good health to enjoy the repose to which you are justly entitled after so many years of continuous labour.

We are gratified to know it is not from enfeebled health or failing energies that you are leaving the service of the Company, but rather from the natural feeling that after an active and busy life there should come a time of relaxation and rest from the anxieties and cares which the duties of your position necessarily entailed.

We are also pleased to know it is your intention to reside in Ireland, which we trust will afford us the opportunity of continuing the same friendly feelings which in the past subsisted between us.

We beg your acceptance of the accompanying gift as a souvenir of our friendship, and wishing that time as it passes along will deal gently with yourself and the members of your family.

We are, Dear Mr. Atock
Yours very sincerely.

Signed on behalf of the Subscribers

Chairman of Committee
Geo: Wm. Greene,

Edward Cusack Hon. Secretary
George B. Cleugh Hon. Treasurer

Presentation made to Martin Atock on the occasion of his retirement on 31st March, 1900 from the post of locomotive engineer of the MGWR. Note signatures of George William Greene, the Company Secretary from 1876 to 1902, and Edward Cusack, the Chairman's son and Martin's successor.

Katherine Atock Collection

Enfield to a system of 538½ miles, holding second place in Ireland in those terms and employing 3,200 people. Martin then went on to outline the many developments in the workshops, locomotives and carriages. In the latter context he referred to the comfort provided for passengers in 1895 compared with that of 50 years previously. Following his speech, Martin called for a toast to the Institute. In replying to this, John Higgins, chief foreman at Broadstone, commented on how the Institute had grown from small beginnings. He also took the opportunity to propose a vote of thanks to Thomas Atock (Martin's son, and a locomotive inspector with the company), who had unstintingly organized concerts to raise money for charity. The evening concluded with songs and recitals, Martin being one of those who contributed.

Martin decided to retire in March 1900, by which time he would be 66 years of age. His retirement was prompted by the feeling that his energies were by then somewhat impaired after close on 40 years of railway service. The retirement of James Rowe in December 1899, on grounds of poor health, may also have been a factor influencing his decision. In the event, Rowe was to outlive his chief, passing away on 20th March, 1910 at the age of 69, at his residence, No. 25 St Andrew's Terrace, North Circular Road, Dublin. Martin Atock was the recipient, on 17th April, 1900, of an address and presentation from the Directors and principal officers of the MGWR and the foremen of the Locomotive Carriage & Wagon Department. The address was presented by Martin's successor, Edward Cusack, son of the Chairman of the MGWR and Secretary of the Testimonial Committee. Reference was made to the respect and esteem in which Martin was held by all and he was wished many years of good health 'to enjoy the repose to which you are entitled after so many years of continuous labour'.

A presentation was then made, consisting of a horse and trap, harness, etc. In reply, Martin thanked his friends and 'old comrades' for the very handsome gift, which was well chosen and would be put to good use exploring the charming scenery around his new abode beside the sea at Killiney in south County Dublin. He went on to refer to the employees generally, thanking them for the good feeling that they had always displayed towards him in what was a difficult job, trying to please both his Board of Directors and the men. According to C. Hamilton Ellis in *The Trains we Loved*, Martin was one of the gentlest and most courteous of locomotive superintendents.

It is to be regretted that Martin did not live for very long to enjoy the scenery of south County Dublin. On returning from a visit to London in the autumn of 1901 he took ill and passed away at his residence, Lower Killiney Lodge, on 28th November. After the funeral service, which was attended by many of his old colleagues, not only from the MGWR but from the railway community generally, he was interred in Mount Jerome Cemetery, Dublin. A vote of condolence was proposed at a meeting of the Institution of Civil Engineers of Ireland by its President, Edward Glover and seconded by William Hemmingway Mills. An Obituary in the Newsletter of the Bethesda Church stated that Martin Atock had been a member of the choir there for almost 30 years. Although he had moved to Killiney in 1900, he had still retained a keen interest in the church's welfare.

Dr Arthur Atock took over from his brother, Martin Henry, as assistant medical officer to the GS&WR Sick Fund in Dublin. On Dr Tweedy's retirement in 1899, Arthur was appointed chief medical officer to the GS&WR, a post which he held until his sudden death in March 1936.
Alex Atock Collection

Chapter Seven

Another Generation of Railwaymen

The move from Limerick to Dublin resulted in the Atock family taking up residence at Royal Canal House on Phibsborough Road. The property adjoined the MGWR terminus at Broadstone and was used as the residence for successive locomotive superintendents up until Martin's retirement. At the time, Martin and Eliza had five young children, Martin Henry (11), Arthur (9), Esther (7), Thomas (4) and Amy (1) and Eliza was expecting their sixth child. Eliza must have remained in Limerick for a while as George was actually born there on 22nd May, 1872. Once settled in Dublin there was one final addition to the family, another daughter, Florence Bowbank, who was born in Dublin on 14th September, 1874. The subsequent career of Martin Henry is dealt with in Chapter Nine and that of George is covered in Chapter Eight.

Arthur, like Martin Henry before him, would have commenced his early schooling in Limerick, but would have completed it in Dublin. He decided on a career in medicine, which was to be in a railway environment. He obtained his MD in 1885 and MS in the following year, both from the Royal University of Ireland. Arthur was first registered as a doctor on 4th December, 1885. Around this time he moved away from home and was living at Ardevin Terrace in Inchicore. A GS&WR Traffic & Works Committee Minute dated 3rd March, 1886, in connection with the resignation of his eldest brother Dr Martin Henry Atock from the company's Sick Fund, confirms the appointment of Arthur, as assistant to Dr H.C. Tweedy in his place. Dr Tweedy wrote to the Board in November 1889 stating that the Sick Fund had become difficult to manage owing to increased patronage. He suggested that the Dublin (Kingsbridge) and Inchicore Districts should be separated and £150 a year allocated to each, instead of the gross sum of £270 then paid. The Board agreed to his recommendation, appointing him to look after the Kingsbridge District whilst at the same time giving Dr Arthur Atock responsibility for the Inchicore and Sallins District.

Arthur wrote to Henry Ivatt, the locomotive superintendent* at the end of January 1896 seeking increased accommodation at the Dispensary in Inchicore. The Board ordered that a plan and estimate be prepared for the necessary work. In the meantime Arthur had met Marion Louise (Marie), the youngest daughter of Thomas Lewers, a District Inspector with the Royal Irish Constabulary. Although they were married at St George's church, Dublin, on 10th December, 1888, it was not until 27th October, 1897 that their first child, Arthur George, was born. A sister, Esme Violet, followed on 1st September, 1905, both children being born at their parents' home, Hampden House, situated at the Goldenbridge end of Tyrconnell Road in Inchicore.

* Ivatt had by this time accepted the position of locomotive superintendent of the GNR at Doncaster to replace Patrick Stirling who had died suddenly at the age of 75. He was working out his notice and was replaced by Robert Coey as from 1st March, 1896; Coey had been works manager at Inchicore under Ivatt for the previous 10 years.

Dr Tweedy retired in 1899 and was replaced as the company's Chief Medical Officer by Arthur. Further correspondence with the Board took place in November 1904 in relation to the boundaries of the Sick Fund's two districts. By that time the Kingsbridge District had about 550 men with 900 at Inchicore. The Board now decided to re-combine the two districts, allocating a sum of £270 per annum to Dr Atock. Medical matters appear to have run smoothly for the next 20 years or so as there are no further references to be found in the GS&WR minute books.

With the formation of the Great Southern Railways (GSR) in 1925, consideration had to be given to the much larger area of responsibility now involved. The MGWR had its own Medical Officer in Dublin, as did the Dublin & South Eastern Railway (D&SER). It was agreed that the MGWR's Dr Redmond should in future look after the employees on the D&SE section, his remuneration being increased by £75 to £325 per annum to reflect his increased responsibilities. As regards the former GS&WR area of responsibility, it was decided to continue the existing arrangements with Dr Atock, under which he received fees for the examination of applicants for employment, for medical examinations during illness and for other similar services. Once again everything must have run smoothly, as over the next 11 years there are no further references to the Medical Officer.

A mischievous and quite untrue story circulated around Inchicore during Arthur's time as Medical Officer. The story went that no matter what illness or accident befell one, whether it be a cold or a sprained ankle, Dr Atock would prescribe a bottle of his patent medicine, always the same remedy. The recipients would regularly throw it into the pond on their way down from the Dispensary, and in time the rumour got around that the build-up of medicine in the pond killed off the resident swans. The large pond in question was situated behind the Railwaymen's Institute at Inchicore, better known simply as 'The Club.' It was surrounded by trees and shrubs and was for many years home to ducks and swans; it appears that Alexander McDonnell went as far as having a special swan-house erected. However, the demise of the swans was more likely a result of poisoning, the pond water having been polluted by discharges emanating from the works.

The *Irish Times* and the *Irish Press*, in their editions of Thursday 12th March, 1936, both refer to the sudden death of Dr Arthur Atock on the previous evening. It appears that shortly after 4 pm his chauffeur, James Coburn, entered his office at Kingsbridge to take him up to the Locomotive Department dispensary at Inchicore. Coburn found him lying on the floor beside his desk, holding a fountain pen in his hand and a half-completed report on his desk. Arthur, who was 72 years of age, was immediately removed to Dr Steeven's Hospital directly across the road from the Kingsbridge terminus, but was pronounced dead on arrival; he was a diabetic and had apparently been suffering from influenza. Surprisingly the only reference in the GSR General Board Minutes is one dated 3rd April, 1936 which confirmed that Dr Charles Joseph O'Reilly of Temora, Booterstown, Co. Dublin had 'been unanimously elected to the position of company Doctor, vacated by the death of Dr Atock, at a salary of £700 per annum, with effect from 1st May, 1936'. One would have thought that some further mention might have been made since Arthur had given some 50 years in the service of the company.

Arthur had been Governor of the Apothecaries' Hall in Dublin in 1903-04, and had also been involved with a number of other institutions during his lifetime. These included being Medical Referee to both the Prudential and Scottish Amicable Assurance companies, Medical Officer to the Drummond Institute, Physician to Cheeverstown Convalescent Home, and Medical Adviser to the National Health Insurance. He was also a Fellow of the Royal Institute of Public Health. For some 50 years he had been a member of St Jude's parish in Inchicore. He was the superintendent of the Sunday School for no less than 46 years and a member of the Select Vestry for 45 years, all but one of which were as its secretary. He was also involved with the Men's Society and the Temperance Alliance. An obituary in the St Jude's parish magazine referred to Arthur Atock as 'a marvel of efficiency and conscientiousness in his professional work, but we think of him beyond all else as a Christian man', surely a tribute to which any of us would aspire. Arthur was a prolific traveller in later life, making a total of seven overseas journeys between 1923 and 1934. Destinations included Manaus in Brazil, Rangoon (twice), Bermuda, Athens and Las Palmas (twice). His wife Marion travelled with him on each occasion, sometimes being accompanied by his daughter Esme. On one occasion he took his two nieces, Elizabeth and Violet Doris to Athens.

Arthur's son, Arthur George, was educated at Mountjoy School, at that time situated at Nos. 5-8 Mountjoy Square on the north side of Dublin. School records are sparse but we do know that he obtained a third prize in the Junior Grade in the Religious Knowledge examinations in 1910, improving to a second in the following year, while he was awarded a certificate in middle grade in 1912. The year 1913 saw Arthur George pass some general subjects but failures came in arithmetic and algebra. He later studied engineering at Trinity College, but it is not known if he intended to pursue a career in the railways.

Arthur George Atock sitting on his father's motorcycle, a 500 cc side-valve New Hudson, carrying the Dublin registration RI-1830, indicating that it was first registered in 1913.
Alex Atock Collection

Arthur George Atock in the uniform of the Black Watch Regiment in which he served for a brief period in 1916, when he was based at Perth. He returned to Ireland briefly in August 1916 before joining the Royal Engineers. *Alex Atock Collection*

Below: Wooden cross marking the temporary grave of Arthur George Atock in France. *Alex Atock Collection*

Bottom: Gravestone for Arthur George Atock. *Alex Atock Collection*

Arthur George became a Cadet with the Engineering unit of Trinity College and enlisted with the 11th Battalion, 9th Black Watch Regiment of the Royal Highlanders on 10th March, 1916 as a private based in Perth. He was promoted lance corporal on 3rd June and was based at Catterick and Dunfermline. He then returned to Ireland and on 7th August, 1916 became an officer cadet with the 7th Officers' Cadet Battalion at the Curragh Camp in Co. Kildare; he also trained at Fermoy in Co. Cork during this period. Arthur George was formally discharged from the Royal Highlanders on 18th December and commissioned in the 11th Battalion of the Royal Dublin Fusiliers, with which he remained from 19th December, 1916 until 2nd December, 1917.

The 11th Battalion of the Royal Dublin Fusiliers was mobilised to France in February 1917. Later that year, on 3rd December, Arthur George transferred to the 155th Field Company of the Royal Engineers. The 155th Company was part of the 16th Division of I Corps R.E. under the command of Lieut-Col F. Summers, and was transferred from First to Fifth Army on 20th September, 1918. Lieut. Atock was twice awarded parchment certificates for bravery in the field. The first occasion was for leading forward his section and destroying the gun team of an enemy machine-gun that was harassing retiring troops. On the second occasion, when the company was in danger of being cut off in a village, Arthur George remained behind with his section, fighting from house to house while the remainder of the company was being withdrawn.

Having been wounded on 29th August, 1918, he was advised to go down the line for rest, but he insisted on rejoining his unit. Fifteen days later, when making a road reconnaissance on 13th September, 1918, 2nd Lieut A.G. Atock was killed by a booby trap in a recently vacated German trench. In writing home to his parents, his Commanding Officer stated, 'I cannot adequately express my sorrow at the loss of such a gallant young officer. He was as brave as a lion and always extraordinarily cheerful and beloved by all his brother officers and the men of the Company'. He was only 20 years of age and was posthumously awarded the Military Cross for his bravery in the field. The MC is the third highest gallantry award, after the VC and DSO. Arthur George was buried in the British Military Cemetery at Houchin in Pas de Calais, France. Houchin is a village situated between Barlin and Bethune, about 5 km south of the latter.

Arthur George's sister, Esme, joined the British Army Catering Corps during World War II and went with the allied armies into France following the D-Day landings. She remained in Germany for many years post-war, being based at Osnabruck. She retired in the early 1960s and returned to Ireland, where on 7th March, 1963 she married her cousin, Charles McDonogh, a radiologist and consultant in Sir Patrick Dunn's Hospital in Dublin; he also practised privately from the couple's home in Fitzwilliam Place, Dublin. When Charles retired they moved to live at Ballysheman near Rathdrum in Co. Wicklow. Ballysheman was an old shooting lodge. After Esme moved, the new owners opened a deer farm there. For 10 years following his death in April 1976, Esme remained at Ballysheman before moving again, to Clonmannon, near Rathnew, in Co. Wicklow. She died there on 23rd April, 1996 following a short illness and was buried next to Charles in the cemetery adjoining Enniskerry parish church. In

Awarded the Military Cross.

****

Temporary Second Lieutenant Arthur George ATOCK,

155th Field Company, Royal Engineers.

****

For conspicuous gallantry and devotion to duty. When an enemy machine gun was harassing the retiring troops from a wood, this officer led forward his section and destroyed the gun team. Later, when the company was in danger of being cut off in a village, he remained behind with his section, fighting from house to house, while the remainder of the company was being withdrawn.

Extract, London Gazette,
16th September, 1918.

****

The Military Cross awarded to Lieut Arthur George Atock in September 1918 for 'conspicuous gallantry and devotion to duty'. The accompanying citation gives further details. The MC is now in the possession of Arthur George's nephew, Alex.

Alex Atock Collection

A portrait photograph of Tom Atock in his later years.

Davis of Dublin, courtesy Alex Atock

Portrait photograph of Thomas Atock's wife, Bessie.

Katherine Atock Collection

her will, Esme left a legacy to the Irish branch of the Royal British Legion, with which was founded the Arthur G. Atock Memorial Trust in memory of her brother.

As already recorded, Thomas Atock was born in Limerick on 8th June, 1868, but before looking at his career, this is an opportune moment to take note of Martin's three daughters. Esther married a John Baird on an unknown date; she died at the Adelaide Hospital in Dublin on 16th June, 1934. Amy Isabel married Maj. Charles Mitchell on 14th December, 1905 at St George's church in Dublin. Charles and Amy had one child, also named Charles, born in Dunlavin, Co. Wicklow on 22nd October, 1906. Tragically, Charles Junior passed away on 17th April, 1912 at the age of 5½. Martin's youngest daughter, Florence Bowbank, never married and later moved to England, passing away at Tunbridge Wells in Kent on 15th December, 1950.

As a young boy Thomas became friendly with Lincoln A. Lang, who was born in Dublin of Scottish parents in March 1867 and educated at Bective College. Lincoln Lang's mother was related to the famous railway engineer George Stephenson, and for as long as he could remember he had been interested in engineering matters. Through his friendship with Thomas the boys were able to enlist Martin Atock's good offices to visit the works at Broadstone on many occasions. However, when he was only 16 years of age Lincoln's father took up a position as manager of a cattle ranch in North Dakota, a move which could have spelled the end of any aspirations which the young Lincoln might have had to pursue an engineering career in Ireland. He took up an apprenticeship in the firm of McConway & Torley in Pittsburgh, but the onset of severe deafness brought this to a halt. Undeterred, the young Lincoln set about designing a form of radial valve gear, which in due course was patented and used in marine engines. Were it not for his friendship with young Thomas Atock and his introduction to steam engines at Broadstone, his career might have been totally different.*

We do not know where Thomas received his early education, but for his secondary education he had attended the High School, Dublin, where his tutor was a Mr Roberts. In 1883 he entered the MGWR at Broadstone as a pupil under his father, and in April 1885 he commenced engineering studies at Trinity College as a fee-paying student, graduating with a BA in the summer of 1891. After completing his engineering apprenticeship in 1888 he gained much experience on the MGWR, firstly as a draughtsman and secondly as a locomotive inspector in the Locomotive Running Department. Thomas was elected a member of the ICEI on 7th January, 1903.

Thomas had married Elizabeth Matilda (Bessie) Smith in the parish church of Finglas, just north of Dublin, on 13th August, 1894. Bessie was the eldest daughter of Robert Smith, a Justice of the Peace, of Johnstown House, Glasnevin. Robert was the founder of the well-known firm of sales masters, Messrs Smith Griffin & Co. of Dublin, and was a member both of the Cattle Traders' Association and the Royal Dublin Society. He was widely known as a thorough businessman and for his honourable dealings throughout his life. In addition to his 'home-farm' at Johnstown, Smith also had a grazing farm at Ashgrove.

* The *American Shipbuilder* for 30th November, 1899 contains an article describing the Lang Radial Valve Gear and its application to marine engines.

Right: Four generations in Dublin. At rear, a young Martin Leslie Atock in his mother's arms. In front are his great grandmother and grandmother on his mother's side.

Alex Atock Collection

Below: Tom Atock with Doris, Bessie, Ronald and Martin Leslie in their back garden. *Alex Atock Collection*

Thomas' marriage and career might well have been cut short by a potentially serious incident that occurred on the night of 9th May, 1895. Shortly before 11 pm, Thomas and his expectant wife Bessie, who had been out together for the evening, returned to their home at No. 10 Cabra Parade. On entering the house, Thomas got a smell of gas. In the front parlour he found two gas jets burning in the chandelier and, assuming that the water in the seals might require renewing, he turned off the gas, filled the tubes, and then called for Bessie to bring him a light. There followed a massive explosion, which ripped down the doors separating the front and back rooms and blew out the front window, glass from which was found on the far side of Cabra Parade. A crack appeared in the front wall, window frames were forced from their seatings and ceiling plaster fell down.

Despite the enormity of the explosion, Thomas was only slightly injured, Bessie, two sisters-in-law and a servant escaping with nothing more than shock. It was probably the fact that the front window was rather large that saved them from more serious injuries as it allowed the force of the explosion to escape to the atmosphere. The family had to move in with Martin, at Royal Canal House, pending repairs to the house at Cabra Parade, but they were back home by the time their first child, Martin Leslie, was born there on 18th September, 1895. A daughter, Gladys Mabel, born prematurely on 12th July, 1897, tragically died on 1st May, 1898. Thomas and Bessie had two more children, Violet Doris, born on 5th May, 1899, and finally Robert Charles (Ronald), who arrived on 18th September, 1908.

Martin Atock's decision to retire at the end of March 1900, and consequent changes in the Locomotive Department of the MGWR, resulted in promotion for Thomas. The Board at its meeting on 3rd January, 1900 resolved that 'Henry Edward Cusack be nominated to succeed Atock from 1st April, 1900' and pending Martin's retirement he was to fill the position of first assistant locomotive superintendent vacated on Jimmy Rowe's retirement. Meanwhile the Board sought 'a fully qualified person to be appointed First Locomotive Superintendent', the job to include the responsibilities of both chief draughtsman and works manager. From the foregoing it would appear that Cusack lacked competency in the areas of design and of workshop organization and methods; his principal qualification for the job appears to have been the fact he was the Chairman's son!

The Board had obviously decided that Thomas was not ready for a senior position. It may have been that the poor health that he was to suffer in later years had already manifested itself by 1900. Whatever their reasons, they decided that the appropriate role for Thomas was that of second assistant locomotive superintendent, and he was appointed to that position from 1st January, 1900 at a salary of £300 pa. Perhaps because he felt he had been overlooked, Thomas applied for the position of locomotive superintendent of the West Clare Railway at the end of 1902, following the resignation of George Hopkins, who had been a draughtsman on the MGWR until 1891.

By 7th March applications for the post of first locomotive superintendent had been received from three candidates: John Basil Hope, North Eastern Railway; John Adams, South Eastern & Chatham Railway; and James Parker, Great

NOTE—These Instructions must be kept strictly Private and must only be communicated to those persons in the service of the Company who, in the discharge of their duty, require to know and act upon them; and those persons must not give any information whatever to any one respecting the hours or other arrangements set forth in these Instructions.

Midland Great Western Railway

MANAGER'S OFFICE, BROADSTONE,

DUBLIN, *20th January.* 1905.

CIRCULAR—IMPORTANT.

Visit of His Royal Highness the Prince of Wales to Ballinrobe.

TUESDAY, 24th JANUARY, 1905.

Arrangements and instructions regarding the working of the Royal Train and Pilot Engine which is to precede it. These instructions must be strictly carried out by all concerned.

Train Arrangements.

		PILOT ENGINE	ROYAL TRAIN
Dublin (Broadstone)	DEP.	**11 35 a.m.**	**12 0 noon**
Liffey Junction	PASS.	11 38 ,,	12 3 P.M.
Blanchardstown	,,	11 42 ,,	12 7 ,,
Clonsilla	,,	11 46 ,,	12 11 ,,
Lucan	,,	11 49 ,,	12 14 ,,
Leixlip	,,	11 54 ,,	12 19 ,,
Maynooth	,,	12 0 P.M.	12 25 ,,
Kilcock	,,	12 6 ,,	12 31 ,,
Ferns Lock	,,	12 8 ,,	12 33 ,,
Enfield	,,	12 16 ,,	12 41 ,,
Nesbitt Junction	,,	12 18 ,,	12 43 ,,
Moyvalley	,,	12 23 ,,	12 48 ,,
Hill-of-Down	,,	12 30 ,,	12 55 ,,
Killucan	,,	12 38 ,,	1 3 ,,
Mullingar	ARR.	**12 51** ,,	**1 16** ,,
,,	DEP.	**12 54** ,,	**1 19** ,,
Castletown	PASS	1 5 ,,	1 30 ,,
Streamstown	,,	1 10 ,,	1 35 ,,
Moate	,,	1 19 ,,	1 44 ,,
Athlone	ARR.	**1 32** ,,	**1 57** ,,
,,	DEP.	**1 35** ,,	**2 0** ,,
Kiltoom	PASS.	1 44 ,,	2 9 ,,
Knockcroghery	,,	1 53 ,,	2 18 ,,
Ballymurry	,,	1 58 ,,	2 23 ,,
Roscommon	,,	2 3 ,,	2 28 ,,
Donamon	,,	2 13 ,,	2 39 ,,
Ballymoe	,,	2 24 ,,	2 51 ,,
Castlerea	ARR.	**2 31** ,,	**2 59** ,,
,,	DEP.	**2 34** ,,	**3 2** ,,
Ballinlough	PASS.	2 44 ,,	3 13 ,,
Ballyhaunis	,,	2 54 ,,	3 24 ,,
Claremorris	ARR.	**3 11** ,,	**3 41** ,,
,,	DEP.	**3 14** ,,	**3 50** ,,
Hollymount	PASS.	3 27 ,,	4 3 ,,
Ballinrobe	ARR.	**3 29** ,,	**4 15** ,,

Both Pilot Engine and Royal Train will cross Up Limited Mail at Claremorris, and Specials of Stock from Claremorris Pig Fair where necessary.

Page 1 of timetable and instructions issued under the signature of Joseph Tatlow in connection with the visit of the Prince of Wales to Ashford Castle in January 1905. Tom Atock travelled on the Royal Train engine in both directions.

Author's Collection

Central Railway. It was decided that all the candidates be requested to attend the following Board meeting on Wednesday 14th March, and it was suggested that if they could arrive in Dublin on the Tuesday they would have an opportunity of visiting the Broadstone works. On 21st March the Board resolved to appoint Basil Hope as first assistant locomotive superintendent at a salary of £400 pa on the explicit condition that 'he devote his entire time to the Company's affairs'. Hope subsequently applied for reimbursement of his removal expenses from England and the MGWR agreed to pay the relevant railway charges, but not those of a carrier.

Despite their efforts to find 'a fully qualified person' for the post of first assistant locomotive superintendent, it quickly became apparent that Hope did not have the required experience to be the MGWR chief draughtsman. According to the late R.N. Clements, all accounts indicated that Hope was 'more ornamental than useful' and he appears to have had a strong objection to doing anything that might have involved dirtying his hands or clothes. However, the way was opened at the beginning of July 1900 for changes in the drawing office at Broadstone. It is not clear how William Herbert Morton, a Leeds man, came to be appointed chief draughtsman on the MGWR, but all that needs to be said here is that he arrived at Broadstone in August 1900.

Morton must have made a good impression on the MGWR right from the start for he was indeed a very competent railway engineer and this was soon proved as his area of responsibility increased. Brief mention might be made of the MGWR Royal saloon, built at Broadstone works in 1903. Although its design has been attributed to Edward Cusack, it was probably a product of Morton's drawing board, and was acknowledged as the best vehicle ever turned out of the works. It was 56 ft in length and ran on six-wheel bogies. The vehicle was entered by centrally-placed double doors opening into a vestibule, on one side of which was a large reception room that led to a small smoking and observation compartment. The end wall of the latter was bowed with curved glass windows providing the occupants with magnificent views of the passing scenery. To the other side of the vestibule were a lavatory and a 15 ft dining room, the latter with two round tables, each seating four persons at movable chairs, served by a small 4 ft 6 in. kitchenette. The carriage was painted externally in royal blue with white upper panels and gold lining with the MGWR crest and royal arms on the sides. The well-known Dublin firm of Millar & Beatty provided the interior decorations and furnishings. It was first used for the visit of King Edward VII in 1903.

The Prince of Wales (later King George V) paid a visit to Ireland in January 1905. He travelled by special train from Broadstone station to Ballinrobe on Tuesday 24th January, and thence by horse-drawn carriage to Ashford Castle, in Cong, Co. Mayo where he spent a week with Lord Ardilaun. The special train consisted of a first class saloon, dining saloon, Royal saloon and a passenger brake van in that order. The Royal Train was preceded by a pilot engine, which departed Broadstone at 11.35 am, and it ran through to Ballinrobe, being due there at 3.29 pm. The Royal Train left Broadstone at 12.00 noon and was worked as far as Athlone by one locomotive, where a change of locomotives was made. When the Royal Train arrived at Claremorris, the locomotive was uncoupled and turned for the journey up the branch, the train reaching Ballinrobe at 4.15 pm.

Map of the Midland Great Western Railway.

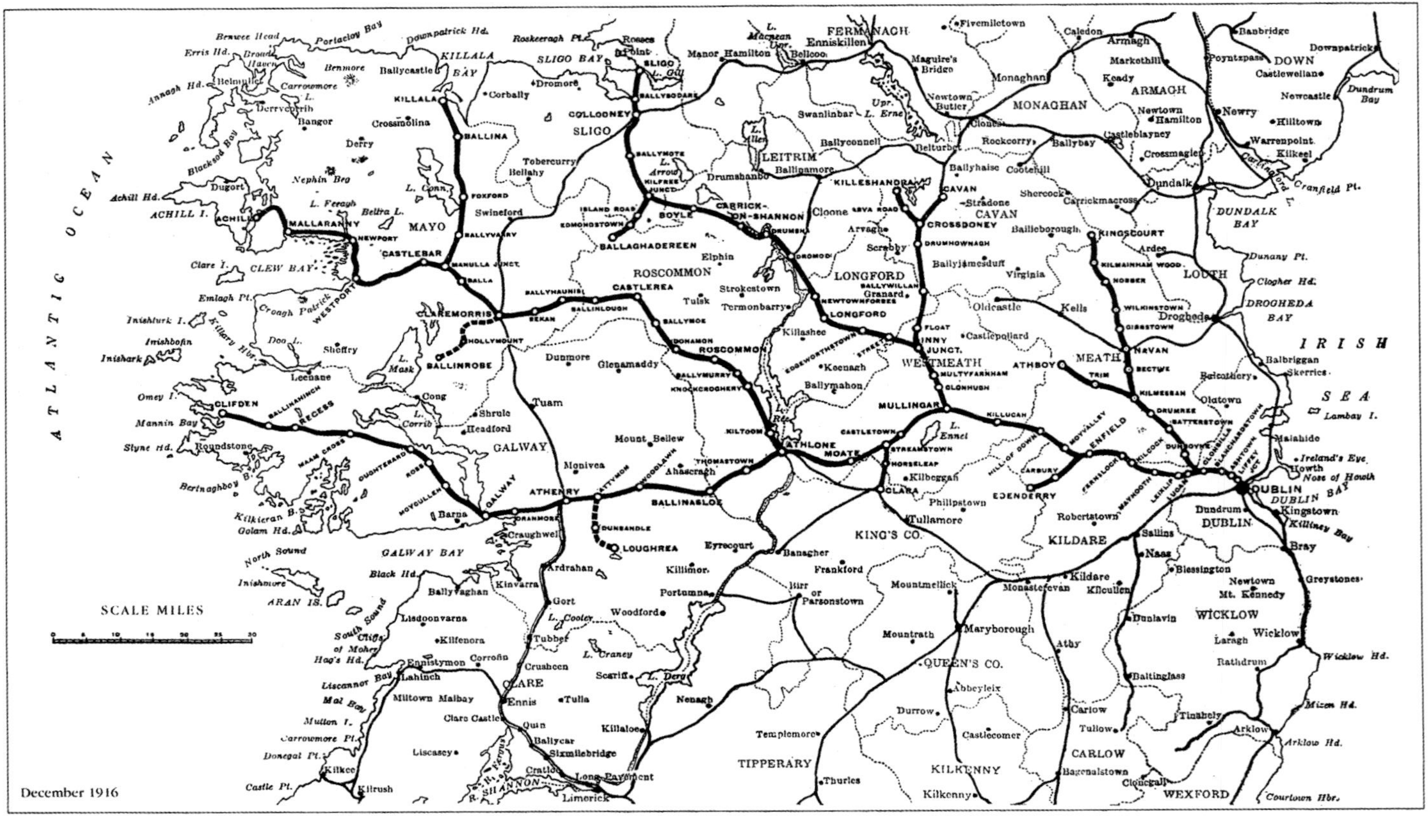

Lines owned by the MGWR — Lines leased to the MGWR — Lines over which the MGWR had running powers — Other railways — County boundaries

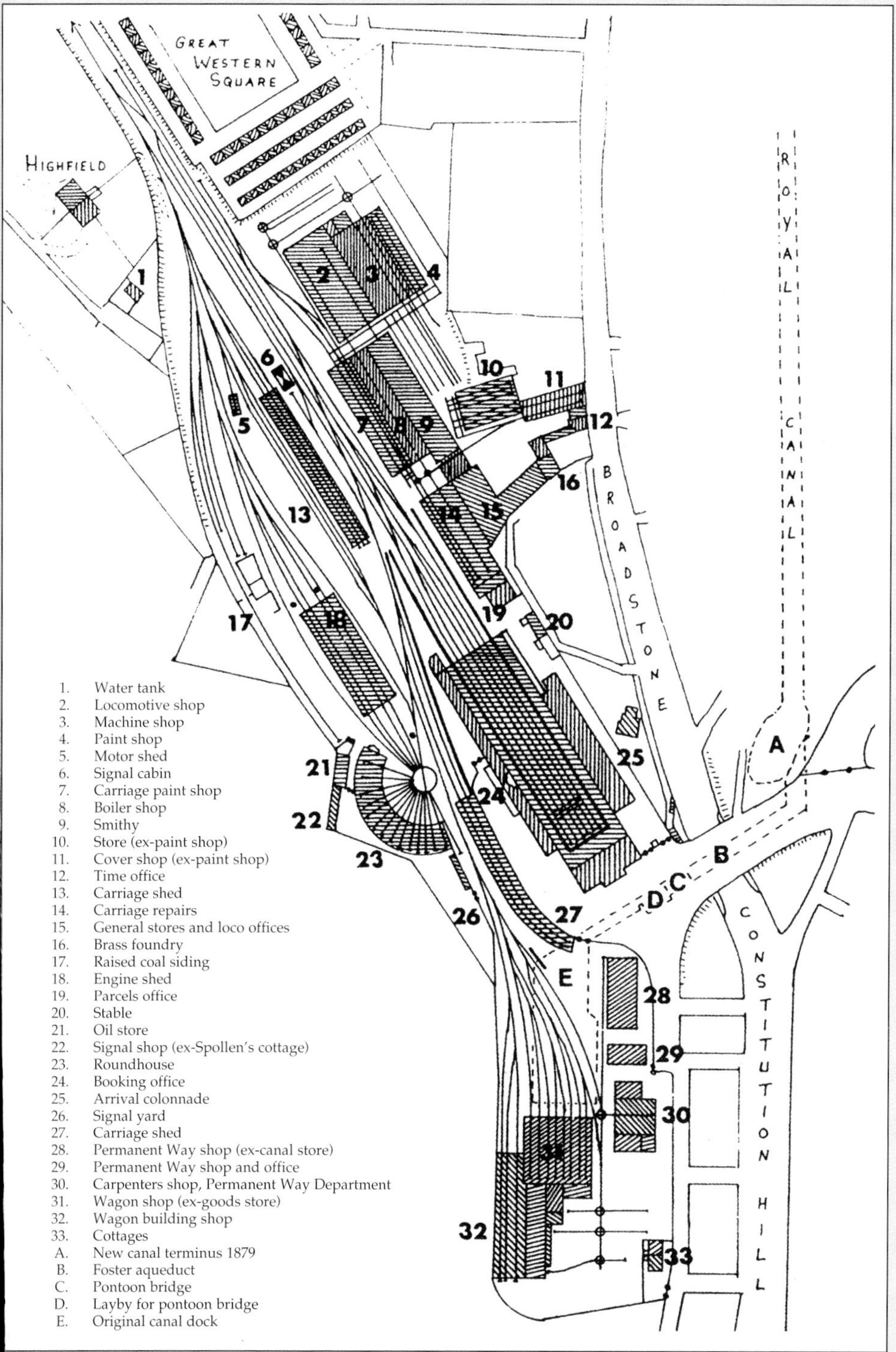
GREAT WESTERN SQUARE
HIGHFIELD
ROYAL CANAL
BROADSTONE
CONSTITUTION HILL
1. Water tank
2. Locomotive shop
3. Machine shop
4. Paint shop
5. Motor shed
6. Signal cabin
7. Carriage paint shop
8. Boiler shop
9. Smithy
10. Store (ex-paint shop)
11. Cover shop (ex-paint shop)
12. Time office
13. Carriage shed
14. Carriage repairs
15. General stores and loco offices
16. Brass foundry
17. Raised coal siding
18. Engine shed
19. Parcels office
20. Stable
21. Oil store
22. Signal shop (ex-Spollen's cottage)
23. Roundhouse
24. Booking office
25. Arrival colonnade
26. Signal yard
27. Carriage shed
28. Permanent Way shop (ex-canal store)
29. Permanent Way shop and office
30. Carpenters shop, Permanent Way Department
31. Wagon shop (ex-goods store)
32. Wagon building shop
33. Cottages
A. New canal terminus 1879
B. Foster aqueduct
C. Pontoon bridge
D. Layby for pontoon bridge
E. Original canal dock

Broadstone in 1920. *Herbert Richards*

It was reported that despite the inclement weather many spectators turned out to greet the Prince as he travelled by horse-drawn carriage from Dublin Castle to Broadstone; many of them 'cheered or uncovered [removed their hats!] as the Prince drove past'. He was met at Broadstone by a number of the Directors, including Sir Ralph Cusack, who had only a month previously announced that he was stepping down as Chairman, at the age of 84. Also in attendance were a number of the company's officers. William Purcell O'Neill, the Chief Engineer, Joseph Tatlow, the Manager and Edward Cusack, locomotive engineer, travelled on the train so as to ensure there were no hitches in the arrangements. In addition, Thomas Atock travelled on the footplate through to Ballinrobe. We are also told that the Inspector-General of Constabulary, Col Sir Neville F.F. Chamberlain, joined the party 'with the object of personally directing such dispositions of the police force as may be deemed necessary'.

A week later the party returned to Dublin, the first class saloon being replaced in the formation by another passenger brake van. The empty train had been worked down from Broadstone the previous day and stabled overnight in Ballinrobe. The following day the pilot engine left Ballinrobe at 11.45 am, being followed half an hour later by the Royal Train, once again with Thomas on the footplate. The operating notice for the return trip makes no mention of a change of locomotives at Athlone so we must assume that the one locomotive worked through to Dublin. The press reported that the approach to the station and the exterior of the building at Ballinrobe were handsomely decorated with flags and evergreens. The Royal party was met there by a guard of honour of 40 men of the Royal Irish Constabulary under the command of District Inspector Lowndes.

TIME TABLE
FOR
SPECIAL TRAIN
WITH
His Royal Highness
THE
Prince of Wales
FROM
BALLINROBE
TO
DUBLIN (Broadstone)
On Tuesday, 31st January, 1905.

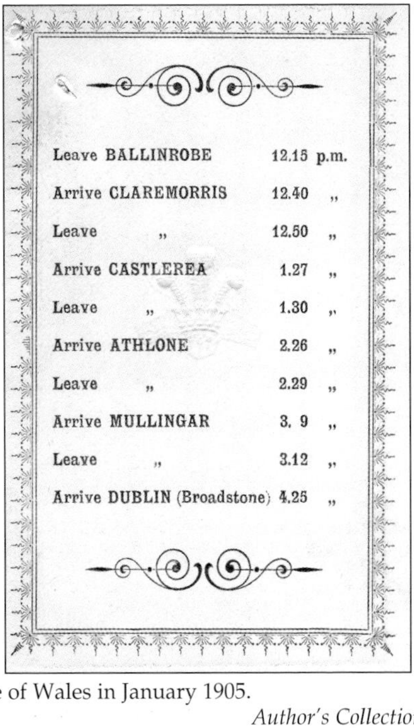

Leave	BALLINROBE	12.15	p.m.
Arrive	CLAREMORRIS	12.40	"
Leave	"	12.50	"
Arrive	CASTLEREA	1.27	"
Leave	"	1.30	"
Arrive	ATHLONE	2.26	"
Leave	"	2.29	"
Arrive	MULLINGAR	3. 9	"
Leave	"	3.12	"
Arrive	DUBLIN (Broadstone)	4.25	"

Extract of timetable for the visit of the Prince of Wales in January 1905.
Author's Collection

Family group on holiday in Norway in 1925. *Left to right*: Bessie Atock, Marion Atock, Tom Atock, Kathleen Baird, Charles McDonogh (senior), Ronald Atock, Bessie Smith, Arthur Atock. *In front*, Doris and Esme Atock. *Alex Atock Collection*

On 1st October, 1906 Thomas and Basil Hope swapped positions, i.e. Thomas took charge of Broadstone works, while Hope replaced him in the Locomotive Running Department. This change was formalised on 7th January, 1907 when Thomas was appointed works manager at a salary of £375 pa. However, Thomas' supervision of the works was not as effective as it ought to have been owing to illness, and on 11th June, 1907 the Traffic & Works Committee recommended that Francis H. Litton be employed for three months to assist him in his duties. F.H. Litton had been locomotive superintendent on the Tralee & Dingle Railway from February 1902 to July 1903 before taking a post in China. Basil Hope obviously felt that he had been pushed aside and handed in his notice on 1st July, 1907. Dr Coleman and Dr Redmond submitted a certificate on 29th December, 1910 advising the MGWR that Thomas was suffering from a nervous breakdown. They suggested that he should have a month's leave of absence, which was presumably granted. However, following a protracted period of ill health, Thomas resigned his position with the MGWR at the end of 1911.

Although Thomas enjoyed more than 40 years of retirement, his wife Bessie passed away suddenly on Wednesday 3rd April, 1929, at the age of 62. She had helped to decorate Zion Church for Easter and had attended Holy Communion on Easter Sunday, only three days prior to her death. Almost exactly a year later, on 5th April, 1930, Thomas married Margaret Ethel (Pearl) Maconkey, the only daughter of the late Henry and Mrs Maconkey of Drumbraine, Ashfield Park, Terenure in Dublin. Pearl had been a long-time friend of the Atock family. She was a keen musician and was for many years Secretary of the Feis Cheoil.* Tom took his new wife, 30 years his junior, on a cruise from Southampton on the Blue

* In this capacity she may well have met the author's father who was awarded various Feis Cheoil medals for singing during the late 1920s and early 1930s. The Feis Cheoil is a national music festival founded in 1897.

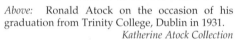

Above: Ronald Atock on the occasion of his graduation from Trinity College, Dublin in 1931. *Katherine Atock Collection*

Above right: Ronald and Marjorie Atock at his father's house in Dublin. Kathleen Marjorie was the only daughter of Mr and Mrs William Lister of Kippax. *Katherine Atock Collection*

Right: Tom Atock relaxing with his pipe in his garden in July 1950. Tom took early retirement from the MGWR almost 40 years previously on the grounds of poor health. *Alex Atock Collection*

Star Line *Arandora Star* in the following June, taking a second cruise on the same vessel in September 1931. Despite his earlier health problems, Thomas lived on in retirement until his death at his residence, De Grey, No. 11 Bushey Park Road, Rathgar, on 24th December, 1952; he was buried in Mount Jerome Cemetery.

Regarding Thomas' children, Martin Leslie's career is dealt with in Chapter Eight. Violet Doris (known by the family as Doris) joined the Women's Royal Air Force during World War I and became a motor driver based at Shawbury Aerodrome, some eight miles north-east of Shrewsbury. Whilst serving there, Doris met with a nasty accident, sustaining injuries to her wrist and a broken collarbone. The Medical Officer at Shawbury apparently administered nothing more than first-aid treatment, sending Doris home to Shrewsbury to rest up. Not having received any further instructions from the Medical Officer and being in considerable pain, Doris consulted a local general practitioner. Thomas, hearing of his daughter's plight, travelled to Shrewsbury and sought permission from the RAF to take her back to Dublin. This they agreed to, but refused to pay either the doctor's fee of £3 13*s.* 0*d.* or subsequent medical expenses incurred in Dublin amounting to £11 5*s.* 0*d.*; this led to an article appearing in the periodical *John Bull* dated 6th December, 1919 questioning the grounds on which the RAF authorities repudiated all responsibility for injuries received in the service of the Crown. In the event, Doris subsequently made a full recovery.

Thomas' youngest son, Robert (Ronald) Charles was educated at St Andrew's School in Dublin, where he was a keen tennis player and one of the first King's Scouts. He entered Trinity College Dublin, aged 17, to read both Engineering and General Arts, graduating with a BEI and MA in April 1931. This being the time of the Depression it was difficult to find work and he went first to Scotland to the Lochaber Project* but found the working conditions appalling (for example a colleague was blown off the Laggan Dam to his death while surveying) and left after three months. (His daughter, Katherine, believes that it was this experience which inspired him to eventually join the Factory Inspectorate.) He applied to join the Royal Engineers but he was regarded as being too old at the age of 24 so he travelled to England and taught science at Seaford College, a boy's school near Brighton, for two years. The headmaster's reference described him as a good teacher and a successful master.

October 1935 saw him back in Ireland with the GSR as an assistant under agreement with G.J. Murphy, Chief Engineer of the GSR, based at Westland Row, Dublin, but within a year he had decided against a railway career and in June 1936 he resigned. In the preceding month he had applied for a position with the Home Office in London. He was successful in his application and was appointed to the North London District of the Chief Inspector of Factories based at No. 324 Gray's Inn Road, London with effect from 14th July, 1936. On the outbreak of World War II, Ronald was posted to Leeds, where he met Marjorie Lister, who was a secretary in the same office. The couple were married on 24th May, 1941 at St Mary's church, Kippax in Yorkshire and honeymooned in the Lake District.

* The Lochaber Project, finally completed in 1943, comprised a network of dams and tunnels across the area and included the creation of Loch Laggan by the building of the 900 ft Laggan Dam. The project culminated with the construction of a 45 ft diameter tunnel for 15 miles through the Ben Nevis range to emerge 600 ft above Fort William. Water flowing down the hillside pipes was used to generate electricity for Fort William's aluminium industry.

Above: Ronald Atock in New Delhi in November 1947 in connection with a training course for factory inspectors. Ronald is seated, *third from right*.
Katherine Atock Collection

Right: Ronald Atock standing in front of the Taj Mahal during the period when he was resident in India.
Katherine Atock Collection

Chapter Eight

Far East and Latin American Exploits

George Atock, Martin Atock's youngest son, was born in Limerick on 22nd May, 1872. His secondary education was divided between Arnold College Blackpool and the High School Dublin. He attended the latter from October 1888 until June 1889; how well he studied in Blackpool is not known but his year at the High School appears to have been, if anything, below average, as shown by a report in April 1889 from his Form Teacher, Mr H.G. Morris, who remarked that George was 'very slow' (perhaps he was having too good a time in Blackpool and resented being brought back to Dublin). George was at Arnold College at the same time as George Henry Attock, and one family tradition has it that he was sent to school at Blackpool with his first cousin 'to heal the (family) rift'. It is not clear what this was about and at that stage it is unlikely to have had anything to do with the change of the spelling of the name a generation earlier.

George served a five-year pupilage under his father on the MGWR at Broadstone, where he passed through the fitting, pattern and erecting shops as well as the drawing office, and during this period he also undertook scientific studies at the Royal College of Science in Dublin. For a brief period in 1894 he was employed as a draughtsman at Messrs Kitson & Co., Leeds, but he was soon back in Ireland and, in November 1895, he was appointed foreman of the Tuam locomotive running district on the WL&WR under J.G. Robinson, a position he retained for five years. Following the absorption of the WL&WR by the GS&WR at the beginning of 1901 George went to work overseas, initially taking a four-year contract as assistant to C.E. Cardew, locomotive superintendent of the Burma Railways Company Ltd.

Cornelius Edward Cardew was born on 18th July, 1851. He commenced a four-year apprenticeship at the Glasgow Locomotive Works of Messrs Dübs & Co. in February 1869 and on completion he stayed with Dübs for a further six months as a draughtsman. He then moved to the Locomotive, Carriage & Wagon Department of the LB&SCR where he remained for just over 2½ years before his next move to India in May 1876. He was elected a member of the Institution of Mechanical Engineers in 1879.

The first part of the metre gauge railway system in Burma was the Irrawaddy State Railway, a 161 mile line between Rangoon and Prome that ran through the Irrawaddy valley. Work on its construction commenced in 1874 and it was opened for traffic on 1st May, 1877. The first locomotive obtained by the company, a second-hand 2-4-0 side tank, was built by Messrs Dübs & Co. of Glasgow in 1871 and delivered to Burma in 1876. Other locomotives included two 0-4-2s, Nos. 5 & 6, supplied by the Vulcan Foundry in 1878. In 1881 the Sittang Valley Railway was established to construct a metre gauge line over the 166 miles between Rangoon and Toungoo, which was completed in four stages during 1884-85. Charles Bernard, the Chief Commissioner of Burma (1880-88), believed that there had to be a railway line to Mandalay following the

Burma Railways 0-6-6-0T Fairlie locomotive. George Atock's sojourn in Burma would have predated this locomotive by only a few years as it was delivered by the Vulcan Foundry in 1906. It was followed by a series of North British-built Mallet tender locomotives, the first Beyer-Garratts not being delivered to Burma until 1924.

Photographer unknown, courtesy G. Beesley Collection

Gokteik viaduct on the Mandalay to Kunlon line in Burma. The viaduct, construction of which was commenced in 1899 and still in use today, is 2,260 ft in length and consists of 17 spans. At its highest pier the rails are 325 ft above the ground, but over the gorge itself they are 825 ft above the stream.

Provenance unknown, courtesy G. Beesley Collection

annexation of Upper Burma in 1885. The line between Toungoo and Mandalay was sanctioned in October 1886 and opened throughout in 1889, providing a 385 mile railway link between Rangoon and Mandalay. These three railways were all constructed by the government of India and leased to the Burma Railways Company Ltd (BRC) in 1896.

The father of the Mandalay-Kunlon railway scheme was F.R. Bagley, Chief Engineer of the BRC. The most formidable obstacle on this direct route connecting Mandalay with the Chinese frontier was the Gokteik gorge. At first it was proposed to use a rack railway for the approaches to the Gokteik viaduct, and Bagley prepared plans for the line in 1892-93 using an Abt type rack inclined at 1 in 12½. This would have permitted a comparatively short viaduct at the natural bridge of the gorge. Later on it was decided to abandon the rack idea and to ease the gradients to 1 in 25 for a normal adhesion track, and a new survey was made on this basis by A.R. Lilley in 1895-96. Further investigation revealed that it would be possible for the approach gradients to be eased to the maximum of 1 in 40 in standard use in Burma, and Bagley made a new survey in May 1898. Mr G. Deuchars, who succeeded Bagley as Chief Engineer in September 1898, carried out further survey work so as to realign the whole of the approaches and curve the ends of the viaduct, thereby reducing the cost of tunnelling and earthworks.

Construction of the line commenced in August 1899. By making use of a temporary three-mile zig-zag line down the side of the gorge it was possible to deliver all kinds of materials to the foot of the viaduct, which greatly simplified the work of erection. It also allowed rails and sleepers to be taken across the gorge on a wire rope way, a procedure that enabled track to be laid to a point 35 miles ahead of the gorge by the time the viaduct was completed. Two locomotives were even transported across in pieces by means of that rope way!

Sir Alexander Rendel & Company, Consulting Engineers to the BRC, undertook the design of the bridgework. The Pennsylvania Steel Company, of Steelton, Pennsylvania, USA won the contract for the viaduct in April 1899. By October the first consignment of materials had arrived at Rangoon and the actual work of erecting the viaduct commenced in December 1899. The 2,260 ft viaduct, which is still in use to this day, was constructed from 4,308 tons of riveted steel and consists of seven spans of 60 ft plate girders and 10 spans of 120 ft triangulated girders. The bridge girders rest on steel towers which are each made up of two trestles 24 ft 6 in. wide at the top, splayed out with a batter of 2½ in. per foot. The two trestles of the tower are spaced 40 ft apart, and are connected at the top by 40 ft plate girders, and the whole structure is securely braced in all directions. At the highest pier the rails are 325 ft above the ground, but over the gorge they are at a height of 825 ft above the Chungzoune stream.

The southern approach to the viaduct begins at a point 2,691 ft above sea level and descends 556 ft on an almost continuous gradient of 1 in 40. After crossing the viaduct the line skirts steep hillsides, passing through two tunnels and some heavy cuttings, and then proceeds to ascend by means of three semi-circular loops. Although the end of the northern approach is at Pinkaw, four miles from the viaduct, the line continues to ascend on steep gradients for a further nine miles, reaching a level of 3,256 ft above sea level between Maymyo and the Salween river, the highest point on the line.

At the opening of the line from Amarapura (the junction point some seven miles south of Mandalay on the main line to Toungoo) as far as Hsipaw in December 1900, Sir Frederick Fryer, KCSI, Lieutenant Governor of Burma, stated in his speech that 'No one who has seen the Gokteik Gorge and the fine structure which now spans it can fail to be impressed with the magnitude of the task which confronted the engineers when it was decided to take the railway across it'. At that stage the river Myitnge, between Hsipaw and Lashio, had also just been bridged and one of the spans, at 200 ft, was the longest in Burma at that time. Progress with the construction of the line was so good that it was anticipated it would be opened through to Lashio by early 1902, but it was to be the following year before the 171 mile line was complete. For working the line Vulcan Foundry supplied five 0-6-6-0 double-Fairlie locomotives in 1900 (Works Nos. 1773-1777).

The isolated Mu Valley railway from Sagaing (12 miles west of Mandalay on the opposite side of the Irrawaddy River) north to Myitkyina, 725 miles from Rangoon, had been completed in 1899. There was a short branch from Mandalay to the river, where a train ferry made the connection with that line and the Sagaing-Mnywa-Alon branch, which was opened in 1900. A branch off the main line at Thazi, which served Meiktila and Myingyan, was also opened to traffic during 1900. In 1902 a railway from Henzada to Bassein was formed and in 1903 a short branch was laid to a point on the west bank of the Irawaddy River opposite Letpadan. From there a connection was made by ferry to the Rangoon-Prome line, on which the BRC workshops were situated just outside Rangoon at Inseine. There was also a 66 mile branch from Henzada to Kyangin, and another ferry connected the 121 mile Pegu-Martaban line with Moulmein. By the time George Atock left the company in 1904-05 BRC had a total of 1,342 miles of lines open for traffic. He was succeeded as assistant locomotive superintendent by Thomas E. Heywood who had arrived at Inseine in 1902 and was later to become the last locomotive superintendent of the Great North of Scotland Railway (1914-22).

The railways were an important contributor to the success of the rice and timber trade. Rice was in great demand in those days and the teak timber was a much sought after hardwood. The railways reverted to the government in 1929 and, with the separation of Burma from India in 1937, they operated under the Burma Railways Board. After Burma gained independence in 1948 the railways were nationalised as the Union of Burma Railways. In 1972 the name was changed once again, to Burma Railways Corporation, and then to Myanmar Railways on 1st April, 1989.

Working for a railway with such amazing engineering features must have proved very interesting for George, but when his term as assistant locomotive superintendent with BRC came to an end, in early 1905, he returned home to Ireland. We next find him in Liverpool, on 23rd September in that same year, boarding the Cunard liner SS *Lucania* bound for New York, where he arrived on 30th September. The 12,952 ton *Lucania* had been completed by the Fairfield Govan yard in Glasgow early in 1893 and, for the first four years of her existence, she was the largest and fastest liner afloat. She was laid up in 1909 but caught fire in Liverpool docks in August of that year and was scrapped in 1910.

It is of comfort to note that the ship's manifest records that George had never been in prison, nor was he a polygamist or an anarchist! Even in those far off days the immigration authorities in the USA had strict criteria, which also applied to those in transit. The manifest also informs us that George's passage had been paid for by the United Railways of the Havana & Regla Warehouses Ltd. George was on the first stage of his passage to Cuba to take up an appointment as chief assistant to C.J. Thornton, locomotive superintendent of the United Railways of the Havana & Regla Warehouses Ltd (URH).

Charles James Thornton, born Cherraponjee, India on 2nd November, 1865, was educated at the United Services College, Westward Ho! from 1875 to 1880, and then privately until 1882 under the Revd E. Walker in Brighton, following which he attended King's College, London for three years. He then completed an apprenticeship with Sharp, Stewart & Co. in Manchester between 1885 and 1888. In January 1889 he was appointed inspector and shed foreman on the Argentine Great Western Railway, followed in February 1892 as locomotive superintendent of the Transandine Railway in Argentina. From there, he went in March 1899 to the Leopoldina Railway in Brazil as chief assistant locomotive superintendent, becoming assistant mechanical engineer of the Rio Tinto Co. from May to December 1900. He was appointed locomotive superintendent of the URH in January 1901 and was elected a member of the Institution of Mechanical Engineers in 1908.

The roots of the British-owned United Railways of the Havana & Regla Warehouses Company were set in the first railway built in Cuba - the Havana & Guines Railway. King Ferdinand II of Spain authorized the construction of this line in October 1834, the Cuban Government raising the necessary capital on the British financial markets. The main purpose of the railway was to provide a better and more economical means of transportation for the sugar industry from the inland plantations. The 27 km section from Villanueva station, Havana, to Bejucal

A busy scene at the URH engine shed in Havana around the turn of the century.
Railway Magazine

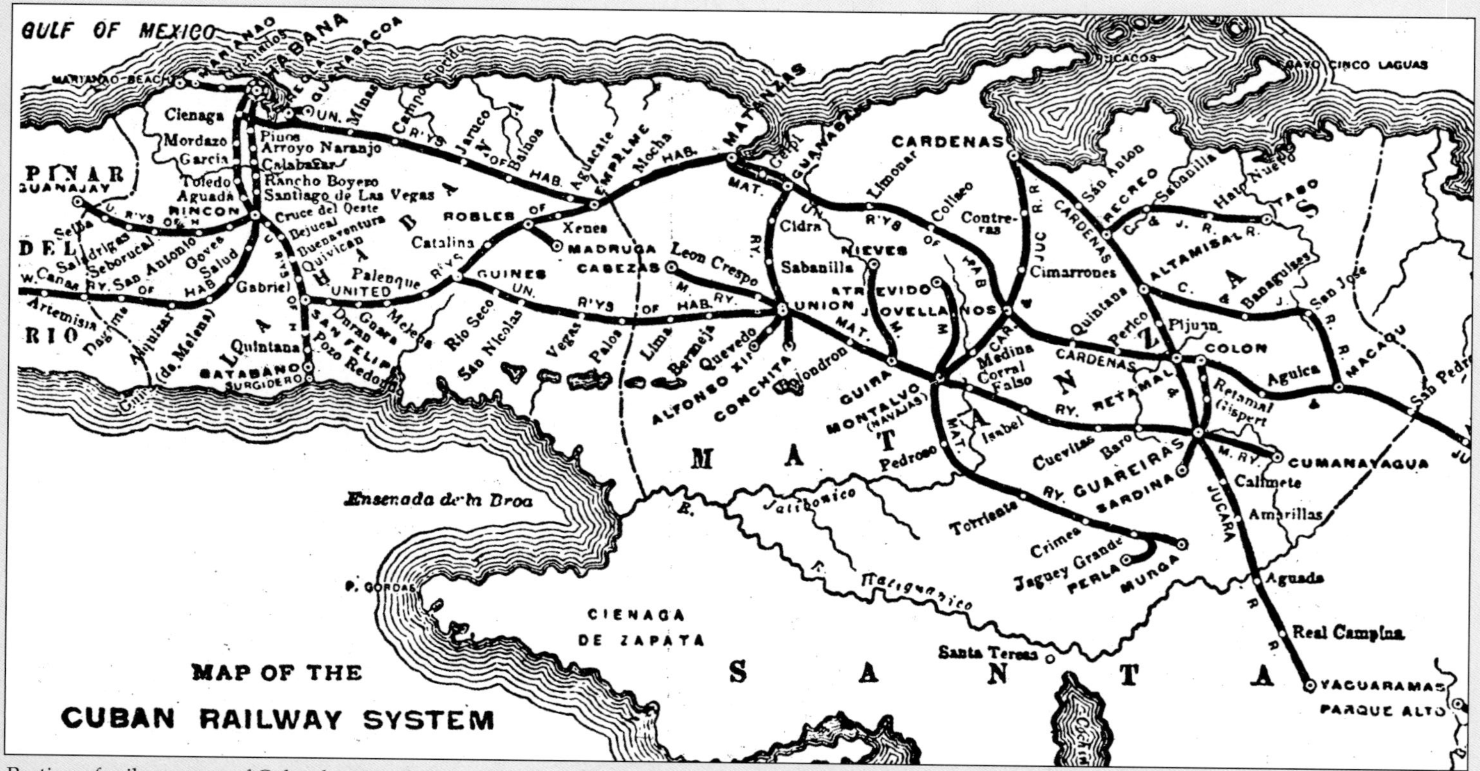

Portion of railway map of Cuba showing the line of the United Railways of the Havana & Regla Warehouses Company.

Railway Magazine

was opened on 19th November, 1837 and the 41 km extension to Guines was brought into use exactly one year later. With the opening of this line Cuba became just the seventh country in the world, after Britain, to have a steam-powered railway. This extraordinary feat was even 11 years ahead of the opening of the first public railway in its mother country of Spain.

Four Bury-type 2-2-0 locomotives were supplied for the opening of the line and were almost certainly built by Messrs Braithwaite at their New Road works in London. They were similar to those in use on the London & Birmingham Railway but Cruger, the American engineer in charge of the line, disliked them and had them shipped back to England where they arrived at the London docks on 12th October, 1839. However, Braithwaite's was in receivership by that time and the subsequent history of these locomotives is unknown. John Braithwaite, the owner of this short-lived locomotive manufacturing company was, as we have noted in Chapter Two, the first locomotive superintendent of the Eastern Counties Railway.

In 1842 the Government disposed of the line by public auction to the Havana Railway Company. The sale was conditional upon the new owners constructing several branch lines, and the network of the Havana Railway Company grew by the following stages:

Section	*Length*	*Opened*
San Felipe-Batabano	15 km	December 1843
Rincón-San Antonio de los Banos	10 km	December 1844
Guines-La Union	49 km	November 1848
San Antonio de los Banos-Guanajay	21 km	August 1849
Guines-Mantanzas (San Luis)	54 km	October 1861

In addition to the aforementioned main routes, there were a number of short branch lines which contributed to the company's total route length of about 260 km.

An URH 2-6-0 locomotive with train at Matanzas station around the turn of the century.
Railway Magazine

The port of Regla was located on the eastern side of the Bay of Havana, opposite the city. From 1843 onwards the Regla Warehouses Company had constructed a large complex of sugar stores which was served by its own internal railway network from an early date. In an effort to consolidate its grip on the sugar export trade, the Bank of Commerce, which had been established in 1852, together with the Regla Warehouses Company, acquired the Bay of Havana & Matanzas Railway, later simply known as the Bay of Havana Railway, by an agreement dated 20th June, 1883. This line had its origins in a concession that was granted in 1857 for the construction and operation of a 92 km line from Regla eastwards towards Matanzas, together with a 5 km branch line from Regla to Guanabacoa. The branch line from Fesser station, Regla, was the first section to open, in 1858. In 1863 the Bay of Havana & Matanzas Railway united with the Coliseo Railway under one management, resulting in a combined system of about 150 km.

In 1889 the Havana Railway Company amalgamated with the Bank of Commerce consortium, then trading under the name of the Bank of Commerce, United Railways of the Havana and Regla Warehouses Company. On 8th February 1898 a new and separate entity, the United Railways of the Havana & Regla Warehouses Ltd, was registered to acquire from the Bank of Commerce and United Railways of the Havana & Regla Warehouses Company the whole of its undertaking of railways, warehouses, etc., exclusive of the banking business.

On 1st January, 1906 the URH acquired the Cárdenas & Júcaro Joint Railways. This entity had been formed in August 1853 by the amalgamation of the Cárdenas & Bemba Railway and the Júcaro Railway. The Cárdenas & Bemba dated from a concession, granted in 1837, for a railway between the two towns named. The first section, from Cárdenas to Contreras, was opened on 25th May, 1840, and the line through to Bemba (now Jovellanos) was completed in December of the same year. The Júcaro Railway was the result of a concession for a line between Júcaro, just east of Cárdenas, to Pijuan (now Itabo). The first section from Júcaro to Recrero (now Maximo Gomez) was opened in September 1842 and Pijuan was reached in 1843. In August 1854 the two separate systems were connected by a short link east of Cárdenas, and the joint company made subsequent extensions to the network, which eventually totalled 338 km.

The URH also operated the 35 km Marianao Railway, which it leased in February 1905. The first section, which ran from Concha station, Havana, was opened in July 1863 and a branch to Marianao Beach followed in 1884. It was electrified in 1910 using a fleet of vehicles purchased from American Car & Foundry. The URH also took control of the Matanzas & Sabanilla Railway from 1906 onwards. The US stock market crash of 1907 enabled the URH to obtain 51 per cent of the stock of Havana Central Railroad Company (HCR), which had been incorporated in New Jersey on 4th April, 1905. The HCR had built electrified lines on direct routes from Havana to Guanajay and Guines, which had opened respectively on 12th November, 1906 and 16th March, 1907. It also built a number of connecting lines around Regla and Guanabacoa as well as acquiring the Regla-Guanabacoa line of the Cuban Electric Railway. The latter had originally opened in 1843, and animals had been used at first for haulage until steam power was introduced in 1884.

The purchase of the controlling interest in the HCR gave the URH control of all the rail lines in the Havana area except the Havana Electric Railway tramway system. The Havana Central lines were operated as a separate division and, probably at the behest of the other shareholders, the original company name was maintained on its vehicles. The transport of sugar cane, tobacco and pineapple from Cuba's rich farm lands to the docks on Havana Bay constituted a large part of the HCR's business and for the heavy freight working it operated ten 40 ton steeple-cab Bo-Bo electric locomotives built for it by General Electric in 1916.

After George Atock had left for Venezuela, the company continued to expand its network. From 1911 it took over the operation of the 14 km Matanzas Terminal Railroad, and in 1912 it obtained control of the Western Railways of Havana, which were amalgamated with the URH in 1921. In June 1914 the 20 km line to Rincón was electrified - this was not the 1837 Havana-Guines route, which was never electrified, but a parallel line built by the Western Railways a few kilometres east. A proposal to acquire the Cuban Central Railways was approved by the shareholders of both companies in December 1913, but it was not fully merged with the URH until July 1920. The Cuban Government, at the request of the British owners, purchased the URH and on 24th July, 1953 the nationalised railways became the Western Railways of Cuba, at which time the total route length of the organization stood at 2,223 km.

Having completed his time in Cuba, George Atock returned to Ireland in the summer of 1909. The first stage of his passage, from Havana to New York, was aboard the American-built, 6,391 ton, SS *Saratoga*, owned by the Unifruitco Steam Ship Co., which arrived in New York on 6th July, 1909. From New York he travelled on the *Cedric*, arriving in Queenstown on 18th July. While home in Ireland he attended the funeral of Robert Smith, his brother Thomas' father-in-law. When, in early 1910, George once again set sail for Latin America he was not heading for Cuba, but to Venezuela where he had been appointed to the position of locomotive superintendent on the La Guaira & Caracas Railway.

The earliest schemes for a railway in Venezuela, linking the port of La Guaira to the city of Caracas, originated with Robert Stephenson's visit to the country in 1824. It was while doing some Parliamentary work in London for the Stockton & Darlington Railway in early 1824 that Stephenson entered into a three-year contract to work in South America. His interest had been stirred by a scheme for a road in Colombia in connection with four silver mines at Mariquita, with which the Colombian Mining Association of London was involved. This concern was headed by a Mr Powles from the company of Grahan, Powles & Herrring of London, who were also interested in a railway line between La Guaira and Caracas. Robert Stephenson set sail from Liverpool on 18th June, 1824 on board the *Sir William Congreve* and disembarked at the port of La Guaira on 23rd July. His first job was to look into the building of the railway to Caracas, but he finally reported that it would cost £160,000 and would never pay its way. He noted that the annual load of 8,000 tons could be transported by the railway, using about 25 horses for pulling purposes.

In 1854, the Venezuelan government decreed that the railway between La Guaira and Caracas should be constructed, and in April 1856 Congress authorized the Executive to enter into a contract for the line, but nothing came of this. In 1867 the government granted a concession to 'The Railroad Company of the Guayra' who were selected to construct and operate the line. The government guaranteed a return of 9 per cent and also granted the company the right to establish a telegraph line along the route, but this scheme also failed.

As a result of an initiative of the government of Gen. Antonio White Guzmán, which proposed that the line should be constructed with State aid, definitive studies were undertaken in 1872. The English engineer Robert Francis Fairlie was contracted as a consultant with F.A.B. Geneste of the firm Alexander, Garland & Pagan acting as resident engineer. Geneste arrived on site in December 1872 to make the necessary surveys, but before his arrival a team of five Venezuelan engineers and one Cuban engineer had begun the work and completed about 75 per cent of the 23 mile route.

On 15th September, 1874 the Venezuelan Ambassador in Spain signed an agreement with George O. Budd and William Lyster Holt, public works contractors, to complete the works, construct the stations and water supplies, and provide the rails, wagons and locomotives. The government agreed to pay £405,752, the balance of the cost of the project being funded by investors, through H.L. Boulton & Co., at the rate of £12,000 per month. This contract was not executed, as the Government was unable to raise its share of finance for the project, which was equivalent to 28 per cent of the national budget.

A new contract was negotiated in Paris, on 27th March, 1876, with Jose M. Antomarchi and ratified by Congress on 5th May. However, the contract was declared null and void on 26th June, 1877 by Gen. Francisco Linares Alcántara, who had seized power from Gen. Guzmán. Following the death of Gen. Alcántara and the revolution of February 1879, Gen. Guzmán returned to power and, on 11th March, 1879, a contract was agreed with Charles J. Badman, which was immediately ratified by Congress. However, Badman was unsuccessful in raising finance and a new contract was agreed, on 22nd October, 1880, with General W.A. Pile, and ratified on 7th April, 1881.

William Anderson Pile was a North American citizen, who had been US Minister to Venezuela (1871-74); he travelled to the United States and Europe in an effort to raise the necessary capital and form a company to undertake the contract. Meanwhile, works continued on the line, facilitated by the balance of State aid that had originally been provided. Pile failed to gain support in the United States, but he was successful in England where the La Guaira & Caracas Railway Company Ltd (LG&CR) was formed. In an agreement dated 10th March, 1882, Pile yielded his rights to the newly-formed company which entered into a concession agreement with the government for the construction and operation of the line. Soon after commencing the works the LG&CR indicated that it could not be completed on time due to the costs being greater than anticipated. To solve the problem, Gen. Guzmán proposed an extraordinary budget provision of an additional £50,000, half of which was to be paid back by the company from returns in excess of the 7 per cent guaranteed to the shareholders.

Although only eight miles from La Guaira, the climb from sea level to Caracas at 2,950 ft required a zig-zag route to produce acceptable grades - back in 1824 Stephenson had even considered cable haulage with machinery located at Caracas. Despite the zig-zag route, the grades on the line varied between 1 in 110 and 1 in 26½. Starting from 10 ft above sea level at La Guaira, the 3 ft gauge line to Caracas first crossed the Maiquetia river by a bridge of 49 ft span. On its route the line passed the small village of Pariata on an embankment and wood viaduct. Its climb continued along mountain ledges and it crossed the Blue Piedra River twice, first by a bridge of 65 ft span and then by one of 29 ft 6 in. span.

In March 1883 the company estimated that the line would be completed by 20th June, but it was 27th June before a preliminary run was made to Caracas behind locomotive No. 2, which departed from La Guaira station at 12.25 pm. The train was made up of three goods wagons and a passenger coach in which Gen. Pile travelled together with three engineers who had been responsible for the work: Muñoz Tébar, John Houston, and Jiménez Y Durand. At a reception held at Caño Amarillo station, Caracas, John Houston was congratulated for the manner in which he had overcome the technical complexities between Mañonga and Peña de Mora and the construction of the Pariata viaduct. Public services commenced on 29th June, 1883 and on 25th July, as part of the centennial celebrations for the birth of the South American liberator Simón Bolívar, the official opening was conducted by President Antonio White Guzmán who, with family and guests, departed Caracas station at 8.10 am in a special train.

The LG&CR never grew beyond its original 23 miles and by 1919 its rolling stock comprised of 15 locomotives, 28 carriages and 117 goods wagons. From 1910 until the end of 1919 the locomotive superintendent was George Atock who, as we have already recorded, had previously held the post of assistant chief locomotive superintendent for the United Railways of the Havana & Regla Warehouses Ltd. During his time with the LG&CR, George applied for membership of the Institution of Civil Engineers of Ireland. His application was sponsored by W. Purcell O'Neill, Chief Engineer of the MGWR, and he was duly elected a member on 3rd December, 1913. Two months earlier George had been joined in Caracas by his nephew, Martin Leslie Atock, who worked with him as assistant locomotive superintendent until May 1916.

Martin Leslie Atock was born in Dublin on 18th September, 1895 and attended Mountjoy School, Dublin and Chesterfield School in Birr in King's County. At the time the Atocks attended Mountjoy School it was located on Mountjoy Square in the heart of the city; it is now known as Mount Temple Comprehensive School and situated on the Malahide Road in Dublin. King's County is now known as Co. Offaly. He served a three-year mechanical apprenticeship with the MGWR at Broadstone, and attended night classes in mechanical engineering at the City of Dublin Technical Schools. His first appointment was with the La Guaira & Caracas Railway. The Atock family was imbued with a strong Christian tradition and it was not long before Martin Leslie became involved with the Anglican community in Caracas. So it was that the Lord Bishop of Trinidad and Tobago, whose remit included Venezuela, issued a licence, dated 6th December 1914, giving authority for Martin Leslie Atock to act as a 'Reader for our Congregation at Caracas'. In addition to allowing him to read prayers and preach sermons, the authority extended to visiting the sick, and even to burying the dead in the absence of the clergyman.

During their combined sojourn in Venezuela the two men met Dorothy Ross Coates-Cole and, apparently, they both fell in love with her. She was the second daughter of the late Dr J.M. Coates-Cole of Maracaibo, Venezuela, and Mrs Coates-Cole of La Maiterie in Jersey. However, it was the elder man who

No. 44

PASSPORT.

By His Britannic Majesty's
Vice-Consul
at
Caracas

These are to request and require in the Name of His Majesty all those whom it may concern to allow

Martin Leslie Atock

to pass freely without let or hindrance, and to afford him every assistance and protection of which he may stand in need.

Given at Caracas
the fourteenth day of April 1916

T. Ifor Rees
H.B.M. Vice Consul

BRITISH VICE CONSULATE CARACAS
CONSULAR SERVICE

This passport is valid for two years only from the date of its issue. It may be renewed for four further periods of two years each after which a new passport will be required.

RENEWALS.

1.

2.

DESCRIPTION OF BEARER.

Age 20 Profession Engineer

Place & date of birth Dublin; September 18th 189[illegible]

Maiden name if widow or married woman travelling singly —

Height six feet — inches

Forehead High & narrow Eyes Brown

Nose Prominent Mouth Large

Chin Round Colour of Hair Fair

Complexion Fresh Face Oval

Any special peculiarities None

National Status British born subject

PHOTOGRAPH OF BEARER.

BRITISH VICE-CONSULATE CARACAS

SIGNATURE OF BEARER.

Passport issued in April 1916 by the British Consul in Caracas to Martin Leslie Atock shortly before his return to Ireland. *Alex Atock Collection*

Martin Leslie Atock as a Reader in the Church of St Michael and All Angels in Caracas on 19th December, 1915. *Alex Atock Collection*

eventually won her hand, and in due course George and Dorothy were married in St Martin's Church in Jersey on 26th May, 1917. George had taken a trip home to Ireland in 1916, sailing from Caracas on board the Atlantic & Caribbean Steam Navigation Company's 1,713 ton vessel, SS *Zulia*, which was on passage from Curaçao in the Dutch East Indies to New York, where it docked on 11th March, 1916. When George returned to Caracas, Martin Leslie took a break, sailing from Cristobal, Panama, to New York aboard the 7,782 ton SS *Calamares*, another Unifruitco Steam Ship Co. vessel. It appears that he initially intended to return as he gave his uncle's details in Caracas as a point of contact. In the event, Martin Leslie, perhaps still trying to come to terms with the loss of Dorothy to his uncle, did not go back and instead enlisted with the Mechanical Transport Section of the Army Service Corps, based at Grove Park Depot, Holland Park Avenue, London.

The LG&CR was not a bad little line, and up to 1914 it had been carrying an average of 3 million tonnes of freight per annum. Passenger carryings were also good with 92,000 persons travelling in 1914. It is no surprise, therefore, that during George Atock's time it was able to return profits, the Directors announcing an interim dividend of 2½ per cent free of tax for the year 1919 - his last year with the company. However, it eventually became impossible to meet the obligations of the concession agreement of 18th April, 1885, and the government agreed to buy the railway from the British owners, the transaction being completed on 26th November, 1926. The line was electrified at 1,500V DC in 1927, English-Electric supplying five small electric locomotives and four electric coaches to work the service. Despite these efforts the line subsequently went into decline, due to rising costs and road competition and, following a landslide in 1949 that caused considerable damage, it finally succumbed to closure in 1951.

Left: Martin Leslie Atock in the uniform of the Royal Army Service Corps with his mother Bessie. The photograph was taken in 1916, shortly after his return from Venezuela.
Alex Atock Collection

Below: Lieut M.L. Atock, *fourth from right front row,* at Base MT repair depot, Italy, February 1918.
Alex Atock Collection

Below right: Temporary Lieut M.L. Atock, *second from right*, with a group of fellow officers at an unknown location in Italy, 1918.
Alex Atock Collection

It is of interest to note that Livesey, Son & Henderson of No. 14 South Place, London E.C. were engineers to both of the Latin American railways for which George Atock worked. This was a position that they also held with the Central Argentine Railway. The relevance of this fact in the context of this family history lies in the appointment of two of F.W. Attock's L&YR colleagues to that railway: J.P. Crouch who became chief mechanical engineer of the Central Argentine Railway in October 1910, and C.H. Montgomery followed him there as his locomotive works manager at Rosario from the end of April 1912. George Atock apparently returned briefly to Ireland as a Cavan & Leitrim Railway Board minute of 21st July, 1920 refers to a Mr Atock applying for the vacant position of locomotive superintendent following the retirement of Thomas H. Shanks who had been in charge since 1896. George spent his last years in Liverpool where at the age of 72 he was acting as a postal censorship examiner in wartime Britain. He passed away on 12th June, 1944 at his residence, No. 73 Menlove Avenue, in the Wavertree district and was buried at Woolton Cemetry. Following his death Dorothy re-married and went to live in Jersey; she was still using the Atock name when she arrived at Southampton from New York on 5th October, 1949, at which time her address was shown as Jersey, the same address as shown for a previous trip from Beira in July 1932.

In January 1917 Private Martin Leslie Atock was passed out as a lorry driver with the Royal Army Service Corps (RASC), but his engineering qualifications were quickly realised and on 25th January he was re-classified as a fitter. On 9th April he went for training with the Officer Cadet Company, Mechanical Transport Section. He was commissioned as a 2nd Lieutenant in the RASC on 3rd June, 1917 and a week later he was assigned to the 606th Mechanical Transport Company. In preparation for duty overseas he was sent to the Mechanical Transport Depot at Bulford in Wiltshire in November and, on 15th December, 1917, the 1034th Mechanical Transport Company was raised for service in Italy, the Company arriving there on 7th January, 1918. By June, 2nd Lt Atock was

Above: Martin Leslie Atock and his new bride, Margaret Alice (Madge) Strain, outside the Standard Hotel, Harcourt Street, Dublin on 25th August, 1927. *Left to right rear*: Alex Strain, Maurice MacAuley (best man), Martin Leslie, Madge, Doris Atock, Tom Atock. *Front row*: Kathleen Strain, Dorrie Strain, June Strain and Bessie Atock.
Alex Atock Collection

Right: Martin Leslie Atock and his wife Madge on a short break at Ashford Castle, near Cong, Co. Mayo. Tragically, Martin Leslie died very suddenly on 14th September, 1941, only two days after this photograph was taken.
Alex Atock Collection

attached to the 166th Auxiliary (Petrol) Company on the Line of Communication, and on 4th December, 1918 he was promoted to the rank of Lieutenant. A medical certificate dated 7th October, 1919 confirms that he was free from infectious disease and fit to travel to Arquata for demobilisation, which took place on 17th October, 1919. At that time Martin Leslie's home address was given as No. 68 Iona Road, Glasnevin, Dublin. He did not go back to work directly for the railways, but took up employment with C.C. Wakefield & Company (Ireland) Ltd. for whom he acted as agent in Ireland for the Wakefield lubricator.*

On 25th August, 1927 Martin Leslie married Margaret Alice (Madge) Strain, the third daughter of Mr & Mrs Alexander Strain of Cliftonville Road, Glasnevin. Originally from Markethill in Co. Armagh, Alex Strain had moved to Dublin at the beginning of the 20th century and established himself as a well-known builder in the Glasnevin area. Alex Strain was involved in the famous Armagh Accident of 12th June, 1889, being one of the 600-odd Armagh Methodist Sunday School children travelling on the special train. He was lucky to have been travelling in the front portion of the train when it was divided and was not injured. He was involved with a great deal of social work, becoming Chairman of the Drumcondra Hospital Management Committee as well as a governor of the Adelaide Hospital in Dublin and a keen supporter of the Marrowbone Lane Fund (a charitable organisation providing assistance for sick and deprived children and their families). He was also a trustee of the Abbey Presbyterian Church, Rutland Square, where the Revd Dr Denham Osborne officiated at the marriage ceremony of Martin Leslie and Madge. The best man was Maurice MacAuley, BL, of Belfast, and the bridesmaids were Martin Leslie's sister Doris and Madge's two sisters, June and Dorrie. It was reported that the bride wore a medieval gown of white satin beauté with a Russian headdress. The reception, attended by about 90 guests, was held at the Standard Hotel in Harcourt Street, which was a notable temperance establishment.

Martin Leslie died suddenly from angina during the course of a holiday to Ashford Castle Hotel, Co. Mayo, on 14th September, 1941. He was only 45 years of age and having just been promoted within the C.C. Wakefield organization, was preparing to move to Leeds. The funeral service, conducted by Mr Breakey and the Revd Canon Campbell, was held at Abbey Presbyterian Church and was followed by burial in Deansgrange cemetery, Blackrock, Co. Dublin.† At the time of his death Martin Leslie was the chairman of the Metropolitan branch of the British Legion and was reported to be popular in both tennis and golfing circles in Dublin. Abbey Presbyterian Church published a glowing obituary, pointing out his remarkable qualities - a sympathetic spirit, uprightness and genius for friendship, and his constant readiness to help people, which endeared him to people of all faiths.

* In the 1890s Charles 'Cheers' Wakefield had patented the Wakefield Lubricator for lubricating the motion of steam locomotives and on 19th March, 1899 he had founded C.C. Wakefield & Co. Ltd in England. In 1909 he registered a new lubricating oil that was destined to revolutionise transport in the first half of the 20th century. The brand was *Castrol*, a name that is still synonymous with premium quality, high performance, leading-edge technology in lubrication.

† Until reading the details of this funeral in newspaper cuttings the author was quite unaware that his late mother had attended this service and may indeed have been acquainted with Martin Leslie through her attendance at Abbey Presbyterian Church.

Chapter Nine

The Australian Branch of the Family

Although there was no career-long railway involvement on the Australian side of the family it was felt that, as Martin Henry Atock made the initial move to the opposite side of the world and albeit that he had but a brief connection with the railways in Ireland, this branch of the family is deserving of some mention. As already recorded, Martin Henry was Martin Atock's first child, and was born in Stratford on 30th June, 1860. The family moved to Limerick a little over a year later and Martin Henry's early education took place in that city. Martin's appointment to the MGWR saw the family move to Dublin in April 1872, and Martin Henry would probably have received his secondary education in that city, but regrettably it has not been possible to establish which school he attended. Unlike his father and grandfather before him, he decided not to pursue a career on the railway but to opt for medicine.

Martin Henry attended the Royal University of Ireland, obtaining his MD and MS in 1882 and was first registered as a doctor on 20th October of that year. The Royal University of Ireland (RUI) was established by Benjamin Disraeli under the University Education (Ireland) Act of 1879 and was an attempt to solve the complex problems of higher education in Ireland. The Queen's Colleges in Belfast, Cork and Galway, and Trinity College, Dublin, were unacceptable to the Catholic hierarchy, while the Catholic University of Ireland had been restricted by lack of state support and its lack of power to award degrees. The RUI was, in effect, a university with a staff but no student body; and students from other institutions were free to sit its examinations. It lasted until 1908 when the Queen's colleges at Cork and Galway were incorporated in the National University of Ireland while at the same time the Queen's College, Belfast, became the Queen's University. Dr M.H. Atock, is shown in Thom's Directories in 1884 and 1886 as a registered practitioner. At that time he was living with his father at Royal Canal House, Broadstone, but it is not clear exactly where he initially practised. What we do know is that a GS&WR Traffic & Works Committee minute for 3rd March, 1886 refers to a recommendation from the company's Chief Medical Officer, Dr Tweedy, that Dr Arthur Atock be appointed his assistant in connection with the Sick Fund instead of his brother Martin Henry who had resigned. It may be, therefore, that his medical career commenced on the railway.

What is certain is that Martin Henry Atock, MD, joined the Royal Navy on 18th February, 1886 and was posted to HMS *Duke of Wellington* at Portsmouth. He was one of several additional officers posted to the 6,071 ton ship for various services. Amongst his duties, he and several other surgeons were assigned for services at Haslar Hospital. On 28th August of the same year, Martin Henry was posted as Surgeon to the 3,653 ton Guard Ship of the Reserve, HMS *Indus*, flagship of the Admiral Superintendent at Devonport. At that time the flagship of the Australian command was HMS *Nelson*, a 7,630 ton, iron armour-plated ship, which had been re-commissioned at Sydney on 15th January, 1885, and Martin Henry found himself posted as Surgeon to this vessel on 27th January, 1887.

Rear Admiral Henry Fairfax assumed command of the Australian station on 20th April, 1887 and the flagship was replaced by a new 5,600 ton twin-screw cruiser, HMS *Orlando*, commissioned at Devonport on 24th May, 1888. When HMS *Orlando* arrived at Sydney, certain of the officers and crew from HMS *Nelson*, including Martin Henry, were transferred to the new flagship.

On 15th April, 1890 Martin Henry married Mary Elizabeth Dunscombe at *Wimbledon*, Five Dock, a suburb to the west of Sydney. Five Dock lies about six miles west of Sydney's central business district, between Parramatta Road and the City West Link Road and runs alongside the Parramatta River. The name is believed to derive from the shape of the bay along the river front. According to the Marine Services Board, the name derives from the fact that at the north-east point of the area known as Canada Bay there were five water-worn indentations that were likened to docks. It was first granted to European settlers in December 1794, one of these early settlers being John Harris, a noted surgeon of his day. Mary Dunscombe attended St Vincent's College for Girls, Sydney's premier Roman Catholic school for girls of the day. The school's annual ball was one of the highlights of the city's academic and social calendar and it is therefore highly likely that visiting Royal Navy officers, including Martin Henry, were invited to attend. It was here in 1889 that the young couple met (he was 29 while she was 12 years his junior) and they fell in love. Mary (or Queenie as she was known to her friends) was described as being very beautiful, musically accomplished and with a bubbly personality whereas Martin Henry was considered to be conservative and rather austere. In any event, the couple married, the ceremony being held at the home of the bride's mother, Ann Dunscombe (neé Johnston) 'according to the Rites of the Roman Catholic Church'. The marriage certificate simply refers to Mary's father, Robert, as a merchant; this hardly does him justice as the family was very wealthy, owning a lot of property in the city and suburbs.

The couple had one son, Vivian Henry, who was born at *Wimbledon* on 15th April, 1891, exactly 12 months to the day following their marriage. Martin Henry and Queenie returned to England on 13th May, 1893, leaving behind Vivian Henry in the care of his maternal grandparents. We do not know whether Martin Henry left the naval service immediately, but he does not appear in the Navy Lists after July 1894. About this time he was apparently living with his brother Arthur at Inchicore, Dublin and the *Medical Directory* for 1895 shows him as a Surgeon RN (retired). Whilst in Dublin, he obtained a Bachelor of Arts in Obstetrics from the Rotunda Maternity Hospital. On his return to Sydney, some two years later, he became Superintendent of St Margaret's Hospital, then the leading Catholic maternity hospital in Sydney.

Martin Henry next appears in the *Medical Directory* for 1898 as a medical practitioner at Bowral* in New South Wales and appears to have worked there for several years as a general practitioner, but by 1906-07 he was at Coolamon, situated about 25 miles north-west of New South Wales' most populous inland town, Wagga Wagga.# He returned to Ireland once more about the end of 1914, again residing

* Bowral lies about 60 miles south of Sydney, and is noted as the place where Sir Donald Bradman, Australia's greatest cricket player, grew up. Coolamon is Aboriginal for 'a vessel for holding water'; the town is situated in a rich agricultural district and otherwise only distinctive for a series of naturally occurring water holes.

Wagga Wagga, known simply as Wagga to the locals, has a current population of about 55,000 and is situated on the Murrumbidgee River; it derives its name from the Widadjuri, the largest of the NSW Aboriginal peoples; Wagga means crow, its repetition signifying the plural.

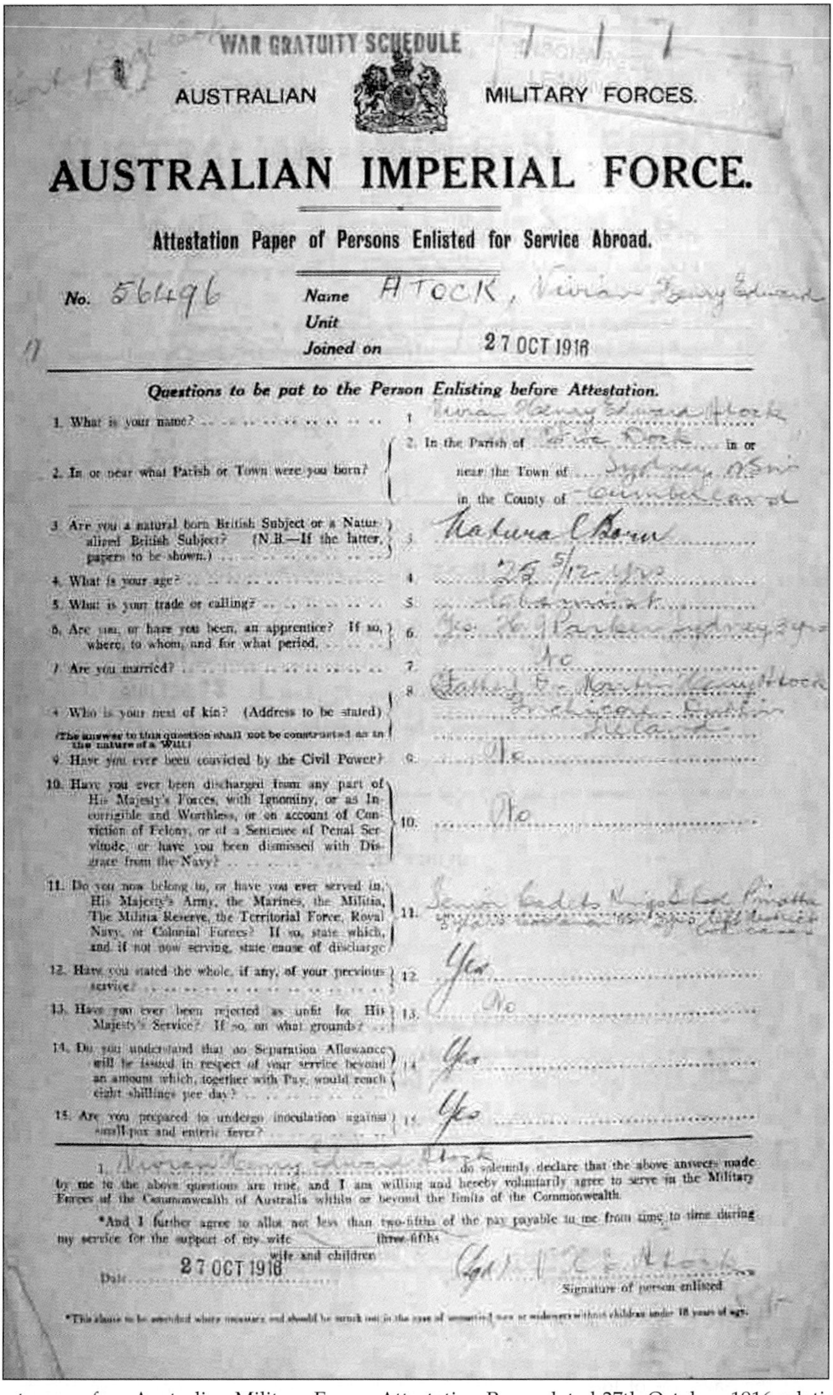

WAR GRATUITY SCHEDULE

AUSTRALIAN MILITARY FORCES.

AUSTRALIAN IMPERIAL FORCE.

Attestation Paper of Persons Enlisted for Service Abroad.

No. 56496 Name ATOCK, Vivian Henry Edward
Unit
Joined on 27 OCT 1916

Questions to be put to the Person Enlisting before Attestation.

1. What is your name? ... 1. Vivian Henry Edward Atock
2. In or near what Parish or Town were you born? ... 2. In the Parish of Drive Dock in or near the Town of Sydney NSW in the County of Cumberland
3. Are you a natural born British Subject or a Naturalized British Subject? (N.B.—If the latter, papers to be shown.) ... 3. Natural Born
4. What is your age? ... 4. 29 5/12 yrs
5. What is your trade or calling? ... 5. Cabinetmaker
6. Are you, or have you been, an apprentice? If so, where, to whom, and for what period. ... 6. Geo. H. Parker Sydney
7. Are you married? ... 7. No
8. Who is your next of kin? (Address to be stated) (The answer to this question shall not be construed as in the nature of a Will.) ... 8. Father
9. Have you ever been convicted by the Civil Power? ... 9. No
10. Have you ever been discharged from any part of His Majesty's Forces, with Ignominy, or as Incorrigible and Worthless, or on account of Conviction of Felony, or of a Sentence of Penal Servitude, or have you been dismissed with Disgrace from the Navy? ... 10. No
11. Do you now belong to, or have you ever served in, His Majesty's Army, the Marines, the Militia, The Militia Reserve, the Territorial Force, Royal Navy, or Colonial Forces? If so, state which, and if not now serving, state cause of discharge ... 11. Senior Cadets
12. Have you stated the whole, if any, of your previous service? ... 12. Yes
13. Have you ever been rejected as unfit for His Majesty's Service? If so, on what grounds? ... 13. No
14. Do you understand that no Separation Allowance will be issued in respect of your service beyond an amount which, together with Pay, would reach eight shillings per day? ... 14. Yes
15. Are you prepared to undergo inoculation against small-pox and enteric fever? ... 15. Yes

I, Vivian Henry Edward Atock do solemnly declare that the above answers made by me to the above questions are true, and I am willing and hereby voluntarily agree to serve in the Military Forces of the Commonwealth of Australia within or beyond the limits of the Commonwealth.

*And I further agree to allot not less than two-fifths of the pay payable to me from time to time during my service for the support of my wife / three-fifths / wife and children

Date 27 OCT 1916

Signature of person enlisted

*This clause to be amended where necessary and should be struck out in the case of unmarried men or widowers without children under 18 years of age.

First page of an Australian Military Forces Attestation Paper dated 27th October, 1916 relating to Vivian Henry Edward Atock. Vivian was to be discharged from the Army before year's end due to his health.

Author's Collection

with his brother Arthur in Inchicore. (His granddaughter, Pam Holmes, comments that Martin Henry was by then suffering from diabetes at a time when insulin was yet to be discovered. He may well, therefore, have returned to be with his family.) We certainly know that he was in Dublin at the beginning of February 1915 as he attended the funeral of Frederick George Smith, the brother-in-law of his brother Thomas. Martin Henry died in Dr Steeven's Hospital in Dublin on 25th September, 1917. His wife Mary, from whom he appears to have been separated for some time, died on 15th April, 1916 at Montrose, Garden Street in the Paddington district of Sydney. She was buried in the Roman Catholic cemetery in Waverley on 17th April. The informant to her death is shown as her son Vivian Henry, then residing at the Railway Hotel at George Street in Sydney.

Vivian Henry attended King's School in Parramatta for three years, following which he spent two years at Coolamon. During his time at the latter location Vivian suffered an acute attack of rheumatism which badly affected his shoulder; at about the same time he had a severe attack of tonsillitis. Subsequently he had numerous attacks of rheumatism. After leaving school he appears to have decided on a legal career, but left those studies after three years in favour of serving a three-year apprenticeship with H.J. Parker in Sydney, in due course qualifying as a pharmaceutical chemist. Vivian was conscripted for war service at the end of September 1916, becoming a Private, No. H56496, in the 18th Battalion at Victoria Barracks in Liverpool, a western suburb of Sydney. There is no mention of his medical history on his initial recruitment papers, but barely a month later he was re-examined at the Garrison Hospital in Sydney, having suffered bouts of tonsillitis and rheumatism. This led to Vivian's medical discharge from the army at the end of November, and so came to a close any aspirations he may have had to serve his country abroad.

Vivian apparently had a relationship with Edna Lois Stewart, aged 22, who was the daughter of the late George Stewart (a bank manager from Redfern in Sydney) and Nina Blanche Manton of Melbourne. Lois's occupation was shown as 'Home Duties'. This resulted in the birth of a son, James Kenneth, on 28th March, 1919. The couple later married on 15th September, 1921 in St Mark's church, Long Bay in Sydney, and about that time, Vivian gave up his pharmaceutical career, becoming a real estate agent. The marriage did not last and, following a divorce, Vivian married again on 14th August, 1928, on this occasion to Marjorie Belle Evans, described as a saleswoman aged 28. The ceremony took place at St Andrew's Anglican Church, Summerhill, and it is interesting to note that Vivian's name is shown on the marriage certificate as James Bradley Atock, an Agent from Potts Point in Sydney, son of Martin Henry Bradley Atock; furthermore he was described as being a bachelor!* With the outbreak of World War II, when the Australian Government encouraged people back into essential industries, which were short of staff because of the numbers joining the armed forces, Vivian returned to pharmacy. In 1931 a half-sister to Ken, Pamela, was born. Pamela knew nothing of Vivian's early medical history and informed the author that in all the years she knew him he had never had a day's illness and had never visited a doctor, and that when he died in 1987 at the age of 96 his mind was as clear as a bell.

* Nowhere in official records is the name Bradley shown for Martin Henry. Marjorie Belle was the daughter of John Jones Evans, originally from Criccieth in Wales. He and his brother Robert married two sisters, Jane Daniels and Elizabeth Marie Hardaker; Jane was Marjorie's mother.

AUSTRALIAN ROCKET SOCIETY 1935

BOX 2038 X G.P.O.

BRISBANE, 25th. Jan. 1937.

Ken Atock Esq.,
Albert Park. Vic.

Dear Sir,

I am in receipt of your letter of the 21st. Inst. and thank you for the enclosures.The photographs are indeed very interesting and form a permanent record of a very difficult experiment.Thanks also for the cuttings and sketch.

We read in a Melbourne stamp paper that there had been a rocket firing in Melbourne and found out from Orlo-Smith that a report had been written in the Herald of Oct. 3rd. We obtained several copies which arrived last week. From covers we purchased from that firm we obtained your address and wrote both you and a Mr/ Hirn. However Mr. Mr Hirn may get in touch with you so you will know how we came to write him.

On behalf of Mr. Young and myself I have pleasure in enc[illegible]es. a set of flown rocket covers to date. You will notice that the first three were conducted by Mr. Young as president of the Queensland Air mail Society before he founded the Australian Rocket Society.We trust you will accept this set as a token of our esteem.Please forward a second set of photographs and let us know cost of same.Mr. Young and I would both like a set for our separate collections. We will send you some photos at an early date but at the present are up to our eyes arranging two experiments which will take place shortly. In addition we are arranging a large public exhibition of the worlds rocket experiments. We have a remarkable collection having acquired it over a period of three years from every country where an experiment has taken place. Would you give us permission to have two of the photos you forwarded enlarged and shown publically in our exhibition. Please give full details as to persons etc. on back of each photo.In all future experiments please forward us copies of everything in duplicate and we will reciprocate if you desire.No, there was no mentuon of your experiment in any of the Brisbane papers. Will write you re. liquid hydrogen later in the week.Again many thanks for your kind letter,

Yours faithfully,

Noel S. Morrison

Noel S.Morrison. Hon. Sec.
Australian Rocket
Society.

Letter from the Australian Rocket Society dated January 1937 addressed to Kenneth Atock, thanking him for sending details of his rocket experiments of the previous October.

Pamela Holmes Collection

Kenneth Atock inspecting mail recovered from his attempted launch of a rocket at Fishermen's Bend near Melbourne on 3rd October, 1936. Standing beside him is his friend Bob Ware, who had helped in the construction of the rocket. Although it never left the ground, the two boys considered the experiment a success. *Pamela Holmes Collection*

No details have survived of Ken Atock's early years, although we do know that he commenced at Camberwell Grammar School in Canterbury, Victoria, in 1930. Quite early on he appears to have developed a keen interest in rockets, experiments leading to an attempt to launch one at Fishermen's Bend near Melbourne on 3rd October, 1936. A local newspaper stated that the original intention was for Ken and his friend, Bob Ware (who had helped to build the rocket), to launch it from a large expanse of open ground at Lilydale with mails aboard to celebrate the forthcoming Coronation. However, the State Explosives' Department refused to give permission for the launch, claiming it would be dangerous, and plans were then drawn up to tow the rocket out to sea. In the event, the Fishermen's Bend site was used. Although the rocket's casing exploded and it never left the ground, Ken considered the experiment a success!

With the outbreak of war in Europe in September 1939 the young Ken Atock enlisted, on 20th October, 1939, in the 2/7th Infantry Battalion, then based at the Parade Grounds in Melbourne. By 3rd November the Battalion had moved to Puckapunayal, a new centre near Seymour about 60 miles north of Melbourne, to carry out basic training. Writing home on 10th November, the day after he had arrived at Puckapunayal, he recorded that the young recruits had had to march the seven miles from Seymour station to the camp. He was soon transferred, probably only temporarily, to the Transport Section to look after the

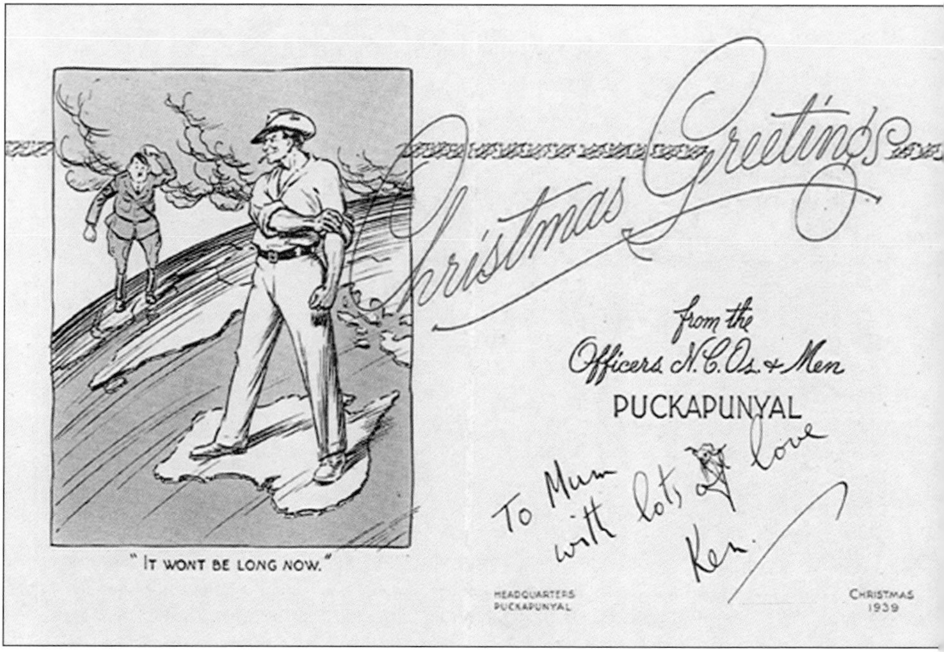
Christmas Greetings
from the
Officers N.C.Os. & Men
PUCKAPUNYAL
" IT WONT BE LONG NOW."
To Mum
with lots of love
Ken.
HEADQUARTERS
PUCKAPUNYAL
CHRISTMAS
1939

A Christmas card sent by Kenneth Atock to his mother in December 1939 whilst he was based at Puckapunyal, about 60 miles north of Melbourne, and preparing to set sail for the Middle East.
Pamela Holmes Collection

Kenneth Atock, *extreme left*, standing with other members of the Battalion at an unknown location.
Pamela Holmes Collection

horses. As early as April 1940 there was intense speculation as to the likely date for the departure overseas of the Battalion; it was about this time that the firing of mortars with high-explosive shells was first carried out.

Addressing the troops on 5th April, 1940, Lieut-Gen. Sir Carl Jess, who had been the colonel of the old 7th Battalion and was now Hon. Colonel of the 2/7th, wished them well with a speedy and safe return. A week later, they were addressed by Lieut-Gen. Sir Thomas Blamey who also wished them well. In his speech he thanked the men for their contribution to the railways 'for the damage done on their return from pre-embarkation leave'. They were exhorted to refrain from 'souveniring' in the future, as it was nothing more than theft, an obvious reference to their recent 'lively' train trip! Following the parade many of the men went into the town of Seymour for what was to be a final night-out before embarkation.

The date chosen for the Battalion's departure was 15th April. The previous two days were taken up with cleaning and washing out the huts, organizing kit and obtaining identity tags. The men were informed that they had been chosen to travel overseas on the same ship as the Divisional Headquarters and some of the senior officers; this ship HMT-Y4 (the MV *Strathaird*) would be the best in the convoy as the other ships had been built specifically as troop carriers.* On the morning of 15th April, Reveille was called at 3.00 am and after breakfast the men were transported to Seymour, departing from there in two special trains, at 7.30 and 8.00 am. On arrival at Port Melbourne the men embarked on HMT-Y4 and were allotted sleeping quarters. The ship cast-off about noon and rendezvoused with the rest of the convoy, viz. three other transports and the Royal Australian Navy ships, HMAS *Australia*, *Sydney* and *Canberra*, together with the 15 in. gun battleship HMS *Ramillies*.

The following day turned out to be particularly rough and it was reported that many of the men were seasick, particularly those in 'A' and 'B' companies who were occupying hammocks on 'H' deck, there not being sufficient cabins available. The next few days were occupied with boat drills, PT and rifle drills. Writing home again, Ken confirmed that 'some of the boys had been hanging over the rail', but he was one of the lucky ones with a bunk, which he shared with his friend Allan Fry, a fellow resident from Hawthorne, which was the next suburb to Camberwell. Conditions on board ship were far superior to those at Puckapunayal with hot baths, water laid on in the cabins, beer at 5*d*. a pint and nurses 'who may be viewed at a distance'!

At 9.30 am on 21st April the convoy entered Fremantle Harbour, general leave being granted from 10.30 am. The men were taken by special trains to Perth, very favourable comments being made as to the hospitality of the residents of that city. The convoy set sail again the following day, many of the men feeling sad at leaving Australia, some probably for the first, and last, time. Once again the days following departure were taken up with drills and lectures, although it was also reported that various games were played aboard ship. One minor problem, which presented itself, was in regard to the supply of beer, both to the officers and men. It was the practice for the men to give their money to their company officer who paid for the beer and stood by when it was being

* Built for P&O Line in 1931 the 22,500 ton *Strathaird* was the first P&O liner to enter the Australian cruise market in December 1932. Along with her sister ship, the SS *Strathnaver*, she was requisitioned as a troop carrier in September 1939, eventually returning to the P&O Line at the end of 1946. Martin Oldacres Attock also sailed to Ceylon on the *Strathaird* when delivering the railcars in 1938 (*see Chapter Fourteen*).

served out from the bar. The problem was, however, that the men had to parade for their beer and had only a short time allowed in which to consume it. It was in due course agreed that they should not have to parade, but that beer could not be issued in the evenings as lights might be switched on and endanger the safety of the convoy.

The convoy steamed into Colombo Harbour, Ceylon, early on the morning of 3rd May, the troops being taken ashore on lighters and water boats. Two days of shore leave was granted; the men were marched to a green near the Galle Face Hotel* where money was exchanged. Battalion strength was increased by one during the Colombo stopover, a monkey being taken on board Y4, the property of Pte Anstis of HQ Company. By the time the ships left Ceylon the weather had turned very hot and a great many of the men appeared on sick parade with colds, due to sleeping on deck. Another letter from Ken to his mother, although undated and simply addressed from 'Abroad', was apparently written shortly after leaving Colombo. He informed her that they were surrounded by 'hydrogen oxide in all directions as far as the eye can see'. He mentioned that they had had a great time at Colombo, and that he had dined at 'one of the biggest hotels in the world' at a cost of about 12*s*., where a foreign prince sat at the next table. Whilst ashore, Ken had bought a couple of uncut moonstones and promised to send them home, although admitting they were of little value.

The convoy reached Aden on 12th May, and shore leave was not granted as they only remained about four hours in port. Two days later, as they passed up the Red Sea, one of the destroyers dropped depth charges and submarine drills were followed, which reminded the troops that they were then approaching the war zone. At least by that time the temperatures had dropped somewhat, due to a strong breeze. The ships finally arrived at El Kantara, Egypt, at about 10.30 pm on the evening of 17th May, the troops being quickly entrained for their onward journey. It was reported that the troop train consisted of two carriages in front for the officers and 20 boxcars for the men, 20 to a car. The train crossed the Egyptian/Palestine border at 7.00 am and arrived at Gaza just under an hour later. Here tents were allocated, these having previously been erected by the men of the 2/3rd Battalion. Blankets, palliasses and floorboards were also handed out. The following few months were taken up with training in both Egypt and Palestine, but it was not until just before Christmas 1940 that the Australians experienced their first campaign, which was against the Italians in eastern Libya.

In the interim several letters home give us some additional information, none of it of a military nature as each letter was censored before dispatch. From Palestine, we hear how they went on three days leave to Jerusalem. On their second day there Ken and some of his friends hired a car and went through Shiloh, then to Jacob's Well and Nablus and other sites of religious significance. Their first view of the Sea of Galilee was spectacular, seen as it was from a height of 1,000 ft. Later, at Haifa, they observed many of the residents being evacuated from the town in convoys of trucks. Another letter provides in-depth details regarding various religious sites in Jerusalem itself. Ken experienced his first camel ride early in

* In Chapter Fourteen we shall again make our acquaintance with this hotel in connection with the marriage of another member of the family, Martin Oldacres Attock. A third member of the family, Ronald Atock, spent some six months there as recorded in the Epilogue.

September 1940, and in endeavouring to dismount, he performed a somersault, ending up under the camel's nose with the saddle on top of him.

A letter dated 19th September confirms that the Battalion had moved to Egypt where they were having 'quite a decent time in spite of the heat and the sand'. By that time they had a choice of two very nice open-air theatres with programmes changed daily. Ken and some of his mates visited Cairo on leave and a trip was planned to see the Pyramids and the River Nile. One of the unpleasant aspects of life in this region was the Khaseem, or desert wind, which caused severe sandstorms - these are also referred to in the Battalion's War Diaries. Ken also mentions having received a letter from Mr Doyle, chief of staff of *The* (Australian) *Argus*, as well as having received some socks from the staff of that newspaper. This, and a later letter from the Editor, makes it clear that Ken had worked for them for a while prior to enlisting, having also submitted articles about rockets.

In the first week of January 1941 the Battalion found itself up against Italian troops in the Battle for Bardia, a number of officers and other ranks being killed or wounded. Following that battle, several days were taken up sorting out and cleaning captured materials; the lull in the fighting was warmly welcomed by the troops. On 9th January the commanding officer, Lieut-Col Theodore Gordon Walker, DSO, left for Tobruk to reconnoitre a new position for the Battalion, a move in convoy to a point some 20 miles east of that place being made later that day. At Tobruk itself one of the first duties was what became known as 'winkling' or the rounding-up of escaped enemy soldiers on the beach. The troops were also allowed to swim, which came as a welcome relief to Ken and his colleagues, as water restrictions had rendered washing rather difficult. Shortly after their arrival, fresh fruit, cream, tobacco and tinned peas were handed out. The weather was by now described as terribly cold and the men welcomed their winter clothing.

The Battalion experienced its first taste of dive-bombing on 18th February, 1941 when it was attacked by eight German bombers, luckily without any casualties. Orders were received on 9th March to move back to Tobruk where several days of rest followed before the Battalion was once again on the move eastwards towards Alexandria. While awaiting embarkation orders, their transport was loaded aboard the *Singalese Prince* for shipping to Larissa, about 210 miles north of Athens. Two ships in this convoy, the *Devis* and the *Northern Prince*, were hit and sunk *en route*. The Battalion itself remained at Amiriya, about 25 miles west of Alexandria, until 9th April, when it moved by train to Alexandria, where the men boarded the *Cameronia*, setting sail the next day for Greece. It was during that period that Ken wrote home again, tragically, as it transpired, for the last time. In his letter he referred to a magnificent seven-course dinner which he had consumed, in Alexandria, with a bottle of champagne. After the meal the group went to see *Spring Parade* starring Deanna Durbin, which he thought 'rather good'. Ken also purchased a birthday present for his mother, a book of antiquities entitled *Pyramid and Temple*. He was at that stage having driving lessons and confirmed that he could drive not only a car but also a tractor, a Bren carrier and an 'Iti tank'. Ken was also being taught to drive a locomotive - perhaps this was by Cpl Taylor whom we will meet shortly.

The convoy arrived off Piraeus harbour on 12th April, the troops being disembarked the following morning by means of rowing boats, they were landed at Phaliron. Two days later the men entrained at the station at Rouf, *en route* to Larissa; progress was extremely slow due to frequent air raid alarms and it was 11 hours later before the train stopped for the night at Dhomokos station. On the following morning the train moved off at 7.30 am but stopped at Krannon for two hours as the locomotive crew refused to go any further. Due to heavy air raids on Larissa between 2.00 and 5.30 am no train crew could be located. Cpl Taylor organized fire lighting of two locomotives with two volunteers, but it is not known if Ken was one of them. One locomotive was left with the firehole door partly open and the blower on, which provided a ready target for enemy aircraft. The second locomotive was manned by the three men who, under incessant bombing attacks, marshalled a rake of wagons into a train which they then moved into position for the troops to board, moving off at 7.30 am.

On the morning of 19th April it was learnt that a train of gun cotton and ammonal was lying in a railway siding at Sophiades, about two miles north of Dhomokos Pass. Two members of the Battalion volunteered to blow it up but, when it was realised that an engine had also been left in the siding, Cpl Taylor and eight other men agreed to raise steam and move the train. During the course of lighting-up the engine, the train was hit by a bomb, which caused it to blow up, Cpl Taylor being blown off the footplate of the engine, luckily without any injuries. Suffering more or less continuous bombing raids, the Battalion began a retreat from the area and eventually arrived at Kalamata Harbour at about 4 pm on 26th April pending their evacuation from Greece. In the interim all transport had been rendered useless before evacuating. At the jetty Ken and his comrades were loaded aboard destroyers and taken out to the troop carrier the SS *Costa Rica*.* In all, some 2,600 troops from a number of Australian Brigades were on board the ship as she left Kalamata.

Shortly after leaving Kalamata the SS *Costa Rica* was attacked by enemy aircraft, no damage being done. However, at about 2.40 pm on 27th April another attack was made, bombs dropping within 8 ft of the port side. Immediately the ship's engines stopped, the Chief Engineer reporting that she was taking water in the engine room. Despite this an orderly evacuation was made with destroyers coming alongside the starboard side of the ship. First HMS *Defender* took as many as possible, pulling away to allow HMS *Hero* and then HMS *Hereward* to come alongside. All the ship's crew and the troops, including Ken, aboard were safely taken off, the *Costa Rica* disappearing beneath the waves about an hour after the commencement of the attack. By then the three destroyers were so heavily laden that it was realised that it would be too risky to attempt to reach Alexandria, as had been intended, and it was decided to make for Crete. In the event troops were landed at Suda Bay later that evening and moved about three miles inland to settle for the night. The unfortunate men had nothing but what they stood up in and had to camp out in the open air under an olive grove.

* The SS *Costa Rica* had previously been owned by the Royal Dutch Steamship Company (KNSM) and had operated pre-war between Amsterdam and Curacao in the Netherlands Antilles.

Life on Crete during mid-1941 turned out to be difficult for the men of the Battalion. The day after landing they moved further round Suda Bay to a concealed position about 1½ miles south of Celebes. Towels, shirts, shorts, socks, cigarettes and soap were issued in replacement for what had been lost during the evacuation from Greece. Severe air raids were encountered on 3rd May, a squadron of about 35 aircraft attacking in the space of half an hour during the afternoon, five of the aircraft being shot down. Later in the month there was heavy bombing of Suda and Retimo, which was followed by troop-carrying aircraft coming in from the sea at a height of between 50 and 100 ft over Suda, which made them sitting targets for arms fire, many being shot down. The Germans suffered extremely heavy losses from the Anzac fire and one particular area became known as 'Death Valley'.

On 25th May the 2/7th Battalion were ordered back to Suda Bay to take up defensive positions. The following evening they suffered a surprise attack, the Germans having broken the English line. A counter-attack was ordered and the Battalion gave a good account of themselves, as did a Maori contingent on the right flank, which had the effect of driving back the enemy. However, it was quickly realised that the position was untenable and a withdrawal was ordered. The decision was now taken for the Allied troops to retreat towards Sphaxia on the south coast, a journey which involved a trek across the mountains, some of which rose to 8,000 ft. The plan had been for the Royal Navy to provide vessels for the evacuation from Sphaxia of all Allied troops remaining on the island.

The Battalion encountered great difficulties in negotiating the descent to the beach at Sphaxia, some members of the Intelligence Section having preceded the main body of men to find the most suitable access. Pte Atock was specifically mentioned by Lieut-Col Walker as being in the Intelligence group and this was confirmed by a friend, Roy Macartney, in a subsequent letter to Ken's mother. By the time the remnants of the Battalion reached the beach most of the ships had departed, only a small number of the men actually getting away. The remainder were later rounded up and taken prisoner by the Germans. In a subsequent report, it was admitted that the fighting units had become scattered owing to faulty administration and liaison between staff officers and the Navy; no effective control was attempted or maintained.

It was to be 9th June before Lois Atock received a telegram from the Minister for the Army confirming that VX5403 Pte K. Atock had been reported missing, the Minister and the Military Board expressing their sympathies. Three weeks later Lois received a letter from Allan Fry confirming that as far as he was aware Ken was now a prisoner-of-war. A letter from the Manager of *The Argus*, dated 4th August, also confirmed Ken's status at that time. Another letter from Allan Fry confirmed that he had recently spoken to two members of the Battalion who had escaped from Crete. They were able to confirm that Ken and a pal, Hugh Jordan, were busy devising methods of cooking their rations in empty jam and fruit tins. It was also confirmed that they were being treated well by their captors, probably due to the high esteem in which the Germans held the Australian troops. Ken Atock decided to make a break for freedom on 13th July, 1941 but, tragically, he was shot dead during the attempt. He was buried in the Military Cemetery at Suda Bay.

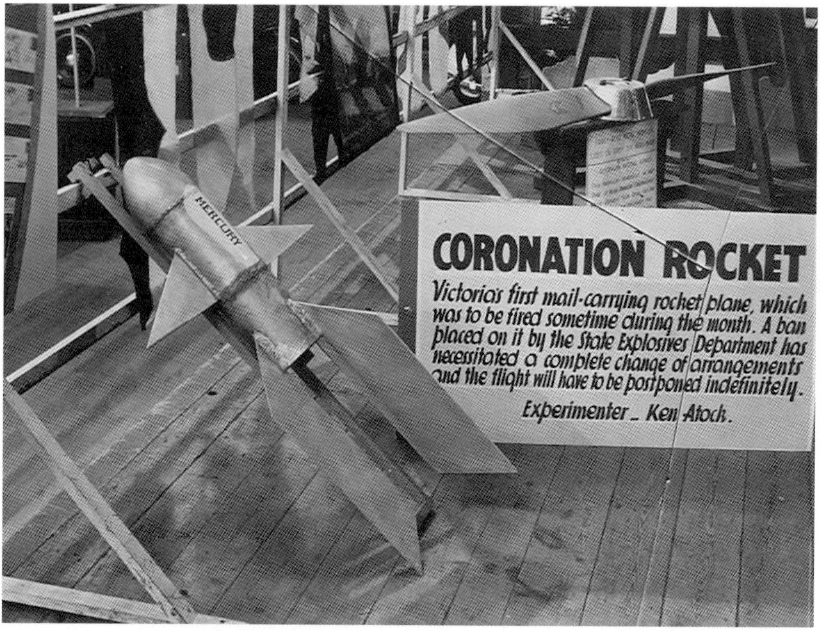

MERCURY
CORONATION ROCKET
Victoria's first mail-carrying rocket plane, which was to be fired sometime during the month. A ban placed on it by the State Explosives Department has necessitated a complete change of arrangements and the flight will have to be postponed indefinitely.
Experimenter _ Ken Atock.

The Australian War Memorial Museum with Kenneth Atock's rocket, *Mercury*. As this appears to differ slightly from the one used in the attempted launch, it is not quite clear whether the latter was rebuilt or a new one constructed. *Pamela Holmes Collection*

Following Lois Atock's death on Christmas Eve 1975, Camberwell Grammar School, where Ken had been in the 1930s, announced that under the terms of her will she had endowed the 'Kenneth Atock Memorial Scholarship Fund'. Advertisements were placed in the local press in October 1976 seeking applications. It was reported that the scholarship was worth approximately two-thirds of the annual tuition fee and was available for the final two years at school. The scholarship was to be awarded to students who showed outstanding academic promise and who intended to study a predominantly Mathematics/Science course. The first award under this scheme was made in 1977, a fitting tribute to Ken Atock, a brave young man.

Chapter Ten

Frederick Attock moves to Manchester

Frederick Attock's application for the position of carriage & wagon superintendent on the Lancashire & Yorkshire Railway was considered, along with other outside candidates, on 5th December, 1876 at a meeting of the sub-committee that had been appointed to consider the matter. During his interview Frederick informed the sub-committee that he had seen the company's new carriage shops at Newton Heath, and he also took the opportunity to advise them of a new planing machine recently installed at Stratford. He informed them that a similar machine, which was capable of planing four sides at the one time, could be seen at the Midland Wagon Company's shops and was available at a cost of £150. Among the other candidates for the position was William Wainwright of the Worcester Carriage & Wagon Co. It quickly became clear, however, that Frederick Attock was the preferred candidate, although William Wainwright obviously had some connections as it was reported that he had already met with some of the Directors.

Born at Leeds in 1833, Wainwright served his apprenticeship with E.B. Wilson of Leeds, from which he moved to the Oxford Worcester & Wolverhampton Railway, becoming locomotive & carriage superintendent in 1860. When that company was amalgamated with the GWR he was appointed to a similar position in the Worcester division before leaving to join the Worcester Carriage & Wagon Co in 1873. In January 1877 he was appointed chief outdoor assistant in the carriage & wagon department of the Midland Railway and in April 1882 he became carriage & wagon superintendent of the South Eastern Railway. He was the father of Harry Smith Wainwright who became locomotive superintendent of the South Eastern & Chatham Railway in January 1899.

Both men were advised to attend a Board meeting in Manchester on 13th December, 1876. At that meeting Frederick was offered the post at a salary of £500 per annum plus a company-owned house at a reasonable rent. The property in question was Somerset House, at North Road (later known as Northampton Road) beside Thorp Road bridge and immediately adjacent to Newton Heath works. However, before a new tenant could move in, repairs estimated at £568 were necessary. Unwilling to spend that amount, the Directors ordered that essential repairs only be carried out at a figure not exceeding £300; the rent was agreed at £40 per annum. Frederick accepted the new position, his duties to commence on 1st February, 1877. At the time of his move to Manchester, Frederick Attock had become a well-settled family man. On 17th April, 1869 he had married Ellen Elizabeth Gardner in Leyton parish church; she had been born in 1845 at Shoreditch in London. Frederick and Ellen Elizabeth had four children all born at Stratford; two daughters, Ellen May, born on 20th March, 1870, and Mary Grace on 5th January, 1872, were followed by George Henry, who arrived on 26th January, 1874, and his younger brother Frederick William, born on 15th November, 1875.

The early history of the L&YR is complex, involving a number of amalgamations and acquisitions, and is clearly beyond the scope of this biography; what follows is no more than a very brief summary of events to set the scene at the time of Frederick's arrival at Newton Heath. The most important constituent of the L&YR was the Manchester & Leeds Railway (M&LR), originally authorized by an Act of July 1836, the proposed line running from a high-level terminus at Oldham Road in Manchester to Normanton, where it was to join the North Midland Railway, reaching Leeds over the latter company's line. Oldham Road was chosen as a terminus so as to avoid the inconvenience of a steep descent into the city. However, the Liverpool & Manchester Railway terminus was at Liverpool Road, 1¼ miles distant and at a rather lower level, and it quickly became obvious that the two lines should be connected. Arguments between the two companies over the best route for a connecting line meant that Parliamentary approval was not obtained until July 1842; a new joint station, known as Manchester Victoria, was finally opened on 1st January, 1844. The new connecting line joined the M&LR main line at Miles Platting where the company's principal locomotive, carriage and wagon works were situated in a very cramped and unsuitable location. The M&LR continued opening up further sections until 1st March, 1841, and acquisitions and amalgamations led to an Act of Parliament dated 9th July, 1847, which authorised a change of title to the Lancashire & Yorkshire Railway Company, but even at that stage the system was far from complete.

The second principal constituent of the L&YR was the East Lancashire Railway (ELR), itself an amalgamation of various concerns. The original line was the Manchester Bury & Rossendale Railway, incorporated by Act of Parliament of July 1844. The M&LR and the ELR had a rather difficult relationship in the early days, with disputes over the use of Clifton Junction by the latter company's trains. Eventually common sense prevailed, with the ELR being absorbed into the L&YR in 1859.

By the beginning of the 20th century the L&YR system compared roughly, at least in terms of mileage, with the MGWR, with a route mileage of 585¼, of which only 39¾ miles were single-tracked; however, this was the only point on which there was any comparability. Out of the total mileage, almost 134 miles were on gradients of 1 in 100 or less, with a further 150 miles between 1 in 100 and 1 in 200; there were no less than 91 tunnels, the longest of which, Summit tunnel on the line between Rochdale and Todmorden, was 2,885 yards in length. There were six other tunnels in excess of 1,000 yards in length. The company owned 260 passenger stations and there were a further 31 jointly owned, but operated by L&YR staff. Signal cabins entirely owned by the company totalled 677, of which seven alone were in the immediate environs of Manchester Victoria station. That station, which encompassed an area of 13½ acres, handled as many as 720 trains a day.

At its greatest extent, the system extended from Liverpool, Blackpool and Fleetwood in the west to York and Hull in the east, the latter reached by running powers over the North Eastern Railway (NER). Although basically a 'business line' the L&YR also catered for extensive excursion traffic. Each year the Whit weekend in particular saw a huge exodus of workers from Liverpool,

Manchester and other towns to coastal resorts such as Blackpool, Southport and Lytham or as far as the Derbyshire Dales. Blackpool had no fewer than four stations to handle the enormous excursion traffic; in its heyday they dealt with almost 400,000 passengers over an August bank holiday weekend. Many Sunday School excursions were also organized for those weekends. Apart from excursion traffic, many race meetings were held, including the famous Grand National at Aintree racecourse, which adjoined the railway and saw trains arrive, not only from all over the company's system, but also from the lines of adjoining companies.

On the goods front, the two principal industries were cotton in Lancashire and wool in Yorkshire. Vast quantities of cotton from America were imported through Liverpool and the same port exported woollen and cotton goods. The principal cotton spinning towns were Oldham and Bolton with weaving in Preston, Blackburn, Accrington, Burnley and Nelson. At one time Bolton held the distinction of being the largest cotton-spinning town in Britain. The Yorkshire woollen industry was centred around Bradford, Leeds, Huddersfield, Halifax and Dewsbury. There were extensive coalfields in both Lancashire and Yorkshire, which served not only the foregoing industries but also the engineering industries in both counties. Coal was also exported through the ports of Liverpool and Goole. Daily fish trains were run from the fishing port of Fleetwood to Manchester and other important centres. All of the towns mentioned were served by the L&YR which also carried mill workers in their millions. Some idea of the company's dependency on the local industries is vividly illustrated by J. Marshall who records that, during and following a strike of cotton workers in October 1908, the L&YR found it necessary to withdraw in excess of 100 trains.

In 1880, receipts at £3,573,702 handsomely exceeded the £1,896,897 expenditure, allowing the payment of a dividend on the ordinary shares of $5\frac{3}{8}$ per cent; however, the figures masked a rather different story. A study of the minute books of the various committees of the Board suggests a harmony in making quick decisions on matters of expenditure. Closer inspection, however, reveals the fact that such decisions rarely involved large expenditure on plant and the casual reader might be forgiven for believing that maintenance was such that heavy capital expenditure was unnecessary. We shall return to this aspect of the company's operations later in our narrative.

On the locomotive front, William Barton Wright had been appointed locomotive superintendent of the L&YR in November 1875 at the age of 47. Barton Wright had begun his career as an apprentice at Swindon, in due course spending three years in charge of the running shed at Paddington. In October 1854 he became locomotive carriage & wagon superintendent of the Madras Railway in India, a post he held until he came to the L&YR.* At the time of his arrival the company had about 800 engines, consisting of more than 30 classes,

* Alexander McDonnell of the GS&WR, along with Barton Wright, was short listed to fill the vacancy of locomotive superintendent on the L&YR. Following his resignation from the GS&WR in 1882, McDonnell moved to the North Eastern Railway at Gateshead to replace Edward Fletcher. McDonnell upset the workforce at Gateshead and he resigned in the autumn of 1884; one can but speculate how he might have got along on the L&YR. Another contender for the position on the L&YR was Henry Appleby who later went to the Waterford & Limerick Railway.

many of which were too small and quite unsuited for their duties. Apart from Miles Platting, already referred to, the company also had the old ELR works at Bury, also very cramped and lacking in up-to-date machinery. Barton Wright immediately realised that it was necessary to introduce a standard set of engines, but he also came to the conclusion that the two works were totally unsuited for purpose. Barton Wright brought about a transformation in the locomotive stock, which in turn had a knock-on effect on timekeeping and reliability.

Insofar as carriage and wagon stock was concerned, Charles Fay had been appointed to the position of carriage & wagon superintendent in October 1846. Charles Fay, born in Dublin in 1812, was apprenticed to T.W. Worsdell, who built carriages for the Liverpool & Manchester Railway. He joined the GS&WR at Inchicore as carriage superintendent on 11th October, 1845, but only remained for a year before accepting the position at Manchester. All of Fay's carriage stock was four-wheeled and was fitted with his design of brake, patented by him in 1856, all passenger trains being fitted with the Fay brake by October 1860. Initially only first class passengers enjoyed the comfort of upholstery on seats and backs, although this was extended in August 1862 to include second-class carriages in ordinary service. During Fay's time carriages were painted in teak colour, although in May 1874 it was reported that 288 excursion carriages had been painted red, with a further 135 to be done after the Whit weekend. By the time of Fay's retirement in January 1877 much of the carriage stock was in poor condition. His retirement was honoured by a dinner held at the Manchester Café under the Old Exchange. Following his retirement, Fay lived with his daughter Ann Eleanor and her husband, James Lawton, a solicitor, at Bowdon near Altrincham. He passed away at Stockport in January 1900 at the age of 88.

On 27th April, 1873 a serious fire had occurred at Miles Platting that resulted in the destruction of the carriage shops. General plans were drawn up in 1874 by Fay for the provision of a new carriage works, the detailed design being left to the company's Engineer, Sturges Meek. The site chosen was at Newton Heath, about two miles north-east of Manchester Victoria station, immediately beyond Thorp Road Junction. The tender of Messrs Robert Neill & Sons of Strangeways in an amount of £98,330 for the buildings, was accepted on 14th October, 1874. However, the total cost of the Newton Heath carriage workshops (including land and machinery) was considerably more, eventually totalling £262,094 18*s*. 2*d*.

From the foregoing brief description it will be seen that, on his arrival in Manchester, Frederick Attock encountered a railway environment that differed considerably from his experience on the GER. Some idea of his new responsibility can perhaps be gauged from the December 1877 rolling stock return, viz. coaching vehicles 2,137, of which approximately 50 per cent were third class carriages, and 18,494 goods vehicles of all categories. It was into this different world at Newton Heath that Frederick and his family arrived at the beginning of February 1877, but bearing in mind the extent of repairs necessary to Somerset House, it seems unlikely that they moved in to their new residence immediately.

Within a week of taking up office the Board requested Frederick to inspect and report on the condition of seven old third class carriages taken over from the

Preston & Longridge Railway; following receipt of his report on 26th February it was ordered that three of the carriages be repaired at an estimated cost of £50, the other four to be broken up. At the same Board meeting Frederick reported that he had inspected 80 old carriages in store at Bispham sidings, just outside Blackpool. He recommended that 50 of them should be broken up. Perhaps still reluctant to place too much reliance on their new superintendent, and perhaps due to their parsimonious approach to such matters, the Directors ordered that only the worst 20 carriages should be broken up, these to be replaced by a similar number of carriages in course of delivery from Messrs Craven Bros. Furthermore, Frederick was instructed to utilise the old under-frames as far as possible in the construction of 36 ballast wagons recently ordered to be constructed.

One of the first ideas introduced by Frederick in 1877 was an order book into which entries were made for each new lot of carriages and wagons built in subsequent years. Shortly after his retirement a second order book was opened in 1896. Regrettably the earlier one has not survived, although many of the orders can be traced from the diagram books, which were introduced in 1893. The Miles Platting fire resulted in the loss of virtually all of Fay's drawings and papers, so new drawings were prepared for the older vehicles. Order numbers were only allocated to new builds and not to rebuilds or conversions. They consisted of a letter and number, e.g. A1, B1 etc., certain letters (I, J, Q, U and X) not being used so as to avoid confusion. The system started with A1, then B1, C1, etc. until Y1 was reached when A2 was used, followed by B2, etc. Similar numbers were used for both carriages and wagons. The scheme continued in use until abandoned by the LMS in 1925, at which time order numbers had reached O61.

It is clear that Frederick was extremely busy during his first few months at Newton Heath, but even at that early stage it is obvious that he quickly came to the conclusion that he should effect savings wherever possible. With that purpose in mind he made various suggestions to the Board. As an example, at the Board meeting held on 28th February, 1877 he suggested the use of pitch pine instead of teak or oak in the construction of carriages and wagons. He had, of course, been using pitch pine quite successfully on the GER;* in the case of wagons he had effected a saving of £5 to £6 per vehicle compared with the use of oak. The Directors, however, deferred a decision for future consideration, apart from the 36 ballast wagons already ordered to be made with pine.

Another item that received his early attention was the question of painting carriages. Frederick had a sample carriage painted up in teak colour, which he claimed would save a figure of up to £8 per carriage. Following an inspection, the Directors confirmed that the excursion stock should be at once painted 'according to the cheaper mode of which he (Frederick) has given a sample'. In addition, he was instructed to paint up several carriages for the ordinary traffic in various shades of colours for further inspection, and on 20th June Frederick was able to confirm that these were ready for viewing. He attended the inspection at Victoria station early in July and explained that a light brown colour would cost about £12 per carriage as against £13 10*s.* 0*d.* for imitation teak and £17 to £18 for the other (unspecified) colours. It was agreed that in future all ordinary stock was to be painted light brown, the same as sample carriage, No.139. In addition the edges

* It was on 1st December, 1874 that the GER Board took the decision to change from oak to pine for wagon underframes. At that time the GER were paying out £11,500 each year for Quebec oak, whereas pitch pine was estimated to cost about £5,000 annually.

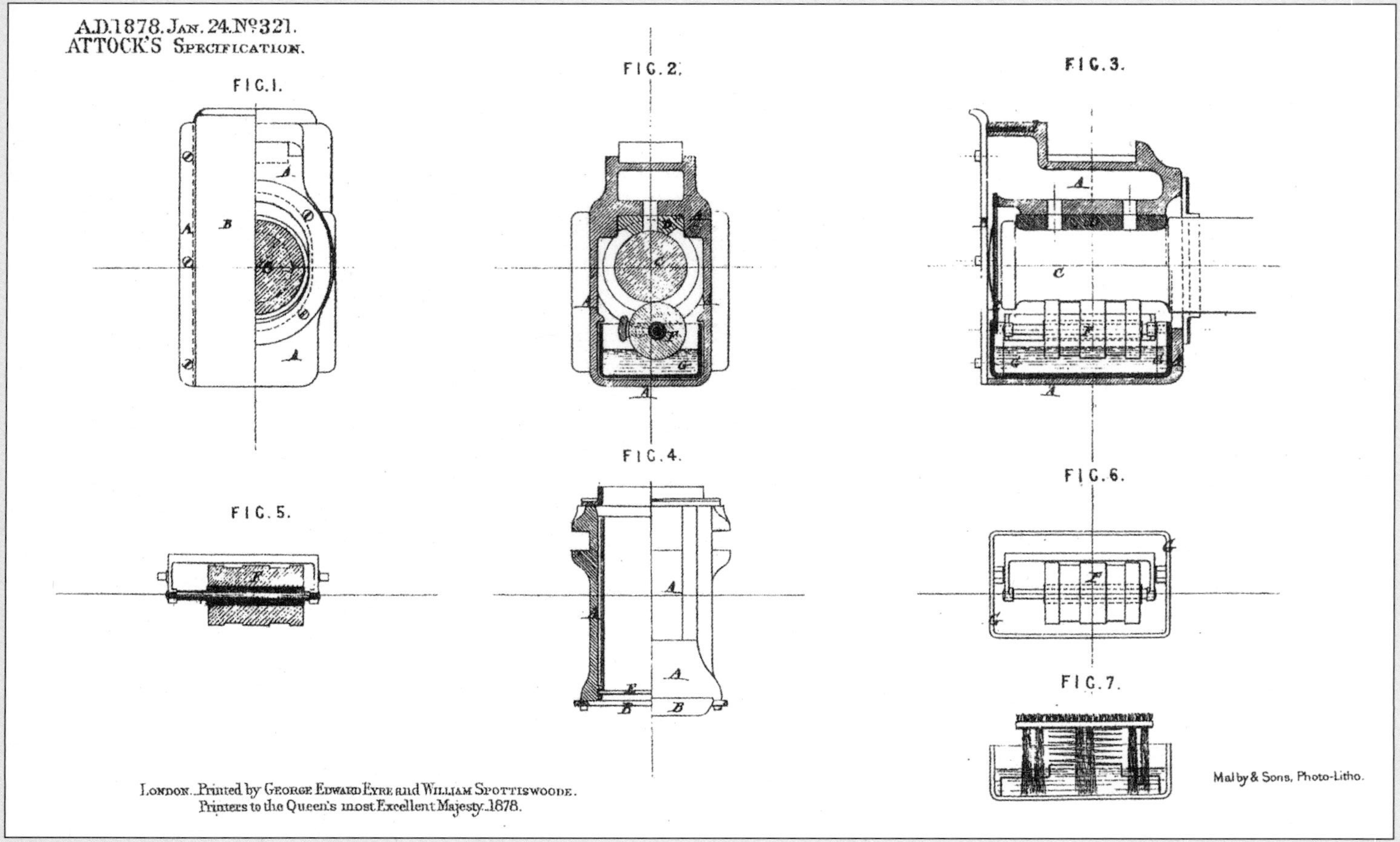

A drawing attached to Frederick Attock's Axlebox Patent of 1878. This was one of a number of patents registered by Frederick while he was with the Lancashire & Yorkshire Railway.
Author's Collection, courtesy British Library

were to receive a beading to distinguish the different classes. A slightly brighter shade of brown was adopted in November 1879 following a recommendation from Mr Hare, chairman of the Rolling Stock Committee.

Aside from rolling stock matters, Frederick found himself closely involved in the final stages of setting up the new works at Newton Heath. This involved the installation of new machinery, the removal and transfer of stores, tools and materials from both the old ELR shops at Bury and the MLR shops at Miles Platting, and the taking down of machinery at Blackburn (some of which was transferred to Newton Heath). Frederick also requested the provision of a small locomotive with a jib crane for use at the new workshops. This matter was referred to Barton Wright for further consideration and approved by the Board on 12th December, 1877 at an estimated cost of £1,200. The foremen at Newton Heath had submitted a memorial, in November, requesting the erection of suitable dwelling houses 'of a rather better kind than those now being erected in the neighbourhood', this matter being referred to Mr Meek to confer with Messrs Attock and Wright and report.

Another concern for Frederick was the lack of suitable storage facilities for timber at the new carriage workshops. At that time a small timber store was provided on the upper floor of a building used for other purposes. He suggested the provision of a separate shed, a plan and estimate for which were duly submitted in February 1878. It would appear that the tenders received were considered to be too costly, and Frederick agreed to the reduction of the size of the building to 200 ft in length. He considered that this would be adequate for the following 12 months, but by then he expected to be in a position to prepare carriage framing for drying, when an extension would be required. At the same time he sought additional woodworking machinery, including sawing, smoothing, planing and jointing machines. Frederick confirmed he had seen the machines he required in use by the LNWR at their Wolverton works, the Board being suitably impressed to order that prices be obtained.

It is clear from studying Frederick's career that he had a keen and inventive mind and he was not afraid to experiment with new ideas and inventions. On 24th January, 1878 patent No. 321 of that year was registered, the first of no less than 10 patents in his name. It was intended as an improvement in axle box design for locomotives and rolling stock. Made in one casting, the Attock patent axle box was entirely open at the front to facilitate access to the axle and the bearing. The front could be closed off either by a sliding shutter or a hinged door. The new design also provided improved facilities for lubrication of the axle with grease. It was widely adopted for use by the L&YR. A further patent of 1892 (Patent No. 2707, 28th May, 1892) brought an improvement in the design, allowing easier removal and replacement of the bearing by keeping the hinged or sliding door open; it included a removable chamber for lubricant in the upper part of the axlebox.

As already stated, all carriages introduced during the Fay era were four-wheeled and Frederick initially followed this policy as he struggled to find his feet. The L&YR traffic manager, William Thorley, submitted a report in January 1878 to the effect that additional carriage stock was required for working new lines. Consultation with the carriage & wagon superintendent followed and it was agreed that 11 first class carriages at £450 each, eight second class at £400 each, and 20 third class at £340 each be provided, in addition to eight passenger brake vans at £330 each. It was agreed that all of the vehicles were to be constructed in the company's workshops at Newton Heath, and Frederick was ordered to submit plans of the new stock to the Rolling Stock Committee. When these were produced at a meeting of the Committee on 10th April it was decided to substitute the firsts and seconds by composites with various compartment layouts. All of the vehicles were to be four-wheeled and it was agreed, on the suggestion of the traffic manager, that six of them should be equipped with the Westinghouse air brake so that they might run on the Midland Railway (MR) line. The Midland Railway had first carried out trials with the Westinghouse air brake in June 1875, but subsequently changed over to the automatic vacuum brake in 1889. A decision on whether or not to fit continuous footboards was deferred pending a report from the Officers; orders were subsequently given on 25th September, 1878 for fitting the same to all new stock and renewals.

Up to 1880 a total of 178 four-wheeled passenger carriages to Fay's designs appeared, viz. 95 composites, 47 second class and 36 first class In addition, no less than 120 four-wheeled passenger brake vans were built between 1875 and 1885. Quite early on Frederick set about persuading the Directors to change over from four-wheeled to six-wheeled carriages. The first six-wheeler was a 29 ft 6 in. first class carriage built in 1878 with four compartments and seating for 24 passengers, but it was not until 1880 that Frederick built six-wheeled stock as standard. His carriages were quite distinctive in appearance, devoid as they were of exterior mouldings apart from a narrow strip running along the sides 3 in. below the tops of the windows. The windows themselves were also distinctive with the upper corners curved and the lower ones square. These same windows were to be found in earlier GER carriages and also in Martin Atock's carriage stock on the MGWR. At one time the author was of opinion that this might have been a design feature peculiar to the Atock/Attock family, but photographic evidence subsequently emerged that showed Ashbury carriages with this feature built for other companies, although the Ashbury vehicles appear to have had curves of a larger radius for the upper corners. The carriage ends were flat with no tumblehome at the bottom and consisted of six vertical panels. In his designs Frederick set the trend for future L&YR carriages, the basic features remaining virtually unaltered until the end of the company's independent existence.

Towards the end of March 1878 Frederick advised the Board that, with the facilities at Bury about to be removed, he wished to have the services of Jonathan B. Mellor as his outdoor assistant, thus allowing him to devote more of his personal time to the workshops. J.B. Mellor resigned in June 1882 and was replaced by James Davies. He also recommended that James Howarth be appointed as his principal foreman in the carriage shop, with Samuel Cooper as assistant. Howarth later rose to become works manager at Newton Heath, a position he retained until his retirement on 28th February, 1902 when he was succeeded by Nigel Gresley. Although it was the company's intention to close the shops at Bury and Southport, Frederick was anxious that they be retained for the lifting and varnishing of carriages; a suggestion, which together with his proposals for staff appointments, received Board approval. A report that he submitted to the Board, in July 1878, listed various matters still outstanding in connection with the new carriage shops. Apart from the new timber shed previously referred to, a paint grinding room and weighbridge were required. In addition, two additional tracks were required, necessitating the widening of Thorp Road bridge, but before approving these alterations the Directors decided to visit and inspect the site.

As with the carriage stock, Frederick brought his own distinctive style to the wagons, amongst which might be mentioned the covered goods wagons, the fruit* or half-box wagons and, probably best known of all his designs, the distinctive goods brake vans, generally referred to as 'Tin Tabs.' Annual rolling stock returns indicate that a total of 11,973 wagons were constructed between 1877 and 1895, and during the same period Frederick was also responsible for recommending the withdrawal of in excess of 6,000 wagons from service. The returns for December 1895 show that 49 per cent of the total stock of 24,423 was 18 years old or less, but annual rate of building had varied a good deal from about 1874 to 1895.

Prior to Frederick's appointment the April 1873 fire at Miles Platting had severely disrupted the building of new wagons, and so the company embarked on purchasing them from various outside contractors, a total of 1,550 coming from various wagon builders in the years 1874 to 1876. However, the Miles Platting fire only explains in part this trend; it was obvious that the Directors, in pursuing their parsimonious approach, had allowed the wagon stock to deteriorate to the extent that much of it was in very poor condition. In addition, the expansion of heavy industry, particularly the cotton and woollen industries as far as the L&YR was concerned, required increased movement of coal and other commodities. Having acquired additional wagons, the Directors appear to have reverted to true form with wagon building dropping back again, reaching a low of 76 new vehicles in 1880.

Among the wagons supplied by outside builders were 175 covered wagons supplied by the Beverley Wagon Co. at £94 10*s.* 6*d.* each, which may have been numbered in the series 7276 to 7450. Reporting on them in December 1877 Frederick commented that his inquiries showed that they had been built in a great hurry, the men working day and night, including Sundays, to complete the order. This resulted in the use of timber that had not been properly dried or seasoned. The inspector who supervised delivery at Goole had apparently not been instructed to inspect them for quality, yet Frederick considered him well qualified for his post. Reporting again in September 1880, Frederick confirmed that all of the Beverley wagons had been put right, and in fact 162 of them were still in service in December 1895.

Another group of vehicles that caused Frederick some concern was the private owner wagons, of which there were a large number in use all over the system. He discovered in September 1877 that they had not been subject to

* It is not entirely clear where the term 'Fruit Wagon' came from but one theory is that it was a corruption of 'Freight Wagon'. A reference is made in May 1883 to their conversion for the carriage of potatoes; this required an increase in depth from 1 ft 8 in. to 2 ft 4 in. at a cost of £4 each, this being approved by the Board.

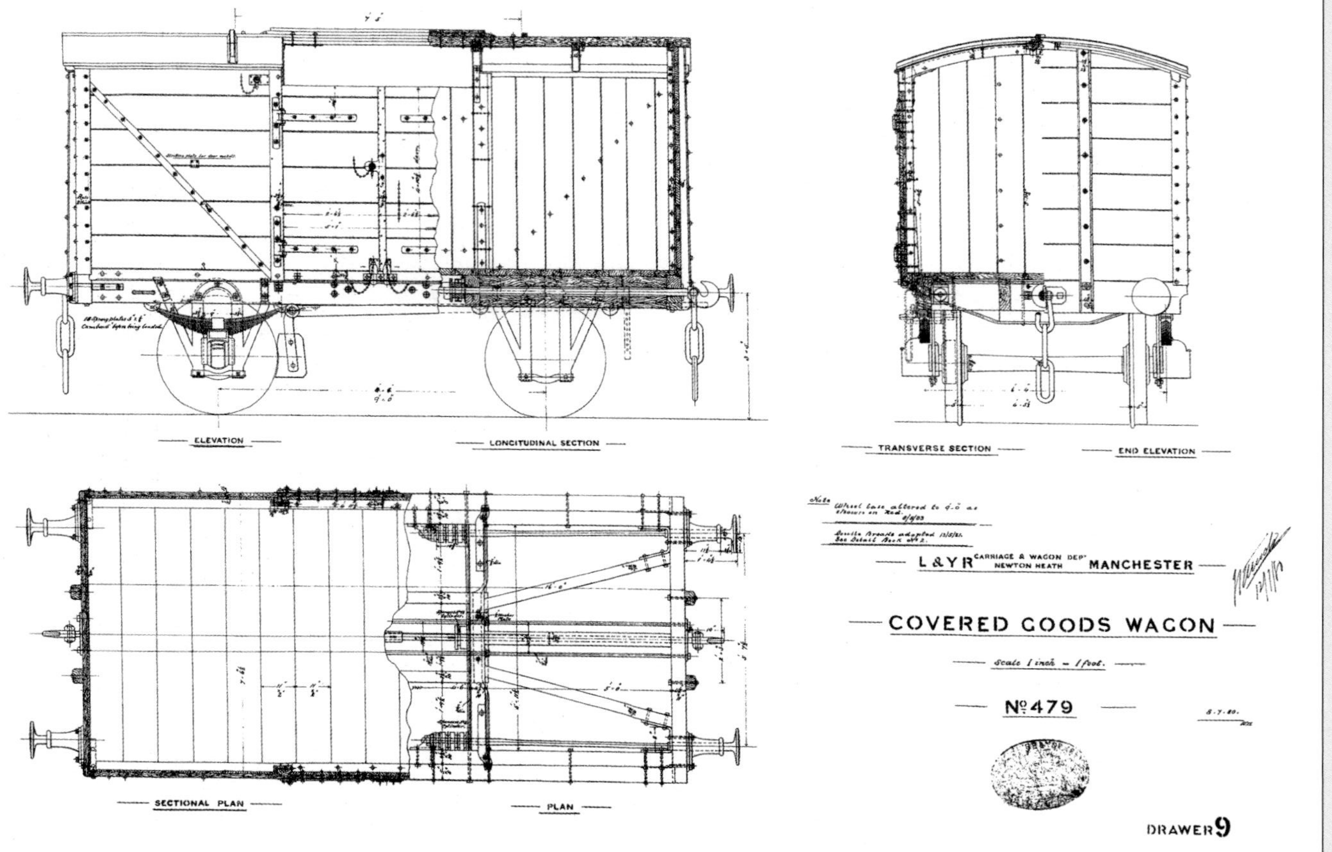

Diagram No. 479 representing a Lancashire & Yorkshire Railway open centre goods wagon to Frederick Attock's design. His signature appears on the right-hand side with the date 8th July, 1880. *B. Weller Collection, courtesy of his Executors and L&YR Society*

periodical examination and he confirmed that he was instituting such a check. Apparently those that were checked had a plate put on the sole bars, but this had proved unsatisfactory when new sole bars were fitted as the plates were not re-affixed and the wagon was once again unplated. The whole situation was so unsatisfactory that, in April 1878, Frederick employed six men specially for the task and by August they had examined some 25,000 wagons. By May 1879 he was able to report that a total of 37,475 private owner wagons had been inspected; of these 1,701 required breaking up while 5,411 had not been plated as they did not conform to L&YR standards. A further 10,810 were at slight variance with the company's requirements, 9,195 required slight alterations, 10,358 fully complied, and all of them had been plated. At that stage it was clear that virtually all private owner wagons running on the L&YR had been inspected.

Considering the condition of the stock that Frederick had inherited, it was inevitable that repair costs would increase, and the Directors turned their attention to this matter, but Frederick was able to easily explain the increase of some £8,000 over the previous year. Following the derailment of a carriage at St Anne's on 3rd July, 1878, caused by a defective Mansell wheel (the second such incident in a short space of time), orders had been given that all carriages coming in for repairs were to have new wheels with Messrs Kitson's patent boss fitted. These cost 10*s*. 6*d*. per wheel, a not inconsiderable sum when applied to several hundred carriages, and those vehicles already modified accounted for £6,915 19*s*. 0*d*. of the £8,000 increase, a fact which quickly silenced any further complaints as regards the cost of repairs! It was, however, decided to re-use the old wheels, with new axles, on wagons coming in for repair.

Frederick constantly encountered problems with the numbers of workmen available for various duties, either too many or too few depending on the whims of the Directors at any particular time. To be fair, what was referred to as 'excursion stock', consisting of a large number of older coaching vehicles, also sometimes referred to as 'trip coaches', lay unused for lengthy periods of the year and was then required at short notice for several months from Easter onwards. These carriages, which had been removed from main line duties, suffered from lying outdoors in sidings and required urgent repairs and re-painting before being put back into use. As an example, in November 1878 Frederick confirmed that he had 1,075 carriages in use on 'ordinary trains' with an additional 350 required for the summer services. There were 192 carriages lying in sidings and 349 awaiting repairs, giving a total of 1,966. Despite this, by the end of November he confirmed that he had given notice to 189 men in the wagon department and no less than 356 in the carriage department; this followed confirmation from the Directors only a month earlier that he might engage up to 70 additional men to carry out outstanding work.

Reports reached the Board, early in December 1878, that coach makers and several other classes of workmen had gone on strike on 28th November. This followed the imposition of a reduction in their wages of 1*s*. 6*d*. per week. Frederick was informed that he could take back any of the men who agreed to accept the reduction, but by early January, with no improvement in prospect, advertisements were placed in various newspapers seeking coach makers. A deputation of the men met with the carriage & wagon superintendent on 12th February and agreed to return to work at the reduced wages. Despite this disruption to work, one of the Directors suggested a five-day working week, this being brought into operation after the Easter weekend. This situation could not continue for long, and we find Frederick seeking a return to full time working after the busy Whit week. In September 1879 the Directors once again sought further reductions in wages and expenses, Frederick reluctantly agreeing to let 200 men go. In the meantime he was ordered to report on a recommendation that the working week be extended to 57 hours. Having dispensed with the 200 men in September, authority was given in January 1880 to take on 50 additional hands to deal with an accumulation of heavy carriage repairs; Frederick must have been a very patient man to cope with such vacillation!

Under pressure, in March 1879, to have additional carriages available for race traffic at Aintree and the usual increase in traffic over the Easter week, Frederick informed the Directors that he had 405 carriages either under or awaiting repair compared with 282 at the same time in 1878. To put between 80 and 100 additional carriages back into traffic, even on a temporary basis, he required an additional 100 men. Reluctantly the Directors agreed that he should engage the additional men and put the men in the carriage shops on full time *pro tem*. At the same time orders had been given to build 18 new first class carriages; the old first class carriages that they replaced, which were regarded as too small for modern requirements, were to be rebuilt as thirds. Likewise, nine composites were to be converted to third class and replaced by new composite carriages. Of the 262 excursion vehicles, 253 had light drawbars and couplings that required replacement, whilst 100 required repairs and re-painting. One can but sympathise with Frederick as he struggled to turn out new and repaired vehicles against the backdrop of constantly striving to reduce expenses. This rather lengthy description of labour problems is given to better acquaint the reader as to how so many complaints were being directed at the company by the late 1870s.

Whilst on the subject of the workforce, another matter had been reported in 1879 when six men working as trimmers were convicted of stealing Morocco skins from the carriage shop. Reporting on the incident following their conviction, Frederick pointed out that the bulk of the material had been pilfered at the time of the removal from Miles Platting to Newton Heath. This period offered anyone so interested an ideal opportunity for such activity as the stores had not been completed at the new location. Again, due to the varied sizes of material cut up and its varying quality, it would have been quite easy for a clever cutter to save one skin out of a quantity without being detected. To guard against this for the future, Frederick proposed to weigh out the skins and to re-weigh them with the scrap when finished. The heaviest sentence handed down was 15 months' hard labour followed by three years' police supervision. There is little doubt that low wages and uncertainty of continuous employment must have been contributing factors in the pilferage by employees.

Chapter Eleven

Tragedy and Change

On 26th June, 1878 Frederick Attock applied for a fortnight's leave 'in order to restore his health', this being granted. It is not clear what the exact problem was at that time, but we do know that his wife, Ellen Elizabeth, passed away at Somerset House in the following year on 13th July, at the young age of 34. Perhaps her health may have been, in part, the reason for needing to get away from the job. The cause of death was shown as heart failure and, rather interestingly, the informant was her brother-in-law, Edward Stevens, who was present at the time. There is nothing in the L&YR Board minutes to suggest that Frederick was away from work at that particular time and, in fact, several of his reports were submitted to the Board towards the end of July. It will be recalled that in Chapter Two we recorded the marriage of Frederick's sister, Phoebe Ann, to William Strutt at Leyton Parish Church on 15th September, 1879, and that one of the witnesses was her mother, Hephzibah. With the last of her children married, there was no reason for Hephzibah to remain in East London, so it was probably at that time that she moved in with Frederick to help with the rearing of his four young children.

Frederick requested that certain alterations be made to Somerset House in August 1879, perhaps in anticipation of the arrival of his mother from Stratford; he offered to pay an additional rent equivalent to 5 per cent of the total outlay. Repairs costing about £370 were carried out in the following month, when the additional rent was fixed at £15 per annum. An interesting aside in relation to Somerset House arose in March 1880 when a contractor, John Faulkner, submitted an account for £50 15*s.* 0*d.* in respect of the fitting of a lightning conductor to the building. When the Secretary sought to find who had requested the work he was unable to do so, the upshot being the arrangement of a special meeting to which Faulkner and various officers, including Frederick Attock, were summoned. This meeting also drew a blank and the matter was closed when Faulkner agreed to accept £35 in settlement of his account.

Following the Newark trials, referred to in Chapter Six, in 1875 the L&YR gave consideration to installing some form of continuous braking system. Trials commenced during the summer of 1878 with two trains, one equipped with Smith's non-automatic vacuum brake and one with the Westinghouse air brake. Trial trains were run between Manchester and Bacup and between Wakefield and Goole, and on 9th October, 1878 Messrs Wright and Attock were ordered to furnish a joint report on the trials, these being further considered at a Board meeting on 6th November. Wright, the locomotive superintendent, was requested to report additionally on Webb's (LNWR) brake and also on the company's own improved brake, and in the previous chapter we have already noted the fitting-up of six carriages in 1878 with the Westinghouse brake so that they would be able to run on the MR. It would appear that no definite decision was taken at that time as Frederick reported in February 1879 that he was fitting new carriages with Fay & Newall's Combined Break [*sic*] with a simpler and more effectual rigging system which was, co-incidentally, also cheaper than the earlier rigging system.

Correspondence was received in April 1879 from an American gentleman, Frederick W. Eames, asking to be allowed to fit up two trains with his new brake at his own expense, this being acceded to by the Board. A train of nine carriages and a van were equipped with this particular design of automatic vacuum brake in February 1880, entering service on the Manchester-Skipton line; a second train commenced running between Manchester and Middleton in April. Mr Eames was quite a colourful individual and further details of him and his brake are outlined in *Appendix Seven*. About the same time a third set of carriages was fitted with Messrs Sanders & Bolitho's automatic brake and was tried out on the Manchester to Bury line. This particular brake had first been used on the GWR in 1876.

The year 1880 was a busy one for the L&YR as far as brakes were concerned as, apart from the foregoing, a further set of carriages had been equipped with a new automatic brake supplied by the Vacuum Brake Co. Braking trials were conducted at Gisburn on the company's Blackburn to Hellifield line on 15th & 16th July, 1880, the trials being supervised by Railway Inspecting Officer Capt. Douglas Galton, who in due course received a sum of £100 for his attendance. Following the trials, and before a final decision was made as to which system should be adopted, Mr Hare, one of the Directors and Chairman of the Rolling Stock Committee, suggested, in September 1880, that the Bradford Express should be fitted with the Westinghouse brake for experimental purposes, this being approved. Ahrons states that the Bradford Express was a market train (initially first class only) which ran both ways between Manchester and Bradford on Mondays and Thursdays during the 1870/80s. A similar train started from Bradford on Tuesdays and Fridays. The term Express was hardly appropriate as average speed was less than 30 mph. Co-incidental with the brake experiment, an agreement was entered into whereby the Westinghouse Continuous Brake Co. was also to equip the train with its new system of gas lighting for a trial period of six months, a decision that was to lead to delays in putting the train into service. Frederick reported in due course that the first trial trip was to take place on Thursday 16th December from Manchester Victoria to Blackpool. It appears that the lighting system proved to be rather less than ideal and the Westinghouse Brake Co. wrote on 28th June, 1881 suggesting its removal from the carriages on the grounds of cost, as it feared that difficulties with it might reflect badly on all its equipment including the braking system.

Mr Hare, Chairman of the Rolling Stock Committee, travelled to London in March 1881 for a meeting at LNWR headquarters, Euston, to discuss the whole question of train brakes; by now the railway companies had realised that some commonality had to be introduced. The three principal parties present, the LNWR, GWR and the LSWR, all expressed their aversion to the Westinghouse brake and their preference for the vacuum brake. Under the circumstances, Hare returned to Manchester expressing the opinion that it would be inexpedient to equip any more carriages with the former system, although it was agreed that some engines in course of delivery from Messrs Sharp, Stewart & Co. should be so fitted to work the Bradford and Blackburn expresses and the Hellifield service in conjunction with the MR; the remainder of the engines were to be fitted with Smith's Automatic Vacuum Brake. In addition, Frederick was ordered to put the Smith's Brake on 100 carriages in course of construction on the Renewal Account. Later, in June 1883, the decision was taken to simply pipe non-passenger coaching stock such as horseboxes and carriage trucks (i.e. fit through pipes only but not brake equipment on the vehicle).

As early as July 1872 the second class carriages were being lined with ribbed cloth, although this was viewed to be rather extravagant by Thomas Fielden who suggested, on 15th January, 1879, that the linings should in future 'come underneath the hats of passengers of average height'. Thomas Fielden (b.1816) took over the family business in 1845 with his younger brother John, and invested heavily in new spinning and weaving machines. He was one of three members of the Fielden family of Stansfield Hall, Todmorden who served as L&YR Directors. Although they were Quakers they were a constant thorn in the flesh to successive L&YR Chairmen, frequently objecting to capital expenditure. A small textile business was started near Todmorden by Joshua Fielden in the late 18th century and by 1832 it had grown to be one of the largest textile companies in Britain. Thomas's son, Edward Brocklehurst Fielden served as MP for Manchester Exchange and later became Deputy-Chairman of the LMS. The firm of Fielden Bros finally ceased trading in 1966. On the other hand, Samuel Fielden's widow was a generous lady who provided funds for the extension of the mechanics' institute building at Horwich, publicly opened on 27th July, 1893.

A fortnight later the Board decided that the current practice should be continued, Fielden requesting, 'that his protest should be entered against this matter being dealt with by a Committee at which only seven Directors were present'. It appears that Fielden himself was absent from that meeting! As a further economy measure, the Stores Department was requested, in May 1879, to seek tenders for the provision of millboard instead of mahogany for the inside roofing of carriages. Even this product must have been considered too expensive as Frederick sought instructions, on 30th July, for the use of stamped paper instead. This material was approved and he was ordered to adopt it for new carriages.

Although it was decided, in January 1880, to fit cushions to all new and renewed third class carriages, excursion stock remained with bare wooden seats. Frederick enquired, on 3rd November, 1880, as to whether he should also cushion the excursion carriages, and it was agreed, on 14th December, that only the best of those vehicles should be lined and trimmed similar to the new thirds. In fairness to the company, and as Marshall points out (*see Bibliography*), third class compartments suffered rough usage by the thousands of mill and factory workers; this was to lead to the use of material woven from horsehair. Reference was first made to this product, on 22nd February, 1881, when it was ordered that horsehair carpets be used in future in second class carriages; hair seating was mentioned on 24th January of the following year when it was decided to fit first class smoking compartments with crimson damask, second class seating to be grey and black. Even the height of the lining above the cushions was considered in May 1884. A survey of other companies' carriages showed the L&YR as having the lowest lined backs at 1 ft 8 in. above the cushions, the best being the Manchester, Sheffield & Lincolnshire Railway (MS&LR) at 2 ft 9 in. The Directors compromised and agreed that in the future all third class carriages should have the seat backs lined up to 2 ft 4½ in. at an additional cost of 20*s*. per compartment.

The application of Utrecht velvet was mentioned in November 1879 but its use was not sanctioned. This material was again referred to in May 1883 after one carriage had been experimentally so fitted for the Bradford Express but, as the cost of fitting up one first class compartment worked out at £8 1*s*. 9*d*. compared to £4 5*s*. 3*d*. for blue cloth then in use, it was decided not to proceed with any further carriages. Blue cloth had been approved for the lining of smoking compartments in June 1881, at which time it was also agreed to fit spring blinds to all new carriages, except third class ones; the latter carriages were finally provided with blinds in July 1884. Frederick again referred to Utrecht velvet in September 1888, but once again its use was not sanctioned on the grounds of cost.

Quite possibly as the result of the various ongoing difficulties, and still not recovered from the tragic loss of his wife, Frederick had sought permission, in February 1880, to be allowed to lodge out of town on two or three nights a week for the benefit of his health. This was agreed to for a period of three months, after which he was to raise the subject again; there is no indication in the Minutes that it was ever raised again. In fact, at the time of the 1881 census the family was shown as residing at Somerset House, but it is interesting to note that Frederick's daughters, Ellen May and Mary Grace, although aged only 11 and 9 respectively, were not at home on that night.

In March 1880 the Traffic Department advised that 64 additional coaching vehicles would be required for the working of new lines comprising 28 composites, 24 thirds and 12 passenger vans. Approval was given for them to be constructed at Newton Heath, but the question was raised as to whether the composites should be four- or six-wheeled. Frederick suggested that if they were six-wheeled vehicles, then an additional compartment could be included in the composite carriages; he and Wright were requested to report their views as complaints had been made as to alleged uneasy running of carriages. Meanwhile Mr Thorley, the traffic manager, was instructed to decide as to the provision of compartments for the various classes. Mr Hare suggested that the brake vans should be made the same width as the carriages so that trains might be more uniform in appearance. Messrs Wright and Attock having submitted their reports, it was decided that carriage wheelbase should not exceed 20 ft; if the additional compartment could not be accommodated within that wheelbase then it was to be omitted.

At about the same time, the traffic manager stated that he proposed to adopt the suggestion of providing Ladies' compartments at Manchester and Liverpool by the simple expedient of labelling compartments when applied for. He reverted to the Board again in September seeking authority for the provision of additional carriages required, in part due to the opening of new lines, but also due to the increase in the number of third class travellers. Although many complaints were being received in regard to the poor quality accommodation, larger numbers of passengers than ever were travelling. It was therefore ordered that 100 additional third class carriages and 10 brake vans be built at Newton Heath.

Frederick had several carriages painted up in June 1880 for inspection, resulting from which a train of third class carriages was painted with the upper panels dark brown. A year later, on 14th June, 1881, it was agreed that the lower panels of all carriages should be painted in lake colour. This livery of umber brown and lake was to be the standard L&YR livery for the remaining 40 years of the company's existence. The body ends were dark brown with a lighter brown stripe all round; roofs were dark grey, officially referred to as white - probably white lead which turned grey when in use. Door and window frames were red, all lettering and numbering being gold with black, vermilion and white lines round, but devoid of shading. A black stripe with a thin white line ran across the bottom of the windows and along the length of the carriage. Non-passenger coaching stock was painted purple-brown all over.

Marshall* refers to a complaint made to the Board in November 1862 regarding some of Fay's carriages being too wide for use on the Manchester-Bolton line, with reports of lamp irons being knocked off vehicles by passing trains in Farnworth tunnel. Farnworth tunnel was situated on the Pendleton to Blackpool line between Kearsley and Bolton; another tunnel complained of was Spring Vale on the Ribble Valley line (Bolton to Hellifield) between Entwistle and Darwen. At the time Fay had reported that certain wider than normal branch line carriages had inadvertently been used on the Bolton line. Similar complaints were made in January 1880, Frederick reporting that no alterations had been made in the position of lamps on carriages nor could any of his staff recollect any alterations having been made during the previous 15 years. A suggestion was made by one of the Directors that lamps should be placed at a different height on one side of carriages. As Frederick delicately pointed out, however, this was an impractical suggestion as carriages were frequently turned.

The men in the wagon department applied for a trip at reduced fares in August 1880. Around that time it was quite a common feature for railway companies to grant their servants an annual outing, usually restricting it to places on the respective company's own system. In response to the request the Secretary explained that prior to the year 1873 the Directors had granted a cheap trip to the men at reduced fares, but that the privilege had been abused, and in consequence it had been withdrawn. After some discussion it was decided to decline the application on the grounds that the concession was liable to abuse.

Although oil had been used for carriage lighting in the early days, Marshall states that James Newall had, in 1860, invented a system of gas lighting supplied from a flexible gas container in the guard's van with iron tubing along the carriage roofs and flexible connections between the carriages. When, in late 1880, Frederick recommended the renewal of the entire carriage stock in use on the Liverpool-Southport line (with the exception of the Express trains) he made reference to the replacement of 11 gas vans. However, he went on to say that these could be converted into thirds and 11 brake vans built in lieu. The Board were obviously satisfied with the compressed gas system, and, on 23rd August, ordered that the new Southport line carriages be so equipped. In September 1881 Frederick suggested that some trains using Victoria station should also be lit by compressed gas and it was agreed that the necessary apparatus be provided.

* *The Lancashire & Yorkshire Railway*, Vol. 3, p.102, John Marshall, David & Charles, Devon.

Messrs Pope's gas system was first mentioned in November 1881 when it was agreed to fit out one of the new trains in course of construction for the Southport service and it was not long before this apparatus was in widespread use on the company's trains. A further step forward in lighting came in January 1882 when it was ordered that all compartments in third class carriages were to be provided with lamps; prior to that third class passengers travelled in the dark at night. Complaints were made from time to time as to the quality of Pope's lighting, George Armytage, the Deputy Chairman, pointing out twice in 1886 that the lights on the Yorkshire trains were not satisfactory. Ramsbottom, a Director, put this down to 'the admission of air with the gas which, however, will remedy itself in a short time'. By the end of 1886 about 500 carriages had been equipped with Pope's apparatus, Frederick confirming that a further 500 would be completed by the end of February 1887; by then a total of 327 carriages would still be lit by oil lamps.

Mr Hare reported, in November 1881, on a recent visit he had made to London where he had inspected not only Pope's system, but also gas lighting by Messrs Pintsch and also a system of electric lighting being offered by a French Company, La Force et la Lumière, who offered to fit up two trains at their own expense. The Secretary was instructed to enquire if they would equip four trains for a fair comparison with the gas lighting but, as there is no further reference to a trial of electric lighting, it is assumed that it was not proceeded with. Another firm, the Brush Midland Electric Light & Power Co., offered an electric lighting system in July 1884 but once again nothing transpired. Electric lighting of carriages was, however, finally introduced in 1901.

An interesting item was raised at the Board meeting held on 8th March, 1881, namely an order to Frederick to prepare and submit, as early as possible, drawings of a train for the Southport line on the American principle. Frederick got to work quickly and his report with a design of the proposed carriages was submitted on 22nd March. A report was also read from Messrs Mulook & Davis giving their observations regarding American railway carriages. It was ordered that the traffic manager obtain particulars from the Midland Railway of the train built by them and also to enquire whether that company would be disposed to lend their Pullman cars to the L&YR for a trial. There is no evidence to suggest this was ever done.*

John William Grover approached the company in May 1881 with a proposal to the effect that if the L&YR was prepared to construct a train of 10 carriages based on his patent flexible wheelbase system then he would only seek a nominal royalty of £50. If the company subsequently decided to adopt the system he would charge a royalty of £15 per vehicle. Grover was politely informed that the company was quite unprepared to consider his proposal

* Following an extensive tour of North America in 1872, James Allport, the General Manager of the MR, was apparently very impressed with the Pullman cars in use and it was decided that George Pullman should provide, at his own expense, a number of carriages built to the British loading gauge. The first of these, a sleeping car, was assembled at Derby in January 1874. A Pullman special ran from Derby to St Pancras on 17th March, 1874 carrying the MR Directors and officers, and a Pullman car express began operating between St Pancras and Bradford on 1st June.

unless he made a considerable reduction in the royalty charges. Frederick advised the Rolling Stock Committee in June that whilst Grover's system had been considerably improved he was still seeking too high a royalty. Grover approached the Board again saying he would like to try out the system on one of the Liverpool to Southport trains, a decision being deferred at the time.

However, Grover was informed in July that the company would have no objection to him trying out his system provided he would allow a train of seven carriages to be fitted free of cost. If the company subsequently agreed to adopt his patent, then they proposed to pay a sum of £1 per carriage. It is not entirely clear what was agreed, but a Rolling Stock Committee minute of 29th May, 1883 ordered Frederick to report his recommendations on the five out of the seven carriages not yet built on Grover's system. In his report dated 8th June Frederick stated that the two carriages 'now built' were too long for Grover's purposes and suggesting that they be fitted with bogies. He then went on to say that three composites should be built 36 ft long and four others (presumably also composites) at 32 ft on the principle of Grover's flexible wheelbase. It was ordered that the carriages be built as suggested.* In the meantime, James Cleminson had written seeking permission to try out his flexible wheelbase, this being declined.

Early in 1882 Frederick converted one of the company's carriages into an invalid carriage but when the Directors made an inspection of it in March it was considered to be 'unnecessarily elaborate'. He was then instructed to convert another carriage into an invalid carriage 'somewhat similar to the old one, but to have such alterations as were suggested on the spot'. About the same time Frederick submitted a tracing of a new saloon built by the MR, this being intended for the use of the Directors. He was duly instructed to fit up, roughly, the body of a saloon for the Directors' inspection, once again in accordance with suggestions made. One wonders whether they deemed the design of their saloon was 'unnecessarily elaborate'. It is not clear, however, whether a purpose-built Directors' saloon was actually put into service at that time.

A labour problem of a quite different kind confronted Frederick when it was reported that an employee in the carriage shop, a Mr J.G. Woodhouse, had been struck on the head by a piece of wood from a circular saw on 27th June, 1882 and fatally injured. An inquest was held and the jury returned a verdict of accidental death; they did, however, recommend that the company should take steps to prevent such accidents in future by having the saw repaired. Frederick, however, pointed out that he had carefully examined the saw in question but did not consider it required any alteration. Nevertheless, the saw was removed as it was and retained pending the outcome of a compensation claim made by Woodhouse's widow. A piece of better news for Frederick in 1882 was his election as an Associate Member of the Institution of Civil Engineers, his sponsors including William Adams, S.W. Johnson, J.C. Park (North London Railway) and W. Barton Wright. He became a full member of the Institution in 1890.

* The term 'bogie' which was sometimes applied to Grover's six-wheel system - the 'Grover bogie'- has in the past been confused with normal carriage bogies, resulting in short vehicles being shown as 12-wheelers. This is incorrect; the Grover bogie was akin to the Cleminson system, i.e. a steerable six-wheel underframe.

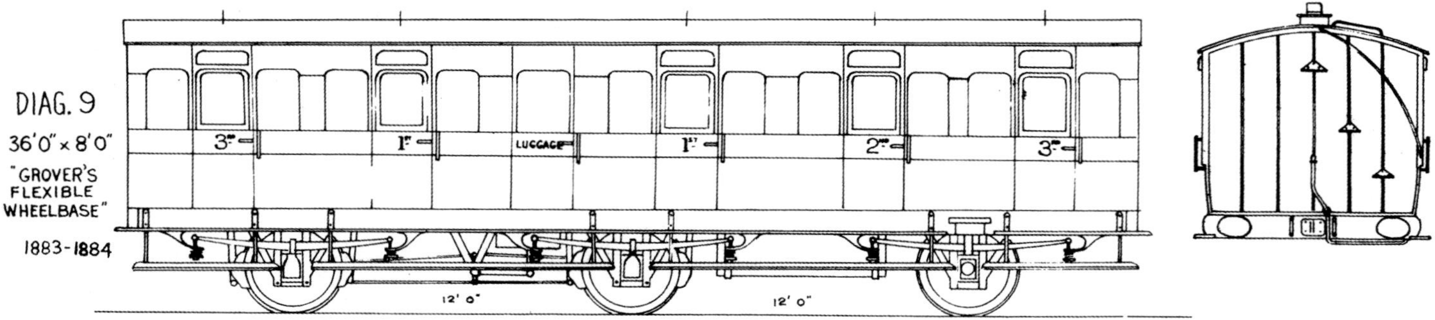

Six-wheeled 36 ft luggage tri-composite, three of which were built in 1883 and three in 1884; the former batch had no luggage compartment and were 35 ft long. Running numbers unknown. Equipped with Grover's Patent flexible wheelbase. *R.W. Rush*

An unusual livery was suggested by Messrs Ashbury & Co. in March 1883 for use on carriages passing through the 713 yds-long Heaton Park tunnel on the Manchester to Bury line, namely luminous paint. Frederick was not in favour of this, on the grounds that it would take a minute or two before the paint would give any illumination, by which time the train would be out of the tunnel. Also, early in 1883, a Mr Kneale offered to supply his patent heating apparatus for carriages but it was decided not to adopt his system and incur the expense of the patent. Frederick carried out heating experiments with eight carriages in the autumn of 1884, further consideration of the matter being postponed *sine die*. In December 1885 one of the Directors, Mr Fielden, called the attention of his fellow Directors to the unsatisfactory state of footwarmers in use on the Bradford train; apart from drawing Frederick's attention to the matter nothing further was done at that time.

In the previous chapter it was noted that reasonable dividends were being paid to the shareholders in the late 1870s, but a study of day-to-day operations gives a rather different picture of what O.S. Nock in his History has described as 'a squalor and decrepitude in equipment that was only matched by the chaos and ineptitude of the traffic working'. For a true insight into the affairs of the L&YR in the 1870s and early 1880s we must turn to the celebrated railway historian, Ernest Leopold Ahrons, who, with his acute eye for detail and a delightful sense of humour, beautifully encapsulated the L&YR of the period, describing it as 'probably the most degenerate railway in the kingdom' in the mid-1870s. He went on to state that the L&YR of 1876 'was a railway of ugly inconvenient stations, of old broken-down engines and dirty carriages, and of a superlative unpunctuality to which no pen could do justice'. Commenting on the works at Miles Platting, which dated from the early days of the M&LR, he stated that they were overcrowded inside and outside with no room for extensions.

So bad had the problems become that the shareholders considered the matter at their half-yearly meeting in February 1883, a decision being taken to elect a new Chairman who would also fill the new post of chief executive. John Pearson, a colliery owner, was duly elected at the next meeting in July and he quickly set about making changes; George Armytage was elected Deputy-Chairman. At the July meeting of shareholders Pearson had this to say:

> No doubt, gentlemen, mistakes have been made and opportunities of developing the line have been allowed to go by, but we must bear in mind that some at any rate of those errors in judgment have arisen from an over desire to consult the wishes of the shareholders. For instance, it would have been better if, instead of paying the good dividend of former years, a portion had been retained for the renewal of rolling stock and stations, and in making proper arrangements for facilitating the conduct of the traffic.

One of the early changes made was the appointment, for 12 months from 18th October, 1883, of John Ramsbottom on a consultancy basis to assist Barton Wright. Ramsbottom, who had been responsible for much of the development of the Crewe works of the LNWR, retired from that company on grounds of ill-health in 1871; retirement had allowed him to recover his health and he relished the idea of working with Barton Wright. The two men appear to have got on

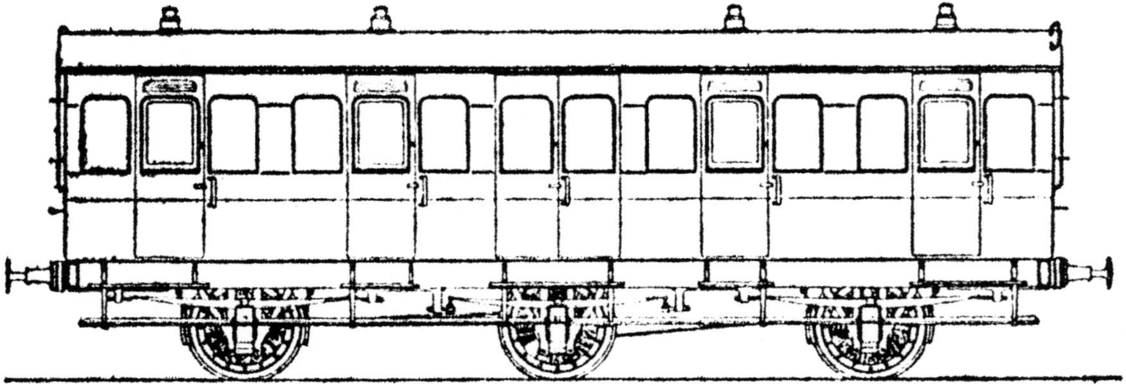

L&YR carriage drawing of a typical six-wheeler to Frederick Attock's design. Note windows which have rounded upper corners and square lower corners, a feature also found on Martin Atock's carriages on the MGWR. This feature may, however, predate the family designs and have originated with Messrs Ashbury. *Ian Allan Ltd*

very well. He also appears to have had a good working relationship with Frederick Attock. Pearson's thinking was that the Board would still stall when it came to making serious decisions on capital investment. Ramsbottom quickly undertook a tour of inspection of all the locomotive facilities along with Barton Wright; the upshot of this visit was the purchase, at auction, in May 1884, of a 650 acre estate at Horwich, some five miles west of Bolton, and the establishment on a green-field site of a completely new locomotive workshop. A good portion of the estate was later sold for development, in effect meaning that the setting-up of the works there cost the L&YR virtually nothing. The state of the wagon shops at Miles Platting was the subject of some discussion at a Board meeting, on 9th October, 1883, when Frederick informed them that the works could be put into, what he referred to as, 'a trustworthy condition' for a sum of about £320 by utilising good sound second-hand timber. Frederick was instructed to proceed, not spending any more than his estimate.

A proposal was put forward, on 26th September, 1883, for the joint operation by the L&YR and the LNWR of traffic between Liverpool and Scotland. This necessitated the provision of the Farington Curve to enable direct running between Liverpool and Preston. The extension, 1 m. 9½ c. in length, was authorized by a L&YR Act of 16th July, 1885 and was opened for traffic on 1st July, 1891. At a Board meeting on 20th November, 1883 Mr Hare stated that the Traffic Department would require carriages equipped with lavatory accommodation for the joint service between Manchester and Glasgow 'in order to compete with other companies'. This may seem a strange reason for providing such facilities on a train that was scheduled to cover a distance in excess of 200 miles, but is an indication of the advances made in respect of on-train passenger amenities by other railways compared to the L&YR. In 1884 the LNWR requested that two through carriages and a spare vehicle be equipped with both vacuum and Westinghouse air braking systems for the Scottish traffic, Frederick being ordered to obtain the necessary materials from the Vacuum Brake Co. and proceed with the work. A month later he confirmed that the latter company had agreed to supply Westinghouse brake fittings at £6 per set, these being duly ordered.

Frederick communicated with the Board again on 9th September, 1884 when he enquired whether it was intended to build any more saloons for the Scottish traffic. It was decided that the Directors should inspect the new saloons, then in course of construction, when they were ready and make a decision at that time. Tracings of the new composite carriages for the Scottish traffic were only submitted to the Board in December for consideration and approval, and presumably lavatory accommodation was included.

Frederick Attock's signature on a L&YR drawing.

B. Weller Collection, courtesy of his Executors and L&YR Society

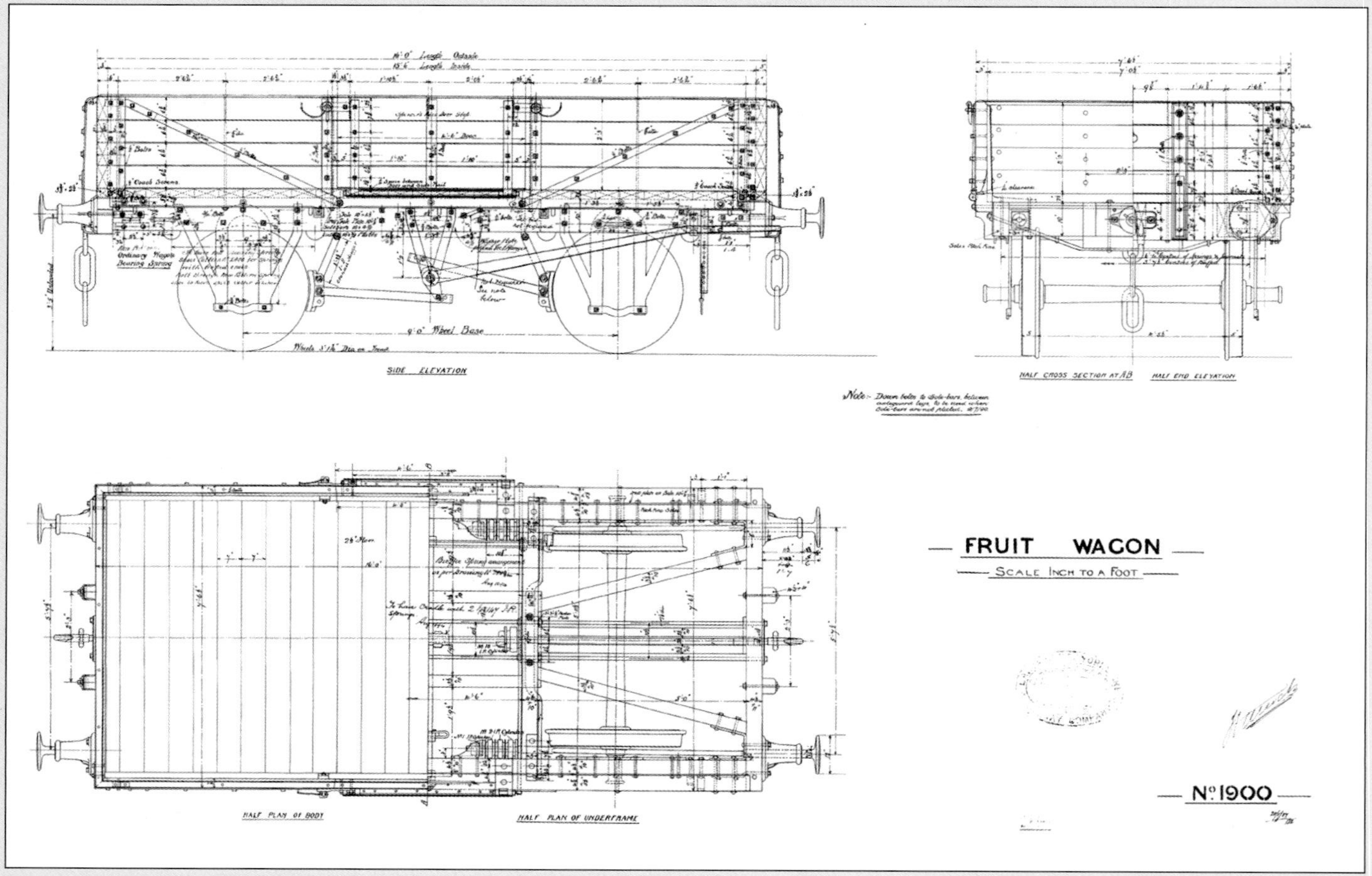

Drawing of a Lancashire & Yorkshire Railway four-plank open wagon, generally referred to as fruit wagons by the L&YR. The origin of the term is unknown, but it has been suggested that it may be a Lancashire corruption for freight wagon. *B. Weller Collection, courtesy of his Executors and L&YR Society*

Chapter Twelve

The Family Rift is Healed

The tradition of a rift in the family was first mentioned in Chapter Two in the context of Martin Atock's decision, in October 1861, to leave Stratford and move to Ireland, and at the same time adopt the ancestral spelling of his surname. That a rift occurred there can be no doubt, but the exact cause remains a mystery. The story that has been handed down is that some sort of disagreement occurred between Frederick and his older brother George. Frederick had joined the ECR as an apprentice on his 14th birthday in February 1860, and, as the youngest son, his mother probably favoured him, especially as he was born following the infant deaths of two previous sons in Liverpool. He may have been too young to become seriously involved in whatever disagreement there was, but his mother might have taken his side. Perhaps Hephzibah also disapproved of Martin's wife or a prospective wife-to-be for George. In any case, by April 1861 George was living at Brighton and had adopted the Atock surname. He never married and does not appear to have had any further contact with the family, apart from going to live with his married sister, Elizabeth, for at least the last four years of his life.

Frederick's brother George died on 14th January, 1885 at just 47 years of age, and his early death would have come as quite a shock to both Hephzibah and Frederick. There may have been a feeling of remorse in the household over the fact that it was then too late to do anything about healing the rift with George himself, but perhaps his death was the catalyst for a family reconciliation. That all was not well at Somerset House became evident just six months later when Frederick requested permission to reside away from the works for a period of three months. There is no record of the particular reason for this request, but we do know that Hephzibah was living at Pleasant View, South Shore, Blackpool, at the time of her death, a few months later, on 15th February, 1886. Blackpool was some 51 miles distant by rail from Manchester, and becomes all the more significant in our story when we consider what we have already noted in Chapter Eight about Martin's son, George, and Frederick's son, George Henry, being together at Arnold College, Blackpool, in the 1885-87 period. A personal letter giving some family history details concludes with the following comment 'Tom (Martin Atock's third son) was sent to school with Frederick William (Frederick's second son) at Manchester Grammar School to heal the rift.' However, this statement does not stand up to scrutiny due to the age difference of 7½ years between the two boys and the known fact that Tom's secondary education was all undertaken at the High School in Dublin. What is significant is that the statement supports the known evidence of one of Martin's sons being at school with one of Frederick's sons.

It is quite possible that Hephzibah was heartbroken at not having seen George before his death, and she may also have been troubled by the fact that since 1861 she had been distanced from Martin's wife who had died on 14th May, 1883. So it appears that, in her last days, Hephzibah made an effort to ensure that two of her younger grandsons did not grow up under a family shadow. The family reconciliation must have met with some degree of success, as we know for certain that Martin stayed with Frederick at Manchester in April 1891 and that the latter sent his condolences when Martin passed away in November 1901. It is also known that Tom Atock and Frederick William Attock subsequently became good friends, sending gifts to each other on the occasions of their respective weddings.

The years 1885-87 also brought significant changes for Frederick on the work front. Ramsbottom's appointment had been extended for a further 12 months from October 1884 and then, in September 1885, he was appointed to the Board, becoming Chairman of the Rolling Stock and Locomotive Works Committees. Barton Wright announced his resignation on 23rd June, 1886, having decided to return to India. The L&YR was lucky to attract John Audley Frederick Aspinall as his replacement. He came from the GS&WR at Inchicore with a strong recommendation, his appointment being confirmed, with the new title of chief mechanical engineer (the first such in Britain), at the Board Meeting held on 14th July. Aspinall initially carried on with Barton Wright's standardisation, but was later to stamp his own unique authority on L&YR locomotive matters.

Reference was made in the previous chapter to the appointment of John Pearson as Chairman and Chief Executive in July 1883 and his subsequent efforts to improve the state of the L&YR. Tragically, Pearson took seriously ill and died in June 1887, but his deputy, George Armytage, who was to be an able successor, replaced him. In previous years Frederick had doubtless seen Armytage as a thorn in the flesh on those occasions when he complained of dirty carriages, poor lighting and the like. Despite the loss of both Pearson and Barton Wright much had already been done, and matters were not going to be allowed to drift back into the slovenly ways of earlier years. Frederick was happy to play his part along with the new men. Aspinall was so well thought of that Armytage later persuaded him to accept the post of General Manager of the L&YR in May 1899. This was another first for Aspinall, as it was at the time unknown for a locomotive man to cross the divide into general management.

A Board decision to establish new wagon shops at Fazakerley near Liverpool led to orders being placed in January 1885 for additional machinery. The equipment ordered included drilling and screwing machines, a double wheel lathe, a circular saw bench and a 10 hp horizontal engine. The question of lighting the new shops was raised in the following September. Pearson, in a report to his fellow Directors, pointed out that the Fazakerley shops were located some 2,600 yards from the Liverpool Corporation gas supply at Cinder Lane and that the cost, to the company, of laying pipes would be in the region of £227. Pearson, seeing the bigger picture, suggested bringing the pipes a further 682 yards to serve Fazakerley station, and went on to state that the Railway Signal Company was desirous of obtaining gas from the same source, and had offered a payment of £25 per annum for the use of the pipes and 3*s*. 6*d*. per 1,000 ft^3 of gas; his proposal was approved by the Board.* Following an

* The Railway Signal Company was established in early 1881 by George Edwards, who was formerly of the Gloucester Wagon Co. Land was purchased in April 1881 adjacent to the L&YR main line and a manufacturing facility set up. The new company was registered on 3rd June, 1881 on the strength of an agreement to supply signalling equipment to the L&YR, which it did until 1889-90.

inspection of the wagon shops by the Directors, in September 1888, Frederick was censured for having erected a fence between the land occupied by his department and the line. He was informed that, before executing any such work in the future, he should obtain the sanction of the Rolling Stock Committee. The question of further accommodation at Fazakerley was raised in September 1894, and the Rolling Stock Committee recommended that the Board sanction the covering-in of various lines at an estimated cost of £900.

The Board Minutes for 22nd April, 1884 noted that a 42 ft-long bogie carriage, which had been built in the workshops and which could run over any portion of the line, was ready for inspection by the Directors. This is the first recorded reference to a bogie carriage on the L&YR, but the first bogie carriages to be produced in any numbers were the tri-composites built to Diagram 11 in 1886, one of which was shown at the Liverpool International Exhibition in that year. These carriages were also the longest vehicles to be built during Frederick's time at Newton Heath, being 51 ft long on two 11 ft 6 in. wheelbase bogies at 29 ft 6 in. centres. Despite the introduction of bogie carriages, six-wheeled stock continued to be built in quite substantial numbers right up until 1895. Indeed, various small batches of special six-wheeled passenger carriages were even built after that date, four first-class saloons to Diagram 20 introduced in 1899 being a typical example. Also, in September 1887 Frederick had an opportunity to show off his new six-wheeled invalid carriage at the Manchester Exhibition, a venue which attracted more than a million visitors.

Up until the 1880s the Manchester to Liverpool service was operated via Bolton and Wigan. The former location represented a serious bottleneck to the passenger traffic and, in addition, there were lengthy and steep gradients on either side of Wigan. As a result of these constraints the L&YR was simply unable to compete on equal terms with the LNWR and Cheshire Lines Committee (CLC) who also operated passenger services between the two cities. The L&YR Directors, under Pearson's chairmanship, took the bull by the horns and decided to build a completely new line from Windsor Bridge Junction, 1.8 miles from Manchester Victoria, to Crow Nest on the existing Lostock Junction to Wigan line, a distance of 13 miles, which was opened in stages between 13th June, 1887 and 1st October, 1888. A second short deviation of 3½ miles, known as the Pemberton Loop, by-passed Wigan, and was opened on 1st June, 1889.

Thorley and Attock submitted a joint report to the Board, on 29th March, 1887, which stated that for the company to be able to secure a fair share of the passenger traffic between Liverpool and Manchester it would be necessary to run an hourly service from, say, 8.30 am until 8.30 pm with perhaps four or five slower trains before and after those times. Thorley pointed out that the LNWR ran 22 trains in 45 minutes, nine in 50 to 60 minutes and 10 in 65 to 113 minutes, while the CLC ran four trains in 40 minutes, 29 in 45 minutes and seven in 65 to 95 minutes. The journey by the new L&YR route would take 45 minutes and the report suggested departures half-hourly from each end of the line.

Frederick suggested that the new Liverpool and Manchester trains should consist of four vehicles providing seating for 32 first class, 20 second class and 100 third class passengers. He had considered the use of bogie carriages but, after some deliberation, had decided it would not be desirable to introduce a

A.D. 1892. FEB. 11. Nº 2707.
ATTOCK'S COMPLETE SPECIFICATION.

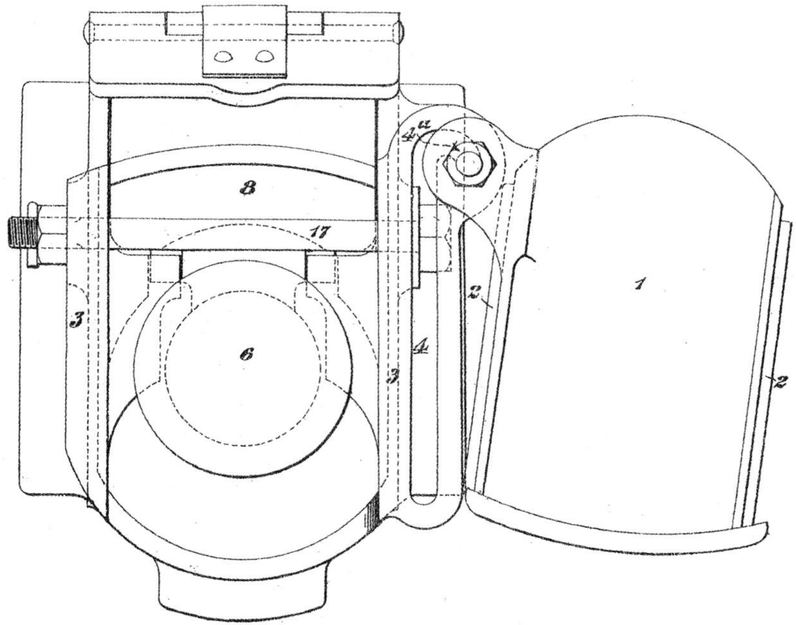

A drawing attached to Frederick Attock's Axlebox Patent of 1892. This was one of a number of patents registered by Frederick while he was with the Lancashire & Yorkshire Railway.
Author's Collection, courtesy British Library

different type of carriage after spending so many years endeavouring to get the stock of a uniform character. In addition, he considered that bogie carriages would not afford the same facilities for exchange as the existing stock and therefore more spare carriages would have to be kept for strengthening trains. The proposed number of trains would require four sets of carriages daily, in addition to which it would be necessary to have a spare set at each end of the line to cater for accidents or irregular running. It would also be desirable to have two further sets to use during repairs, making eight sets in total or 32 carriages, the estimated cost of which was £15,600. The Rolling Stock Committee recommended the Board to sanction the construction of six trains at a cost of £11,700; the carriages were to be six-wheeled, with the first-class compartments seating three aside and equipped with movable armrests.

The question of the future of the carriage repair shop at Southport was raised in September 1888, Frederick informing the Board that the repairs carried out there consisted of painting, varnishing and trimming in addition to work on brakes and gas fittings. The work applied mainly to carriage stock on the Liverpool to Southport service as well as to other vehicles running to and from the latter place. Southport's atmosphere was apparently particularly conducive to the varnishing of vehicles, and Frederick stated that he had currently 106 men employed there. He was ordered to prepare a report showing the number of men employed at the various outstations, indicating their various duties; he was also requested, if possible, to devise a scheme whereby repairs could be concentrated at Newton Heath.

When he reported back to the Board in October, Frederick confirmed that the number of men employed at Southport had increased during the previous five years from 74 to 106, this being accounted for, in part, by an increase of eight in the number of trains, but also due to the fact that the entire stock of passenger carrying vehicles was now fitted with vacuum brakes and Pope's gas lighting apparatus. The shops at Southport also repaired a varied assortment of ancillary vehicles, including road lurries [*sic*], sack trucks, platform trucks, handcarts, luggage carts and parcel carts belonging to the Passenger and Goods Departments. Previously these had been loaded and dispatched to Manchester for repairs. Frederick was of the opinion that to remove the repair facilities to Newton Heath would necessitate the provision of additional stock, but, having considered the matter, it was decided to close the Southport workshops except for day-to-day running repairs; this resulted in two men being dispensed with and the transfer of 35 others to Manchester.

Reference was made in Chapter Ten to Frederick's grease axlebox patent. Two further patents were registered in 1885, one in conjunction with pattern maker Peter Morris, for an improvement in the method of coupling wagons together originally propounded by Frederick two years earlier.* The 1883 patent allowed the coupling of wagons from either side without the necessity for shunters to go between wagons. This was effected by elongating the last link of a standard coupling to enable it to pass over the drawbar hook, allowing it to be hung up out of the way on a separate hook. The elongated link was also provided with a rigid lever at each side that extended outwards, the handle of which was placed at a suitable height for use by the shunter. This patent

* Patents A.D. 1883, 20th January, No. 342 *Coupling of Railway Wagons etc.* & A.D. 1885, 31st October, No. 13,155 *Improvements in Coupling Apparatus for Railway Wagons and other Vehicles.*

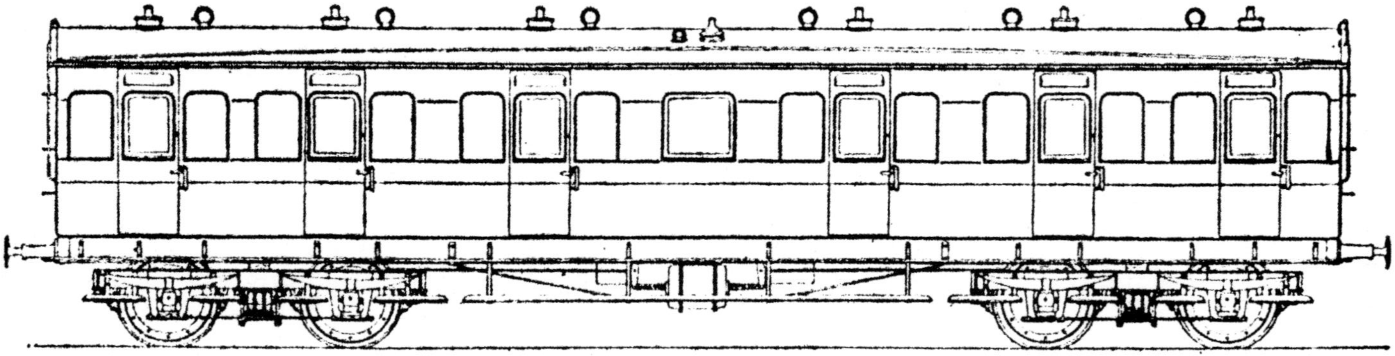

A 46 ft lavatory composite, 30 of which were built in 1894/95 to Diagram 28. Seating for 42, compartments being arranged 3.1.1.T.T.1.1.3. Numbered in series 281 to 614.

Courtesy Ian Allan Ltd

demonstrated that Frederick also had the welfare of the men at heart. The second of his 1885 patents related to the construction of a table capable of folding up into the smallest possible area, thus enabling it to be easily carried.* The table was fitted with a set of 'umbrella ribs' at one end of a metal tube. The table was enabled to stand by virtue of a slide passing up through the inside of the tube to which a set of three or more legs were hinged, which folded close together and passed up through the tube; when drawn out and distended by springs they formed a stable support for the table.

Always conscious of improving passenger comfort, Frederick also turned his attention to improvements in carriage sliding windows so as to prevent them rattling in their frames and, at the same time, excluding draughts. First introduced in May 1881,† his idea consisted of applying to the upper framework of the window opening a bar of wood or other suitable material, which was so shaped and mounted in position that its upper edge constantly pressed against the fixed framework. Meanwhile its lower edge pressed against the upper part of the framework or sash of the sliding window when it was closed, this being accomplished by means of two or more screws or studs fixed to the inner face of the bar. Not entirely happy with his original arrangement, Frederick produced an improvement in 1887;# this consisted of a metal flap hinged or pivoted so as to close the opening when the window was in the closed position.

Frederick's address was still officially shown as Somerset House in June 1887 but by October 1890 he was living at No. 185 High Street off Oxford Road, Manchester; he was still there in April of the following year, but by the end of 1891 he appears to have moved to No. 131 Palatine Road, Fernyhurst in the Didsbury district of the city, where he remained until he retired nearly four years later. To complete the story of Somerset House, it was finally demolished in 1896 in connection with extensions at Newton Heath workshops and the erection of new houses on the site.

It is worth making some mention of various staff matters, which reflect Frederick's approach to his men. He wrote to the Board in November 1883 to ask if, in a limited number of cases, he would be allowed to take on apprentices who would pay a premium. It was agreed to consider the question in both the Locomotive and Rolling Stock Departments. The issue was raised again, in December 1886, when Frederick mentioned that there were no premium apprentices and in fact ordinary apprentices received wages of 6s. per week. The Rolling Stock Committee considered that the same system should be adopted in the Carriage & Wagon Department as applied in the Locomotive Department, with the company's servants having preference over outsiders. Frederick was ordered to report the number of apprentices he proposed to appoint and the premiums he recommended, the question of the disposal of the latter being postponed. Reporting further, in June 1887, Frederick informed the Committee that he had received £50 from two apprentices, which he suggested should be handed over to the Carriage & Wagon Institution & Dining Room Fund, this being approved.

* Patent A.D. 1885, 14th November, No. 13,915 *An Improved Construction of Folding Portable Table.*

† Patent A.D. 1881, 5th May, No. 1954 *Sliding Windows of Railway Carriages, Tramcars etc..*

Patent A.D. 1887, 9th June, No. 8319 *An Improved Draught and Dust Excluder or Closing Device Applicable to Railway Carriage Doors and otherwise.*

An unusual case involving an accident to a Mr W. Jones in the carriage shops on 26th March, 1886 was referred to, on 23rd November, when Frederick reported that Jones was still in the Infirmary & Convalescent Hospital, and that the broken bone in his leg had not knitted and by that time it was considered that it never would. It was ordered that Frederick be given authority to obtain, from the Provident Surgical Appliance Society of London, an instrument for easing the lower part of Jones's leg, this to be paid for out of the Benevolent Fund. The Fund was called on again, in June 1888, to pay £10 to the widow of J.B. Lance, late foreman at Cheetham Hill gas works, who had died, 'from the effects of coughing and pains in the head caused by inhaling some of the vapours of gas'.

A memorial presented to the Rolling Stock Committee, on 10th March, 1887, requested the restoration of the 7½ per cent reduction in wages that had been applied to the men in the Carriage & Wagon Department about 15 months previously. Consideration of the matter was postponed, but Frederick made reference to it again a year later when he recommended that in giving the men back 5 per cent, he proposed only giving it to those who 'are quite worthy of it' and that this would cost £5,000 per annum. To meet the cost he intended making reductions in prices paid for piecework. Authority was given for Frederick to grant, to those men he deemed fit, 5 per cent for a period of 12 months. However, this was at a time when railway wages were on the increase, it being reported in July 1888 that the MS&LR, Beyer, Peacock and other Manchester shops had conceded an increase, while the L&YR men had served notice seeking an advance by 28th July. Frederick informed the Board that it would be almost impossible to avoid conceding the advance and he felt that an extra 5 per cent should be paid, from the previous April, to those men in his department whose wages had been reduced in 1885, as it was the men's understanding that the percentage was to be reinstated. It appeared that the Carriage & Wagon Department men's wages had been reduced a year before those in other departments, hence their call for an additional 5 per cent for a year. The Directors, however, recollected differently and were quite satisfied that there was never any intention on their part to reimburse the men.

Another aspect of the men's welfare was referred to in October 1890 when permission was sought by the Manchester, Salford & District Temperance Union for them to give a short address to the men in the shops once a week. Frederick suggested that the Union should communicate with the Manchester & Salford Mission on the subject, as the latter body already held a weekly service and might be disposed to occasionally give a Temperance address to the men. The Secretary was duly instructed to write to the Temperance Union on the subject. Also in October, the Dining Room Committee asked to be allowed to pay the full cost of a library facility for the men at Newton Heath. This suggestion was intended to be in lieu of paying an annual rent of 5 per cent of the cost of the renovations. The Board declined to agree with the suggestion, but they instructed Frederick to inform the Committee that they would accept a rent based on 4 per cent of the cost.

Wagon building was retained at Miles Platting following the opening of the Newton Heath workshops. The workshops at Miles Platting were far from adequate for new wagon building and, on 7th January, 1889, Frederick submitted a report to George Armytage regarding construction of a wagon shop at Newton

Heath at an estimated cost of £11,400. He suggested that this should be built on surplus land thus freeing-up more valuable land at Miles Platting. He added that the building of such a facility would also enable the carriage & wagon superintendent to utilise his work force to better effect, as he could divide their time between repairing the excursion stock for the summer traffic and then put them on to wagon building in August and September when they would otherwise be laid off. Frederick estimated that the removal of the wagon works from Miles Platting to Newton Heath would result in an annual saving of £4,000. The proposals were approved in principle in April, Mr Hunt submitting his detailed plan and estimate for £10,305 in May 1889. It was ordered that tenders be obtained and matters had proceeded sufficiently by June 1890 for Aspinall to have selected machinery at Miles Platting which might be of use at Horwich. Frederick was ordered to obtain the best price he could for redundant machines, this in due course bringing in a sum of £450. In August it was recommended that four additional sidings be laid down at Newton Heath for goods wagons awaiting repairs, this being approved by the Board at a cost of £800. The total cost of the transfer of the wagon works to Newton Heath was quoted as £11,558 and, in January 1891, Frederick confirmed that the actual saving during the first 12 months had worked out at £4,811, or some £800 in excess of his estimate.*

The subject of wheelbase arose, in March 1889, in connection with locking bars on point work. A joint report from Messrs Thorley, Hunt and Attock recommended that a BoT Order of 28th May, 1879 limiting the wheelbase of carriages to 18 ft should be rescinded. It was pointed out that a large number of locking bars were from 27 ft to 32 ft 6 in. in length, and throughout the L&YR system there were by March 1889 only 177 locking bars between 18 ft and 26 ft long, which would require replacing to permit the general use of a longer wheelbase; their replacement was estimated at £2,555. Frederick commented that if those locking bars were replaced it would allow for carriages being built in a more convenient and safe form. Indeed, he went on to say that the company already had two boiler trucks in use with wheelbases of 22 ft 8 in. and 24 ft 4 in. as well as other companies' stock with wheelbases up to 31 ft 10 in., none of which appeared to create any problems. It was agreed to suggest to the Board of Directors the sanctioning of these recommendations.

Matters do not appear to have improved as regards lavatory accommodation in the carriage stock, as a joint report of 7th May, 1889 from the traffic manager and the carriage & wagon superintendent refers to constant calls for the provision of such accommodation. There were only 13 carriages so equipped in service at that time, which were in use on the Yorkshire service, although it appears that summer travellers to and from Scarborough were denied the facility. Frederick had 16 composite carriages about to be rebuilt and he suggested that they should now be provided with lavatories at a cost of £95 each. This suggestion was approved on the understanding that drawings were to be submitted in advance of any work being carried out. The subject came up

* Newton Heath had another claim to fame. Workers from the Carriage & Wagon Department formed Newton Heath Football Club sometime in 1878, the club being known as 'The Heathens'. With professional football being introduced in 1895 the club attracted quality players with the bonus that they could obtain a job in the works. Financial difficulties led to a new club being formed in 1902, the players now wearing red shirts, white shorts and black socks. Such were the origins of the world famous Manchester United.

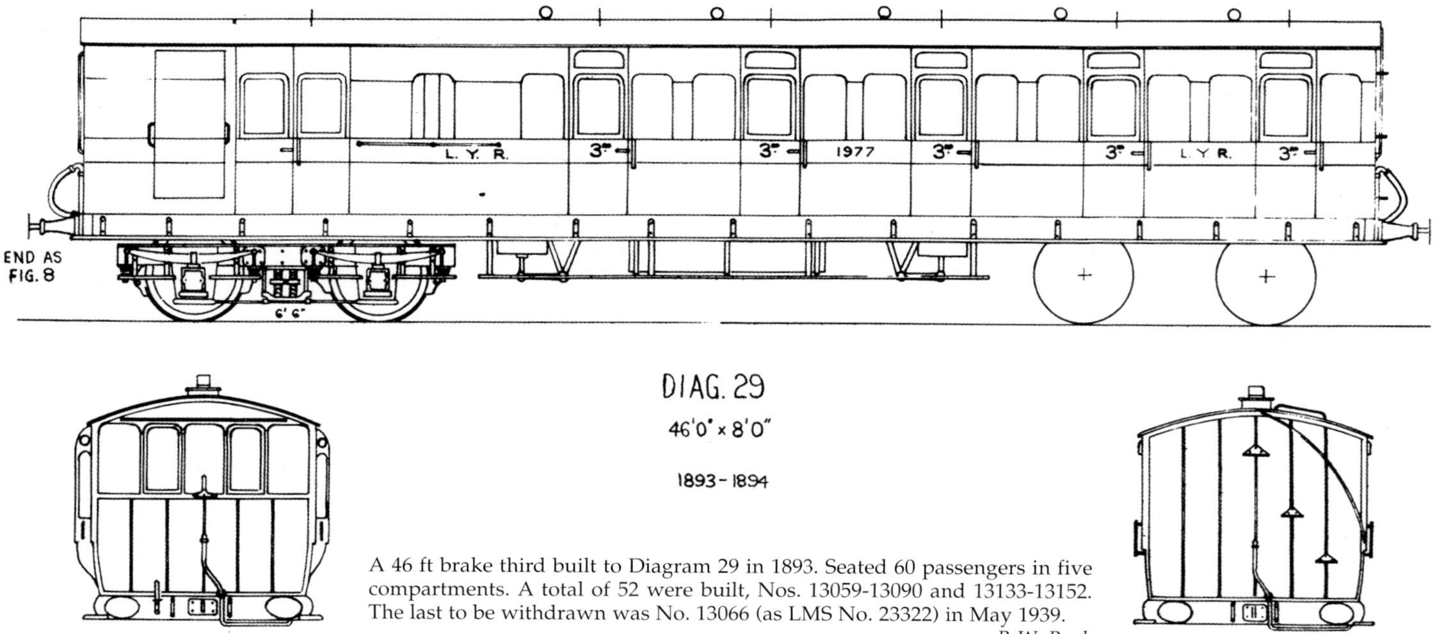

A 46 ft brake third built to Diagram 29 in 1893. Seated 60 passengers in five compartments. A total of 52 were built, Nos. 13059-13090 and 13133-13152. The last to be withdrawn was No. 13066 (as LMS No. 23322) in May 1939.

R.W. Rush

again, in August 1890, in the context of new first class bogie carriages in course of construction for the Manchester to Liverpool service. Once again there were 16 carriages involved, and it was estimated that the additional work would cost £84 per carriage, or £1,344 in total; this was also approved and they were built to Diagram No. 36 between 1893 and 1898.

It appears that carriages were not always lit when passing through tunnels in daytime, as a deputation from Blackburn met with the Rolling Stock Committee, on 18th June, 1889, asking for this to be done on trains passing through the 434 yard Blackburn tunnel. Frederick was asked to report on the matter, and he confirmed in October that all of the Yorkshire trains were run with full lighting during daylight hours at a cost of £14 12*s*. 0*d*. per week; if run at reduced light he estimated it would cost £10 14*s*. 6*d*. He went on to say that, if the Blackburn trains were run with full lighting during daylight, it would cost £3 6*s*. 0*d*. per week as against £2 5*s*. 7*d*. for reduced lighting. The Board ordered that these trains be run in future with reduced lights. It also emerged that the Goole and Doncaster line trains were still lit by oil, an order being given to convert them to gas at a combined cost of £954 15*s*. 0*d*. It was reported that, in addition, a pair of travelling receivers, or gas tank wagons, would be required at a cost of £150. In his *L&YR Wagon Diagrams* book Coates shows four such wagons under Diagram 29, with the building date queried as 1885; it is possible that two of them were built in 1889. Initially these vehicles carried two cylinders, this being increased to three about 1906.

A review of the carriage stock, carried out in January 1885, showed that, as of the end of the previous month, 449 vehicles had been fitted with the vacuum brake and 434 had the company's 'latest improved hand brake'. This left 1,928 vehicles, including excursion stock, without any brake for which the cost of providing the vacuum brake was estimated at £29 per vehicle, representing a total outlay of £55,912. In addition, the 434 vehicles with handbrakes only would cost a further £8,680. Following the passing of the Regulation of Railways Act of 1889, Frederick was able to confirm, in November of the same year, that all but 24 vehicles had been fitted with the continuous automatic vacuum brake, 22 of which were cattle drovers' carriages, the remaining two being the Engineer's and Directors' saloons. It is of interest to record that, whilst Frederick quickly confirmed that the two saloons had been fitted with the vacuum brake and orders were given to fit tool vans, the Secretary was instructed to enquire of other companies what they intended doing as regards drovers' carriages and ballast brake vans!

Frederick registered two patents related to the design of a combined movable armrest and headrest for passenger comfort. In his patent of December 1890* the apparatus was arranged such that when the arm-rest was not required for use it could be turned up, and, at the same time, the head-rest would automatically be raised clear of the seat's occupant. He produced a slight modification in 1893† to provide a rather larger movement of the headrest. This was accomplished by means of a 'lazy tongs' device mounted on a fixed pivot.

* Patent No. 20490, A.D. 1890, 16th December *An Improved Arm and Head-rest Combined, applicable to Railway Carriages, Tram-cars, Ships' Berths and other Seats.*

† Patent No. 885 A.D. 1893, 9th December *Improvements in or relating to Movable Arm and Head Rests Combined, applicable to Railway Carriages, Tram Cars, Ships' Berths and other Seats.*

A.D. 1893. Jan. 14. N°. 885.
ATTOCK'S Complete Specification.

Fig. 1.

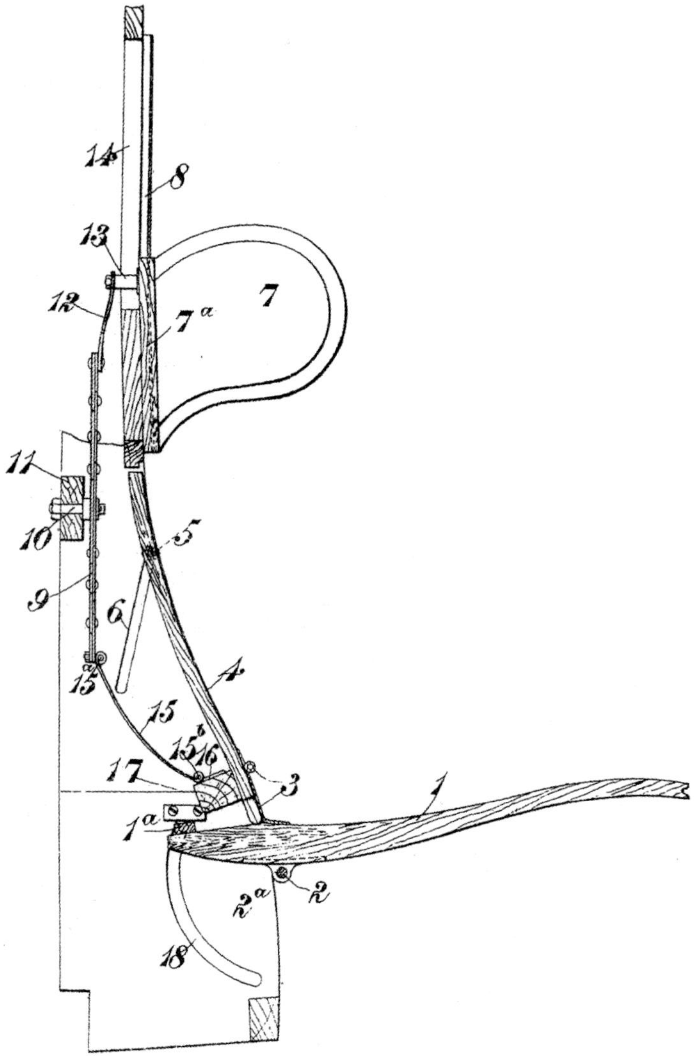

Diagram accompanying Frederick Attock's Patent No. 885 of 14th January, 1893 for an improved combined movable arm and head rest. This patent was accepted on 9th December, 1893.

Courtesy British Library

Frederick's final two patents related, respectively, to a device for lifting engines and rolling stock so as to more easily enable the withdrawal of bearings for examination and/or replacement, and improvements in bogie design.* This latter patent† introduced improvements enabling the springs, upon which the bogie bolster directly bore, to be placed further apart, thus reducing vibration and oscillation imparted to the carriage body at high speeds over points and crossings or when negotiating curves.

The question of the men's hours became an issue, in May 1891, when strike notice was served. It was agreed to concede a 53 hour week and it was announced that Newton Heath workshops would, from then on, close at 11.30 am on Saturdays rather than at 12.30 pm as previously. Frederick reported, in May 1893, that Mr Gibbons, a labourer in the Carriage & Wagon Department, aged 77 years, had been employed in that Department for 39 years but was now unfit for further service. The Revd Fergus Hill had written to the company appealing for some assistance on Gibbons' behalf, stating that he had obtained a gratuity of 6s. per week from Booth's charity. It was agreed to allow a sum of £10 from the Benevolent Fund, 'the amount to be dealt with by Mr Attock'. The sum of £10 appears to have been a standard gratuity made from the Fund at that time.

Experiments had been carried out, in the winter of 1892, with a train on the Southport line fitted with a system of heating involving the circulation of hot water from the locomotive through a series of coils in the carriages, the used water being returned by means of a second pipe to the tender. A second train fitted with the 'American Gold' system was tried out on one of the Bradford trains for comparison and proved to be most successful. As a result Frederick recommended the equipping of five additional train sets with this apparatus so as to provide complete and exhaustive trials. The cost of both systems was the same, viz. £20 for each ordinary carriage; in addition Messrs Laycock & Sons of Sheffield, who held the patent for the 'American Gold' apparatus, agreed to supply wrought-iron train piping for carriages of up to six compartments at a cost of £15 each. It was agreed that five trains be so fitted.

Following extensive trials Frederick reported back to the Board, early in May 1894, commenting that the 'American Gold' heating had performed well throughout the winter with virtually no trouble encountered. He pointed out that the best course of action appeared to be to maintain a constant temperature of not less than 60°F within the carriages. Passengers were given the option of using the window ventilators, as no controls were available to them for turning off the heat. Frederick also pointed out that both the GNR and the MS&LR were well pleased with the American system. It was recommended that the Board should authorize the fitting of about 60 carriages. It was not until after Frederick's departure that the decision was taken to equip newly-constructed carriages with steam heating rather than retrofitting them. H.A.V. Bulleid, in his biography of Aspinall, suggests that this was a nettle that Attock had failed to grasp, but in fairness to him it may also have been, in part, reluctance on the part of the Directors to pay for it.

* Patent No. 22,140 A.D.1891, 18th December *An Improved Portable Grip Lifting Jack for Railway Engines, Carriages, Wagons, Tram-cars, and other like Vehicles.*

† Patent No. 16,293, A.D.1893, 7th October *Improvements in Bogies for Rolling Stock.*

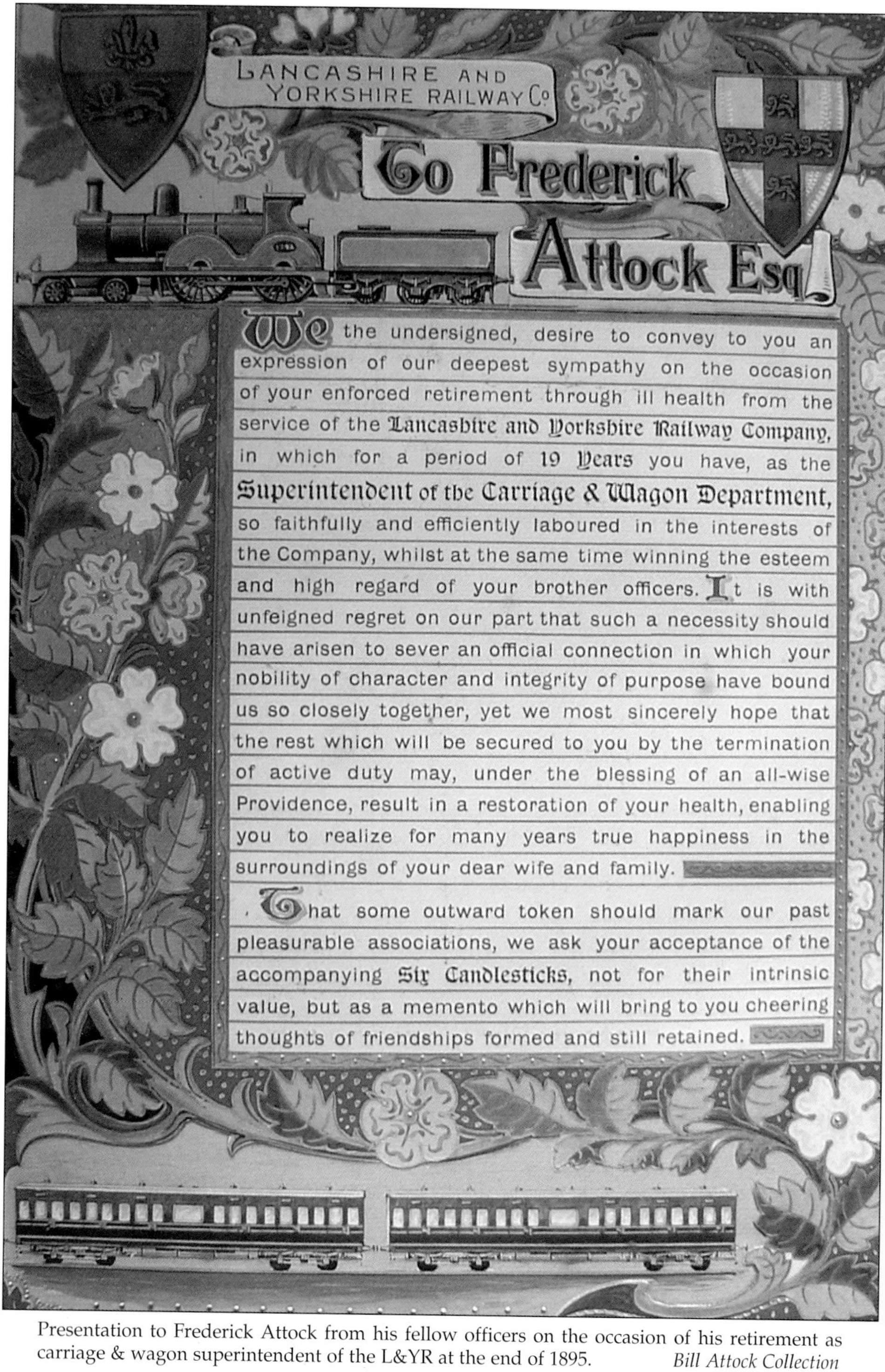
LANCASHIRE AND YORKSHIRE RAILWAY Co

To Frederick Attock Esq

We the undersigned, desire to convey to you an expression of our deepest sympathy on the occasion of your enforced retirement through ill health from the service of the Lancashire and Yorkshire Railway Company, in which for a period of 19 Years you have, as the Superintendent of the Carriage & Wagon Department, so faithfully and efficiently laboured in the interests of the Company, whilst at the same time winning the esteem and high regard of your brother officers. It is with unfeigned regret on our part that such a necessity should have arisen to sever an official connection in which your nobility of character and integrity of purpose have bound us so closely together, yet we most sincerely hope that the rest which will be secured to you by the termination of active duty may, under the blessing of an all-wise Providence, result in a restoration of your health, enabling you to realize for many years true happiness in the surroundings of your dear wife and family.

That some outward token should mark our past pleasurable associations, we ask your acceptance of the accompanying Six Candlesticks, not for their intrinsic value, but as a memento which will bring to you cheering thoughts of friendships formed and still retained.

Presentation to Frederick Attock from his fellow officers on the occasion of his retirement as carriage & wagon superintendent of the L&YR at the end of 1895. *Bill Attock Collection*

Frederick married again on 28th June, 1893; his bride was Elizabeth Nowall, a 39-year-old widow and daughter of William Andrews (deceased) of 34 Nicoll Road, Harlesden, the ceremony taking place at St Michael's Church, Willesden, Middlesex. It was around that time that he submitted plans for proposed additions to the works at Newton Heath. Henry Shelmerdine, the company's architect and land agent, was instructed to enquire whether land on the east side of Thorp Road bridge could be purchased, also land to the north of the existing works; in the latter context Shelmerdine was also asked to enquire whether the roadway (presumably North Road) might be abolished. In November 1894 Frederick submitted a report advising on how many additional carriages could be turned out at Newton Heath if the wagon shops were utilised for that purpose, but he urged the Directors to consider the erection of a new shop with accommodation for 150 carriages. Shelmerdine was ordered to continue his negotiations with the Deans and Canons, with authority to purchase the necessary land at a price not exceeding 3*s*. 4*d*. per square yard. The land in question, to the east of Thorp Road bridge, was purchased in January 1895, the additions to the works being opened in 1898 after Frederick's retirement. From that time onwards, carriage building was concentrated in the new shops, wagons being largely dealt with in the older buildings to the south-west of Thorp Road bridge.

Frederick does not appear to have enjoyed good health during his time at Manchester and he again took some sick leave in the autumn of 1895, Aspinall taking charge of the Carriage & Wagon Department during his absence. It therefore probably came as no surprise when Armytage read a letter at the Board meeting on 22nd October, 1895, from Frederick Attock, tendering his resignation owing to his continuing ill health. In his letter he appealed for some consideration in view of his long service and also for the use by the company of his various patents. The Board unanimously approved a gratuity of £500. At the same Board meeting it was decided to place the Carriage & Wagon Department under the chief mechanical engineer. Aspinall recommended that George Hughes, who was at the time in charge of the Gas Department under him at Horwich, be appointed his assistant carriage & wagon superintendent at a salary of £400 per annum, which was approved.

The staff and employees at Newton Heath workshops made a presentation of a gold watch and chain to Frederick in recognition of his 'hearty support in matters in which their interests have been involved'. The memorial presented to him also referred to his 'urbanity & kindness in the treatment of all questions affecting their welfare'. A second presentation was made at the end of December, on behalf of Frederick's fellow officers, consisting of six candlesticks, 'not for their intrinsic value, but as a memento which will bring to you cheering thoughts of friendships formed and still retained'. It is abundantly clear that Frederick was well liked not only by his fellow officers, but also by the workmen at Newton Heath. Certainly the references in the L&YR minute books show a caring individual with the interest of his men very much to the fore.

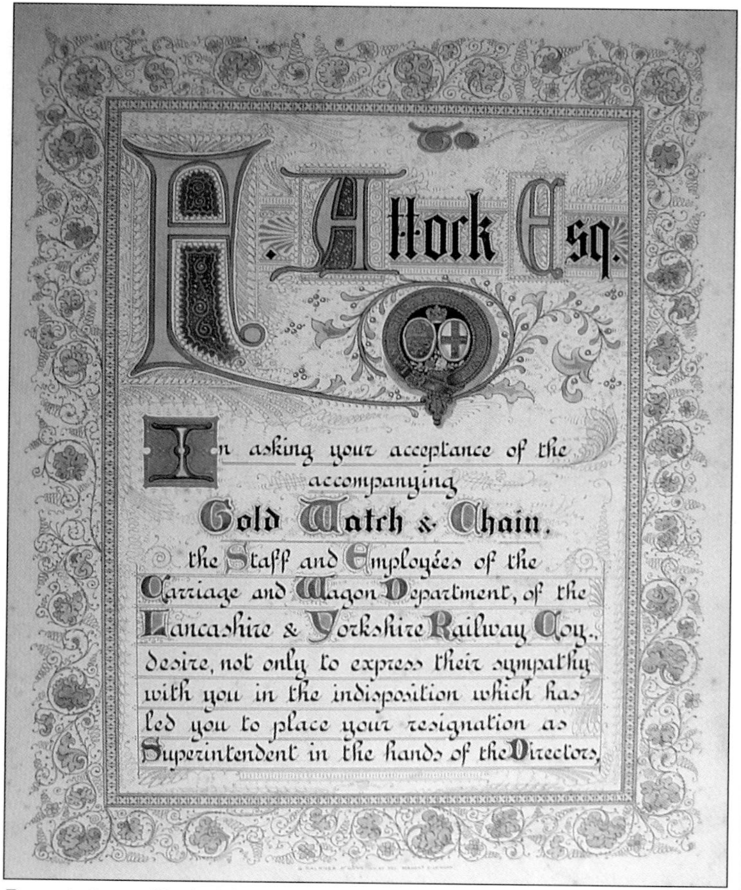

To

F. Attock Esq.

In asking your acceptance of the accompanying

Gold Watch & Chain.

the Staff and Employées of the Carriage and Wagon Department, of the Lancashire & Yorkshire Railway Coy., desire, not only to express their sympathy with you in the indisposition which has led you to place your resignation as Superintendent in the hands of the Directors,

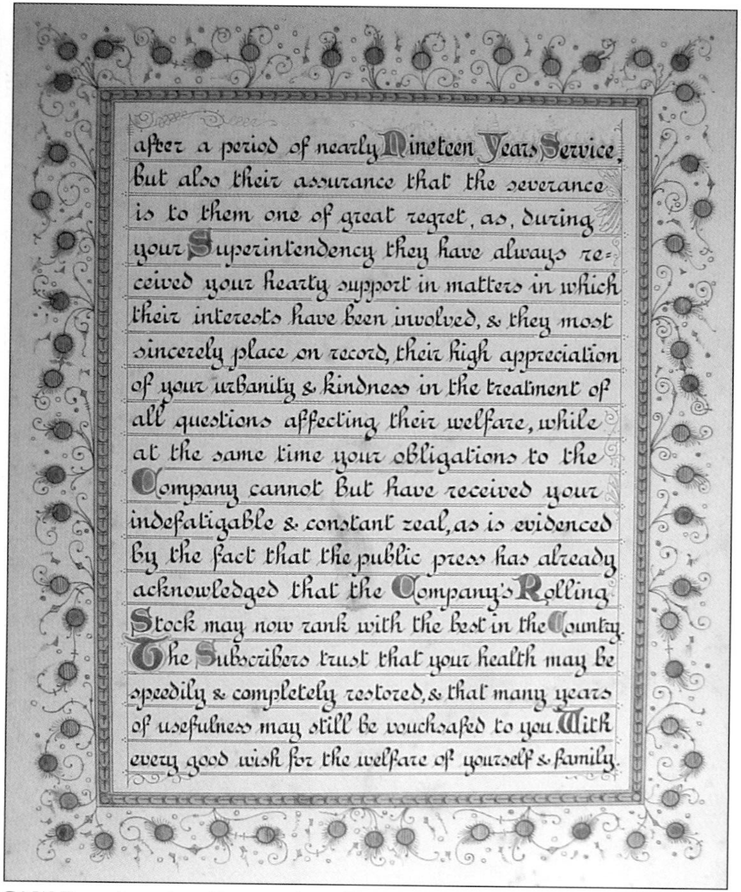

after a period of nearly Nineteen Years Service, but also their assurance that the severance is to them one of great regret, as, during your Superintendency they have always received your hearty support in matters in which their interests have been involved, & they most sincerely place on record, their high appreciation of your urbanity & kindness in the treatment of all questions affecting their welfare, while at the same time your obligations to the Company cannot but have received your indefatigable & constant zeal, as is evidenced by the fact that the public press has already acknowledged that the Company's Rolling Stock may now rank with the best in the Country. The Subscribers trust that your health may be speedily & completely restored, & that many years of usefulness may still be vouchsafed to you. With every good wish for the welfare of yourself & family.

Presentation to Frederick Attock of a gold watch and chain by the staff of the C&W Department on the occasion of his retirement. *Bill Attock Collection*

Chapter Thirteen

A Tale of Two Brothers

In Chapter Eleven we recorded that Frederick Attock, his wife Ellen Elizabeth, and their four children had moved to Manchester, taking up residence at Somerset House, in Newton Heath, at the beginning of February 1877. At the time of the move their third child, George Henry, had just turned three years of age and his younger brother, Frederick William, was an infant a little more than a year old. In their new home the two young boys would have been exposed, on a daily basis, to the sights and sounds of trains passing virtually in front of the house, not to mention the activities associated with the adjacent carriage and wagon works. Tragically, their mother died in July 1879 while they were both still very young, but their grandmother, Hephzibah, moved to Manchester, and was on hand to assist Frederick in bringing up his four young children. Both of the boys decided to follow their father into the railway industry, and we shall now take at look at their respective careers.

Taking George Henry first, we know nothing about his early school education but in 1884 he was sent away to Arnold House College in Blackpool where, as we have noted in Chapters Eight and Eleven, his Irish cousin George Atock had also been sent at about the same time. In 1887 George Henry moved to Leamington College where he remained until 1890. For the following five years he undertook an apprenticeship in the workshops and drawing office at Newton Heath. Whilst there, he also attended Manchester Technical School during 1891-92 to further his technical education. By that time George Henry had left home and was lodging at No. 561 Oldham Road, the home of John C. Dent, a foreman coach painter, and his wife, Ann. Having completed his apprenticeship, George Henry was, in 1896, appointed a draughtsman at Newton Heath and later he became an assistant to the locomotive works manager on the L&YR. He remained in that position for only a year, as in 1897 we find him managing his own saw milling business at the Old Forge Mill at Cunsey, Satterthwaite, on the west side of Lake Windermere.

One can but speculate as to the motivations behind this strange move and the fact that George Henry was in severe financial difficulties only five years later. In the previous chapter we have already related how his father, Frederick, had resigned his position as carriage & wagon superintendent at Newton Heath, on 22nd October, 1895, on the grounds of ill health. Not quite 50 years of age, Frederick was a comparatively young man and it is possible that he may have been looking for a business in which to invest for his retirement. We have also previously noted that, following the death of his first wife, Frederick had re-married. It is not clear whether Frederick and Elizabeth moved out of Manchester at the end of 1895. What we do know is that tragedy had struck a second time when, at the young age of 45, Elizabeth died at No. 89 Barkston Gardens, Brompton, on 27th March, 1899. There is no evidence to confirm that they were living in London at that time, and it may simply be that Elizabeth had family in Brompton as, at the time of her marriage to Frederick, less than six years previously, her address had been shown as nearby Harlesden.

Following Elizabeth's death, Frederick and his two daughters, Ellen May and Mary Grace, moved north to the Lake District to live at Garden Hill, Undermillbeck, on the east side of Lake Windermere. This was little more than two or three miles as the crow flies from where George Henry had set up his sawmill. It seems unlikely that at the age of 23 George Henry would have had the means to invest in the sawmill business, but Frederick could have used his retirement gratuity to help fund the venture, placing its management in the hands of his son. Frederick died of kidney failure at Garden Hill on 21st May, 1902, probably never having recovered from the loss of his second wife. We do not know the reason why, but the sawmill business was in severe financial difficulties by the end of 1902, only some seven months after Frederick had passed away.

In March 1903 an assignment was made of George Henry's estate and effects 'apart from necessary wearing apparel and bedding of himself, his wife and family' to Haydn Bernard Dawes, an auctioneer of Windermere, to enable debts to be cleared. The largest sums were due to three members of the Howson family, while it appears that two of George Henry's brothers-in-law, Frederick James and Harry Oldacres, had also invested in the business. In total, debts amounted to in excess of £1,400, a not inconsiderable sum in 1903. George Henry had married Jessie Oldacres at Monks Kirby on 18th September, 1901. The church has been described as a very impressive building dominating the village of the same name. As the name implies, the village had monastic origins, their involvement having been brought to an end during the reign of King Henry VIII. It is unclear how George Henry and Jessie met, but the Oldacres family can be traced back to at least the mid-16th century when one Thomas Oldacres was born in Alrewas in 1559. Alrewas, meaning 'alluvial land where alders grow', is close to the River Trent about 5 miles north-east of Lichfield in Staffordshire. Later, in the 18th and 19th centuries, the family was to be found living further to the east, in Churchover, roughly midway between Rugby and Lutterworth in Warwickshire.

The only known photograph of George Henry Attock, *third from right, front row.*

H.A. Gee, courtesy Bill Attock Collection

The financial upset had come at an inopportune time for the young couple as Jessie was pregnant and gave birth to their first child, James Frederick Everard Attock, at Cunsey on 8th April, 1903, only a couple of weeks after the assignment. With the sawmill business gone, George Henry decided to revert to his engineering expertise and joined the firm of Taite & Carlton of London, consulting engineers. In one of those remarkable co-incidences that keep cropping up in the family story, he found himself at Lutterworth in Leicestershire, where he was made personally responsible for the layout, equipment and management of the Wycliffe Follsain malleable castings foundry, then under construction in that village. Lutterworth, situated just to the south-west of Leicester immediately adjacent to Junction 20 on the present-day M1 motorway, is believed to date from Anglo-Saxon times, the name 'Lutter's Vordig' meaning Luther's Farm. Although an important posting station for stagecoaches on the London to Chester turnpike, it had few industries prior to the coming of the railway. In fact, railway communication came late, having to await the arrival of the London extension of the Great Central Railway (GCR).

The roots of the GCR lay in the Manchester Sheffield & Lincolnshire Railway, an east to west cross-country line formed out of an amalgamation of various companies with its headquarters at Manchester. Parliamentary approval was granted in 1893 for the construction of a line from Annesley, 10 miles north of Nottingham, to a junction with the Metropolitan Extension Railway at Quainton Road. Running powers were to be exercised over the latter company's system to Finchley Road, and the London terminus of the GCR was to be on the Marylebone Road. The line was opened for coal traffic on 25th July, 1898, for passenger traffic on 15th March, 1899 and for general goods traffic on 11th April of the latter year. A station was provided on the new line just to the east of the town of Lutterworth; previous to this the nearest station was at Ullesthorpe on the Rugby to Leicester line of the Midland Railway.

The opening of the new railway line soon attracted industries to the town. In 1902 George Spencer established the Vedonis hosiery factory, which quickly became one of Lutterworth's major employers. During World War II that factory was used to produce munitions. Two foundries were also established in the town, the Wycliffe Foundry with which George Henry was associated, and the Ladywood Foundry. The latter closed during the 1930s, but later became better known for F.W. (later Sir Frank) Whittle's pioneering work carried out there, on the development and testing of the jet engine, between 1937 and 1945.* The name Wycliffe derives from John Wycliffe, a past rector of the local parish from 1374 until his sudden death in December 1384. It was he who was responsible for the first translation of the Bible into English, and was sometimes referred to as the 'Morning Star of the Reformation'. Some 40 years after his death, in an attempt to stamp out moves for further reforms which Wycliffe's teachings had inspired, the Council of Constance ordered his bones to be exhumed, publicly burnt and his ashes thrown into the nearby River Swift. To this day there is a legend that a spring where some of the ashes fell never dries up and never freezes over.

With the opening of the Wycliffe Foundry in 1905, George Henry was appointed the first foundry manager, remaining in that role until 1908. In the latter year he severed his connections with both the foundry and Messrs Taite & Carlton Ltd,

* A replica jet aircraft was erected in May 2003 on the Lutterworth's southern bypass roundabout to commemorate Sir Frank Whittle's connections with the town.

The Wycliffe Follsain Foundry in Lutterworth, for which George Henry Attock was responsible as regards the layout, equipment and management. With the opening of the foundry in 1905, George Henry was appointed its first manager, a post which he held until 1908.

Photograph courtesy Lutterworth Museum

The interior of the Wycliffe Follsain malleable castings foundry in Lutterworth.

Photograph courtesy Lutterworth Museum

and for the next six years he represented Messrs Snowdon Sons & Co. of Millwall and other agencies for railway and general engineering specialities. Then in 1914 he joined Messrs C.C. Wakefield & Co. Ltd as engineering assistant engaged in the design and application of mechanical lubricators for use on engines and machinery. He was also involved in experimentation and testing of lubricants generally. During his time with C.C. Wakefield & Co. George Henry was elected an Associate Member of the Institution of Mechanical Engineers in 1920. His proposer and seconder were none other than George Hughes, chief mechanical engineer (CME) of the L&YR, and Francis Edward Gobey, his carriage & wagon superintendent. The application was supported by George Henry's brother Frederick William and by David Gibson, both also L&YR officers. David Gibson was apprenticed at Horwich locomotive works but left the L&YR on completion of his apprenticeship. Having gained marine experience, including his certificate as Extra Chief Engineer, he became a draughtsman in the marine department of the L&YR at Fleetwood. In 1900 he was placed in charge of the outdoor machinery department, and in January 1922 he became assistant works manager at Horwich under George Nuttal Shawcross on the 'greater' LNWR. He was appointed superintendent marine engineer LMS in April 1928 but died just seven months later, whilst travelling, on 8th December.

Three more children were born to George Henry and Jessie, two during their sojourn in Lutterworth and one following their move to Rugby. A daughter, Joan Leila, was born on 26th January, 1906 when the family were living at The Laurels in Bitteswell Road, Lutterworth. A second son, Martin Oldacres, arrived on 25th March, 1909, by which time the family had moved the short distance to Elm Cottage on Coventry Road and, finally, Priscilla Rosalind was born at Rugby on 14th October, 1920. George Henry retired from C.C. Wakefield & Co. in 1929 and spent his remaining years at No. 31 Bilton Road in Rugby. However, he was not content to sit back and watch the world go by. Both Frederick and Joan trained as teachers, in due course becoming principals, respectively, of Longrood School and Tower Lodge School in Rugby. George Henry maintained an interest in woodworking, building caravans as a hobby, and he also taught carpentry and drawing at the two schools. He suffered from heart trouble in his later years and he died suddenly at his home on the morning of Friday 26th May, 1939. The local rector, the Revd S. Morris, conducted the funeral service at the nearby Bilton church.

George Henry's younger brother, Frederick William, received a private education until he was nearly 17 years of age, which was followed by a year of study at Manchester Technical School. Between March 1893 and August 1896 he was a pupil with Messrs W.J. Galloway & Sons at their Knott Mill Iron Works in the Ardwick district of Manchester. Two brothers, William & John Galloway, established the firm in 1835, a large boiler works being constructed at Ardwick in 1872. They built a viaduct over the Leven estuary for the Ulverston & Lancaster Railway between 1855 and 1857 and Southport pier in 1859-60. Leaving Galloways he obtained, on 17th August, 1896, a situation as a fitter in the locomotive department of the L&YR, spending a year at Newton Heath locomotive shed. From there he moved to take up a position as assistant foreman at Wakefield running shed on 16th August, 1897. The 10-road locomotive shed

MR. F. W. ATTOCK,
Chief Assistant, Outdoor Locomotive
Department, Horwich.

The only known portrait of Frederick William Attock. *Courtesy Railway Magazine*

was situated ¾ mile to the east of Wakefield station and dated from about 1890. Facilities included a breakdown train with a 30 ton travelling steam crane. On the basis of the duties it had to cope with for the heavy coal traffic from the South Yorkshire coalfields, Wakefield shed was probably only second in importance on the L&YR system to that at Newton Heath. There would, however, only have been a few passenger engines allocated there for working secondary services.

Shortly before Wakefield shed took delivery of a number of Aspinall's new 0-8-0 coal engines, Frederick William was promoted, on 17th June, 1898, to the post of foreman at Normanton shed. This was hardly a surprising move, as he would have added considerably to his knowledge and experience during his short stay at Wakefield. Normanton was a sub-depot to Wakefield and was located just to the east of the passenger station on the line to Goole, adjoining the roundhouse jointly used by the Midland Railway and North Eastern Railway. The L&YR facility was a medium sized straight-road shed used for servicing mainly 0-6-0 goods engines and radial tanks. It might here be mentioned that Normanton and Wakefield were two of only six locations on the entire L&YR system where siding accommodation was provided for in excess of 1,000 wagons, which gives some indication of their importance. Normanton shed was closed in 1924 as an economy measure.

Having proved himself to his superiors, Frederick William returned to the centre of operations at Horwich with his appointment on 6th October, 1899 as junior assistant in the Outdoor Locomotive Department. His immediate superior was Arthur Dansey Jones who, on the preceding 1st July, had been appointed assistant to Charles O'Keefe Mackay, chief of the Outdoor Locomotive Department. The CME, Henry Hoy, proposed Frederick William for membership as a Graduate of the Institution of Mechanical Engineers (IMechE) on 15th January, 1900, the proposal being seconded by Charles O'Keefe Mackay and supported by George Hughes, Arthur D. Jones and Hawthorn Thornton. Frederick William remained in his position for 4½ years, in the meantime becoming an Associate of the IMechE in 1901, about which time he was boarding at No. 167 Victoria Road, Horwich, the home of Fred Morton, a storekeeper on the L&YR.

Henry Hoy wrote to the Board of the L&YR, on 10th February, 1904, tendering his resignation following his appointment as General Manager of Beyer, Peacock & Co. in Manchester.* Hoy was allowed to leave the company on 12th March; George Hughes, who had been works manager at Horwich since 1st July, 1899, was promoted to the vacant position of CME. Hughes continued to hold that position for the remaining years of the L&YR's independent existence, and, in January 1922, he was appointed CME of the combined LNWR and L&YR. Following the Grouping he was appointed CME of the London Midland & Scottish Railway, which post he held until his retirement in October 1925. The promotion of Hughes to the top job at Horwich led to a number of consequential appointments and promotions. Oliver Winder, who had held the position of assistant carriage & wagon superintendent, was appointed works manager, Horwich and deputy to Hughes. Nigel Gresley was appointed in place of Winder, he in turn being replaced as works manager at Newton Heath by C.H. Montgomery, who had been the outdoor assistant in the Carriage &

* Hoy was responsible for the re-organization of the Beyer, Peacock works at Gorton. He died only six years later, on 24th May, 1910, at the comparatively young age of 55.

Wagon Department. These appointments all dated from 12th March, 1904, but Montgomery's old job was not filled at the time, it being decided to make an appointment at a later date.

At a Board meeting held on 26th April, 1904 it was, on the recommendation of the Rolling Stock Committee, decided to appoint F.W. Attock as outdoor assistant in the Carriage & Wagon Department, at a salary of £160 per annum. Within less than a year Gresley was to move to the GNR at Doncaster and a distinguished and brilliant career, which has been adequately described in Geoffrey Hughes's excellent biography (*see Bibliography*). Following Gresley's move to Doncaster, in January 1905, another reshuffle took place, Frederick William finding himself becoming assistant to A.D. Jones in the Outdoor Locomotive Department as from 18th February in place of John Peachy Crouch, who became assistant carriage & wagon superintendent. Frederick William's appointment necessitated another move of office, this time from Newton Heath to Hunts Bank, Manchester. One consolation was that his salary was raised to £250 per annum, this being further increased to £275 in the following December.

We have already met the Oldacres family earlier in this chapter. Old James Oldacres, born in May 1803, was a wealthy landowner farming 680 acres at Cestersover House near Monks Kirby and in 1881 was employing 15 labourers and 6 boys; there was also a mill on the estate close to the house with a resident miller. When James died in 1886 the estate passed to his son, also James, who had been born on 11th February, 1836. He married twice and had three or four children by his first wife, Kate (née Eccles). His second wife, Priscilla (née Moxon), had eight children, amongst whom were Jessie, who was born on 13th June, 1873, and her younger sister Evelyn Mary, born in 1882. We do not know how or exactly when Frederick William met Evelyn Mary Oldacres, but, as she was his sister-in-law, he would certainly have known her since the time of George Henry's marriage in 1901.

What we do know is that the happy couple married, on 1st September, 1908, at All Saints' church, Norton near Daventry in Northamptonshire, Frederick William's address at that time being shown as Lever Bridge, Bolton. The Rector of Norton, the Revd J.H. Churchill-Baxter, assisted by the bride's uncle, the Revd George Oldacres, Rector of Illingworth in Yorkshire, conducted the ceremony, one of the witnesses being the Rector's daughter, Mabel Maria Baxter. At the time of his marriage Frederick William's salary had just been increased to £300, sufficient to support himself and his young bride. Among the guests attending the ceremony and subsequent reception were some of his colleagues from the L&YR, including John Peachy Crouch and his wife, Arthur Dansey Jones, Oliver Winder and his wife, and Charles Hubert Montgomery. The couple received a large number of gifts, these including one from the clerical staff of the Locomotive Department and a separate one from the works staff at Horwich.

A.D. Jones submitted his resignation to the Board of the L&YR in March 1912, leaving to take up the post of running superintendent on the South Eastern & Chatham Railway, and, on Hughes's recommendation, it was resolved to appoint F.W. Attock to the vacant position of head of the Outdoor Locomotive Department, at a salary of £425 per annum, with effect from 1st March, and to appoint H. Housley as his assistant. Frederick William attended the Officers'

Monthly Conference, held at Manchester on 22nd April, for the first time in his new capacity, although he had previously stood in for Jones in July 1911. In his new position he was responsible for all L&YR locomotive running matters. This covered the operation of 1,550 engines and the supervision of almost 6,000 staff involved in crewing, preparation and disposal, and running maintenance, including 300 fitters and assistants. Geographically his area of responsibility encompassed 32 engine sheds, details of which are given in *Appendix Four*.

Frederick William was transferred to the grade of Member of the IMechE, in 1913, on the proposal of J.P. Crouch, seconded by Henry Fowler. Not long after that event one of his sheds was closed, in 1914, the locomotives and crews at Doncaster being accommodated at the GNR shed. On 21st December, 1918, Frederick William was also elected to membership of the Institution of Locomotive Engineers (ILoco.E). On 28th February, 1919 a meeting, presided over by George Hughes, was held at the College of Technology in Manchester for the purpose of inaugurating a Local Centre of the ILoco.E for the Manchester district. A provisional committee had been formed at the suggestion of the main body in London, amongst whom was F.W. Attock. Hughes commented that many of those present had attended previous meetings of the 'Civils' and the 'Mechanicals' in London and would have noted how very popular locomotive subjects had been. He went on to point out that the latter were by then being dealt with almost exclusively by the Locomotive Institution.

Hughes then called on Mr A.T. Houldcroft, secretary of the Leeds branch, to outline the progress to date of the branch there, the first to be set up outside London. The latter gentleman confirmed that the branch had been set up during the war and had already attained a membership of 100. The members found that the various railway companies serving Leeds had been most helpful when approached and there was little doubt that the same would apply in Manchester. A motion in favour of forming a Local Centre of the ILoco.E was carried unanimously, and it was proposed that Hughes be appointed to the office of chairman. He declined the honour, due to work commitments, but proposed F.W. Attock in his stead. The proposal was seconded by J.W. Smith of the Great Central Railway, and also carried unanimously. Smith was elected as vice-chairman, and the committee formed included representatives not only from all of the railway companies serving Manchester, but also from various railway equipment manufacturers located in the area.

The first ordinary meeting of the new centre was held at the Manchester College of Technology on 4th April, 1919. F.W. Attock was unavoidably absent, owing to urgent business in London, the chair being taken by Smith who read out a prepared statement by the chairman. In it Frederick William noted that the membership had already reached 50 and he hoped that more prospective members would soon join. He also reported that George Hughes had kindly consented to the members visiting the L&YR works at Horwich; it was hoped that this would be the first of a number of visits to facilities in the Manchester area.

At the meeting held on 5th March, 1920, with Frederick William in the chair, W.A. Barnes read an interesting paper entitled 'Electric Traction for Railways'. Barnes was Assistant at Clifton Junction Power House from July 1915. In summing-up afterwards Frederick William put forward some interesting points, from which it was clear that he was not totally convinced of the merits of electrification in all circumstances. He was of the view that many of the arguments put forward as regards the economic benefits of electric traction were based on the working of sections of line where the best conditions obtained. He felt that a minimum traffic density was required as well as something approaching a constant load, so that the machinery might be fully occupied. If steam engines were confined to busy sections where there was constant work on full load, more favourable results would be recorded. Much was said about radiation losses from steam locomotives, but he was convinced that there was also considerable loss due to leakage from third rails; one had only to observe steam coming off the third rail in wet conditions to realise that! He considered that another point to be taken into account was the working of branch lines connecting into electrified main lines. If the latter only were electrified, there had to be a change from electric to steam traction at each connecting point unless the branches were also converted; this would take from the economic benefits. The biggest objection, however, to electric traction in Frederick William's view was the scenario of a total failure of power which would bring the entire system to a halt, unless there were steam locomotives to bring out in such emergencies.

In October 1920 Frederick William's senior colleague, Col H.E. O'Brien, DSO, presented his classic paper entitled 'The Management of a Locomotive Repair Shop' to the Manchester Centre of the ILoco.E. O'Brien was works manager and assistant chief mechanical engineer at Horwich at that time. Frederick William contributed to the ensuing discussion, and made reference to the fact that, in his view, the majority of engine repair shops were far too small. Col O'Brien referred to the employment of inspectors to oversee repairs and renewals. Frederick William had no problem with this concept, but he was of the opinion that inspectors should focus their attention on an efficient repair rather than having as their primary consideration economy in the use of materials, etc. In concluding his remarks, Frederick William congratulated the author of the paper on putting into practice an efficient policy of boiler renewals and repairs at Horwich.

By 1920 the largest shed on the L&YR system was Newton Heath, with an allocation of 219 engines, and the smallest was Barnsley with just three. More than half of the sheds were relatively new buildings, the company having built 10 new ones and rebuilt seven others between 1884 and 1900 in order to improve efficiency of locomotive preparation and disposal, matters of daily concern to Frederick William. When the LNWR and the L&YR were amalgamated on 1st January, 1922 the respective locomotive running departments became the 'A' and 'B' Divisions of the enlarged company. As the person responsible for motive power operations on the L&YR, Frederick William effectively retained his position as running superintendent of the 'B' Division. Both he and F.W. Dingley, his opposite number at Crewe on the 'A' Division, reported to George Hughes.

A year after the LNWR/L&YR merger the Grouping took place and the newly formed LMS at once adopted Midland Railway organizational structures, separating the Locomotive Running Department from the control of the CME and placing it under a chief motive power superintendent who reported directly to the General Manager. The four divisions within the Running Department were based on the former operating areas of the constituent companies of the LMS and were designated as Western (LNWR), Central (L&YR), Midland (MR) and Northern (Caledonian, Glasgow & South Western and Highland Railways) Divisions. James Edward Anderson, the former deputy CME of the MR, was appointed chief motive power superintendent, Frederick William Attock becoming divisional superintendent, Central Division. Not only had responsibility for locomotive running matters been taken away from Hughes, but with the transfer of Frederick William's Division to Anderson, he had also lost one of his long-standing immediate subordinates and colleagues from L&YR days.

After the Grouping, Blackpool (Talbot Road) was merged with Blackpool (Central), and Hellifield and Leeds (Wortley Junction) were merged into the nearby ex-MR sheds, respectively, on 7th November, 1927 and 9th July, 1928. It was also on the latter date that Horwich shed was reduced to a depot only for the works shunting engines. The small sheds at Normanton and Barnsley had already succumbed prior to 1925. In the last years of Frederick William's tenure major development work was carried out at several sheds. Trackwork was altered, mechanical coaling and ash handling plants were installed, and new turntables of increased diameter were provided at Wakefield (1930-32), Blackpool (1932) and Bank Hall (1933). A 70 ft diameter turntable had previously been installed at Agecroft in 1926.

In a paper presented to the ILoco.E in London on 22nd November, 1923, and also read a month later in Manchester, Frederick William spoke from his personal experience on the lay-out of locomotive sheds, a subject which appears to have been well received at both venues judging by the lively discussion that followed, even though some of those who contributed were at odds with Frederick William in his views. For the purposes of his paper, Frederick William took as an example a shed of average size, which had to supply 60 engines for mixed classes of traffic to maintain a daily service, with a staff of some 400 employed in maintaining and working the engines. Of the total allocation, he was of the view that for every two engines on the daily roster, a third must be provided to allow for boiler washing, running repairs and periodical works repairs; this meant that the shed would probably have about 90 engines allocated to it, of which 10 would always be away at the works for repair. Allowing for engines being in traffic throughout the 24 hours, he deemed it unnecessary to provide covered accommodation for more than 50 engines.

Frederick William referred to three types of shed in use on the LMS system, viz. the 'interior turntable' shed with 'dead-end' roads, the parallel road shed with 'dead-end' roads and the parallel road shed with through roads. Whilst the first type had the advantage that engines could be taken out in any order, the main drawback, in his view, was that an accident to the turntable could trap a large number of engines, thus seriously disrupting traffic. Frederick William's preference was for the second type, which was comparatively cheap to build; the disadvantage of the through road shed was that it required more roads leading into and out of the shed to facilitate engine movements. Apart from the provision of sidings for locomotives, he pointed out that additional accommodation was also required for locomotive coal wagons. Taking 20 ton capacity wagons as being the normal in use at that time, he reckoned that a typical three days supply of coal would require in excess of 500 ft of siding space, not to mention requirements for holiday periods, stockpiling, and empty wagons awaiting return to their destinations.

It was Frederick William's belief that many existing sheds had been built wherever spare ground was available, without any consideration being given either to future expansion or to the proper provision of ancillary services such as ash disposal, coaling and watering. The location of these services in relation to the shed itself required careful planning if congestion and unnecessary engine movements were to be avoided. Ideally, the movement of engines should, as far as practicable, be continuously in one direction. In his view, the sequence of operations on entering the shed yard should be: inspection and ash disposal, coaling, turntable and finally shed. Inspection, which should be carried out either by the incoming driver or an appointed member of the shed staff, should be completed within 15 minutes; it would then normally take about 30 minutes more to drop the fire.

Water columns, he stated, should ideally be placed at the exit end of the ash pits. Coaling of engines differed considerably between sheds, being dependent on the size of the depot which, in turn, dictated the method of coaling. Larger depots would inevitably have mechanical coaling facilities, whereas smaller ones would have to rely on manual coaling. In between would be depots with elevated wagon stages, enabling coal to be tipped direct from wagons into the tender. In regard to turntables, Frederick William felt that they should be as large as possible to allow for the introduction of larger engines; in addition, larger turntables allowed better balancing of locomotives when turning.

In Frederick William's view the layout of shed buildings was also important, his suggestion being that, in laying out a shed, room be left on one side for future extensions. Buildings could be simple and rectangular in shape with offices, stores and mess rooms along the side rather than at the ends; and again, these should be on the opposite side to that left free for extensions. He proposed that the office accommodation would house the district locomotive superintendent and the shed foreman, who would therefore be on site to carry out their supervisory duties. If placed in front of the shed, the offices would give unrestricted viewing of engine movements in the yard. He considered that the mess room and signing-on area, followed by the stores, should be located adjacent to the offices but that, although he considered the foregoing as being the ideal, it was quite obvious that local conditions would dictate the actual layout.

Having given the LMS notice of his intention to retire in November 1934, Frederick William concluded his affairs with the company at the end of the year and moved shortly afterwards, to live at Cross-in-Hand just to the east of Uckfield in East Sussex. Frederick William and Evelyn had three children, Elaine (born 1901), Eric (1913) and Rowan (1918), all of whom became teachers. Eric married Dorothy May Crane in 1943 and they had two children, Thelma born in 1947 and Brian born in 1944. Brian became a doctor whilst Thelma also not only took up teaching herself, but also married a teacher, Victor West. Evelyn Mary Attock died in the District Hospital at Tunbridge Wells on 2nd February, 1950 and, almost a year to the day later, Frederick William Attock passed away at his home, Five Ways, Cross-in-Hand, on 1st February, 1951 at the age of 75.

Chapter Fourteen

A Career with English Electric

Martin Oldacres Attock commenced his secondary education at Oakfield School, Rugby, in the summer term of 1920. In May 1923 he transferred to Rugby School, where he stayed until December 1925. He began a four-year mechanical engineering apprenticeship at the Willans Works of English Electric, Rugby, on 25th March, 1926. This included time in the pattern shop and foundry (six months in each) and 12 months in the machine shop where he gained experience of marking off, milling, grinding, and turning, the latter using both centre lathes and capstan lathes. The following 12 months were spent in the diesel engine section of the drawing office, and his apprenticeship concluded with six months in the diesel engine fitting & erecting shop and six months in the diesel engine design department. During his apprenticeship he attended Rugby Technical College, his studies resulting in the award of a National Certificate in mechanical engineering.

The English Electric Company Limited was formed in 1918 and during that year and the following acquired control of Dick, Kerr & Company Ltd in Preston, Willans & Robinson Ltd in Rugby, and the Phoenix Dynamo Manufacturing Co. Ltd of Bradford. It also purchased the Stafford premises of Siemens Bros Dynamo Works Ltd. After the acquisition of the various concerns the traction activities of the new company were concentrated at Preston, but the diesel engine work remained at Rugby. In 1930 the manufacture of electrical traction equipment was transferred to Bradford, with body assembly retained at Preston, although frame construction was often sub-contracted to R. & W. Hawthorn, Leslie Ltd, Newcastle-upon-Tyne. The locomotive manufacturing department of Hawthorn, Leslie was taken over, in 1937, by Robert Stephenson & Co., Darlington and the restyled Robert Stephenson & Hawthorns Ltd was acquired in 1944 by the Vulcan Foundry Ltd of Newton-le-Willows, which in turn became part of the English Electric Group when they were taken over in 1955.

On completion of his apprenticeship Martin Oldacres was appointed an assistant in the diesel engine design department, on 26th March, 1930, where he was engaged on the development of high-speed diesel engines. He was seconded to British Thomson-Houston (BTH), Rugby, from May to October 1933, where he worked in their refrigeration test department. On his return to English Electric he immediately became involved in the testing of the demonstrator diesel-electric railcar *Bluebird*, the first of the diesel engines produced at the Willans Works specifically for railway traction having been installed in that vehicle. It was a six-cylinder four-stroke engine with a rated output of 200 bhp at 1,500 rev./min., believed at the time to be the highest rotational speed of any internal combustion engine in use for railway traction.

The diesel engine was installed above the floor and direct-coupled to a 135 kW direct-current generator, an auxiliary generator being chain-driven from the main shaft. Two nose-suspended traction motors of the self-ventilating type,

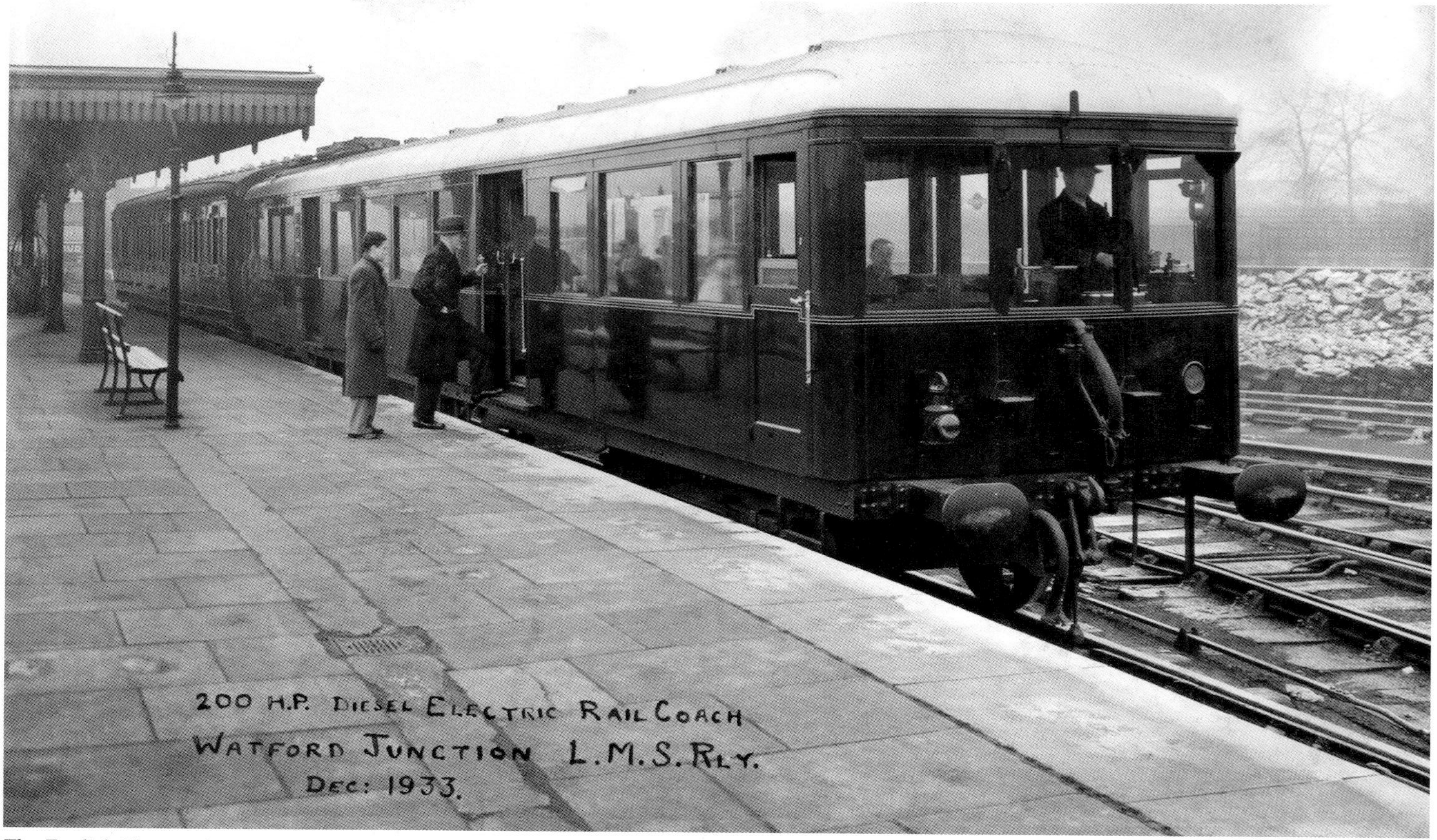

The English Electric demonstrator railcar *Bluebird* photographed at Watford Junction in December 1933 while working on the St Albans branch. On this service it was coupled to a standard LMS bogie carriage which had a driving cab fitted at one end. The railcar, allocated Works No. 859, was built at the Dick, Kerr works in Preston.

Bill Attock Collection

producing a maximum tractive effort of slightly over 6,000 lb., were mounted in the motor bogie under the engine compartment. The electrical equipment came from the company's Phoenix Works at Bradford and the mechanical portion, including the underframe and two four-wheeled bogies of the spring-bolster type with SKF roller bearing axleboxes, was assembled at the former Dick, Kerr Works, Preston. The body of the railcar had outer panels of steel with ash fillings in the pillars. Passenger entrance was via sliding doors in the centre of the carriage on each side, giving access to two third-class compartments. These were finished in mahogany and bubinga,* with chromium plated metal fittings and upholstery in figured moquette. There was a small luggage compartment between the passenger compartment and the engine room.

When completed the railcar underwent preliminary trials on the English Electric test track at Preston. This was followed by in-service trials on branch lines of the London Midland & Scottish Railway, during which Martin Oldacres was responsible for the care of the diesel engine. Out-road trials commenced on 2nd October and were conducted on the Rugby to Market Harborough line for the first week. In order to keep operations within close range of the Willans Works the initial in-service trials were carried out on the Warwick to Northampton route, via Rugby. *Bluebird* operated five round trips per day, and it was reported that speeds in excess of 60 mph were achieved. By the end of five weeks on the Warwick to Northampton route the railcar had run a total of 5,880 miles, and it was decided to transfer it to the Watford Junction to St Albans branch. For working on that line it was coupled to a 27 ton trailer coach fitted with a driving compartment, the additional load reducing the maximum speed obtainable to 45 mph. *Bluebird* appears to have been successful in service, and, by the end of 1933, it had accumulated approximately 12,000 miles.

On 26th January, 1934 a special non-stop demonstration run was made from Euston to Watford with W.A. Stanier, CME of the LMS, C.E. Fairburn,† his electrical engineer, and H.N. Gresley, CME of the LNER, on board. At Watford the trailer coach was uncoupled for the return to Euston during which Stanier drove the railcar, which achieved a speed of 60 mph at one point. After six months of trials *Bluebird* had accumulated 19,000 miles and it was withdrawn in March 1934 for an examination. Everything was found to be in good order and it was put back into service on the Burton-Tutbury line. Later it was reported that the engine suffered a big-end failure and that there was also excessive camshaft wear. It may have been those problems that led to the experiment being discontinued and, in any event, the LMS was not inclined to purchase the railcar.

* Bubinga is a dense, fine-grained, hardwood, also known as African Rosewood, and is found in Central Africa. When first harvested it exhibits a pinkish rose coloured appearance, which turns a beautiful burgundy red when fully aged. It was in the past used for both domestic and commercial application where a dark red wood colour was required.

† Charles Edward Fairburn was born in Bradford in 1887 and became a pupil under Henry Fowler at the Midland Railway at Derby in 1910. He joined the Research Department of Siemens Dynamo in 1912 and was involved as assistant to the resident engineer on the North Eastern Railway's Newport to Shildon electrification between 1913 and 1916. In 1919 he joined the technical staff of English Electric and was involved in building-up the electric traction department, later becoming the chief engineer of that department. He would undoubtedly have known Martin Oldacres Attock from those days. Fairburn joined the LMS in 1934 as electrical engineer, succeeding as CME on Stanier's retirement in 1944.

The prototype English Electric shunter for the LMS at work in Rugby marshalling yard in April 1934. She is yet to receive her LMS number, 7079. *Bill Attock Collection*

LMS diesel-electric 0-6-0 shunting locomotive No. 7069 in the English Electric works at Preston. Martin Oldacres Attock can be seen looking out of the cab window. *Bill Attock Collection*

Following the trials with the railcar, Martin Oldacres assumed a similar responsibility for the English Electric demonstrator diesel-electric shunting locomotive when it entered service at various locations on the LMS between April 1934 and July 1935. R. & W. Hawthorn, Leslie & Co., Newcastle-upon-Tyne, manufactured the frames and some other mechanical parts, but English Electric undertook final assembly of the locomotive and installation of the diesel engine and electrical equipment at Preston.* It was equipped with a 300 bhp English Electric 6K medium-speed diesel engine direct-coupled to a main generator that supplied current to two self-ventilating nose-suspended traction motors which powered the outer two of the three axles. Because the design of the locomotive incorporated outside frames, fly cranks and coupling rods were adopted to transmit power from the outer axles to the centre axle, resulting in an 0-6-0 wheel arrangement.

Initial trials were conducted on the Preston Docks Railway before the locomotive was sent to commence in-service trials at Rugby during the week ending 7th April, 1934. Martin Oldacres accompanied the locomotive as the LMS put it through its paces in goods yards at Rugby, Camden, Birmingham, Crewe, Beeston (Nottingham), Toton, Salford, Speke (Liverpool), Healey Mills, Wakefield, Sheffield, Rotherham, Carlisle, and Glasgow, where it covered almost every type of shunting duty. When in Glasgow a trial was even conducted on the Glasgow Underground system, between Glasgow Central and Bridgeton Cross, to ascertain if diesel traction might provide an answer to the problem of smoke and fumes in tunnels. Whilst the trials showed some promise, the noxious diesel exhaust proved to be an equally distressing problem. However, a trial made from Rutherglen to Glasgow Central on 13th January, 1935 produced very satisfactory results.

During this period one person who visited English Electric, and would most probably have met with Martin Oldacres, was W.A. Smyth, mechanical engineer of the Ceylon Government Railways (CGR). William Addison Smyth, who was born in Dublin in 1902, joined the MGWR in 1920 as a pupil of W.H. Morton at Broadstone works. After a spell with the MGWR and GSR, he left Ireland in 1929 to take an appointment as assistant mechanical engineer (Manufacturing) on the CGR. On 1st April, 1931 he was appointed deputy mechanical engineer and succeeded to the position of mechanical engineer on 6th February, 1935. (Further details of his career may be found in the *Journal of the Irish Railway Record Society*, Vol.14, pp117-128.) While he was on leave in England, in 1934, he carried out an investigation of the position of diesel traction on Britain's railways, visiting all of the principal diesel engine manufacturers. The significance of this visit, in so far as Martin Oldacres' career is concerned, will become apparent later in this chapter. Although there is no record of the demonstrator diesel–electric shunting locomotive being tested on the Southern Railway or the Great Western Railway (GWR) in 1935, the latter company did purchase one standard diesel-electric shunting locomotive from English Electric. GWR No. 2 was delivered in June 1936 and was put to work in the goods yard at Acton. Frames and bodywork for three shunting locomotives were constructed by the Southern Railway at Ashford in 1937 and delivered to the works at Preston for installation of diesel engines and electrical equipment by English Electric.

* Although English Electric took the lead in producing the demonstrator shunting locomotive, the Maker's Plates bore the inscription 'English Electric – Hawthorn Leslie 1934' and carried a Hawthorn Leslie works number (3816).

Great Western Railway 0-6-0 shunter No. 2 on load-hauling trials prior to delivery from English Electric. *Bill Attock Collection*

English Electric 350 hp 0-6-0 diesel-electric shunting locomotive delivered to the GWR in 1935. *Bill Attock Collection*

A batch of production diesel-electric shunters for the LMS in various stages of construction in Preston. In the background can be seen the English Electric demonstration railcar *Bluebird*. *Bill Attock Collection*

The LMS had earlier agreed to procure 10 locomotives of this type in their 1935 programme (LMS Nos. 7069-78), while the demonstrator was purchased from English Electric in 1936, becoming LMS No. 7079. The latter locomotive appears to have been the subject of a disagreement with English Electric, the LMS requiring that it should be altered and upgraded, so as to be identical to the production batch, at a cost of not more than £5,000. The manufacturers disagreed and supplied the modified equipment, leaving it to the LMS to carry out the work at Crewe. Nos. 7069-73 and 7079 were allocated to Crewe South, the remainder going to Willesden depot in London. These locomotives were the precursors of the BR class '08' shunting locomotive, of which more than 1,000 units were built between 1952 and 1962.

On 19th February, 1935 Martin Oldacres was attached to the outside department of English Electric and attended a three month course on the electrical aspects of diesel-electric railway traction at the Phoenix Works, Bradford. Thereafter he was appointed superintendent for the erection and testing of diesel-electric locomotives at the Dick, Kerr Works at Preston. His first tasks included the assembly of the aforementioned 350 hp diesel-electric shunting locomotive for the GWR and 320 hp diesel-electric freight shunting locomotives for New Consolidated Gold Fields in early 1936. The first half of 1936 also saw work in hand at Preston on the assembly of two similar locomotives for Sudan.

Construction of the first railway line in Sudan, to connect Khartoum with Wadi Halfa was commenced at the latter place in 1875; however, only about 30 miles were completed. Later, in 1884-5, the British Army extended the line to Akasha, but this section was abandoned shortly afterwards. It was subsequently re-instated, but closed again in 1905. The Wadi Halfa to Khartoum

320 hp diesel-electric shunting locomotive for the Consolidated Goldfields Company in South Africa. *Bill Attock Collection*

Consolidated Goldfields 0-6-0 shunter No. 1 preparing to leave Preston by road for export to South Africa. *Bill Attock Collection*

Consolidated Goldfields 0-6-0 No. 1 in service at a mine in South Africa in 1936.
Bill Attock Collection

military railway was meanwhile constructed by Lord Kitchener and handed over to the Sudan Government in 1900, being extended five years later to Port Sudan, where a harbour was constructed. Various extensions to the system were made from 1907 right up until the 1960s.

Sudan Railways ordered five diesel locomotives in 1936 and, in addition to the two English Electric locomotives, two were supplied by Hawthorn, Leslie with McLaren engines and one by Harland & Wolff of Belfast equipped with its own design of engine. The two English Electric locomotives, Sudan Railways Nos. 401 & 402, were to the maker's standard design, but adapted to the 3 ft 6 in. gauge. On 10th July, 1936 Martin Oldacres arrived in the Sudan as the English Electric engineer in sole charge of commissioning the two diesel-electric locomotives for Sudan Railways. Upon delivery to Sudan the locomotives were based at Atbara for initial trials, later being transferred to Port Sudan, where they were employed on heavy and more continuous shunting duties. Martin Oldacres' visit to Sudan coincided with the introduction of a class of Beyer Garratt locomotives of the 4-6-4+4-6-4 wheel arrangement. These locomotives had bar frames, Walschaerts valve gear and Belpaire fireboxes with arch tubes. Four locomotives, Nos. 250-253 (Works Nos. 6798-6801) arrived at Port Sudan in 1936, a further six arriving in the following year (Nos. 254-259). They worked mainly on the Port Sudan to Atbara section which included a stretch of 16 miles at a gradient of 1 in 100; they also worked between Atbara and Wadi Madani. Post-war dieselisation and the laying of heavier track made the Garratts redundant and they were sold in 1949 to Rhodesia Railways, who in turn sold them on again in 1964-5 to Caminhos de Ferro e Transportes do Estado de Moçambique (CFM). At that time much of the Sudan Railways' track in use weighed only 50 lb. per yard, hence the choice of that particular type of locomotive to keep axle loads to the minimum.

New Beyer-Garratt locomotive being unloaded at Port Sudan in 1936/37. They were put to work on the Port Sudan to Atbara line, a line which included 16 miles at a gradient of 1 in 100 and with rails weighing only 50 lb. per yard. *M.O. Attock, courtesy Bill Attock*

Sudan Government Railways 4-6-4+4-6-4 Beyer-Garratt locomotive shortly after delivery in 1937. Ten of these locomotives were supplied by Beyer, Peacock of Manchester. They were sold to Rhodesian Railways in 1949, becoming class '17'; they were sold on again in 1964-65 to the Caminhos de Ferro Moçambique, becoming that company's Nos. 921-30.

M.O. Attock, courtesy Bill Attock

Sudan Railways shunter No. 405, supplied in 1937 by Harland & Wolff of Belfast, with the first of a batch of main line Co-Co locomotives from English Electric. It is not known whether Martin Oldacres Attock was directly involved with these locomotives. *Bill Attock Collection*

A crowd surrounds one of the English Electric Co-Co diesel-electric locomotives of Sudan Government Railways. The second and third coaches on the train provide first class accommodation. *Bill Attock Collection*

The President of Sudan boarding one of the new English Electric main line Co-Co diesel-electric locomotives. *Bill Attock Collection*

Sudan Government Railways shunter No. 2 shortly after entering service in 1937.
Bill Attock Collection

Sudan Railways 3 ft 6 in. gauge 0-6-0 diesel-electric locomotive No. 2, one of two supplied by English Electric in 1936/37. Two were also supplied at the same time by Hawthorn, Leslie and one by Harland & Wolff of Belfast. *Bill Attock Collection*

One of the new railcars for Ceylon on the English Electric test track at Preston. No date is shown but it was probably November or December 1937. *Bill Attock Collection*

CGR Railcar No. D2 being unloaded at Colombo Docks. Note minor sea damage sustained *en route* from England. Also note the CGR initials, which at first glance could be mistaken for the English GWR. *Bill Attock Collection*

When he returned from the Sudan at the end of April 1937 Martin Oldacres was attached to the Traction Department of English Electric where he was responsible for supervising the erection and testing of three 4-car diesel-electric trains, which the CGR had ordered in 1936. Previously, in 1935, two 880 hp diesel-electric locomotives had been loaned to CGR by Sir W.G. Armstrong Whitworth & Co. (Engineers) Ltd; trials with these locomotives showed the economies in operation which might be expected from diesel-engined units, thus leading to the decision to order railcars from English Electric. The project involved activities at both the Rugby and Preston works, and, in November, Martin Oldacres sailed out to Ceylon on the SS *Strathaird* in order to prepare for the arrival of the railcars. In December 1937, while he was making preparations in Colombo, Maj. J.L. Kotelawala, the Ceylonese Minister for Communications & Works, visited Preston to see the new diesel trains. The new railcars were unique in two respects, viz. they were the first contract where one firm was responsible for carrying out the entire job, holding full responsibility for the design, manufacture and final performance of the trains; secondly, they were the first all-welded, diesel-electric, articulated trains to be built in Britain.

The first set arrived in Colombo harbour, on Wednesday 5th January, 1938, aboard the SS *Clan Murray* where it was offloaded the next day, and on 7th January it was moved to the locomotive workshops at Ratmalana. The original CGR workshops were located at Maradana and, by 1913, had expanded into a facility consisting of 13 shops. A.E. Williams of the Indian State Railways had been commissioned, in 1928, to reorganize the railway workshops and it was

P&O Lines MV *Strathaird* of London on which Martin Oldacres Attock sailed to Colombo in November 1937 in connection with the delivery of the three railcar sets to CGR. Some 2½ years later, the young Kenneth Atock sailed with the Australian 2/7th Infantry Battalion on the same vessel, as the Troopship HMT-Y4, from Australia to the Middle East. *Bill Cook Collection*

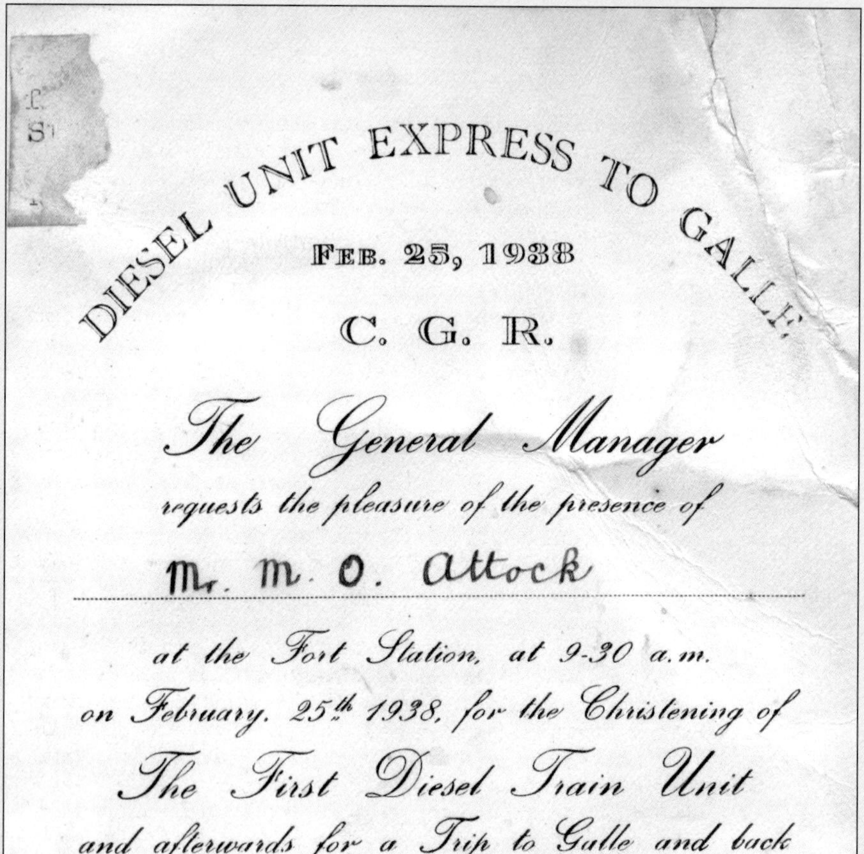

DIESEL UNIT EXPRESS TO GALLE

FEB. 25, 1938

C. G. R.

The General Manager

requests the pleasure of the presence of

M. M. O. Attock

at the Fort Station, at 9-30 a.m.

on February. 25th 1938, for the Christening of

The First Diesel Train Unit

and afterwards for a Trip to Galle and back

leaving Fort at 9-55 a.m. & arriving Galle, 12 noon

Lunch at N. O. H. Galle

Return trip leaving Galle, at 2-07 p.m.

and arriving Fort at 4-12 p.m.

R. S. V. P.
General Manager,
C. G. R.

This card should be presented
at Fort and Galle
Railway Stations.

An invitation to Martin Oldacres Attock to attend the naming ceremony of the first CGR railcar on 25th February, 1938 and a subsequent run to Galle, where a lunch was held.

Bill Attock Collection

decided to re-locate and modernise the facilities. An excellent 77 acre site was found at Ratmalana and removal commenced in 1931, with the transfer of the machine shop. By 1937 the entire facility, which comprised 33 shops, was functioning as a complete unit. The management organization was also restructured with two workshop superintendents (one who had responsibility for locomotives and the other for carriages and wagons) and a design draughtsman, all reporting to the mechanical engineer.

The first trial trip with the railcars was carried out, on 19th January, from Ratmalana to Pandura, and three days later a 62 mile run took place which departed Ratmalana at 8.17 and arrived at Galle at 11.31 am - an amazing 29 minutes under the normal scheduled time. The return journey departed Ratmalana at 1.40 pm and was completed in 20 minutes under the schedule. Among the CGR officials who travelled on the train with Martin Oldacres were W.G. Hills, acting General Manager; J.G. Smith, Acting Deputy General Manager (Operations); and H.W.F. Freer, acting mechanical engineer.

Harold William Farquharson Freer was born in Dublin in 1900 and completed an apprenticeship with the GS&WR at Inchicore in 1921 following which he was appointed a draughtsman. He later served as an assistant in the works manager's office, but left the GSR in 1930 to take an appointment as works superintendent of CGR. He became assistant mechanical engineer on 1st April, 1931, and in December 1935 he was appointed deputy mechanical engineer following the promotion of W.A. Smyth to the position of mechanical engineer of the CGR. Freer succeeded to the latter post when Smyth returned to the UK in 1937; he resigned from CGR in February 1949 and moved to a senior executive post with Commonwealth Railways in Australia.

On 29th January the Governor of Ceylon, H.E. Sir Andrew Caldecott, boarded the new railcar set at Colombo Fort station, which departed at 10.30 am for Ratmalana workshops. He travelled in the cab of the railcar and, following its arrival at the workshops, he was pleased to take part in a ceremony in which one of the CGR steam locomotives, 4-6-0 No. 295, was named *Sir Andrew Caldecott* in his honour.

CGR 4-6-0 No. 295 at Ratmalana on the morning of 29th January, 1938 with one of the new railcars, probably No. D1, in the background. Later that day the Governor of Ceylon, His Excellency Sir Andrew Caldecott, would have the honour of naming the steam locomotive after himself. *M.O. Attock, courtesy Bill Attock*

A group of railway officials and representatives from English Electric in front of one of the new railcars, interestingly numbered 502. Martin Oldacres Attock is in the centre front (wearing wreath) with Joyce to his left. On the other side are Mr and Mrs Cook. The English gentleman seated beside Joyce may well be Harold Freer, the CGR's CME. *Bill Attock Collection*

Bill Cook, who later became Martin Oldacres Attock's father-in-law, taking some light refreshments during one of the early CGR railcar trials. *Bill Attock Collection*

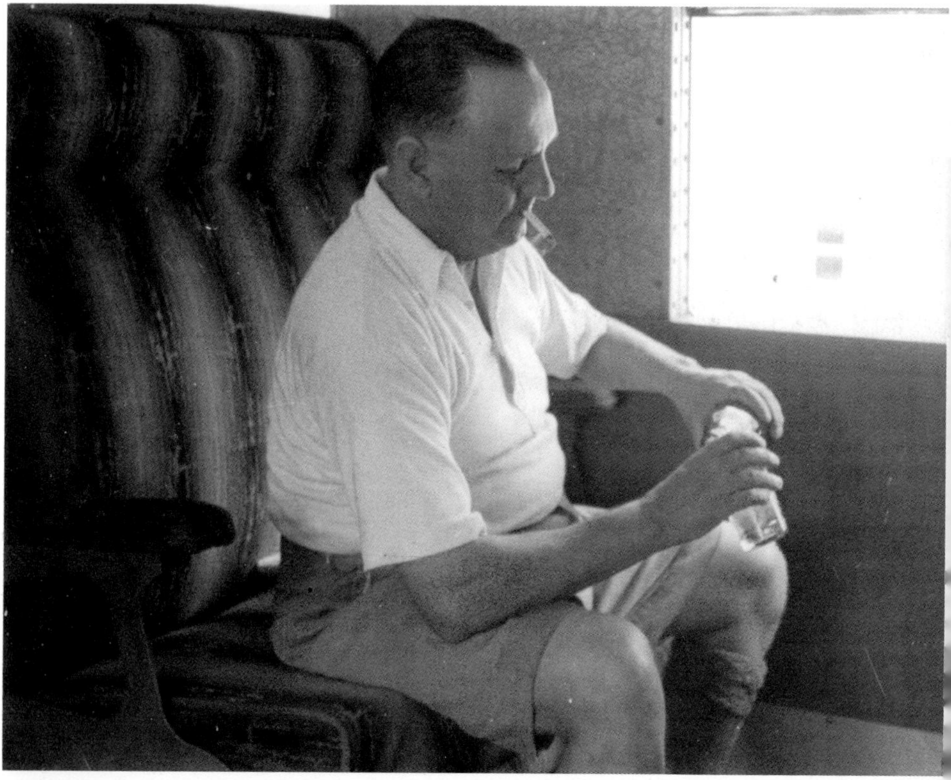

Maradana running shed just outside Colombo with the three four-coach diesel-electric railcar sets delivered in 1938. *Bill Attock Collection*

Looking suspiciously like the aftermath of a collision with buffer stops, CGR Unit No. 2 is in fact undergoing routine overhaul in shop 16 at Ratmalana. The workshops here, eventually totalling 33 shops, were commenced in 1931 and were fully operational by 1937 and replaced the previous workshops at Maradana. *Bill Attock Collection*

Two CGR four-car railcar sets coupled together for the heavy Christmas traffic of December 1938. Photographed just outside Colombo Fort station. *Bill Attock Collection*

Eight-car railcar set with unit No. D3 leading at Mount Lavinia, a short distance south of the capital, Colombo, on the line to Galle and Matara. The date is December 1938.
Bill Attock Collection

The second railcar set arrived a few days before St Valentine's Day, having sustained some sea damage *en route*. The first trial run with the second set, on 18th February, was marred by a failure at Maggona station due to a problem with the electric horn. In fact, complaints were made that the horns were not sufficiently distinguishable from road vehicles and did not therefore warn trespassers on the railway in sufficient time. The units were subsequently fitted with two-tone horns. A factor unique to these railcars was that they were the first trains in Ceylon to have upholstered seats in the third class compartments. The colour scheme adopted was aluminium grey for the roof and body sides down to waist level, with green below.

At 9.30 am on 25th February, 1938 the new diesel train service was launched with a ceremony conducted by Minister Kotelawala. The first railcar set was named *Silver Foam* and at 9.55 am it set off on its first official run to Galle. Amongst those who were in attendance at the ceremony was a Mr R.W. Urie, possibly a grandson of Robert Wallace Urie, the last CME of the London & South Western Railway. Just two days prior to this auspicious event Martin Oldacres Attock had been elected an Associate Member of the Institution of Locomotive Engineers. Martin Oldacres must have been delighted with the two events and to see the introduction of the new diesel trains bring about a reduction of one hour in the 4½ hour schedule between Colombo and Matara. The second and third units were named, respectively, *Silver Mist* and *Silver Spray*, and with their arrival a second diesel service was inaugurated, on 14th March, 1938, on the line to Kandy, 'The Hill Capital'. The introduction of the railcars gave the Ceylonese railway passengers their first experience of comfort, speed and cleanliness in train travel.

Normal train formations consisted of a power car at each end with two intermediate trailers between, except on the hill section to Kandy when one trailer was removed. The approach of the Hindu and Sinhalese New Year and the Easter holidays brought about abnormal traffic on the Coast Line, and resulted in the CGR combining two units into an eight-car train, from 7th April, 1938, for the morning express from Matara to Colombo and the afternoon return working. The new trains were so popular that it soon became necessary to issue special tickets with a supplementary fare in an attempt to avoid overcrowding - it was recorded that instances had occurred when up to 1,000 passengers had managed to crowd in.

Silver Mist was involved in an accident with a tree at about 8.15 am on 26th April. The London *Daily Express* reported that a giant coconut palm had fallen on the train and cut it in two, the flying pieces of the shattered tree severely injuring three men and a woman standing 20 yards from the track. The damage to the train may have been substantial, or other problems might have arisen, as two of the three sets were reported to be out of action by 23rd June. Another incident was reported, in September 1938, when what was initially believed to be a stone tied to a tree hit the windscreen of one of the railcars between Colombo and Galle. Further investigation showed it to be a 7 lb. lead weight which was believed to have been hung from the tree by hirelings of some local bus operators, whose traffic the railcars had succeeded in capturing. On the plus side, it was reported that the toughened windscreen successfully withstood the impact, and that the driver's 'deadman' controls operated exactly as intended.

With three sets in service, and technical problems increasing, English Electric sent out H.L. Troughton to assist Martin Oldacres in remedying defects. A long-

CGR railcar set No. D1 on a pilgrimage special at an unknown location early in 1939. Crowding was a perennial problem on CGR trains, particularly on special occasions such as this.
Bill Attock Collection

Colombo Fort station showing a large crowd of passengers preparing to board railcar set No. D3. Severe overcrowding led to supplementary fares being charged for travelling on the railcars.
Bill Attock Collection

distance trial run was made with *Silver Foam* to Talaimannar Pier and back on 25th January, 1939, but despite this spectacular run there were still problems with the units. In a talk to the Engineering Conference in Colombo, on 10th August, 1939, Harold Freer, noted that 'Failure of the fuel pump governor and the advance and retard mechanism has proved to be the most persistent defect and it continues at the time of writing'. However, the CGR were sufficiently pleased with their new acquisitions for the Crown Agents for the Colonies to place a further order with English Electric, for eight single-unit railcars in September 1939, but delivery was later suspended because of the war. By February 1940 one of the original units had completed a total of 140,000 miles in service, with only one mechanical failure in the preceding 12 months.

As well as commissioning the diesel railcars, Martin Oldacres also 'commissioned a wife'. Whilst working with CGR he had met Joyce Cook, who was born in Lewisham on 10th February, 1917. She was the daughter of William G.A. Cook, acting assistant mechanical engineer (locomotives), CGR, and they were married on 21st December, 1939. The ceremony took place at St Peter's Church, Fort, Colombo with the Revd A. Kendall Baker officiating. The bride, who was given away by her father, wore an ivory satin gown with full skirt forming a petalled line with the flowing train. The bridesmaid was Harold Freer's daughter, Maureen, the best man was J.K.J. Brown and Derek Briggs was the page. The ceremony was followed by a reception at the Galle Face hotel.

Wedding party outside the Galle Face Hotel in Colombo on 21st December, 1939. *Left to right*: Bill Cook (bride's father), Maureen Freer (bridesmaid), Joyce Attock (née Cook), Martin Oldacres, Derek Briggs (pageboy), Mrs Cook. *Bill Attock Collection*

REGISTERED OFFICE:
QUEENS HOUSE,
KINGSWAY, LONDON, W.C.2.

WORKS	SIEMENS WORKS, STAFFORD	DICK, KERR WORKS, PRESTON	WILLANS WORKS, RUGBY	PHOENIX WORKS, BRADFORD
TELE PHONE / GRAMS	700 STAFFORD. ENELECTICO, STAFFORD.	5231 PRESTON. ENELECTICO, PRESTON	2211 RUGBY. ENELECTICO, RUGBY.	9260 BRADFORD. ENELECTICO, BRADFORD.

THE ENGLISH ELECTRIC COMPANY LIMITED.

ALL COMMUNICATIONS TO BE ADDRESSED
TO THE COMPANY, NOT TO INDIVIDUALS.

STAFFORD.

CABLES: "ENELECTICO, STAFFORD".
CODES: BENTLEYS, A.B.C. 6TH EDITION.

OUR REFERENCE

YOUR REFERENCE

TO WHOM IT MAY CONCERN: 26th November, 1940.

THIS IS TO CERTIFY THAT MR. M.O. ATTOCK IS RESPONSIBLE FOR TAKING THE CRUISER TANK MARK V. NO.T,15295 FROM STAFFORD BY ROAD, FOR DELIVERY TO CHRISTCHURCH, HAMPSHIRE.

HIS OFFICIAL PHOTOGRAPH IS ATTACHED HERETO.

THIS MOVEMENT IS IN COMPLIANCE WITH AN ORDER OF THE MINISTRY OF SUPPLY AS INDICATED IN THEIR LETTER OF 21ST NOVEMBER AND CARRIED BY MR. ATTOCK.

...LISH ELECTRIC COMPANY L...

GENERAL MANAGER, STAFFORD.

A letter dated 26th November, 1940 from English Electric in Stafford confirming that Martin Oldacres Attock is responsible for taking a Mark V Cruiser tank No. T.15295 by road from Stafford to Christchurch in Hampshire. *Bill Attock Collection*

A charming scene caught by Martin Oldacres with a 2 ft 6 in. gauge 2-4-0+0-4-2 Beyer-Garratt No. 293 in the Kelani Valley on the independent Colombo to Opanake line, where gradients of 1 in 24 were encountered. No. 293 was designed to replace two 0-4-2Ts which previously worked the line. She had an all-up weight of only 39 tons and axle load of 7 tons. *M.O. Attock, courtesy Bill Attock*

Time spent in Ceylon also enabled Martin Oldacres to see some of the CGR's steam locomotives in operation. These included the country's only Beyer-Garratt, a rather diminutive 2 ft 6 in. gauge 2-4-0+0-4-2, which worked on the Colombo to Opanaike line in the Kelani Valley. This locomotive, delivered in 1929 (CGR class 'H1', No. 293), was designed to replace two 0-4-2Ts which previously worked the line, on which there was a ruling gradient of 1 in 24. No. 293 had outside plate frames; 10 in. x 16 in. cylinders; 2 ft. 6 in. driving wheels; and boiler pressure of 175 psi. Weight in working order was 39 tons, and the water tanks were noteworthy in having rounded tops.

With the problems on the railcars put to bed Martin Oldacres returned to England, but he was only with the Traction Department for the month of September 1940 when he was appointed chief production engineer at the Armoured Fighting Vehicle Works which English Electric had established at their Stafford facility. In this capacity he was responsible, *inter alia*, for acceptance trials on new tanks. As an example we have a report which he submitted describing a run, in November 1943, from Stafford to Chobham in Surrey, a distance of 176 miles. The tank in question left Stafford on Thursday 11th November, travelling as far as Banbury without incident, the journey onwards to Chobham being completed the following day. On the following Monday the tank, with weights added to simulate battle conditions and weight (40 t 8 cwt), ran to Long Valley at Farnborough; this was followed by a 19 mile cross-country run in deep mud. It was reported that a ¼ mile run from a standing start produced an average speed of 19.6 mph, with a flying ¼ mile averaging 22.8 mph.

Covenanter Tank on trial. This was one of a number of classes of tank turned out by the English Electric Stafford works during World War II. Martin Oldacres was responsible for the delivery and testing of tanks during the war years. *Bill Attock Collection*

General Charles De Gaulle standing on a tank while addressing the workforce of the English Electric works at Stafford in 1940. On his left is George (later Lord) Nelson, Managing Director of English Electric. *M.O. Attock, courtesy Bill Attock*

Chapter Fifteen

Dieselisation at Home and Abroad

By February 1945 Martin Oldacres was back with the Traction Division at Bradford and Preston, and once again became involved with commissioning new locomotives and dealing with problems that had developed on locomotives already in service. At the same time the LMS was beginning to consider the question of diesel traction for main line operations. C.E. Fairburn was the chief mechanical engineer of the LMS at the time, and whilst he was most likely in favour of the idea, Sir Harold Hartley, the LMS Vice-President, was opposed to it on the grounds of first cost. Nevertheless, on instructions from Fairburn's assistant, H.G. Ivatt, the Derby drawing office sketched several schemes. Following Fairburn's death, Ivatt, who succeeded him, began seeking support for schemes centred upon the English Electric 16SVT engine.

As chance would have it, Sir William Wood, the LMS President, paid a visit to Derby, in December 1945, and Ivatt took the opportunity to bend his ear. This led to authority being granted for negotiations to take place with British Thomson Houston, Crompton Parkinson and English Electric. Ivatt decided to stick with English Electric for the main project because, firstly, the LMS already had experience of its equipment in the diesel-electric shunting locomotives, and, secondly, the Derby proposals were based around the 16SVT engine. Following a meeting with representatives of English Electric, on 20th May, 1946, tentative agreement was reached for the building of a trial diesel-electric locomotive, in the form of two bogie-mounted units, each of 1,600 hp, which could be coupled together to work as a single unit. Under this arrangement English Electric agreed to provide the diesel engines and electrical equipment; the actual date of contract for the supply of components was 29th November, 1946.

It appears that the locomotives were originally intended to be of the A1A-A1A type, but English Electric insisted on all axles being powered, hence the Co-Co arrangement.* The LMS commenced work on the main frames at Derby on 10th July, 1947, and the electrical equipment began to arrive from English Electric later that month. The first locomotive, No. 10000, was put on its bogies on 21st November, entered the paint shop on 1st December, and was started up for the first time on 4th December, 1947. No. 10000 officially entered traffic on 13th December and went to Euston three days later, in charge of driver Burton, where it was inspected alongside No. 6256, the latest main line steam

* The UIC classification for describing the wheel arrangement of locomotives uses upper-case letters to designate the number of *consecutive* driving axles, starting with 'A' for a single axle. Numbers are used to designate *consecutive* non-driving axles, starting at '1' for a single axle. For electric and diesel-electric locomotives carried on bogies, the bogie designations are separated by a hyphen, and where all axles on a bogie are individually driven by electric traction motors, this is indicated by the addition of a lower case 'o' as a suffix to the driving wheel letter. Thus, Co-Co means that the locomotive is carried on two three-axle bogies with all axles individually-driven by traction motors, and A1A-A1A means that the locomotive is carried on two three-axle bogies, of which only the two outer axles on each bogie are individually-driven by traction motors, etc.

Britain's first main line diesel-electric locomotive, 1,600 hp LMS No. 10000. Martin Oldacres is standing immediately left of the 'M'. *Bill Attock Collection*

The second main line locomotive, No. 10001 did not actually appear until after the formation of British Railways. Here she is seen leaving St Pancras on her first revenue-earning service in August 1948. *Bill Attock Collection*

LMS No. 10000 working a passenger train at 80 mph, the picture presumably taken to show how steady she was at speed. The locomotive is in charge of driver Burton who was responsible for much of the early running with No. 10000. *Bill Attock Collection*

Former Southern Railway 1-Co-Co-1 No. 10203 at Salisbury, one of three locomotives introduced by the SR in 1951-54. Although they used the same engine as No. 10000/1, it was uprated to 1,750 hp. *Bill Attock Collection*

February 1946 is the date and the location the English Electric works at Preston, showing one of the 23 new single unit railcars for the CGR. The destination indicator on the side reads Maradana, Colombo's second station situated about 2 km from Colombo Fort.

Bill Attock Collection

Flying boat on which Martin Oldacres Attock made the first part of his trip to Ceylon in 1947. From Karachi he travelled to Colombo on an Air India 'DC3'. *M.O. Attock, courtesy Bill Attock*

locomotive, before taking a five-coach test train to Watford and back. No. 10000 began regular service on 23rd February, 1948, by which time the LMS had become British Railways (London Midland Region), on the 8.55 am from Derby to St Pancras, returning at 2.15 pm down. No. 10001 emerged from Derby in July 1948, soon replacing No. 10000 on the above turn, while the latter entered the works for interim repairs. The two locomotives began working in multiple for the first time, on 5th October, 1948, on the 1.00 pm Euston-Glasgow express, with loads up to 530 tons as far as Crewe. Martin Oldacres was closely involved in the commissioning of the two locomotives and would have travelled between Derby and London with driver Burton on many occasions.

The late 1940s was a very busy time for Martin Oldacres, for in addition to his involvement with the LMS main line locomotives, he was overseeing the delivery of additional diesel-electric railcars for CGR and diesel-electric locomotives for Malaya, Tasmania and Egypt. Once hostilities ceased and materials became available, the 1939 order for CGR had been re-activated but, by that time, their requirements had changed and the order was increased to 23 single-car units. The CGR satisfaction with the original 1938 railcars was adequately illustrated by Harold Freer, in 1947, when he reported that the three trains had run a total of 1,253,000 miles, between 1938 and the end of 1946, with an overall average fuel consumption of 2.62 train miles per gallon. In their first full year in service, 1939, average running costs worked out at 46.4 cents per mile and availability in that year was 90.3 per cent. Even in 1946 availability at 82.3 per cent was considered to be very satisfactory in view of the difficulties associated with obtaining spare parts during the war years; indeed, one consignment was lost at sea and had to be duplicated.

The first five new railcars arrived in Colombo in early August 1947, and the balance was delivered at the rate of three per month. The new railcars bore many similarities to the earlier units but were intended for operation between Matara and Galle, and also possibly between Kandy and Colombo, as single cars or as trains of two-cars, working as a multiple unit, controlled from one driving cab. Each car was powered by the same 180 bhp EE 6HT engine as was previously used, the traction equipment also being similar to that of the earlier units, and the colour scheme was the same as the 1938 railcars. As delivered they bore many similarities to the earlier units; the principal difference was that they provided only third class accommodation for 80 passengers. Martin Oldacres had returned to Ceylon for the delivery of the new railcars and, on that occasion, he sampled a new form of travel, from Southampton to Karachi by BOAC Hythe class flying boat, and from Karachi to Colombo by Air India DC3. On 4th August a trial run was made from Colombo to Alutgama with two of the new railcars coupled together. The 37 mile run was made in just over an hour, including a stop at Ratmalana, a maximum speed of 50 mph being achieved; on board for the trial was the Minister of Communications & Works, Mr J.L. Kotelewala. The first of the new railcars entered service shortly afterwards.

Later in the same month, Martin Oldacres was in Malaya overseeing the delivery and commissioning of twenty 350 hp diesel-electric shunting locomotives. That order, which had been placed with English Electric in late 1945, marked the beginning of the Malayan Railways dieselisation programme.

Malayan Railways 0-6-0 diesel-electric shunter No. 151.01 as built by English Electric in 1947 for operation on the metre-gauge system. Twenty of these shunters were delivered.

Bill Attock Collection

Egyptian State Railways five-coach diesel-electric railcar set on trial on British Railways track near Birmingham. *Courtesy Diesel Railway Traction*

Known as the '15' class, and built to the metre-gauge requirements, they were delivered through Port Swettenham and put into service in 1948; the first unit carried the number 151.01. Port Swettenham later became known as Port Klang, one of the world's busy seaports. Formerly Kelang, it is situated about 30 miles west of Kuala Lumpur. The Malayan Railways administration placed a further order with English Electric, in 1956, for twenty-six 1,500 hp Co-Co diesel-electric locomotives, which for many years were the most powerful units on the railway. Erection of the '20' class was split between the former Dick, Kerr works at Preston and the works of R. & W. Hawthorn, Leslie at Newcastle-upon-Tyne. They were delivered in 1957 and the whole class was named after Malayan flowers, the first unit being named *Bunga Raya* after the national flower.

By November 1948 Martin Oldacres was in Cairo for the commissioning of twelve 1,600 hp diesel-electric locomotives for Egyptian State Railways (ESR), the first of which had been shipped from Preston in October. These twin-cab locomotives had an unusual wheel arrangement of 1A-Do-A1, with a traction motor powering each of the four axles on the rigid wheelbase and one motor on the inner axle of each bogie. All axle journals ran in Timken roller bearings and the locomotives were equipped for multiple-unit operation. The diesel engine used was the same 16SVT model as had been installed in the main line LMS locomotives, and the electrical equipment was also the same. Six of these locomotives were built at Preston, the remaining six being assembled at the former Vulcan Foundry Works at Newton-le-Willows.

ESR were sufficiently satisfied with the main line locomotives to order 19 articulated, five-coach, diesel-electric railcar sets from English Electric for delivery in 1950. These units were intended for use on the 130 mile section between Cairo and Alexandria, with possible extension of services to Luxor. English Electric was responsible for the design and manufacture of the engine and electrical equipment, the construction of the underframes and bodies being sub-contracted to the Birmingham Railway Carriage & Wagon Company, Smethwick. Power for each set was provided by two English Electric type 4SRKT engines producing 400 hp at 750 rpm, one at each end of the train; these engines were pressure-charged with a blower driven by an exhaust gas turbine. In each power car the main generator was direct-coupled to the engine, power from the generator being taken to two, series-wound, reversible type, traction motors mounted in the respective power bogie. The bogie wheels were of the solid, rolled-steel, disc type pressed on to the axles, which ran in Timken roller bearings; air-actuated, clasp brakes provided braking.

The coach bodies were of all-metal construction, the underframes being welded-up from rolled steel sections and plates. Exterior panelling was of steel sheeting spot-welded to the body frame members. Windows were double-glazed and the first class compartments were air-conditioned, while second class had ventilating fans; a buffet was provided in the centre vehicle of the train for serving light meals. The first trial run of the new ESR railcars was carried out on the British Railways network, on 10th December, 1950, from Birmingham (Snow Hill) to Droitwich and back, a distance of 57 miles; a maximum speed of 76½ mph was achieved on that run. It was reported, in August 1951, that four of the 19 units had been delivered and were in service between Cairo and Alexandria and between Cairo and Port

Group at Bulac, Cairo on the occasion of the delivery of the first of the English Electric 1,600 hp main line 1A-Do-A1 diesel-electric locomotives in 1948. Martin Oldacres Attock on left.

Bill Attock Collection

One of the 19 five-coach diesel-electric railcar sets for operation on the Alexandria to Cairo section of Egyptian State Railways. They were powered by two 400 hp 4SRKT diesel engines, one at each end of the train. Seating was provided for 172 passengers.
Courtesy Diesel Railway Traction

Diesel-electric 1,600 hp 1A-Do-A1 locomotive for Egyptian State Railways in the English Electric works in Preston just prior to the start of its journey to Cairo. *Bill Attock Collection*

South Australian Railways class '900' A1A-A1A No. 900 on a freight train at an unknown location. One of 10 locomotives designed and built at the company's facility at Islington with equipment supplied by English Electric in 1951. They were powered by 16SVT engines and were rated at 1,588 hp. No. 900 was named *Lady Norrie*, after the wife of the State Governor, Sir Willoughby Norrie. *Bill Attock Collection*

South Australian Railways '900' class No.902 on shed at Adelaide. These locomotives were employed on the *Overlander* interstate express trains as well as on heavy interstate freight duties. *Bill Attock Collection*

Said. About that time an alteration was made in the order, only 10 main line sets being then required, the remaining nine being re-configured for suburban services in the Cairo area; later, a further 11, three-coach, suburban sets were also ordered.

The first Australian railway to use English Electric equipment was the South Australia Railways (SAR). Not long after the end of World War II it prepared its own design for 350 hp, diesel-electric, shunting locomotives and contracted with English Electric to supply a pair of 6KT diesel engines and associated electric traction equipment. The two locomotives were built at SAR's Islington workshops, the first one entering service on 7th June, 1949 and the second one two weeks later. Officially designated the '350' class, they initially worked in the Adelaide freight yards but, soon after their arrival, a national coal strike saw them pressed into use on Adelaide suburban passenger services.

At the same time as SAR was building the two diesel shunting locomotives, the Western Australia Government Railways (WAGR) was constructing six, three-car, diesel-electric railcar sets in its workshops at Midland. An English Electric 6H engine rated at 209 hp coupled to a 132 kW traction generator was mounted at each end of the 'ADF' class power cars, which contained a centrally located baggage compartment. Two traction motors were mounted in each of the three-axle power bogies resulting in an A1A-A1A wheel arrangement, which was unique for diesel railcars. In addition to the power car, each set comprised two 'ADU' class passenger trailer cars. The six units, Nos. 490-495, entered service between August 1949 and June 1950, the first trial run being made, on 23rd August, over the 54 mile Perth to Pinjarra section. They were named after Western Australian native flora - *Boronia, Crowea, Grevillea, Leschenaultia, Hovea* and *Banksia*.

Because Australian locomotive builders had not acquired rights to manufacture overseas diesel locomotive equipment at that time, Australia Iron & Steel (AI&S) decided to build eight, 730 hp, diesel-electric locomotives to its own design using power equipment imported from English Electric. Commonwealth Engineering of Sydney undertook to assemble the units, D1 entering service, on 4th May, 1950, as Australia's first main line diesel locomotive type. The 'D1' class totally revolutionised coal haulage on the AI&S Wongawilli and Kemira colliery traffic.

The Tasmanian Government Railways (TGR) was the first government-owned railway to introduce main line, diesel-electric locomotive power. In 1947 they placed an order, with English Electric, for 10 general-purpose locomotives to be powered by six-cylinder turbo-charged SRKT engines developing 660 bhp. A further 10 were ordered in 1948, followed by 12 more in 1949. The first batch was assembled at the Vulcan Foundry Works, but some later units were constructed at Preston. The first unit entered service in September 1950, and by March 1952 all 32 were in traffic. Between 1961 and 1968, five members of the class were equipped with lower gearing and rewired to provide better operation at low speeds, becoming 'XA' class in the process; in their original form they were liable to overheating when hauling heavy trains over long adverse gradients and these modifications made them more suitable for operation on the southern portion of the TGR main line. TGR anticipated that they would become independent of coal supplies from New South Wales with

Western Australian Government Railways diesel-electric railcar set. Each power car was powered by a pair of English Electric 6H engines rated at 209 hp and coupled to a 132 kW traction generator. The power bogies each had two traction motors on the outer axles, resulting in an A1A-A1A wheel arrangement, unique in diesel railcars. Six units, Nos. 490-95, entered service between August 1949 and June 1950; they were named after West Australian native flora. *Courtesy Diesel Railway Traction*

Tasmanian Government Railways 3 ft 6 in. gauge 660 hp Bo-Bo locomotive No. X4 with another, unidentified member of the class, on a test run shortly after their delivery in 1950. Powered by an English Electric 6SRKT engine, these locomotives were fitted for multiple working on freight trains over the steeply-graded Launceston to Hobart line. *Bill Attock Collection*

their introduction. It was also hoped that it would be possible to withdraw the remaining steam fleet, although steam locomotives actually still saw occasional use on passenger, goods and shunting duties up to 1975, 25 years after the introduction of the 'X' class!

The 'X' class locomotives were capable of being operated in multiples of up to three units. The diesel engines were direct-coupled to six-pole DC generators that supplied traction current to four, axle-hung, traction motors; an auxiliary generator providing current for control circuits, lighting and battery charging, and for running the compressor for the locomotive's air brakes and exhauster for vacuum train braking. The underframe and superstructure were of welded steel construction, the bogies being fabricated from steel plate sections. The locomotives were of the single cab type, arranged for right-hand operation. A removable roof section enabled the diesel power unit and generator equipment to be easily removed for maintenance.

As delivered, the 'X' class was painted in plain, dark green, and Martin Oldacres was on hand in Tasmania when the first two locomotives arrived aboard the MV *Stentor** in August 1950. They were put into service between Launceston and Hobart, a line that is, in parts, steeply-graded, and the diesel locomotives were found to be capable of hauling loads of approximately 100 tons more than the most powerful steam locomotives then in service. Furthermore, they could be worked for 23 hours a day and 6½ days a week. In connection with their delivery, Martin Oldacres personally organized a mobile training school for the TGR in a converted railway coach.

The 10 SAR '900' class were the first main line diesel-electric locomotives to be operated by that railway. They were introduced to traffic following an elaborate ceremony held on 10th September, 1951 at the Islington workshops, where they had been designed and built. Diesel engines and electrical traction components were obtained from English Electric, the locomotives having been constructed to replace steam power over the heavily graded Mount Lofty section on the Adelaide - Tailem Bend main line. They quickly took over the working of 'The Overlander' interstate expresses and became firm favourites for heavy, interstate, freight work. Resplendent in maroon livery with stainless steel panels, the first unit was named *Lady Norrie,* after the wife of the State Governor, Sir Willoughby Norrie. The first unit entered service on 10th September, 1951 hauling the *The Overlander,* and all 10 units of the class were in traffic by July 1953.

Victorian Railways (VR) turned to English Electric for help when the need arose for diesel locomotives for its own shunting operations and for State Electricity Commission (SEC) exchange siding shunting activities. Known as the 'F' class, they were based on the standard English Electric 350 hp 0-6-0 diesel-electric shunting locomotive design, but constructed to 5 ft 3 in. gauge. The 16 units were built at Preston and went into traffic during 1953; 10 with VR, and

* The MV *Stentor* was built by Caledon of East Dundee in 1946 for the Blue Funnel Line. A single-screw vessel of 10,203 GRT, she was a fast Empire class ship completed to Alfred Holt requirements. Transferred to Glen Line in 1958 and renamed *Glenshiel,* she reverted to Blue Funnel Line in 1963 and was again named *Stentor*. She was sold for scrap in 1975 and brought to Taiwan for breaking up.

Queensland Railways 3 ft 6 in. gauge 1,290 hp English Electric Co-Co locomotive as delivered to Queensland in 1953. Ten were built, numbered 1200-09. *Bill Attock Collection*

Queensland Railways '1200' class No. 1202 on a traditional freight train of the time. Delivered in 1953, the class comprised ten 1,290 hp Co-Co locomotives for the 3 ft 6 in. gauge. They were built at the Bradford works of English Electric and were initially used on Queensland Railway's top express passenger trains. *Bill Attock Collection*

the other six allocated exclusively to SEC duties, all later passing into full-time VR service. Uniquely amongst this type of locomotive, used in the UK and elsewhere, they were equipped with sideboards to protect shunting staff from getting caught up in the outside coupling rods.

The Queensland Railways (QR) '1200' class diesel-electric locomotives were the only true cab-type units in the state until 1988. Manufactured at English Electric's Bradford plant, and delivered in July 1953, they quickly found use working QR's top expresses such as the 'Sunshine Express' and the 'Inlander'. In addition to the aforementioned diesel electric locomotives, English Electric supplied twenty-five 2,400 hp, 1,500V-DC Co-Co electric locomotives to VR. The first unit was delivered to Melbourne towards the end of January 1953 but, although all had been delivered by August 1954, the electrification of the 128 km Dandenary-Traralgon line was not complete and about 12 of the units were stored at the Newport railway workshops for a time.

Although there is no evidence to confirm when Martin Oldacres visited Australia during 1951-53, we do know for certain that he was on that continent, and in New Zealand, during January and February 1955 in connection with complaints regarding diesel engines and ancillaries. The 3 ft 6 in. gauge New Zealand Railways (NZR) first became involved with English Electric, in 1922, when they ordered five Bo-Bo electric locomotives for working the 1 in 30 grade line through the narrow-bore 5½ mile tunnel crossing the Southern Alps between Arthur's Pass and Otira on the west coast of the South Island, which was opened in 1923. Known as the 'Eo' class, the five 1,500 hp units were built at the Dick, Kerr Works, Preston, where six smaller 'Ec' class locomotives were also constructed, which English Electric delivered in 1929, for the Christchurch to Lyttelton electrification scheme; another line that ran through a long tunnel.

In 1937 an electric locomotive was also ordered from English Electric for service in the Wellington area of the North Island. This first member of the 'Ed' class entered service in May 1938 at Wellington depot. During 1939/40 seven identical locomotives were assembled at the NZR Hutt Shops, Wellington, and two others at the Addington Shops in Christchurch. They worked the newly-opened Tawa deviation and over the electrified line from Wellington to Johnsonville, which had become just a branch line as a result of the deviation. In July 1938 English Electric supplied six, 2-car, electric-multiple-units, each comprising a 'DM' class motor coach and a 'D' class trailer, also for the steeply graded and multiple-tunnelled Johnsonville branch. Due to growth of traffic three more motor coaches and two more trailers were ordered in 1942, but delivery was delayed until 1946 due to the war. In the late 1940s NZR ordered a further 40 motor coaches and 71 trailers for expansion of the Wellington suburban services on the lines to Paekakariki and Upper Hutt, which English Electric delivered between 1949 and 1954.

In 1946, NZR had entered into an agreement with English Electric for the supply of all their diesel motive requirements for a period of 10 years. The first diesel-electric locomotives delivered by English Electric to New Zealand were the 'De' class. These 15 Bo-Bo units, which were manufactured at Preston, were equipped with the 6SRKT engines rated at 660 hp. The first four arrived at Wellington, in December 1951, and were commissioned in 1952, the rest of the

New Zealand Railways class 'Ed' 1-Do-2 electric locomotive outside the Preston works of English Electric being prepared for its road journey to Liverpool for shipment to New Zealand. Nine identical locomotives were assembled at the NZR Hutt and Addington works in 1939/40.
Bill Attock Collection

Brazilian Railways electric locomotive in the English Electric works at Preston prior to delivery. Although this photograph appears in Martin Oldacres' collection, there is no evidence that he had any involvement with this locomotive. *Bill Attock Collection*

units following in 1952-53. They were purchased with the intention of utilising them on heavy shunting and transfer duties and also for some freight and passenger train work. A number of them worked in pairs, hauling Royal Trains when Queen Elizabeth II visited New Zealand in 1953.

It was originally intended to procure 31 'Df' class 2-Co-Co-2 locomotives equipped with the 1,500 hp Mk2 12SRKT engine and double-cabs, but the order was altered to 10 'Df' class and 42 'Dg' class. The 'Df' class, which were the first mainline diesel-electric locomotives in New Zealand, were delivered by English Electric during 1954 and were used only on the North Island, revolutionising main line freight trains when they were introduced. The 'Dg' class A1A-A1A units were half-power single-cab editions of the 'Df' class equipped with the Mk2 6SRKT engine rated at 750 hp. The first 20 were built at the Robert Stephenson & Hawthorns Works at Darlington and the second batch of 22 at the Vulcan Foundry Works. They were all delivered, during 1955-56, for use on the North Island, but 11 of the class subsequently had their springing adjusted to increase the loading of the motored axles and, as the 'Dh' class, were put to work on the South Island.

The NZR English Electric diesel locomotives were the subject of various problems, including failures of big-end bearings and superchargers, excessive lubricating oil consumption, and unsatisfactory exhaust systems. The Tasmanian locomotives were also suffering from cracked cylinder heads, and it was complaints of failures with Australian and New Zealand locomotives that led to the aforementioned visit to the region by Martin Oldacres at the beginning of 1955, on which a Mr Cottam accompanied him. The most common problems centred on dirty engines, heavy lubricating oil consumption, big-end bearing failures and supercharger failures. The report of their visit led to a series of high-level meetings later in the year with George Nelson, the Managing Director of English Electric, and to the establishment of the Traction Technical Service Department at English Electric. Martin Oldacres was appointed Chief of that newly formed department in April 1955.

In a lengthy report on the subsequent meetings, H.G. Nelson relates the problems associated with a continuous succession of locomotive failures in both territories. This was particularly unfortunate for English Electric, as both General Motors and General Electric were aggressively marketing their products at that time with a considerable degree of success. Whilst it was appreciated that both American manufacturers had the advantage of extensive operating experience on their home railways, Nelson stressed that it was essential that English Electric be in a position to offer locomotives that were fully competitive in every way. During the course of the meetings, Nelson made it very clear that everywhere he went he had heard nothing but praise for the excellent work which Attock and Cottam had done during their visit to the various railways.

English Electric realised it was necessary to have a local presence to satisfy the scope of business available in the southern hemisphere. A new company, English Electric - Australia, was established in 1955 with locomotive manufacturing facility at Rocklea, Brisbane. The first locomotives actually ordered from Rocklea were the SAR '800' class. The '900' class had delivered positive economies for SAR and as a result of that experience they decided to order 10, heavy, 660 hp, Bo-Bo diesel-electric locomotives for broad-gauge shunting duties. Their design closely followed that of the AI&S 'D1' class, and they were initially mounted on specially built standard-gauge bogies for out road testing between Clapham and Kagaru. When delivered, in 1956, they were regularly employed in the busy Gilman yard, on transfer duties through the Port Adelaide area and to Mile End and Dry Creek. As part of an Australian $78-million expansion plan for the Port Kembla steel mill, announced by AI&S in 1955, an order was placed with the Rocklea Company for seven B-B diesel electric locomotives, and the first unit of the 'D9' class was tested, to nearby Greenbank, in August 1956. The subsequent history of the Rocklea plant is outside the scope of our story, but suffice to say that they continued to produce locomotives for the Australian railways and NZR until the early 1970s.

It was probably also as a result of Nelson's report that Martin Oldacres paid a visit to Canada, in August and September 1956, making a trip through the Rockies between Calgary and Revelstoke with Canadian Pacific Railway. This trip was most likely a fact-finding mission to observe American locomotives in service, as English Electric never supplied any locomotives to Canada. We also know that Martin Oldacres visited Kenya at some stage, presumably in 1960, in connection with delivery to East African Railways & Harbour Corporation (EAR) of 10 1Co-Co1 class '90' locomotives. Built at the former Robert Stephenson & Hawthorns Works, Darlington, these units were equipped with type 12CSVT engines of 1,840 hp. Following the split-up of the EAR as a result of the dissolution of the East African Community in 1977 they became Kenya Railways Corporation/Tanzania Railways Corporation class '87'.

Martin Oldacres Attock visited Canada in August and September 1956 on a fact finding mission to observe American-built locomotives in service, at a time when English Electric were experiencing engine problems. This photograph was taken in the Rocky Mountains and shows four General Motors Bo-Bo units hauling a load of 3,345 tons. The only locomotives which can be identified are Canadian Pacific Railway Nos. 8491 and 8412.

M.O. Attock, courtesy Bill Attock

Martin Oldacres was the joint inventor of Patent No. 35009/46, dated 26th November, 1947, *Engine-driven Electric Generating Plant*. This was a control system in which engine speed and fuel injection were automatically maintained constant at every running position of the controller, a scheme that was adopted by English Electric for practically all diesel-electric locomotives and trains built since that date. He was also joint inventor with Paul Alistair Angus of Patent Specification No. 803,945, filed on 15th December, 1954, *Improvements in Engine-driven Electric Generating Plant*. This referred to the control system first used on the prototype 'Deltic' locomotive in the UK.

Apart from the above patent, Martin Oldacres does not appear to have had any involvement with the development of the prototype Deltic. With the amalgamation of D. Napier & Son with English Electric, George Nelson had decided to build an experimental locomotive using two, lightweight, high-speed, Napier Delta diesel engines in a single body shell. The original prototype locomotive was built at English Electric's own expense and was, at the time, the world's most powerful single locomotive with its two 1,650 hp engines. The 'Deltic' was a tremendous act of faith in the field of new railway motive power on the part of English Electric. The prototype was a striking looking machine in its distinctive livery of blue, cream and silver.

The 'Deltic' began its trials on the London Midland Region of British Railways (BR), working on a freight train from Garston Dock to Runcorn on 24th October, 1955, and, in November, it was working passenger trains from Edge Hill to Preston, via St Helens, making two double-journeys each day. It then worked the Edge Hill to Camden fitted freight until 9th December before being transferred to the 'Merseyside Express' working, which it commenced hauling on 13th December, returning from Euston on the down 'Shamrock'. In August 1956 the 'Deltic' was transferred to work north from London (St Pancras) over the arduous Settle & Carlisle route, as BR was contemplating electrification of the West Coast main line and therefore had no need of powerful diesel locomotives for that route. However, there were no plans at that time for electrification of the East Coast main line and it was decided to order 22 'Deltic' locomotives for the Eastern Region. Originally scheduled for delivery in 1960, it was 23rd February, 1961 before the first of them was delivered to Finsbury Park, with the last delivery of the order arriving at Haymarket shed on 2nd May, 1962.

During the BR modernisation programme, Martin Oldacres' department operated a training school for railway personnel at the Vulcan Foundry works and for several years he attended the BR School of Transport at Derby to lecture on English Electric locomotives and advise on maintenance problems. The function of his department was described in detail in a paper entitled *Recording and Controlling Faults on Diesel-electric Locomotives*, presented at the ILocoE by S. Fletcher,* a member of his staff. Martin Oldacres was joint author, with S. Fletcher, of a paper entitled *Some Ideas on the Maintenance of Diesel-Electric Locomotives*† for which they won the T.A. Stewart-Dyer award. This paper was translated and published in the International Railway Congress Association Bulletin. On 2nd February, 1967 Martin Oldacres presented a paper to the Stafford Engineering Society, on the Traction Division service organization in

* Paper No. 640 Jnl ILocoE, Vol.52, 1962.

† Paper No. 610, Jnl. of ILocoE, Vol.50, 1960.

The prototype English Electric 'Deltic' locomotive approaching Preston, where she was built, while on trials with British Railways London Midland Region. The original 'Deltic' always looked superb in her blue and silver livery. Subsequently, British Railways ordered 22 of these locomotives for use on the Eastern Region. *English Electric, courtesy Bill Attock Collection*

Martin Oldacres Attock sitting in his beloved Austin Seven, registration No. PY8410. The tax disc indicates that the photograph was taken in 1972, the year Martin retired from English Electric. *Bill Attock Collection*

English Electric. He was also the author of *The Diagnosis of Faults in Roller Bearings in Traction Service*, an article that appeared in the English Electric Journal* and which was also noted in the 4th April, 1968 edition of *New Scientist*.

Aside from work, Martin Oldacres had a passion for vintage cars and was a member of the Vintage Car Club of Great Britain, which he joined in 1947. His first vintage car was a two-cylinder Wolseley, which was followed by a Bullnose Morris, the latter later sold for £1 0*s*. 0*d*. At the time of his retirement, in January 1972, he owned a 1927 Austin Seven (Reg. No. PY 8410) and a 1929 Alvis Silver Eagle (Reg. No. GC 2309), both of which were in regular use. In fact, each day for the last 4½ years of his working life he drove one or other of them from his cottage in Hesketh Bank to the works at Preston, while at weekends he drove home across the Pennines to Bradford. He entered the Alvis in the Oulton Park Concours every single year, from its earliest days up to and including the year of his death, a remarkable achievement for which the Vintage Car Club presented him with a pint tankard on his 25th appearance.

At the beginning of September 1975, Martin Oldacres was approached in connection with a search for vintage cars to take part in the film *It shouldn't happen to a Vet* about to be made in the Richmond area of Yorkshire. Based on the successful James Herriot vet stories, and sponsored by Readers' Digest, it was to star John Alderton as James Herriot, Colin Blakely as Sigfried Farnon, and Lisa Harrow as Helen Herriot. Filming began on 15th September with Martin Oldacres, taking part as an extra, driving the Alvis. The Gala Premiere of the film, which was distributed by EMI, took place in London's Shaftesbury Avenue on 8th April, 1976.

Following the integration of the ILocoE into the IMechE as its Railway Division, Martin Oldacres was admitted as a Fellow on 22nd July, 1970, a fitting tribute to his contribution to the railway engineering profession. He retired from English Electric-AEI Traction at the end of January 1972, and enjoyed 10 years in retirement. Martin Oldacres died peacefully, following a heart attack, on 10th July, 1982, after working in his garden. Tragically, not quite 18 months later, his widow Joyce was killed in a car accident close to her home on the morning of 14th January, 1984.

* English Electric Journal, Vol. 23, No. 1, January-February 1968.

Epilogue

To bring the story of the Atock/Attock family up to date we need to trace the progress of the three branches of the family. Taking first the Irish (Atock) branch, we pick up the story with Martin Leslie, who died in 1941. Following this sudden and tragic event his widow Madge immersed herself in charitable work, firstly for the Soldiers, Sailors and Airmen & Families Association, then with the National Association for Cerebral Palsy in Ireland (NACPI), to which the Marrowbone Lane Fund had made a donation in 1948, enabling it to establish a regular clinic at the Children's Hospital in Harcourt Street. Finally, she was a founder member of the Parents and Friends of Mentally Handicapped Children in Ireland, an organization that she was to remain with as Honorary Secretary until her death from lung cancer in May 1974.

Martin Leslie and Madge had one child, Martin Alexander (Alex), born in December 1932. Alex was educated at Castle Park School in Dalkey and Portora Royal School in Enniskillen and entered the Veterinary College in Ballsbridge, Dublin, where he qualified as a veterinary surgeon in 1958. He initially worked in general veterinary practice, both in Ireland and England, before acquiring his own practice in Dundrum, Co. Dublin. In 1972 Alex became Steward's Secretary (Veterinary) of the Irish Turf (Jockey) Club, but moved to Berne in Switzerland 10 years later as head of the Veterinary Department of the International Equestrian Federation (FEI), which later moved its headquarters to Lausanne.

Retirement from the FEI in 1995 saw Alex appointed Official Veterinary Officer to the United Arab Emirates (UAE) Equestrian & Racing Federation, a post that he held for three years (1995-1998). However, full-time retirement still eluded Alex who then became a consultant to the International League for the Protection of Horses (ILPH) based in the UK. Following the appointment of a full-time officer to this post, Alex spent one more season (2003/4) in the UAE, but now confines himself to some consultancy work for the FEI, ILPH and Peden Bloodstock. Married to Sherley (née Hamilton), they have three children, Sandra Juliet, Martin Hamilton and Philip Garratt. All three are married and followed in their father's equine footsteps. Of these Martin Hamilton was educated at St Columba's College, Dublin, and completed a stud management course at the Irish National Stud prior to commencing work in the horse transport business. Now, as Managing Director of Peden Bloodstock, he has been responsible for planning and handling the shipment of horses for major equestrian events including World Championships Equestrian Games and the Olympic Games since the early 1990s.

We last encountered Martin Leslie's sister, Doris, following her return from the RAF at the end of World War I. On 28th June, 1929 she married Ian Thomas Bryce at Zion Church in Rathgar, Dublin, the ceremony being conducted by the Rector, the Revd Louis Parkinson Hill. Ian Bryce was the fourth son of the late Mr & Mrs James Bryce of Clontarf on the north side of Dublin. Ian fought in the Far East during World War II, being torpedoed twice and being taken prisoner by the Japanese. Released at the end of the War, he took up a position with the British Phosphate Company (BPC) mining phosphates on the tiny Ocean Island, also known as Banaba.* Labourers were brought in from China and the Caroline Islands to work the mines.

* The Australians first discovered phosphates on Banaba and Nauru in 1898. The Anglo-German Pacific Phosphate Co initially carried out mining on Banaba. After the island was transferred to Australian administration in 1920, the BPC, jointly owned by the Australian, New Zealand & United Kingdom governments, began mining operations in Nauru in that year.

Ian and Doris lived for many years on Ocean Island with their son Denis Ian who was born at Benmore Nursing Home in Dun Laoghaire on 20th April, 1929. Following Doris's death in Putney, London, on 2nd December, 1959, Ian and Denis remained on Ocean Island and continued mining there. Ian died on 19th April, 1965 at Elsternwick, near Melbourne, Australia. In the interim, Denis had married Shirley Mary Maynard at All Souls' (Anglican) Church at Sandingham, Melbourne on 14th April, 1962. They have four children, Gaynor, born 18th May, 1964, Dale, born 23rd April, 1966, both of whom trained as nurses, and Darren, born 23rd July, 1972, and who is in the Police Force. Sadly, Richard, born 21st May, 1968, died on 30th June, 1996. The other three are all married. Gaynor and Dale have three and two daughters respectively, while Darren and his wife, Lynley Irvine, have a son born on 16th May, 2007. Denis and Shirley initially retired to New Zealand but now live in Queensland, Australia. Although their children and their families remain in New Zealand, they maintain close contact with their parents.

Meanwhile, in 1946 Ronald was sent to New Delhi as Deputy Chief Advisor of Factories to the Government of India under Sir Wilfred Garrett. His work included overseeing the tea plantations and tea factories, with a visit to Darjeeling being the highlight of his travels. In New Delhi the couple lived in Man Singhi Road, very close to the residences of Gandhi and Nehru. On one occasion he and Marjorie went to hear Gandhi speak. The Mahatma was carried on a great white cushion, being by then too weak to walk, and spoke in Urdu with no translation. At Partition, when there were terrible riots in New Delhi, Ronald and a neighbour managed to save their two Muslim servants by locking them into the boot of a car and driving them to safety at a compound outside the city. It was strictly against government rules to take any part in the political situation.

Ronald and Marjorie returned to England by sea aboard the Anchor Line's 11,200 ton TMV *Circassia,* which departed from Bombay for Liverpool on 7th May, 1949 under the command of Capt. David Blair. The couple's only child, a daughter, Katherine Elizabeth, was born in Sutton Coldfield, Warwickshire on 18th June, 1950.

In 1952 the MV *Staffordshire* took the new family back to the Far East, this time to Ceylon, again for Independence, as Ronald was Chief Inspector of Factories for the Colombo Plan for Technical Co-operation in South East Asia. For the first six months the family lived at the Galle Face Hotel* in Colombo, later moving to their own bungalow where Doris and Denis were welcome visitors. Ronald's work in Ceylon was mainly concerned with the production of tea, rubber and coconuts and at the end of his tour in 1954 he wrote a well reasoned and passionate article on 'The safety of factory work people' for the *Ceylon Labour Gazette* (Vol. V No. 9). This called for urgent changes to be made in the field of accident prevention and in the whole sphere of industrial safety, health and welfare in Ceylon.

Returning from the Far East, Ronald was sent to the port of Hull, Yorkshire to oversee the docks and five or six years later he was promoted to Whitehall.

* As mentioned elsewhere in the text, two other members of the family had connections with the Galle Face Hotel, Ken during his transit through Ceylon on his way to the Middle East and Martin Oldacres who held his wedding reception there.

The Galle Face Hotel in Colombo which played host to three members of the Atock/Attock family. It was here that Martin Oldacres and Joyce Attock held their wedding reception in December 1939, while only a few months later Private Kenneth Atock had a meal there *en route* to the Middle East. Finally, Ronald Atock lived with his family at the hotel for six months during 1952. *Bill Attock Collection*

He would often take his own Court cases and much enjoyed this aspect of his profession. It was said of him, 'You're a lucky man if you have Atock for a friend, but God help you if he is your enemy'. He rose to become Deputy Superintending Inspector of Factories but tragically died of cancer on 18th May 1967, aged only 58, at his home in Northwood in Middlesex, much loved and sadly missed by his family and friends.

Following his death Marjorie moved to Buckinghamshire to be near June Phillips, Madge Atock's sister, and later to Cambridge where she died in February 2006. Daughter, Katherine, became a primary school teacher. Grandson, Robert, took a first in Classics at Oxford in 2001 and a PhD in Cambridge in 2006 and now lectures at York University, Toronto, Canada. Granddaughter, Charlotte, works as a secretary in Cambridge and studies Arts with the Open University.

In relation to the Australian branch of the family, Vivian's daughter Pamela visited the UK in 1954 where she met Patrick Rowland Holmes, a merchant navy officer from Coventry. The couple married in 1956 and then moved back to Australia, where Patrick became a lawyer in the Civil Service. They had two children, Louise born on 12th January, 1959 and Warwick Rowland Atock born in Sydney on 8th December, 1961. Louise married twice, her first husband being tragically killed in a car accident in 1982. She has two children, Lauren and Alexander, born respectively in 1981 and 1989.

Warwick attended King's School in Parramatta and graduated from Sydney University with two degrees in Science and Engineering. He appears to have inherited Kenneth's flair for rockets and began his career in May 1986 with British Aerospace at Stevenage in Hertfordshire, remaining with them for nearly four years. While there, he became a member of the European Space Agency's (ESA) Olympus project,* writing software for system level tests and

* Olympus was a telecommunications technology demonstrator satellite which utilised very new (for its time) and risky technologies which are now used routinely in modern telecommunications satellites. When built, Olympus was the largest and most complex telecommunications satellite for its time (1989).

performing electrical flight hardware unit integrations. Two years followed with Fokker Space in Amsterdam, before Warwick joined Aerospatiale Espace in Cannes, where he was engineer in charge of all attitude and orbital control subsystems (AOCS) for the ESA infrared space observatory (IOS)* spacecraft.

Since March 2003 Warwick has been with ESA as an Avionics System Engineer, with primary responsibility for managing the design, review, development, testing and operations of spacecraft avionics systems. He and a group of fellow Australian space engineers were dispatched to the ESA's Kourou spaceport in French Guiana and put in charge of vital navigation systems on board a spacecraft attempting to make a landing on a deep space comet named Wirtanen (also known as 46P). The International Rosetta Mission was originally approved by ESA in November 1993. The main focus of the mission was to study the composition and physical properties of comets, which have been regarded by many scientists as debris left over from the birth of the planets 4.6 billion years ago. The spacecraft, named *Rosetta*, was to have been launched aboard an Ariane-5 rocket† in January 2003. A number of spectacular failures involving Ariane-5, including one only weeks prior to the launch date, led to the scrubbing of the mission, as Wirtanen was not going to be in correct alignment with earth for a further 170 years. It then looked as if *Rosetta* was destined to be no more than an expensive museum exhibit.

However, *Rosetta* received a new lease of life when space engineers found a new target, an almost unknown comet called Churyumov-Gerasimenko (Comet 67P); first discovered in 1969, 67P is only 5 km in diameter and orbits between earth and Jupiter. This comet is named after the two Russian astronomers who discovered it in 1969 - Klim Churyumov and Svetlana Gerasimenko. It has only been observed six times since this first discovery. It has been calculated that its orbit was significantly modified by Jupiter in 1840, drawing the comet from a very distant outer solar system orbit closer to the sun. Its orbit was again significantly modified in 1959, bringing it to the inner solar system and visible to astronomers for the first time. The 3,000 kg spacecraft was finally launched at 7.17 am on 2nd March, 2004 and is expected to rendezvous with 67P on 22nd May, 2014. To enable it to reach the comet, *Rosetta* required to orbit the earth three times and Mars once to put it into the correct trajectory. All going well, it will, on 14th November, 2014, drop a 100 kg lander called *Philae* on to the surface of Comet 67P.

Warwick returned to Australia in June 2005 and completed a postgraduate Masters degree in Technology & Project Management in the University of New South Wales in Sydney. He graduated from there on 23rd March, 2007. He hopes to return shortly to Europe and the ESA.

As far as the Attock family is concerned, reference has already been made in Chapter Thirteen to Frederick William's children. Martin Oldacres had two children, George William (Bill), born in Stafford, on 3rd June, 1942, and Rosalind Jane, born in Bradford on 3rd April, 1947. Bill was educated at Fulneck School in Pudsey, and later attended Bradford Technical College. During his first long

* IOS is an orbiting telescope which makes images from the infrared part of the light spectrum. It focuses on the formation process of stars before their birth when large dust clouds collapse to form a star.

† For the technically-minded, Ariane-5 is 52 metres in height with a lift-off mass of 710 tons. Each booster provided 630 tons of thrust and burned for 2 minutes and 10 seconds, separating at an altitude of 55 km. Boosters burn fuel at the rate of 2 tons per second, with a combustion pressure of 61 Bar.

Warwick Holmes photographed with the *Rosetta* Lander in August 2002. At that point it had been confidently expected that the spacecraft would be successfully launched from French Guiana in January 2003. However, due to major problems associated with the Ariane-5 launch vehicle, this was postponed until 2nd March, 2004. Rendezvous with the Comet 67P is now scheduled for May 2014. *Warwick Holmes Collection*

Warwick Holmes addressing a conference in July 2003 in relation to the *Rosetta* space project, in which he has been closely involved in charge of the spacecraft support team responsible for the engineers configuring the spacecraft prior to its launch and during the critical countdown sequence. *Warwick Holmes Collection*

summer break from College, he got a holiday job with Messrs E.A. Heap & Co. Ltd, a family business of motor factors in Bradford. The 'holiday job' turned out to be permanent and he remained with the company for 16 years, eventually becoming its Sales Director. When the Heap family sold the business in 1976, Bill and a partner, John Eastwood, started up a wholesale motor parts business, this in turn being sold in 1988. Bill is now semi-retired, although he and John are Directors of a car parts importing business and also a property company.

In another of those coincidences in the family, Bill married Maureen Elaine Toft from Kippax in Bradford Cathedral on 8th March, 1969. A Mary Atock married William Toft in Kippax on 6th July, 1801. They currently live in Harden, a village near Bingley and have two children, Martin Frederick and Clare Wendy. Martin lives in the United States with his wife, Emma, and their two children, Lucy Rowan and James Frederick. Wendy is married to Mathew Donnelly, a City banker; they have a daughter, Isabel May, with another baby due in August 2007.

Bill's sister, Rosalind went to Hanson Girl's School in Bradford and, after a short office career, met and married John Bright. They live in Patley Bridge, near Ripon in North Yorkshire, with their two children, Kathryn and John.

Finally, a word about Martin Atock's locomotives in the post-1900 period would not go amiss. Little could he have realised that they would enjoy such a long life, some of them surviving right up to the end of steam traction on the CIE system. Dealing first with the 'L' class, No. 575 (formerly MGWR No. 92 *Bittern*) got a spare 'L' boiler with Belpaire firebox in 1930 along with a spare cab of square profile. In 1940 the same locomotive was fitted with a GSR 'X' superheater boiler and, thereafter, was based at Mullingar until withdrawn in October 1956. It was the longest-lived of any MGWR locomotive, having been built in 1876; that said her total mileage was only 1,554,000. Conditions on the MGWR always required a large stock of locomotives to be available for special duties (cattle trains etc.), so individual mileages were never very high. No. 575 was amongst a large batch of locomotives disposed of early in 1957, nominally as a working engine, being sold to Ensidesa steelworks at Aviles in Spain. A ban on the export of scrap iron from Ireland was in force at the time, but this did not apply to working locomotives. Those for Spain had, therefore, to be shipped from the North Wall in full working order and suitably invoiced.

Several of the 'L' class suffered damage during the Civil War, including No. 64, which was wrecked at Streamstown Junction in January 1923. This particular incident is mentioned purely to illustrate how journalists can allow their imaginations run away with them in the pursuit of sensationalism, one newspaper account of the incident reporting that a land mine had been placed in the boiler! The boiler in question was in fact put into sister locomotive No. 55 only a couple of months later. Six members of the class were equipped for oil burning during the fuel crisis of 1947, all reverting to coal burning within six months. Towards the end of their lives these locomotives carried out rather more passenger work than they had done on the MGWR, including the working of Dublin & South Easern section suburban trains. At one stage it was intended to retain three of the class (Nos. 598, 599 and 603) in reserve after the end of steam traction, and although nominally held in stock, they were eventually scrapped in 1963-64.

The re-boilering of the 'LM' class is a complicated story and not easy to follow,

An 'L' class standard goods 0-6-0 No. 56 *Liffey*, a Broadstone product of 1885. She has been heavily rebuilt with a new boiler and new cab. One has to feel sorry for the unfortunate fireman - note large lumps of coal which will have to be broken up before firing!

H. Fayle, courtesy Irish Railway Record Society Collection

and is therefore beyond the scope of this narrative. One of the class, No. 593, having received a 'tightening-up' in Cork in 1962, was to have been retained as a reserve steam engine, but was scrapped in 1965. 'LN' class No. 53 was one of two locomotives to be fitted with the Cusack-Morton top-feed superheater, trials of this device having previously been undertaken with the Avonside engine No. 99 commencing in January 1914. A drawing of this device is to be found in the author's history of the MGWR (*see Bibliography*). No. 53 left shops in September 1919 equipped with a slightly modified version of the superheater based on the earlier trials with No. 99. From what little is known of the experiments, this superheater does not seem to have been as good as the earlier one, and No. 53 was back in shops for its removal in August 1924. A new boiler with a Schmidt superheater was installed in June 1925, and finally the locomotive received a GSR 'X' boiler in 1942, remaining in service until April 1950.

It was probably in 1922 that 'P' class locomotive No. 102 was fitted with armour plate and sent to Mullingar for use by the Railway Protection & Maintenance Corps who unofficially named her *King Tutankhamen*; the armour plate was removed in August 1923. The Milne Report of 1948 condemned the 'P' class as being non-standard and three of them were quickly withdrawn. However, it was realised that there were no other locomotives suitable for shunting at North Wall and two were retained; the last to go being No. 617 (formerly MGWR 103) in August 1959.

Reboilering of the 'E' class commenced in 1911. A weak point in all of Martin Atock's designs was the valve spindles, which were always liable to bend. For the 'E' class these were made stronger from 1915 onwards. By 1922 the class was reported to be in a very poor state with a number of locomotives out of service. A completely new boiler was designed by W.H. Morton in 1923, all but three of the class (which had already received new boilers between 1911 and 1914) receiving these. In GSR days the 'E' class tank locomotives (GSR 'J26' class) were used on more varied duties. Three of them were transferred to the Dublin & South Eastern section to work the Shillelagh branch, but their restricted water capacity was soon found to be a problem. In 1932 No. 560 was sent to the isolated Waterford & Tramore section, being joined later by two more of the class. Four were based at the Rocksavage depot of the Cork, Bandon & South Coast section; their duties included passenger specials and beet trains on the Courtmacsherry branch. One of the class, GSR No. 560, travelled further west in 1956 to work the re-opened Tralee & Fenit branch.

The 'K' class 2-4-0s remained largely on the Sligo road until finally replaced by diesels, their last passenger job being the up and down night mails on 15th September, 1956. Following the withdrawal of the 'D' class 2-4-0s they also worked the Mayo road as well as the Meath and Cavan branches. In 1926, two of them were allocated to Bray shed for the Dublin & South Eastern section. One was tried out on the main line trains to Wexford, but it was on the Harcourt Street line that they found favour. As many as six of the class were allocated simultaneously to Bray during the 1950s for suburban work; a final tribute to the versatility of Martin Atock's 60-year-old design.

In comparing the various Atock locomotive types, it is generally accepted that the 'K' class were the best locomotives ever to work on the MGWR, although the late Bob Clements considered the 'LM' class might run them a close second. The 'K' class continued working in the latter years of steam, despite indifferent

CIE 'G2' class 2-4-0 No. 653 at Broadstone. Ex-'K' class No. 19 *Spencer* of 1894, she survived until 1963, having been intended as one of a small number of steam engines held in reserve.
Seán Kennedy

maintenance, and there could be no greater tribute to their basic reliability than the way they kept going under such conditions. Certainly, Martin would have been pleasantly surprised to see how many locomotives of all his classes ran through almost to the end of steam on the CIE system.

Some of the finest work was done by the 'K' class in their last days when deputising for failed diesel railcars. They not only proved capable of running to the accelerated diesel timings between stops, but they were also able to maintain the overall diesel schedules, in spite of extra time required for taking water. As one driver expressed it, 'One notable feature about them was their ability to run shut off. They would run down a bank as free as a bicycle, their balancing must have been just right'. He added that, 'They were a great engine to hold their feet on a bank as well'. These comments came from a 'Midland' man and might therefore be considered to be biased in favour of that company's locomotives. However, as late as 1951, an ex-Cork driver, who had risen to become a locomotive inspector on the MGW section, said he wished that more of them had been built, as nothing like them had been built since. This was tribute indeed to a design which was then almost 60 years old, and to their designer, Martin Atock.

Appendix One

W&LR Locomotives & Rolling Stock 1864-72

Locomotives

Nos.	*Wheels*	*Built*	*Maker*	*Works No.*	*Cyls.*	*Driving wheel dia.*	*Boiler pressure*	*Heating surface*	*Grate area*	*Weight t-cwt*
28	2-2-2	1864	Kitson	1213	15″x22″	5′9″	140	882	14.58	28-00
29	0-4-0ST	1865	Sharp, Stewart	1653	12″x17″	4′0″	120	344.5	8.7	20-00
3/7	0-4-2	1872	Kitson	1783-4	16″x24″	4′6″	140	1010.6	13	26-17

Carriages

Nos.	*Built*	*Class*	*Wheels*	*Builder*
7/8	1865/6	Third	6	W&LR Limerick
1-3	1872	Second	4	Ashbury

Wagons (Capital builds)

Nos.	*Built*	*Type*	*Builder*
444-49	1864	Open	W&LR Limerick
534-560	1866/7	Open	W&LR Limerick
561-63	1872	CGOC	Metropolitan C&W Co.

W&LR 0-4-0ST No. 29 at Limerick. No. 29 was purchased from Sharp, Stewart in 1865 for shunting duties at Waterford. However, she appears to have spent most of her working life at the Limerick end of the line, where she was unofficially named *Darkie*. Despite this being unofficial, she was so referred to in the Board Minutes on several occasions.

H. Fayle, courtesy Irish Railway Record Society Collection

Appendix Two

MGWR Locomotives introduced by Martin Atock 1872-1901

Class	*Nos.*	*Bldr.*	*Wks Nos.*	*Built*	*Type*	*Cyls*	*Driving wheel dia.*	*Boiler pressure*	*Heating surface*	*Grate area*	*Wheelbase*	*Weight t-cwt*	*Remarks*
D (1873)	13-24	N	1784-95	1873	2-4-0	15″x22″	5′7″	130	743	15	13′11″	31-12	
D(1876)	30-4	D	905-9	4/1876	2-4-0	16″x22″	5′7″	130					
L	86-95	S	2284-90 2305-7	1876	0-6-0	17″x24″	5′2″	130	1015		14′11″		
LN	49-54	B	-	1879-80	0-6-0	18″x24″	5′0½″	130	1073	16¼	14′11″	32-10	Renewal of old class '12'
H	96-9	A	1211-4	1/1880	0-6-0	18″x24″	4′9″				15′ 0″	32-10	
D(1880)	2/3,25/6,36/7	BP	1960-5	1880-1	2-4-0	16″x22″	5′8″	130	771½	15	14′11″	32-09	
P	100-3/5	B	-	1881-90	0-6-0T	18″x24″	4′6″	130	1073	16¼	14′11″	35-10	Replacements for North Wall pilots
D(1883)	1/4/5/6,41-6	B	-	1884-7	2-4-0	16″x22″	5′8″	130	907	15	14′11″	32-09	
D(1886)	35/8/9	K	2901-4	1886	2-4-0	16″x22″	5′8″	130	907	15	14′11″	32-09	
L(1885)	55-72,85,104	B	-	1885-9	0-6-0	18″x24″	5′3″	130	1075	16½	14′11″		19 of these replacements
7-12	7-12	B	-	1889-90	2-4-0	17″x24″	6′3″	150	1118		15′ 0″	39-02	Replaced class '18'
E	106-8,112-7	K	Vars.	1891-4	0-6-0T	15″x22″	4′6″	150		13	13′ 3″	35-07	
E	109-11	SS	3693-5	1891	0-6-0T	15″x22″	4′6″	150		13	13′ 3″	35-07	
LM	73-84	B	-	1891-3	0-6-0	18″x24″	5′3″	150	1068	16½	14′11″		Replacements for last of Ramage 0-4-2s
LM	130-4	SS	4057-61	1895	0-6-0	18″x24″	5′3″	150	1068	16½	14′11″		
LM	135-9	K	3584/5/6 3599,3600	1895	0-6-0	18″x24″	5′3″	150	1068	16½	14′11″		
K	13-24,27-34	B	-	1893-8	2-4-0	17″x24″	5′ 8″	150	1118	16½	15′ 0″	38-10	17 replacements for 1873-6 'D'
D(Bogie)	2/3,25/6,36/7	B	-	1900-1	4-4-0	16″x22″	5′ 8″	150	1083	16½	19′11″	40-09	Replaced 'D' (1880)

Builders: A = Avonside; B = Broadstone (MGWR); BP = Beyer, Peacock; D = Dübs; K = Kitson; N = Neilson Reid; S = R. Stephenson; SS = Sharp, Stewart.

Appendix Three

MGWR Rolling Stock introduced by M. Atock

Carriages

Year built	*Class*	*Length*	*Compartments*	*Seats*	*Qty built*
1875-78	Third	22′6″	2 third		44
1879	Family saloon	30′0″	2 first, 1 second + luggage		2
1879-89	First	30′0″	4 first	32	17
1880	Second	30′0″	5 second	50	5
1881-83	Third	31′0″	6 third	72	15
1883	Stores van	30′0″			1
1884-90	Second	30′0″	4 second + luggage	40	12
1885-93	Composite	29′0″	2 first, 2 second + luggage	16	35
			2 second	20	
1885	TPO	29′0″	PO, luggage & brake		4
1887-90	Third brake	30′0″	2 third + van & guard	24	21
1887-88	TPO	30′0″	PO + guard		4
1888-1900	Pass. brake van	30′0″			26
1890-1900	Third	30′0″	5 third	60	78
1892-94	Second	30′0″	4 second, 2 lavatories	40	8
1893-94	First coupé	31′0″	3½ first, 2 lavatories	28	8
1900	Tri-composite	53′0″	2 first	16	4
			2 second	20	
			2 third, 2 lavatories, luggage	24	

Capital Additions to MGWR Wagon Stock 1872-1899

Nos.	*Qty*	*Type*	*Builder*	*Year built*
1580 – 1679	100	Covered goods wagons	MCW	1872-73
1680 – 1691	12	Timber trucks	MCW	1873
1692 – 1711	20	Coal hopper wagons	MCW	1874
1712 – 1897	186	Covered goods wagons	MCW	1876-77
1898 – 1947	50	Open coal wagons (Loco)	MCW	1877
1948 & 1949	2	Boiler & furniture trucks	ASH	1877
1950 – 1975	26	Ballast wagons	BCW	1878
1976 – 2025	50	Open cattle wagons	MGWR	1889
2026 – 2125	100	Open cattle wagons	ASH	1890
2126 – 2175	50	Open box wagons	MGWR	1890
2176 – 2275	100	Covered goods wagons	MGWR	1891
2276 – 2375	100	Open cattle wagons	BCW	1891
2376 – 2395	20	Open coal wagons (Loco)	?	1892
2396 & 2397	2	Boiler & furniture trucks	?	1892
2398 – 2403	6	Timber trucks	MGWR	1892
2404 – 2453	50	Covered goods wagons	MGWR	1892-93
2454 – 2553	100	Open cattle wagons	MCW	1895
2554 – 2653	100	Covered goods wagons	MCW	1895-96
2654 – 2683	30	Covered cattle wagons	MCW	1899
2684 – 2713	30	Open coal wagons (Loco)	ASH	1899

Appendix Four

L&YR Engine Sheds

Shed No.	*LMS code**	*Location*	*Date opened*	*Notes*
1	C1	Newton Heath	1876	
2	C2	Low Moor	1865/66	Rebuilt 1888
3	C3	Sowerby Bridge	1852	Rebuilt 1885/87
4		Leeds (Wortley Jn)	1859	Rebuilt *c.*1886 and again in 1900
5	C5	Mirfield	*c.*1857	Rebuilt 1884/85
6	C6	Wakefield	1848	Rebuilt 1899
7		Normanton	1882/83	
8		Barnsley	1849/50	
9		Knottingley	?	Closed 01-07-1922
10	C10	Goole	*c.*1850	Rebuilt 1871. Replaced with new shed on different site in 1889
11		Doncaster	*c.*1848	Closed 1914. Thereafter locomotives stabled, first, at LNWR/NER shed and later at GNR shed
12		Hull	(NER)	
13	C13	Agecroft	1888/89	
14	C14	Bolton	1874	Rebuilt 1889
15	C15	Horwich	1870	Replaced by new shed on different site in 1887. Closed 9.7.1928, except for works shunters
16	C16	Wigan	before 1868	Rebuilt 1877/78, 1885/86 and 1905
17	C17	Southport	1891	L&YR locomotives were transferred from the 1855 shed to this new shed which was built on the site of an old ELR one
18	C18	Bank Hall	*c.*1850	Rebuilt 1873/74. Named Sandhills prior to 1920
19	C19	Aintree	1886	
20	C20	Bury	*c.*1846	Rebuilt 1875/76
21	C21	Bacup	1882	
22	C22	Accrington	1888/89	New shed on different site
23	C23	Rose Grove	1899	
24	C24	Colne	1900	
25	C25	Lower Darwen	1891	
26	C26	Hellifield	1881	Prior to opening of this shed L&YR shared the LNWR shed at Preston
27	C27	Lostock Hall	1881	
28		Chorley	1868	Replaced by a new shed on different site in 1873. Closed 01-07-1922
29	C29	Ormskirk	*c.*1858/60	Rebuilt 1893/94
30	C30	Fleetwood	?	
31		Blackpool (Talbot Rd)	*c.*1846	
32	C32	Blackpool (Central)	*c.*1885	

* After the merger of the LNWR and L&YR.

Appendix Five

L&YR Carriages introduced by F. Attock

Date	*Dia. No.*	*Order No.*	*Type*	*Length*	*Width*	*Compartments*	*Seats*	*No. built*
1879	27	T1	Tri-composite	40′1″	8′0″	1 first; 2 second; 3 third	56	1
1879-82	113		Covered carriage truck	16′1″	7′9″			6
1879-87	8		Third	32′0″	8′0″	5 third	50	506
1879-88	108		Horse box	16′1″	7′9″			65
1879-1904	107		Open carriage truck	16′0″	7′9″			91
1880-82	6		First	30′6″	7′10″	4 first	24	24
1880-85	24		Composite	32′0″	8′0″	1 first; 3 second; + lugg.	38	39
1881-85	3		Composite	30′6″	7′10″	2 first, 2 second	36	202
1882-86			Third brake	32′0″	8′0″	3 third + van & guard	30	86
1882-94	6		First	32′0″	8′0″	4 first	24	82
1883	9		Composite	35′0″	8′0″	2 first, 3 second	46	3
1883	22	V3	Engineer's saloon	35′0″	8′0″	Saloon	24	1
1883	27	E3	Tri-composite	42′0″	8′0″	1 first, 2 second, 3 third	56	2
1884	9		Composite	36′0″	8′0″	2 first, 3 second + lugg.	46	3
1884	26A	C5	Composite	46′0″	8′0″	2 first, 3 second + 3 lavs	37	2
1884	27A	D5	Composite	40′6″	8′0″	2 first, 3 second + 3 lavs	29	2
1885-90	25		Composite	33′0″	8′0″	2 first, 3 second + 2 lavs	34	26
1885-92	7		Composite	33′0″	8′0″	2 first, 3 second	46	105
1886	11	H5	Third	51′0″	8′4″	8 third	96	8
1886	43A	H5	Officers saloon	51′0″	8′4″	2 saloons + lav.	22	1
1886	141	H5	Invalid saloon	51′0″	8′4″	3 saloons + 2 Lavs	16	1
1886-90	1A	E7	Parcel van	33′0″	8′0″			9
1888	5		Composite	33′0″	8′0″	2 first, 2 second, 1 lav. & lugg.	36	12
1889-99	21	P6/S8	First	33′0″	8′0″		15	9
1889-1909	113		Covered carriage truck	21′0″	7′9″			23
1890-96			Third brake	33′0″	8′0″	3 third + van & guard	30	150
1890	13	F8	Third saloon	33′0″	8′0″	Saloon & lav.	30	12
1891	14	P7	Third saloon	33′0″	8′0″	Saloon & lav.	30	8
1891	26	T7	Composite	46′0″	8′0″	4 first, 2 second + 2 lavs	52	16
1891-97	2		Parcel van	32′0″	8′0″			40
1891-97	10		Third brake	33′0″	8′0″	2third + van & guard	20	90
1892-95	109		Horsebox	16′1″	8′0″			47
1892-97	8		Third	33′0″	8′0″	5 third	50	236
1893			Special van	32′0″	8′0″			1
1893	29	Various	Third brake	46′0″	8′0″	5 third + van & guard	60	52
1893-98	36	M13/O9	First	46′0″	8′0″	6 first	36	16
1893-99	115		Prize cattle truck	18′9″	8′0″			7
1894	26	Various	Tri-composite	46′0″	8′0″	2½ first, 2 second, 2 third	64	44
1894	29A	M9	Third brake	46′0″	8′0″	4 third + van & guard	48	20
1894	29B	K9	Third	46′0″	8′0″	7 third	84	9
1894-95	28	S9/D10	Composite	46′0″	8′0″	6 + 2 lavs	42	30
1894-96	31	Various	Third brake	49′0″	8′0″	6 third + van & guard	72	23
1894-96	33	Various	Third brake	49′0″	8′0″	5 third + van & guard	60	50
1894-99	30	Various	Third brake	49′0″	8′0″	4 third + van & guard	48	257
1894-1905	34	Various	Third	49′0″	8′0″	8 third	96	806
1895-99	20	F10	First	33′0″	8′0″	4 first	24	8
1895-1900	32	Various	Composite	49′0″	8′0″	3 first, 4 second	64	67

Appendix Six

L&YR Wagons built during F. Attock's time

Dia. No.	*Type*	*Length*	*Tare weight*	*Capacity*	*Built*	*No. built*	*Wheelbase*	*Remarks*
1	Low goods	16'0"	4t-15c	10t	1870s-1922	9000	9'0"	
2	Low goods	17'6"	4t-17c	10t	1890	120	9'0"	
3	CGOC	16'0"	6t-1c	10t	1870s-1903	3621	9'0"	Built from late 1870s.
4	Coal (High-sided)	16'6"	5t-10c	8t	1870s-1890	500	9'0"	Orig. Tfc, later Loco. Coal.
5	Coal	16'6"	6t-8c	12t	1892-1902	600	9'0"	Loco. Coal.
6	Coal (End doors)	16'6"	6t-6c	10t	1893	10	9'0"	Experimental.
7	Ballast	14'0"	4t-6c	10t	1870s-1903	235	8'8"	Permanent way use.
8	Sand	16'6"	5t-6c	10t	1892&1900	32	9'0"	Loco. Sand. Fixed sides.
9	Implement	18'6"	5t-18c	12t	1880?	2	10'0"	For agricultural machinery etc.
10	Implement	20'0"	6t-18c	15t	1881?	4	13'0"	Improvement on Dia. 9. Six-wheeled.
11	Piece van	16'0"	5t-0c	9t	1883	6	9'0"	Carriage of road vehicles. No ends.
12	Pitch wagon	15'0"	5t-4c	10t	1870s-1900	1750	9'0"	Standard half-box. One tip-end.
13	Fish wagon	16'0"	6t-0c	9t	1880s-1903	80	9'0"	Could run with passenger trains.
14	Furniture van	16'0"	5t-3c	10t	1880-1920	40	9'0"	Carriage of containers.
15	Fruit wagon	16'0"	5t-1c	10t	1892-1902	1722	9'0"	Falling sides. General merchandise.
16	Fruit wagon	16'0"	5-5c	10t	1870-1902	1827	9'0"	General merchandise.
17	Covered cattle	16'0"	6t-12c	10t	1870s-1892	160	9'0"	Medium cattle wagon
18	Covered cattle	13'8½"	6t-5c	9t	1890	20	8'6"	Small cattle wagon.
19	Covered cattle	18'7½"	7t-2c	9t	1880-1920	650	10'0"	Standard cattle wagon.
20	Meat van	16'02	6t-15c	9t	1870s-1900	20	9'0"	Unrefrigerated. Painted carriage umber.
21	Goods brake van	15'6"		10t	1870s-1902	550	9'0"	Total for iron-bodied GBVs.
22	Ballast brake van	26'0"			1880-1908	26	15'0"	Four-wheeled brake van & travelling mess hut.
23	Tranship van	18'0"	6t-9c	10t	1884 & 1896	6	10'2"	Sliding doors. Never really took off.
24	Goods & tranship	17'10¼"	6t-9c	9t	1890	3	9'0"	Attempt to improve on Diagram 23.
25	Tranship & brake	22'0"	11t-16c	6t	1893 & 1900	6	13'6"	As Diagram 24 but with brake compartment.
25	Tool van	22'6"	8t-18c		1893?	1	13'6"	Tool van for signal gang.
26	Sleeper wagon	19'02	6t-6c	10t	1870s-1896	5	10'0"	Transport of large quantities of sleepers.
26a	Sleeper wagon	19'0"	6t-12c	10t	1898-1920	68	10'0"	Improvement on Diagram 26. Falling sides.

Dia. No.	*Type*	*Length*	*Tare weight*	*Capacity*	*Built*	*No. built*	*Wheelbase*	*Remarks*
27	Hydrocarbon tank	16′0″	7t-9c	1,580galls	1890	2	9′0″	Tank enclosed by pitched wooden roof.
28	Tank wagon	12′2″	5t-19c	8t	1880-1902	15	7′6″	Cover-all diagram for 15 different wagons.
29	Gas receiver wagon	16′2″	10t-18c	408 cu. ft.	1885?	4	9′0″	Used for supplying gas to carriages.
30	Gas receiver wagon	16′0″	4t-17c	265 cu .ft.	188?	3	9′0″	Used for supplying Fleetwood buoys.
31	Rail/sleeper wagon	25′0″	8t-5c	15t	1870s-1922	649	18′0″	Six-wheeled. Used for permanent way & general work.
32	Bolster wagon	22′9″	6t-7c	9t	1875?	?	12′0″	Double bolster wagon.
33	Boiler wagon	40′0″		40t	1885?	2	30′6″	Bogie wagon for heavy specialist loads.
33	Boiler wagon	30′0″		25t	1885?	1	24′9″	Replaced in 1904.
34	Boiler wagon	28′4″	12t-17c	25t	1888	1	22′8″	Used in connection with Belfast steamers.
34	Boiler safety wagon	10′6″	4t-2c	10t	1892 & 1898	6	6′0″	Runners for long loads.
35	Truck for coach	35′0″	7t-18c	7t	1885	1	20′0″	Six-wheeled. For loading coach bodies.
35	Boiler wagon	24′0″	7t-6c	22t	1885?	8	18′0″	Six-wheeled.
36	Boiler wagon	36′0″		30t	1892?	2	23′6″	Second attempt at bogie boiler wagon.
36a	Twin timber wagon	28′11½″			1882-1920	304	13′3½″	304 pairs.
38	Boiler wagon	36′0″	16t-9c-3q	36t	1894 & 1897	6	23′6″	
38	Well wagon	24′0″		6t	1893	6	16′0″	For conveyance of show vans etc.

Appendix Seven

The Eames Brake

Frederick William Eames was born in Kalamazoo in Michigan in 1843, the son of Lovett Eames, a farmer cum mechanic. F.W. had apparently just entered college when the Civil War broke out and he decided to enlist in the Infantry, later becoming a Lieutenant. He left the military, in 1863, and was appointed to a post in the Revenue Service patrolling the Mississippi river. Another source states that he went to New York, in 1861, to instal a pumping system of his own design. In that year his father and an uncle (Moses) jointly purchased Beebee Island and established a machine shop there in an old stone building. F.W. Eames took out his first patent in 1874* and established the Eames Vacuum Brake Co., on 14th February, 1876, and began manufacture at his father's factory on Beebee Island. Apparently he also invented an automatic governor and cut-off for marine engines, a steam pump and various other mechanical devices. Within two years of setting up the business, Eames is reported to have interested no less than 29 US railroad companies in the Eames brake, one of which was the Denver South Park & Pacific Co. (DSP&PRR) which fitted 700 cars with the device in 1880; in the next year the Union Pacific Railroad, which had purchased the DSP&PRR, bought further Eames equipment for their freight stock. By 1881 it was stated that 57 different companies in nine countries were using it.

Eames travelled extensively to market his product and as already referred to in Chapter Eleven he had written to the L&YR in April 1879. He wrote again, on 19th September, 1881, offering to fit his brake to any engines and carriages already fitted with the Westinghouse brake, provided the materials from the latter were handed over to him; consideration of this matter was deferred. At about the same time the question of paying a royalty for the air brake was referred to the company's legal department for a ruling. The Westinghouse Company in fact took a legal case against the L&YR in 1882, orders being issued in June for the removal of all their fittings from rolling stock. It is interesting to note that the Vacuum Brake Co. offered to supply all necessary materials provided the old fittings were given to them. Westinghouse also sued the New York Air Brake Co.

Mr Eames continued to feature in correspondence. A request came from him, in January 1882, for authority to re-erect his engine at his own expense. In 1881, in connection with his brake experiments, Eames had purchased a 4-2-2 locomotive from the Baldwin Locomotive Co. of Philadelphia; it had been built in 1880 for the Philadelphia & Reading Railroad who, for financial reasons, had not taken delivery of the engine; it was named the *Lovett Eames* after his father. It was one of a very few 'single' driving wheel express locomotives to run in the United States. It apparently worked for a short time between New York and Philadelphia equipped with the Eames brake. He then had the locomotive dismantled and shipped to England, it being apparently re-assembled at Newton Heath. It first ran on the L&YR, on 15th March, 1882, between Manchester and Leeds. Frederick Attock was ordered, in January 1882, to furnish the engine with a new cab at Eames' expense; one wonders if this was similar to the cab fitted to an engine and used by Aspinall for travelling round the system. In May Eames requested the platform of a four-wheeled passenger carriage on which to mount his brake gear for an exhibition at Alexandra Palace, the request being turned down as 'it would be inconvenient to the Company'.

Ahrons states that the *Lovett Eames* remained in the GNR shed at Leeds for nearly four months apart from a few odd journeys, eventually ending up being shedded at Wood Green in London, where it was broken up in the spring of 1884. Ahrons also stated that the bell from the engine was preserved for many years at King's Cross running shed. A

* U.S. Patent No.153,814 dated 4th August, 1874.

4-2-2 locomotive *Lovett Eames*, built in 1880 by Baldwin Locomotive Company for the Philadelphia & Reading Railroad. It was purchased in 1881 by F.W. Eames in connection with his brake experiments. It was shipped to England and operated for a short while during 1882 on the L&YR. It was then stored in the GNR shed at Leeds, later being removed to Wood Green in London. It was broken up in the spring of 1884.

Provenance Unknown

Board minute dated 10th July, 1883 refers to a report from Frederick Attock regarding the old cab, which had been taken off the engine, and was still in the workshops and he enquired how it should be disposed of 'owing to the death of Mr Eames'. Eames had apparently returned to America to discover that a New York company had made a claim for $47,000 against him. They had been successful in the sense that they had been awarded his old factory premises, of which they had taken possession. Eames counter-sued and was granted back the factory. However, when he endeavoured to take possession he was shot and killed by an occupant of the factory!

Appendix Eight

English-Electric Deliveries with which M.O. Attock was associated

Diesel-Electric Locomotives

Year	*Railway*	*Gauge*	*Class*	*Type*	*Engine*	*hp*	*Weight*	*Road Nos.*
1934	LMS	4′8½″		0-6-0	6K	300	47t 0c	7079
1935	GWR	4′8½″		0-6-0	6K	350	51t 10c	2
1936	VGMA	3′6″		0-6-0	6K	320		1, 2
1936	LMS	4′8½″		0-6-0	6K	350	51t 0c	7069-7078
1936	SGR	3′6″		0-6-0	6K			401, 402
1947	LMS	4′8½″	34	Co-Co	16SVT	1,600	127t 13c	10000, 10001
1947	Malaya Ry	1000mm	15	0-6-0	6KT	350	44t 0c	151.01-151.20
1948	ESR	4′8½″		1A-Do-A1	16SVT	1,600		
1949	SAR	5′3″	350	Bo-Bo	6KT	350	49t 2c	350, 351
1950	AI&S	4′8½″	D1	Bo-Bo	8SRKT	730	84t 6c	D1-D8
1950	TGR	3′6″	X	Bo-Bo	6SRKT	660	56t 18c	X1-X32
1951	SAR	5′3″	900	A1A-A1A	16SVT	1,588	119t 12c	900-909
1951	VR	5′3″	F	0-6-0	6KT	350	49t 10c	F201-F216
1951	NZR	3′6″	De	Bo - Bo	6SRKT	660	52t 0c	501-515
1953	QR	3′6″	1200	Co-Co	12SVT	1,290	88t 0c	1200-1209
1954	NZR	3′6″	Df	2 Co-Co 2	12SRKT	1,500	110t 0c	1500-1509
1955	NZR	3′6″	Dg	A1A-A1A	6SRKT	750	70t 0c	750-791
1956	AI&S	4′8½″	D9	B-B	6SRKT?	378	60t 0c	D9-D15
1956	SAR	5′3″	800	Bo-Bo	6SRKT	660	72t 0c	800-809
1957	Malaya Ry	1000mm	20	Co-Co	12SRKT	1,500	90t 0c	201.01-201.26
1958	Midland Ry	3′6″	F	Bo-Bo	6SRKT	685	63t 18c	F40-F46
1958	Midland Ry	3′6″	G	Co-Co	8SVT	950	75t 0c	G50, G51
1959	QR	3′6″	1250	Co-Co	12SVT	1,388	89t 0c	1250-1254
1959	AI&S	4′8½″	D16	Bo-Bo	8SRKT	790	91t 0c	D16-D19
1960	EAR	1000mm	90	1Co-Co1	12CSVT	1,840	120t 0c	9001-9010

Diesel Electric Railcars

Year	*Railway*	*Gauge*	*Type*	*Engine*	*hp*	*Quantity*
1933	Prototype	4′8½″	Single-car		200	1 unit
1939	CGR	5′6″	Four-car	6HT	180	3 sets
1947	CGR	5′6″	Single-car	6HT	180	23 units
1949	WAGR	3′6″	Three-car	6H	209	6 sets
1951	ESR	4′8½″	Five-car	2 x 4SRKT	2 @ 400	19 sets

Bibliography

Ahrons, E.L.: *Locomotive & Train Working in the latter part of the Nineteenth Century* - Vols. 2 & 6, W. Heffer & Sons Ltd, Cambridge, 1954

Allen, C.J.: *The Great Eastern Railway, 5th ed.*, Ian Allan, London, 1968

Atock, M.: *A Combined Machine or Tool for Boring, Turning, and Key Bed Grooving*, British Patent Specification No. 2716 of 1874

Atock, M.: *An Improved Hydraulic Gantry*, British Patent Specification No. 1961 of 1878

Atock, M.: *Tubing Locomotive Boilers*, Trans. ICEI Vol. XIV, 1882

Atock, M.: *Improvements in the Shells or Barrels of Locomotive and similar Boilers*, British Patent Specification No. 10826 of 1888

Atock, M.: *The Wheel Base of Railway Carriages*, Trans. ICEI Vol. XXI, 1891

Attock, F.: *Axleboxes for Locomotives, Railway Wagons, etc.*, British Patent Specification No. 321 of 1878

Attock, F.: *Sliding Windows of Railway Carriages, Tramcars etc.*, British Patent Specification No. 1954 of 1881

Attock, F.: *Couplings of Railway Wagons, etc.*, British Patent Specification No. 342 of 1883

Attock, F. & Morris, P.: *Improvements in Coupling Apparatus for Railway Wagons and other Vehicles*, British Patent Specification No. 13155 of 1885

Attock, F.: *An Improved Construction of Folding Portable Table*, British Patent Specification No. 13915 of 1885

Attock, F.: *An Improved Draught & Dust Excluder or Closing Device Applicable to Railway Carriage Doors and otherwise*, British Patent Specification No. 8319 of 1887

Attock, F.: *An Improved Arm and Head-rest Combined, applicable to Railway Carriages, Tram-cars, Ships' Berths, and other Seats*, British Patent Specification No. 20490 of 1890

Attock, F.: *An Improved Portable Grip Lifting Jack for Railway Engines, Carriages, Wagons, Tram-cars, and other like Vehicles*, British Patent Specification No. 22140 of 1891

Attock, F.: *Improvements in Axle Boxes for Locomotives, Railway Carriages, and other Vehicles*, British Patent Specification No. 2707 of 1892

Attock, F.: *Improvements in or relating to Movable Arm and Head Rests Combined, applicable to Railway Carriages, Tram-cars, Ships' Berths, and other Seats*, British Patent Specification No. 885 of 1893

Attock, F.: *Improvements in Bogies for Rolling Stock*, British Patent Specification No. 16293 of 1893

Attock, F.W.: *Locomotive Shed Lay-out*, Paper No. 156, Jnl. ILocoE Vol.XIII, 1923

Attock, G.: *Assistant Bearing Springs for Locomotive Engines, etc.*, British Patent Specification No. 2145 of 1863

Attock, M.O.: *Engine-driven Electrical Generating Plant*, British Patent Specification No. 35009/46 of 1947

Attock, M.O.: *The Diagnosis of Faults in Roller Bearings in Traction Service*, English Electric Journal, Vol. 23, No. 1, January-February 1968

Attock, M.O. & Angus, P.A.: *Improvements in Engine-driven Electric Generating Plant*, British Patent Specification No.803,945 of 1954

Attock, M.O. & Fletcher, S.: *Some Ideas on the Maintenance of Diesel Electric Locomotives*, Paper No. 610, Jnl. ILocoE, Vol. 50 1960

Attock, M.O. & Fletcher, S.: *Recording and Controlling Faults on Diesel-electric Locomotives*, Paper No. 640, Jnl. ILocoE, Vol. 52, 1962

Bardsley, C.W.: *A Dictionary of English and Welsh Surnames*, Genealogical Publishing, Baltimore, 1967

Bulleid, H.A.V.: *The Aspinall Era*, Ian Allan, London, 1967

Ceylon Government Railways: *One Hundred Years, 1864-1964*, CGR, Colombo, 1965

Clements, R.N.: *Locomotives of the Midland Great Western Railway*, an unpublished manuscript, edited by E. Shepherd

Coates, N.: *Lancashire & Yorkshire Wagons - Vol. 1*, Wild Swan Publications, Didcot, 1990

Coates, N.: *Lancashire & Yorkshire Wagons - Vol. 2*, Wild Swan Publications, Didcot, 2006

Coates, N.: *Lancashire & Yorkshire Railway Wagon Diagrams*, Lancashire & Yorkshire

Railway Society, 2000
Durrant, A.E.: *Garratt Locomotives of the World*, Bracken Books, London, 1981
Ellis, C. Hamilton: *The Midland Railway*, Ian Allan, London, 1953
Ellis, C. Hamilton: *The Trains We Loved*, Ian Allan, London, 1947
Hall, S.: *Railway Detectives - 150 years of the Railway Inspectorate*, Ian Allan, London 1990
Hill, G.: *The Worsdells, A Quaker Engineering Dynasty*, Transport Publishing Co., 1991
Hughes, G.: *Sir Nigel Gresley – The Engineer and his Family*, Oakwood Press, Usk, 2001
Hunt, D.: *LMS Locomotive Profiles, No. 9 – Nos.10000/1*, Wild Swan Publications, Didcot
Irish Railway Record Society.: *Steaming through a Century, 1866-1966, The 101 Class Locomotives of the GS&WR*, IRRS, London, 1966
Jackson, D.: *J.G. Robinson - A Lifetime's Work*, Oakwood Press, Oxford, 1996
Lewis, B.: *The Cabry Family - Railway Engineers*, Railway & Canal Historical Society, Gwernymynydd, Mold, 1994
Lewis, J.: *London's Lea Valley*, Phillimore & Co. Ltd, Chichester, 1999
Marshall, J.: *Biographical Dictionary of Railway Engineers*, Railway & Canal Historical Society, 2003
Marshall, J.: *The Lancashire and Yorkshire Railway - Vol. 2*, David & Charles, Newton Abbot, 1970
Marshall, J.: *The Lancashire and Yorkshire Railway - Vol. 3*, David & Charles, Newton Abbot, 1972
Mason, E.: *The Lancashire and Yorkshire Railway in the Twentieth Century*, (2nd edition), Ian Allan, London, 1961
McGavin, T.A.: *NZR Locomotive List, 1959*, NZR&LS, Wellington, 1959
MGWR: *Directors Reports and Half-yearly Accounts*, 1872-1901
Milne, R.: *Working Class Beauty (A tribute to the TGR X and XA classes)*, Railmac Publications, South Australia, 2000
Nock, O.S.: *The Lancashire and Yorkshire Railway - A Concise History*, Ian Allan, London, 1969
O'Brien, H.E.: *The Management of a Locomotive Repair Shop*, Paper No.86, ILocoE Journal No. 45, Vol. X, 1920
Ó Cuimin, P.: *Wagon Stock of the MGWR*, Jnl. Irish Railway Record Society, Vol. 9, 1970, pp 154-171
Ó Cuimin, P.: *Carriage Stock of the MGWR*, Jnl. Irish Railway Record Society, Vol. 10, 1971, pp.59-71, 112-122
Olberg, L.: *Locomotives of Australia, 3rd. edition*, Kangaroo Press, 1996
Parsons, D.: New Zealand Railway Motive Power, 2002, NZR&LS, Wellington, 2002
Richards, E.V.: *LMS Diesel Locomotives & Railcars*, Railway Correspondence & Travel Society, Long Stratton, 1996
Rowledge, J.W.P.: *Diesel Locomotives of the LMS*, Oakwood Press, Surrey, 1975
Rush, R.W.: *Lancashire & Yorkshire Passenger Stock*, Oakwood Press, Lingfield, 1984
Shepherd, E.: *Midland Great Western Railway, An Illustrated History*, Midland Publishing, Leicester, 1994
Shepherd, E.: *Cork Bandon & South Coast Railway, An Irish Railway Pictorial*, Midland Publishing, Leicester, 2005
Shepherd, E.: *Waterford Limerick & Western Railway, An Irish Railway Pictorial*, Ian Allan Publishing, Hersham, 2006
Simms, W.F.: *Cuban National Railways, Vol.1*, Published by the Author
Smyth, W.A.: *Ballina 1924-5*, Jnl. Irish Railway Record Society, Vol. 13, 1977 pp.72-3
Smyth, W.A.: *My Service on the Irish Railways*, Jnl. Irish Railway Record Society, Vol. 14, 1980 pp.117-128
Stanistreet, J.A.: The Malayan Railway, Oakwood Press, Surrey, 1973
Tatlow, J: *Fifty Years of Railway Life in England, Scotland and Ireland*
The Railway Gazette, London, 1920
The Railway Year Book, Railway Publishing Co. Ltd, London, various issues

Index